Behavioral and Quantitative Perspectives On Terrorism

Pergamon Titles of Related Interest

Amos   THE PALESTINIAN RESISTANCE: Organization of a
   Nationalist Movement
Rapoport/Alexander   THE MORALITY OF TERRORISM
Shultz/Sloan   RESPONDING TO THE TERRORIST THREAT:
   Security and Crisis Management

Related Journals*

ADVANCES IN BEHAVIOUR RESEARCH AND THERAPY
BEHAVIOUR RESEARCH & THERAPY
JOURNAL OF BEHAVIOR THERAPY AND EXPERIMENTAL
   PSYCHIATRY
JOURNAL OF CHILD PSYCHOLOGY AND PSYCHIATRY AND
   ALLIED DISCIPLINES
JOURNAL OF CRIMINAL JUSTICE
TECHNOLOGY IN SOCIETY
URBAN SYSTEMS
WORLD DEVELOPMENT

*Free specimen copies available upon request.

PERGAMON
POLICY
STUDIES

ON INTERNATIONAL POLITICS

Behavioral and Quantitative Perspectives On Terrorism

Edited by
Yonah Alexander
John M. Gleason

Pergamon Press

NEW YORK • OXFORD • TORONTO • SYDNEY • PARIS • FRANKFURT

Pergamon Press Offices:

U.S.A.   Pergamon Press Inc., Maxwell House, Fairview Park,
                     Elmsford, New York 10523, U.S.A.

U.K.   Pergamon Press Ltd., Headington Hill Hall,
                     Oxford OX3 OBW, England

CANADA   Pergamon Press Canada Ltd., Suite 104, 150 Consumers Road,
                     Willowdale, Ontario M2J 1P9, Canada

AUSTRALIA   Pergamon Press (Aust.) Pty. Ltd., P.O. Box 544,
                     Potts Point, NSW 2011, Australia

FRANCE   Pergamon Press SARL, 24 rue des Ecoles,
                     75240 Paris, Cedex 05, France

FEDERAL REPUBLIC Pergamon Press GmbH, Hammerweg 6, Postfach 1305,
OF GERMANY   6242 Kronberg/Taunus, Federal Republic of Germany

Library of Congress Cataloging in Publication Data
Main entry under title:

Behavioral and quantitative perspectives on
  terrorism.

  (Pergamon policy studies on international
politics)
  Bibliography: p.
  Includes index.
  1. Terrorism--Addresses, essays, lectures.
2. Terrorism--Statistics--Addresses, essays,
lectures. 3. Terrorism--Psychological aspects--
Addresses, essays, lectures. I. Alexander,
Yonah. II. Gleason, John, 1942-   III. Series.
HV6431.B4 1981   303.6'2   80-39752
ISBN 0-08-025989-8

Printed in the United States of America

To our parents P.A. and C.A. and
John F. and Ella M. Gleason

Contents

CHAPTER

CONTENTS

Foreword
Ray S. Cline

The shooting of Pope John Paul in front of St. Peter's Cathedral in the Vatican is a late and dramatic illustration of the globalization and brutalization of contemporary ideological and political violence. The Turkish assassin, whose whole life revolved around a career of terrorism, trekked around Europe in and out of many nations, a wanted escaped criminal who had sworn to kill the Pope. The mindlessness of this kind of political or religious fanaticism, the vulnerability of open societies, and the widespread infrastructure for training and supporting professional terrorists are all symptomatic of the times ahead.

Terrorism has clearly become a worldwide phenomenon. From 1970 through 1980 there have been a total of 10,748 domestic and international terrorist operations, with a toll of 9,714 individuals killed, 10,177 wounded, and property damage of $701,839,542. During the first three months of 1981, a total of 594 terrorist operations were recorded, with 1,557 persons killed, 513 wounded, and with a cost of over $60 million.

The deliberate use of terrorism as a technique for disrupting the fabric of civilized order in open societies is one of the most menacing facts of international life today. As a form of "low-intensity" attack below the threshold of what is clearly perceived as regular, organized military aggression, terrorism is seldom recognized as a form of warfare and is rarely met with effective counter-measures in democratic nations. It is a destabilizing element that benefits militants and extremists while putting tolerance, moderation, and political pluralism in peril.

Events in Iran have illustrated that terrorism is a devastating political weapon in the hands of violent revolutionaries of any persuasion. Its consequences can bring about major changes in the world balance of power by destroying regimes aligned with the United States without an outbreak of conventional military hostilities.   Unless Americans become more conscious of the broad strategic dangers reflected in the deliberate international use of terror as an instrument of policy and become more skillful in deterring or countering terrorism, regardless of who the agents of violence and their sponsors may be, the 1980s will be catastrophic for worldwide security interests of the United States and its friends and allies abroad.

This book represents an important scholarly effort at understanding some of the behavioral aspects of this "Age of Terrorism."   By examining the psychology of the terrorist movement, pinpointing its prime geographical targets, and constructing statistical profiles of terrorist incidents, the authors break new ground in defining the scope and motivation of the terrorist threat.   As a major resource of data and analysis it is required reading for all those who are deeply concerned with the nature of the menace to the free world and how democratic societies can and should deal with it.

Ray S. Cline
Senior Associate
Georgetown University CSIS

Introduction
Yonah Alexander
John M. Gleason

The bombing of Bologna's main railroad station, Europe's bloodiest terrorist attack and one of the worst in recent history, and the dramatic takeover of the U.S. Embassy in Tehran and its tragic consequences, once again focused the world's attention on the problem of modern terrorism. Unlike their historical counterparts, present-day terrorists have introduced into contemporary life a new breed of violence in terms of technology, victimization, threat, and response. The globalization and brutalization of modern violence makes it abundantly clear that we have entered a unique "Age of Terrorism" with all its frightening ramifications.

THE TERRORISTS

Responding to destructive and nihilist impulses of utilizing power for the purpose of transforming national structures, or of achieving either limited or broader goals, terrorists are distinct from ordinary criminals because they are ostensibly dedicated to an altruistic ideological and political cause. Nourished by various cultural roots, their spiritual mentors include Robespierre, Bakhunin, Marx, Lenin, Trotsky, Sorel, Hitler, Marighella, Castro, Guevara, Debray, Guillen, Marcuse, Fanon, Mao, Giap, Malcolm X, and, more recently, Khomeini. They consist of ethnic, religious, or nationalist groups, such as the Provisional Wing of the Irish Republic Army; Marxist-Leninist groups, as, for example, the Basque Separatist Sixth Assembly; anarchist groups, including the Red Cells in West Germany; neo-fascist and extreme right-wing groups such as Mussolini Action Squads in Italy; ideological mercenaries of which the Japanese United Red Army is typical; and pathological groups as exemplified by the Symbionese Liberation Army.

MEMBERSHIP IN TERRORISTS GROUPS

Terrorist groups vary in membership from several individuals to hundreds of members. The total membership of all groups is probably in the tens of thousands, if "liberation movements" are included ("Fatah," for instance, the largest of all Palestinian "guerrillas," consists of approximately 6,000 active members). At any rate, in Latin America alone, some 3,460 persons are counted as members of terrorist groups. The total membership of European groups is estimated at 970.

In general, present-day terrorists come from affluent, middle or upper-class families with some social prestige and university education. An increasing number of women are joining terrorist movements, and in recent years are becoming more involved in operational roles. Among the more well-known female terrorists are Leila Khalid of the Popular Front for the Liberation of Palestine, Fusako Shigenobu of the Japanese Red Army, and Ulrike Meinhof, one of the founders of the German Baader-Meinhof organization.

THE NUMBER OF TERRORIST GROUPS

Various estimates indicate that there are anywhere from fifty to several hundred terrorist groups around the world. There are several reasons which explain the differences in these estimates. First, there is a definitional problem of what terrorism is. For instance, some incidents which are attributed to terrorist groups may be misleading because they may have been undertaken by criminals or psychotics. Second, terrorism tends to follow a cyclical pattern. Some groups become dormant only to emerge again, perhaps under a different identity. Third, some "groups" that claim responsibility for a specific incident in reality do not exist. Finally, there are groups that are formed for a particular operation and then disappear completely.

Notwithstanding these shortcomings in compiling accurate statistics, according to one data base, terrorist groups tend to proliferate in certain regions and countries. For example, 217 terrorist groups existed in Europe between 1970 and 1980. In the past two years alone, 128 groups were counted there. In Italy some 60 groups are active, while in Spain some 25 groups were operating in recent years. Similarly, 41 terrorist organizations have been active in Latin America during the same period.   Most of the groups operated in Argentina, Colombia, El Salvador, Guatemala, Mexico, and Nicaragua.

FOREIGN SUPPORT OF TERRORISM

Some of these terrorist groups were able to survive simply because they enjoyed the support of thousands of sympathizers within their own country and abroad, as well as direct and indirect "foreign assistance."

For example, it is becoming increasingly clear that ideological and political violence is, to paraphrase Clausewitz, a continuation of war by other means for the purpose of compelling an adversary to submit to specific or general demands. Indeed, terrorism, is escalating into the struggle for power process as a form of surrogate warfare, whereby small groups with direct and indirect state support are able to conduct political warfare at the national level, and ultimately could even alter the balance of power equation on the international scale.

It is not surprising, therefore, that the strategic thinking of certain states, as exemplified by the Soviet Union's policies and actions, calls for manipulation of terrorism as a suitable substitute to traditional warfare which becomes too expensive and too dangerous to be waged eye-ball to eye-ball on the battlefield.   By overtly and covertly resorting to nonmilitary techniques and exploiting low-intensity operations around the world, the Soviet Union is capable of continuing its "revolutionary process" against democratic pluralism of the Free World as well as against a wider target area.

Apart from communist countries, terrorism has been encouraged by Afro-Asian states, including Algeria, Angola, Iraq, Libya, South Yemen, and Mozambique.   In their view, ideological and political violence is a legitimate tool used by oppressed people in their struggle against "tyranny," "colonialism," "capitalism," and "Zionism."

THE DANGERS OF CONTEMPORARY TERRORISM

It is generally recognized that terrorism poses many threats to contemporary society and is likely to have a serious impact on the quality of life and on orderly civilized existence.   Perhaps the most significant dangers are those relating to the safety, welfare, and rights of ordinary people; the stability of the state system; the health and pace of economic development; and expansion or even survival of democracy.

Indeed, from a total of 293 significant acts of ideological and political violence in 1970, terrorist operations worldwide rose dramatically to a total of 2,629 incidents in 1980. Of particular concern is the fact that of all 10,748 domestic and international actions recorded during 1970-1980 over 60 percent have taken place within the past three years.

Pragmatic and symbolic terrorist acts - including arson, bombings, hostage-taking, kidnappings, and murder - undertaken by subnational groups for the purpose of producing pressures on governments and peoples to concede to the demands of the perpetrators, have already killed or maimed or otherwise victimized over 15,000 innocent civilians. These casualties include government officials, politicians, judges, diplomats, business executives, labor leaders, university professors, college students, school children, travelers, pilgrims, and Olympic athletes. For many victims, the only crime was to be at the wrong place at the wrong time.

Although, thus far at least, no catastrophic casualties have resulted from a single terrorist attack, it is suggested by experts that future incidents could be much more costly. First, there is the extremely difficult problem of protecting people and property. The security of a state depends on the good-will of the people within its borders. The terrorist, however, has the advantage of surprise. Police and citizenry cannot check everyone and every place.

Second, new technology is creating new dangers. Today, conventional weapons, including machine guns and modern plastic and letter bombs, are used by terrorists. Highly sophisticated weapons, such as the SA-7 surface-to-air rockets, which can destroy an airplane and kill hundreds of passengers, are now relatively easily available to various terrorist groups. At Rome in 1973, five Palestinians were arrested in an attempt to shoot down an El Al aircraft with SA-7s. A similar abortive attempt was made in Nairobi in 1976.

In the future, there is also the likely possibility that these groups will have access to biological, chemical, and nuclear instruments of massive death potential. An entire city's water supply can be poisoned with lethal chemicals. Nerve agents can cause hundreds of thousands of fatalities. A single incident involving biological agents, both toxins and living organisms, or nuclear bombs would obviously produce far more casualties.

Thus, the advances of science and technology are slowly turning all of modern society into potential victims of terrorism. The noncombatant segment of society will not be immune; nor will those nations and peoples who have no direct connection to particular conflicts or to specific grievances that motivate acts of violence.

THE THREAT OF TERRORISM TO THE STATE SYSTEM

Terrorism poses dangers not only to individuals but also to the stability of the state system. A characteristic of the state which distinguishes it from other social organizations is its monopoly of power. To the exent that subnational actors remain free to engage in terrorism, the power of the state diminishes. Currently, some states are no longer able to protect their civilians at home and abroad, or to ensure the safety of visiting foreigners. For example, the European-Atlantic community has experienced more terrorism and a greater challenge to its stability than any other region. The recent events in Italy and Spain are classic illustrations of this state of affairs. Moreover, there are now terrorist groups with formidable strength capable of creating states within states, thereby undermining the ability of legitimate govern-ments to rule. Frequently, the anarchy produced by local terrorism escalates into a civil war, ultimately engulfing neighboring countries and even more distant governments and their people. A dramatic example of this situation is the case of Lebanon.

THE VULNERABILITY OF THE BUSINESS COMMUNITY

Terrorism also poses a threat to the smooth functioning of the economic system. Terrorist groups - those ideologically committed to the destruction of the capitalist system and those in need of funding, or both - have selected as primary targets the personnel, facilities, and operations of the business community at home and abroad.

As soft targets, businessmen and corporations are ex-tremely vulnerable. According to available global data, during 1970-1980 approximately 45 percent of the total of 9,557 terrorist incidents recorded were business-connected. Cor-porations have paid millions of dollars in ransom money to release their executives. Business enterprises in some countries, such as Argentina and Italy, have contributed substantial payoffs to terrorist movements in order to secure relative peace.

Also, considerable damage has been inflicted on business property and infrastructure. Terrorists have already used conventional explosives to destroy pubs, restaurants, and hotels; banks, supermarkets, and department stores; oil pipelines, storage tanks, and refineries; railroad stations, air terminals, and jetliners; broadcast stations, computer and data centers, and electric power facilities.

As commerce, industry, transportation, and communication become more complex, they also become more vulnerable to the unpredictable schemes of dedicated and determined terrorists. Since more ideological and political violence can be anticipated, terrorism will continue to challenge business, property, and profit.

THE DANGERS POSED TO DEMOCRACIES

Democracy, too, is seriously threatened by terrorists. Unlike dictatorships that are both physically and emotionally conditioned to deal with opposition forces, democratic societies generally make it possible for terrorist groups to organize, although not necessarily to achieve popular political support. When the challenge of terrorism is met with repression, democracy weakens considerably. Between 1968 and 1971, for example, democratic Uruguay was subject to Tupamaro urban guerrilla warfare. In 1972, President Juan-Maria Bordaberry declared a "state of internal war" against the Tupamaros and granted wide powers to the police and army. The Tupamaros were vanquished, but democracy has not been restored to this South American country. The recent Bolivian military coup, which brought Col. Alberto Natusch Busch to power, was also initiated in the name of "democracy" but, in the process, it ended that country's first civilian government in 15 years.

THE FUTURE

It is safe to assume that terrorism is now an established mode of conflict. It provides a model for those with a variety of causes. The major reason for the continuation and probable intensification of terrorism is the fact that many of the roots of ideological and political violence will remain unsolved and new causes will arise in the coming months and years.

But, in spite of national and international efforts to control the dangers of terrorism, the level of nonstate violence remains high. The reasons for these conditions are diverse, but include at least seven factors: disagreement about who is a terrorist, lack of understanding of the causes of terrorism, the role of the media, the politicization of religion, weak punishment of terrorists, flouting of world law, and the existence of an international network of terrorism.

Because of these factors which encourage terrorism, nations and people of the world can anticipate more explosions, hijackings, kidnappings, and assassinations, possibly through the 1990s. Most governments and people favor control at least in principle, but unless they can find ways to deal realistically with factors which promote terrorism, they will be hostages of global blackmailers forever.

THIS BOOK

The study of terrorism, as a distinct field of research, is a relatively recent phenomenon. The recognized importance of this topic, however, is exemplified by the sheer volume of literature - papers, journal articles, journals, and books - devoted to the subject in the last few years. An examination of the literature reveals that the sources of the majority of the material are the more time-honored, established disciplines. The study of terrorism has been the domain of political scientists, psychologists, sociologists, and individuals with interests in international affairs and criminal justice. This dominance became apparent to one of the editors of this volume when, in 1977, he undertook research of a quantitative nature in this field. A literature review produced practically nothing of an operations research/management science nature.

In an attempt to stimulate more interest in terrorism on the part of operations researchers and management scientists, individuals from several disciplines were invited to participate in three sessions on international terrorism at the Joint National Meeting of the Operations Research Society of America and The Institute of Management Sciences in New York in 1978. Versions of several of the chapters in this volume were presented as papers at that meeting; the papers by Brian Jenkins, Ed Mickolus, Ed Heyman, and Larry Hamilton comprise Chapters 1, 8, 9, and 10 of this book.

The chapters are representative of both behavioral and quantitative approaches to the analysis of terrorism. Indeed, the purpose of the book is to foster further cooperation between those with quantitative interests and those with more traditional interests in the study of terrorism. Ideally, this volume will serve to introduce the reader with quantitative interests to the more traditional (if such a word can validly be used in reference to terrorism) aspects of the study of terrorism. Similarly, the reader with more traditional interests will be provided with an exposure to quantitative analyses of terrorism. Hopefully, the book will serve as a vehicle to encourage more work of an interdisciplinary nature.

I
Definitional and
Typological Approaches

1 The Study of Terrorism: Definitional Problems
Brian M. Jenkins

Terrorism has become part of our daily news diet. Hardly a day goes by without news of an assassination, political kidnapping, hijacking, or bombing somewhere in the world. As such incidents of terrorism have increased in the past decade, the phenomenon of terrorism has become one of increasing concern to governments and of increasing interest to scholars.

In the course of its continuing research on terrorism, The Rand Corporation has compiled a chronology of international terrorism incidents that have occurred since 1968. This chronology now contains over 1,000 incidents. In compiling the chronology, numerous problems of definition were encountered.

The term "terrorism" has no precise or widely-accepted definition. The problem of defining terrorism is compounded by the fact that terrorism has recently become a fad word used promiscuously and often applied to a variety of acts of violence which are not strictly terrorism by definition. It is generally pejorative. Some governments are prone to label as terrorism all violent acts committed by their political opponents, while antigovernment extremists frequently claim to be the victims of government terror. What is called terrorism thus seems to depend on one's point of view. Use of the term implies a moral judgment; and if one party can successfully attach the label "terrorist" to its opponent, then it has indirectly persuaded others to adopt its moral viewpoint. Terrorism is what the bad guys do.

---

*Originally presented to the Joint National Meeting of the Operations Research Society of America and the Institute for Management Sciences, New York, May 1-3, 1978.

The word "terrorism" is also an attention-getting word and therefore tends to be used, especially in the news media, to heighten the drama surrounding any act of violence. What we have, in sum, is the sloppy use of a word that is rather imprecisely defined to begin with. Terrorism may properly refer to a specific set of actions the primary intent of which is to produce fear and alarm that may serve a variety of purposes. But terrorism, in general usage, frequently is also applied to similar acts of violence - all ransom kidnappings, all hijackings, thrill-killings - which are not all intended by their perpetrators to be primarily terror-producing. Once a group carries out a terrorist act, it acquires the label "terrorist," a label that tends to stick; and from that point on, everything this group does, whether intended to produce terror or not, is also called terrorism. If it robs a bank or steals arms from an arsenal, not necessarily acts of terrorism but common urban guerrilla tactics, these too are often described as terrorism. Eventually, all similar acts by other groups also come to be called terrorism. At some point in this expanding use of the term, terrorism can mean just what those who use the term (not the terrorist) want it to mean - almost any violent act by an opponent.

The difficulty of defining terrorism has led to the cliche that one man's terrorist is another man's freedom fighter. The phrase implies that there can be no objective definition of terrorism, that there are no universal standards of conduct in peace or war. That is not true.

Most civilized nations have identified by law modes of conduct that are criminal, among them homicide, kidnapping, threats to life, the willful destruction of property. Such laws may be violated in war, but even in war there are rules that outlaw the use of certain weapons and tactics.

The rules of war grant civilian noncombatants at least theoretical immunity from deliberate attack. They prohibit taking civilian hostages and actions against those held captive. The rules of war recognize neutral territory. Terrorists recognize no neutral territory, no noncombatants, no by-standers. They often seize, threaten, and murder hostages. One man's terrorist is everyone's terrorist.

Terrorism, in the Rand chronology, is defined by the nature of the act, not by the identity of the perpetrators or the nature of their cause. All terrorist acts are crimes - murder, kidnapping, arson. Many would also be violations of the rules of war, if a state of war existed. All involve violence or the threat of violence, often coupled with specific demands. The violence is directed mainly against civilian targets. The motives are political. The actions generally are carried out in a way that will achieve maximum publicity. The perpetrators are usually members of an organized group, and unlike other criminals, they often claim credit for the act.

And finally the act is intended to produce effects beyond the immediate physical damage.

The fear created by terrorists may be intended to cause people to exaggerate the strength of the terrorists and the importance of their cause, to provoke extreme reactions, to discourage dissent, or to enforce compliance.

This definition of terrorism would not limit the application of the term solely to nongovernmental groups. Governments, their armies, their secret police may also be terrorists. Certainly the threat of torture is a form of terrorism designed to inspire dread of the regime and obedience to authorities. Some scholars make a semantic distinction here, reserving the term "terrorism" for nongovernmental groups, while using the term "terror" to describe similar incidents carried out by the state. There are few incidents of state terrorism or terror in our chronology, not because it is considered to be less heinous, but because such terrorism tends to be internal rather than international. However, there are some international incidents of state terrorism: the assassination of a troublesome exile like Trotsky is an example. A more recent example may be the assassination in Washington, D.C. of a former Chilean cabinet minister if it turns out to be true, as alleged, that the killers were operating at the behest of the Chilean security services.

International terrorism comprises those incidents of terrorism that have clear international consequences: incidents in which terrorists go abroad to strike their targets, select victims or targets because of their connections to a foreign state (diplomats, executives of foreign corporations), attack airliners on international flights, or force airliners to fly to another country. It excludes the considerable amount of terrorist violence carried out by terrorists operating within their own country against their own nationals, and in many countries by governments against their own citizens. For example, Irish terrorists blowing up other Irishmen in Belfast would not be counted, nor would Italian terrorists kidnapping Italian officials in Italy. Of course, such terrorism although beyond the scope of our specific research task, is also of common interest and concern as it may lead to actions that will imperil foreign nationals, be carried abroad to other countries, be imitated by other groups, affect the stability of nations individually and collectively, strain relations between nations, or constitute intolerable violations of fundamental human rights, making it a matter of universal concern. Thus, while our research focuses on the specific problem of international terrorism, we find ourselves inevitably trespassing into an area of internal political violence as it bears upon the subject of international terrorism.

The Central Intelligence Agency, in its reports on the subject, makes a distinction between "transnational terrorism," which is terrorism "carried out by basically autonomous non-state actors, whether or not they enjoy some degree of support from sympathetic states," and "international terrorism" which is terrorism carried out by individuals or groups controlled by a sovereign state.   This author, frankly, is somewhat skeptical about our ability to make such a distinction, as a growing number of terrorist operations seem to be virtually commissioned by governments.   This trend will continue.   The CIA also recognizes this problem and in a footnote goes on to say,

> Given the element of governmental patronage that is common to both, the boundary line between transnational and international terrorism is often difficult to draw.   To the degree that it can be determined, the key distinction lies in who is calling the shots with respect to a given action or campaign.   Hence, groups can and do drift back and forth across the line.   For example, even a one-time 'contract job' undertaken on behalf of a governmental actor by a group that normally acts according to its own lights qualifies as international terrorism.

In the Rand chronology, we stuck to the term "international terrorism," and attempted to make no distinction on the basis of government support.(1) This definition seemed pretty straightforward until we actually tried to use it in selecting incidents for our chronology of international terrorism.   The chronology was to provide not only an historical record of international terrorism but was also to give some idea of the scope of the problem and allow the identification of trends.
     We ran into several problems from the start.   We decided that we would exclude incidents of terrorism that occurred in the middle of a war.   There were potentially thousands of incidents of terrorism in Indochina, and in the Middle East, for example, during the civil war in Lebanon, some of international character.   It would, however, be impossible to record all of these as they were submerged in a higher level of violence.   Nor did we wish to engage in an unproductive debate as to whether the shelling of an Israeli kibbutz or the bombing of Hanoi constituted an act of international terrorism.   The major incidents of obvious terrorism - the seizure of hostages in a border settlement, the murder of an official of the Palestine Liberation Organization in Beirut or West European capital - were picked up.   When a Palestinian terrorist operation provoked an Israel military reprisal, we listed both.
     Hijackings presented another problem.   Would we include hijackings of airliners by people seeking political asylum? These certainly are not the same as hijackings by groups to publicize a political cause or coerce governments into making

political concessions. Certainly, the two are not in the same category except that the lives of innocent bystanders are often jeopardized to satisfy basically political goals - asylum or revolution. The borderline separating political motives from highly personal motives and purely criminal motives is not always clear. We decided not to try to decipher motives. We would include all hijackings except those carried out for obvious criminal intent - individuals demanding cash and a parachute.

A further problem arose in deciding whether to include the activities of separatist groups. As mentioned previously, our definition of international terrorism would exclude the Irish terrorists blowing up other Irishmen in Belfast. We would, of course, include IRA operations abroad such as the mailing of a letter bomb to a British official in Washington or the assassination of the British ambassador to the Republic of Ireland. We decided also to include IRA bombings in England; in a sense, this represented carrying the campaign abroad. To maintain consistency, we had to include bombings in New York and Chicago by Puerto Rican separatists. Would we then include actions by Corsican separatists if they took place on the French mainland? We have not done so to date but to remain consistent with our decision in the Irish case, I suppose we should. Must we then also include the terrorist activities of Basque and Breton separatists if they operate outside their own provinces? Even with a fairly precise definition, many decisions quickly become subjective. It becomes slippery around the edges.

Finally, we sometimes chose to list some incidents as one, for example, a single mailing of letter bombings, rather than list it as 40-50 separate acts of terrorism. This decision was made in order to avoid distorting the annual total of incidents. On the other hand, a bombing campaign over a period of time, carried on by a single group, was listed as a series of separate actions.

Despite these definitional problems, which pertain to only a fraction of the total number of incidents, the chronology has been a useful tool in assessing the magnitude of the problem. The results are sometimes intriguing. We discovered, for example, that the level of international terrorism based upon the chronology does not exactly accord with the public's perception of the problem of terrorism nor with government reactions. To illustrate the point, the total number of incidents of international terrorism in 1972 was less than that of 1970, while the number of major incidents was about the same for the two years. Incidents with casualties and the number of deaths caused by terrorists were up in 1972. However, it was two particularly shocking incidents in 1972, the Lod Airport massacre in May and the Munich incident in September, that appalled the world and provoked many governments, including the United States, to undertake more serious measures to combat terrorism.

Similarly, the year 1975 was labeled by many in the news media as the "year of the terrorist." Certainly, 1975 seemed to surpass previous years in the number of dramatic and shocking episodes that occurred. There were continued kidnappings in Latin America and in the Middle East, while in Europe two attempts to shoot down airliners at Orly Field in Paris, the kidnapping of a candidate for mayor in West Berlin, the seizure of embassies in Stockholm, Kuala Lumpur and Madrid, the Irish Republican Army's bombing campaign in London, the assassination of the Turkish ambassadors in Austria and France, the hijacking of a train in The Netherlands and the takeover of the Indonesian consulate in Amsterdam, and the seizure of the OPEC oil ministers in Vienna combined to produce an enormous effect. Certainly, it seemed international terrorism had increased. However, measured by the number of incidents, by the number of major incidents, by the total number of incidents with casualties, and by the total number of casualties, it had, in fact, declined.

Some observers found encouragement in the seeming "downward trend" in 1976. In fact, however, more incidents of terrorism took place in 1976 and there were more casualties. There were more bombings, more assassinations, and even hijackings went up again after declining in earlier years.

Some continued to perceive a decline in the early months of 1977 but, by the end of the year, judging by the number of news articles, television specials, and concern in government, virtually everyone agreed that terrorism was on the rise. In fact, it was not. The figures for 1977 actually show a slight decline.

How do we explain that terrorism often appears to be increasing when it is declining - appears down when it is up? Perhaps we count the wrong things. More likely, the things we can count do not reflect our perceptions of the phenomenon. Terrorism is not simply what terrorists do but the effect - the publicity, the alarm - they create by their actions.

Public perceptions of the level of terrorism in the world appear to be determined then not by the level of violence but rather by the quality of the incidents, the location, and the degree of media coverage. Hostage incidents seem to have greater impact than murder, barricade situations more than kidnappings. Hostage situations may last for days, possibly weeks. Human life hangs in the balance. The whole world watches and waits. By contrast, a death, even many deaths, are news for only a few days. They lack suspense and are soon forgotten. More people recall the hijacking of a TWA airliner by Croatian extremists in September 1976 than recall the bomb placed aboard a Cubana airliner three weeks later.

No one died aboard the TWA airliner (although a policeman was killed attempting to defuse a bomb planted on the ground by the hijackers); while 73 persons died in the crash of the Cubana plane.

The location of the incident is also important. Incidents that occur in cities have more impact than those that occur in the country-side. Incidents in Western Europe and North America seem more important, at least to the American public, than incidents in Latin America, Africa, or Asia. It is a matter of communications. An unseen and unheard terrorist incident produces no effect. The network of modern electronic communications laces Western Europe and North America more thoroughly than the rest of the world. We also tend to exhibit a higher tolerance for terrorist violence in the Third World. Terrorist violence in modern industrial societies with democratic governments jars this bias.

Finally, timing is important. Terrorist violence is easily submerged by higher levels of conflict. Individual acts of violence lose their meaning in a war. It is hard to say how many individual acts of terrorism there were during the war in Indochina or how many individual murders, how many kidnappings there were during the civil war in Lebanon. Even a war in another part of the globe can drown out an act of terrorism. There is only so much time and space for news. Terrorist acts themselves in succession produce the effect of a wave of terrorism but must now crowd each other too closely for world attention lest their impact be diluted.

The fact that each terrorist incident is in itself a complete episode--a bomb goes off, an individual is kidnapped and is either released, ransomed, or killed, plus the fact that there are now over 1,000 incidents in Rand's chronology of international terrorism, makes some type of quantitative analysis attractive. If complete chronologies of the terrorism in Argentina, Northern Ireland, Italy, and several other countries that have experienced high levels of terrorist violence were also available, potentially some quantitative analysis could be applied with even greater confidence.

Hostage situations have been examined quantitatively to determine their likely duration, probable outcomes, the risks to the hostages, and even the risks versus payoffs for the hostage-takers. This information has been used in examining the validity of certain policy assumptions and in actually dealing with such episodes.(2)

Enough airline hijackings occurred to permit the construction of a statistical profile of a typical hijacker, and this was used to reduce the crime.(3) Some work has also been done in constructing the demographic profile of a "typical terrorist" - a well-educated (although, perhaps, a university dropout) male in his early twenties, coming from a middle or upper-class family, the son of a teacher, business executive,

or professional, recruited in a university.(4) Further analysis
may enable us to understand more of his motivations and
intentions.

Much more could be done if sufficient data bases were
created. At the same time, some cautionary comments are in
order. The term terrorism is not only slippery but also
politically loaded. We have seen that it can be difficult to
even grossly estimate the level and impact of terrorism by
counting the number of incidents. The term "terrorist" is also
a loose label applied to political extremists, common criminals,
and authentic lunatics. Finally, we must recognize that we are
dealing with a fast-moving subject. While there seem to be
patterns to terrorist activity, we cannot assume that the historical record offers firm footing for predictions.

NOTES

1. David L. Milbank, International and Transnational
Terrorism: Diagnosis and Prognosis, Central Intelligence Agency, April 1976, iii, p. 9.

2. Brian M. Jenkins, Numbered Lives: Some Statistical
Observations from 77 International Hostage Episodes, The Rand
Corporation, P-5905, July 1977.

3. For a discussion of this research, see Evan Pickrel,
"Federal Aviation Administration's Behavioral Research Program
for Defense Against Hijacking," pp. 19-26, in U.S. Department
of Commerce, National Bureau of Standards, The Role of Behavioral Science in Physical Security: Proceedings of the First
Annual Symposium, April 29-30, 1976, NBS Special Publication
480-24, November 1977.

4. Charles A. Russell and Bowman H. Miller, "Profile of
a Terrorist," Military Review, August 1977, pp. 21-34.

2 Terrorist Activities and Terrorist Targets: A Tentative Typology

Ezzat A. Fattah

Terror can take many forms, be inspired by various motives, and may be directed against different targets. Typologies of terrorism are, therefore, useful in differentiating and categorizing terrorism; in understanding its "causes," manifestations, and impact; in controlling its incidence; and in minimizing its effects.

Terrorism is a vague, ambiguous term, loosely used to designate a wide variety of heterogeneous activities. The present chapter examines current typologies of terrorist acts and attempts to develop a typology of targets.

DEFINING TERRORISM

A typology of terrorism requires a prior definition of the concept and categorization of the different acts which fit the definition. But defining terrorism and qualifying certain acts as terroristic is not an easy task. There is no definition which is universally or unanimously accepted, and attempts to achieve international consensus on what terrorism is have failed. One of the major difficulties in defining "terrorism," "terrorist," or "terroristic" is the relativity of these concepts. Relativity stems not only from the differing perspectives and conflicting interests of those who have attempted to define terrorism but also from the inherent difficulties in reaching a neutral or value-free definition of a concept having strong ideological and emotional overtones. Depending on which side the observer is on in the conflict, identical acts may alternately be labeled "terrorism" or "revolution," and the same individuals may be regarded simultaneously as blood-thirsty terrorists, gangsters, and criminals, or patriots, heroes, commandos, and freedom-fighters. A primary obstacle to reaching an agreement on a definition is clearly described in the aphorism "One man's terrorism is another man's heroism." In the eyes of many countries, Che Guevara was a terrorist and a wanted criminal, but he was hailed as a revolutionary and glorified as a hero in several others.

The failure of international organizations to come up with an acceptable definition of terrorism testifies to the magnitude of the problems involved. For example, the League of Nations Convention for the Prevention and Punishment of Terrorism (1937) defined as acts of terrorism: "All criminal acts directed against a State and intended or calculated to create a state of terror in the minds of particular persons, or a group of persons or the general public." According to the Convention, the category of terrorism includes all acts as well as attempts that cause death or bodily harm to Heads of State or Government, their spouses, and other public figures; that cause damage to public property; that endanger the lives of the public; and that deal with arms and ammunition for the commission of any of these offenses in any state (see Qureshi 1976, p. 151).

This definition is narrow, restrictive, and one-sided. It limits the notion of terrorism to criminal acts causing or likely to cause physical or material harm. But fear and terror may be induced by acts that are not "criminal" in nature; and psychological violence may, in some cases, be more terrorizing than other forms of violence. Moreover, the one-sided nature of the definition is self-evident. It defines as terrorist "all criminal acts directed against a state" but leaves out violent and repressive actions of "duly constituted" governments. As it stands, it does not apply to atrocities committed by certain political regimes in violation of the Geneva Convention, such as the killing of civilians or the torture of prisoners. Nor does it apply to the orchestrated efforts of some governments aimed at intimidating and subjugating minority groups, the members of a particular political party or religious faith, the inhabitants of occupied territories, etc. Even acts of genocide would hardly qualify as terrorist acts under this definition. As Qureshi (1976, p. 157) notes:

> The violence of the resister is termed "terrorist" whereas that of the regime is the enforcement of the law, and what distinguishes one from the other is the condition of legality. As long as the regime observes these conditions its reprisals against the resisters, no matter how harsh, are excluded from the category of terrorism.

Bell (1975, p. 14) believes that state violence is nothing more than authorized terror:

Some regimes also authorize or at least employ techniques to maintain internal order that can be readily recognized by the distant observer as a form of terror: random purges, show trials, torture, internment. In some periods and nations such tactics appear systemic rather than a response to specific provocation.

An adequate definition of terrorism should take into account the nature and impact of activities to be so defined and should apply to the actions of the governors as well as those of the governed, to the crimes of the rulers as well as those of the ruled. The literal usage of the word "terror" would bear this out. Literally, terror means "extreme fear" while "terrorist" is a person or a thing causing such fear. The Oxford Dictionary explains the verb "terrorize" as meaning "to fill with terror," "to rule or to maintain power by terrorism." "Reign of terror" has always been used to describe a period during which a certain community lives in constant dread of death, violence, or outrage. Bassiouni (1975, p. 6) notes that the ordinary meaning of the word terrorism has undergone an evolution since it first came into use at the end of the eighteenth century. While at first it applied mainly to those acts and policies of governments which were designed to spread terror among a population for the purpose of ensuring its submission to and conformity with the will of those governments, it now seems to be mainly applied to actions by individuals or groups of individuals.

In his essay on "Political Violence in the South Asian Sub-Continent," Qureshi (1976, p. 151) comes up with a more acceptable definition of terrorism:

Terrorism is the use of violence in order to induce a state of fear and submission in the victim. The object of terrorism is to secure a change or modification in the behavior of the intended victim himself or to use him as an example for others. The violence or terrorism is the ultimate of coercion, whether actually applied or merely used as a threat. The use of terrorist violence is based on the assumption that the intended victim is unreasonable and incapable of seeing the viewpoint of the terrorist, that the victim cannot be persuaded but only compelled, in a manner by which he has absolutely no choice except to surrender.

The search for a viable definition of terrorism is, in fact, a search for one or more denominators common to all terrorist activities. One such denominator is the use of violence - actual or threatened, physical or psychological - in some extreme form to achieve certain ends. In some cases, violence and/or threats are used as means of coercion to get the victim(s) to agree to certain demands. In other cases, they are used as means of extermination, retaliation, or intimidation; to instill fear and terror in the heart of the victims and to force them into submission. These common threads, present in all forms of terrorism, make it possible to qualify specific acts as terroristic regardless of the motives behind them and regardless of whether they are committed by persons in a weak or strong position of power.

CATEGORIZING TERRORISM

Over the years, several attempts have been made to classify terrorist behaviors according to some specific criteria.

Political and Nonpolitical Terrorism

Terrorist activities may be divided, according to the motives of the terrorists, into political and nonpolitical terrorism. Some acts of terror are clearly committed for political purposes, while others are unmistakably committed for lust or financial gain. In some cases, the motives may not be too obvious or may be a combination of political and nonpolitical ones.

Antigovernment and antistate terrorism is taken seriously by those in power since its main objective is to undermine their authority. Political terrorism has assumed new dimensions in recent years and has taken several new forms. Political kidnapping, a rare occurrence until a few years ago, has increased in frequency and intensity. The kidnapping of political figures, diplomats, and other important persons and their detention as hostages as means of putting pressure on governments to get them to accede to certain political demands has been on the rise in some parts of the world. "Diplonapping" is a new term coined to designate those kidnappings where the victim is a foreign diplomat. Political kidnappings differ from ordinary kidnappings in many respects. In the kidnapping of children of wealthy parents, rich bankers, or industrialists, the act is directed mainly against the kidnapped person himself, his family, his firm, or corporation. Political kidnapping, on the other hand, involves a much larger population since it is directed against governments, political organizations, whole ethnic or religious groups, etc. And, while in ordinary kidnappings the demands are predominantly monetary, political kidnappings involve, most of the time, in addition to the demanding of a huge ransom, political demands such as the release of convicted offenders or politically detained prisoners.

Ordinary kidnapping is, most of the time, a local incident, while political kidnapping generally has national or
international implications.   A nationalist cause or a grievance
of political nature can be greatly dramatized and widely
publicized through a spectacular kidnapping.   The modern
techniques of communication have thus inadvertently contributed to the growing popularity of kidnapping and skyjacking
among political terrorists.   Those who are seeking publicity for
their cause or grievances are assured of international media
coverage and the result is that some incidents are committed
for the sole purpose of the publicity they bring.

Skyjacking is another, relatively new, form of terrorism.
But the hijacking of aircraft is not invariably politically
motivated.   Airplanes have been hijacked for a wide variety of
nonpolitical purposes.   In one such incident which took place
in 1969, the hijacked aircraft was used to flee with a child
awarded to the other parent in a custody suit following a
broken marriage.   There have been incidents of skyjackings
committed for purely lucrative purposes and others to publicize
nonpolitical grievances.   However, according to at least one
estimate (Pourcelet 1971), 70 percent of all skyjacking incidents are political in nature.   In recent years, most political
skyjackings were committed by two or three individuals acting
as a group.   This is in contrast with nonpolitical skyjackings
which are usually the work of solitary hijackers.   The fanaticism and dedication of many political skyjackers put the
victims in a particularly dangerous situation and place an
additional pressure on the governments involved.

Repressive, Defensive, and Offensive Terror

Robert Moss (1972) defines terrorism as the systematic use of
intimidation for political purposes.   He then proceeds to
describe three tactical varieties of terrorism.

1)   Repressive terror is used by a government to
keep its grip over the population or by a rebel
movement as a means of eliminating rivals,
coercing popular support, or maintaining
conformity inside the organization (in other
words, bumping off "traitors" and silencing
critics).

2)   Defensive terror can be used by private groups
like the American vigilantes to keep order or to
uphold the status quo; by patriots against a
foreign invader; or by a community defending
its traditional rights.

3)   Offensive terror is used against a regime or
a political system.   Typical forms of offensive

terror are fights by terrorist groups to win
national independence from a colonial government, to overthrow autocratic regimes, and to
impose their ideologies (communist, fascist or
anarchist) on democratic societies.

National and Transnational Terrorism

Terrorism can be classified as national when the violence and
terror are confined to national boundaries and do not directly
involve foreign victims. When violence and terror are employed inland and abroad, or when they are directed against
the nationals or the belongings of one or several foreign
countries, terrorism is qualified as transnational. Attacks
against foreign diplomats and other representatives of foreign
countries and the hijacking of a foreign aircraft are typical
examples of transnational terrorism which also includes terrorist acts by governments against their own citizens when
perpetrated on foreign territory.
    Bassiouni (1975) notes that international terrorism ex-
cludes activities that are the internal affairs of individual
states, such as the acts of governments within their own
territories in respect to their own citizens. Terrorist activities may be regarded as international when the interests of
more than one state are involved, as, for example, when the
perpetrator or the victim is a foreigner in the country where
the act is done, or the perpetrator has fled to another country.
    Transnational terrorism has been greatly facilitated and
promoted by the new technologies particularly in the fields of
weaponry and transportation. Rockets and missiles can reach
targets far beyond national boundaries while foreign aircraft
can become easy targets to terrorists armed only with small,
easy-to-conceal weapons.

    The modern aircraft - which is perhaps the most
    vulnerable of all the high and complex developments
    of technology, which contains assemblages of people
    from many countries, and which if brought under
    the terrorists' control, offers a speedy and safe
    means of reaching a distant asylum abroad - is often
    a factor in modern forms of international terrorism
    (Bassiouni 1975, p. 10).

Legitimate and Illegitimate Terrorism

As mentioned earlier, terrorism is a relative concept. Acts of
political violence or political repression, therefore, cannot

invariably be defined as criminal or condemned as illegitimate. The goals to be achieved through acts of terror allow a distinction between what may be considered as legitimate resistance and what may be regarded as illegitimate terrorism. Hyams (1974) notes that the British Parliament has always made a clear distinction between those who use violence for their own ends - i.e., criminals - and those who use the same kind of violence for political ends - i.e., revolutionaries.

Governments regard as perfectly legitimate whatever suppressive, oppressive, or repressive means they take to crush revolutions, to quell rebellions, or to forcibly put an end to armed insurrections. In other words, they consider counterterror to be legitimate, lawful, and necessary. The United Nations has frequently pledged support to wars of national liberation and to acts of resistance and struggle by movements recognized as having the right to self-determination.

When terrorist acts are committed as countermeasures against violent aggression or continued oppression, they gain a certain legitimacy resulting from the offensive conduct of prospective victims. This applies to armed conflicts in which peoples are fighting against colonial domination, racial extermination, or foreign occupation. No one ever questioned the legitimacy of terrorist attacks by underground resistance movements in countries occupied by Nazi Germany during World War II.

Does the tyranny of the victim convey any sort of legitimacy upon the act of killing? The killing of the tyrant (tyrannicide) was considered justifiable and hailed as a glorious act by Greek and Roman philosophers. Xenophon reports that the tyrant-killer was never punished, and that grateful people usually placed statues in temples to commemorate his deed (Rapoport 1971, p. 8). Cicero notes that the Romans regarded tyrannicide as "the finest of all glorious deeds, especially if the tyrant had previously been an intimate friend" (ibid.). These opinions persisted among Christian theologians. Thus, St. Thomas Aquinas held that an individual (and, á plus forte raison, a group of individuals) has a "natural law" right to resist tyranny, even by the use of assassinations (Hyams 1974, p. 15). The philosopher John Locke expressed the opinion, in his essay "Of Civil Government," that whosoever uses force without right puts himself in a state of war with those against whom he uses it; and that, in that case, everyone has a right to defend himself against the aggressor (ibid.).

Hyams (1974) points out that terrorism is neither more nor less justifiable than war; the pacifist's position is that neither is justifiable; the position of the nonpacifist who admits the justice of war in certain circumstances is untenable unless he also admits the justice of political terrorism in certain circumstances. As for the innocent victims of terrorism, they are in precisely the same situation as the innocent victims of war.

Other Taxonomies

Qureshi (1976) uses, for the description and analysis of terrorism, the following categories:

1) Explicit, organized, deliberate terrorism
   a) direct - rebellions
   b) indirect - tactical, selective assassinations
2) Random, mass, unorganized.

Qureshi explains that, in the cases of indirect or tactical terrorism, a victim is used to pressure his principals or a third party into conceding to the demands of the terrorist. In this category of terrorism he includes selective assassinations and bombings.

In his book, <u>Transnational Terror</u>, Bell (1975) outlines six varieties of terror:

1. <u>Psychotic terror</u>: this includes threats or attempts on the lives of significant political figures such as the President. Bell notes that all significant American assassination attempts have been by psychotics who rationalized their act with the language of politics. It includes, as well, a number of skyjackings of airliners.
2. <u>Criminal terror</u>: one of the most common manifestations of this variant of terror is air piracy. Kidnapping and extortion for criminal purposes also fall within this category of terror.
3. <u>Endemic terror</u> is that which affects particular societies at certain periods in their development, but it also has transnational implications. In some countries, the security of visitors simply cannot be guaranteed. Other international consequences may take place when suddenly a substantial portion of the world supply of an important commodity can no longer be shipped through or from a particular nation wracked by internal disorder.
4. <u>Authorized terror</u> is a form of state terror which not infrequently extends beyond the borders of the authorizing state.
5. <u>Vigilante terror</u>, such as that practiced by the Ku Klux Klan in the United States or by the death squad in Brazil, has no great effect on international order.
6. <u>Revolutionary terror</u>: Bell notes that this form of terror takes on several aspects which often overlap. The subcategories are:

a) organizational terror: essentially maintaining internal discipline
b) allegiance terror: describes the use of violence in order to create mass support
c) functional terror: employed when, in the course of an armed struggle, it is necessary to gain strategic advantage through specific action
d) provocative terror: is intended to produce an over-reaction by concentrating on exploiting the deed and escalating its impact
e) manipulative terror: is used to create a bargaining situation, in which the terrorists threaten to destroy seized assets or hostages unless they are granted certain demands.
f) symbolic terror: truly symbolic terrorism must go beyond the organizational and functional and must select as a victim a figure who represents the epitome of the enemy. Yet, the deed must be more than simple vengeance.

Though all of the above mentioned classifications are useful tools for the study of terrorism, victimology is particularly interested in classifications based on victimological criteria.

VICTIMOLOGICAL CLASSIFICATIONS OF TERRORISM

Individual and Mass Terror

Acts of terrorism can be highly individualized, directed against one or a few individuals or against a whole group or a total population. The popular targets for individual terror are political or religious leaders (Heads of State, Heads of Government, leaders of political parties, or religious groups); or the representatives of the hostile government or group. Mass terror, on the other hand, is usually practiced against whole communities - the population of an occupied territory; the members of an ethnic, political, or religious minority; government officials; the military; people belonging to a social class; etc. Genocide is the ultimate form of mass terror.

Random and Selective Terror/Discriminate and Indiscriminate Terror

The victims of individual terror are usually carefully selected, while mass terror is usually random and indiscriminate. Momboisse (1970) notes that selective terrorism chooses its victims from among important leaders whose loss will severely

handicap the cause they sponsor. These are the leaders of
civil, religious, trade union, police, and military organizations.
It is also designed to intimidate or impress a specific group.
Momboisse feels, however, that terror in its purest form is
indiscriminately aimed at breaking down all trust, authority,
and security. He describes it as follows:

> This methodical type of terrorism is characterized by
> a high degree of violence, attacking the population
> indiscriminately, killing persons of every sex, age,
> profession, rank, religious belief, and economic
> standing. Some examples of this kind of terrorism
> are the attempts made against public establishments
> (restaurants, movies, hospitals, and religious
> centers, transportation services, and people in the
> streets). Its aim is to spread panic among the
> population. The psychological effect of indiscrim-
> inate terror is much greater than selective terrorism.
> The return on terror expenditures increases in
> direct but somewhat scaled-down proportion to the
> apparent indiscrimination of the terror employed.
> Anything which makes terror more unpredictable,
> and therefore more disorienting, contributes to the
> creation of anxiety. The resonant masses and the
> select groups do not become anxious in the face of
> highly discriminate terrorism, but if they believe
> they are confronted with seemingly indiscriminate
> terror, they will experience the required sense of
> personal involvement, for when it is impossible to
> predict what or whom will be the next terrorist
> target, one does not know whether it will be him or
> his neighbor. The result is to create general
> insecurity.

In contrast to this random, nonselective terrorism directed
indiscriminately against nonspecific targets is the other type of
terrorism - sophisticated, subtle, discriminate, and highly
selective. It is no longer necessary to achieve terrorism's
primary goals, namely publicity and recognition, to have
recourse to mass, indiscriminate terror. Modern technologies
make it possible to obtain maximum publicity and to realize a
great impact with practically no loss in lives or with very few
lives lost. For this reason, Jenkins (1974) advances the
notion that terrorism is a theatre and that terrorists are actors
who perform their activities as an operational drama with the
world as an audience. They want a lot of people watching not
a lot of people dead. If this notion is correct, then one
would expect that, in the future, mass, random, and indiscriminate terror will cede the stage to a more selective but
highly dramatic type of terrorism. Some authors, however,

feel that the new technologies are moving terrorism from the specific to the nonspecific, from the discriminate to the indiscriminate, from the selective to the random. Russell, Banker, and Miller (1977) are of the view that modern technology, coupled with the increasingly fragile, exposed, and interdependent automated systems so essential to our modern society, appear to be leading toward a possible change in terrorist targeting from selected individuals to seemingly larger and less discriminate groups.

Face to Face Terrorism and Terrorism "A Distance"

An important distinction can be made between terrorist acts which necessitate and involve a direct confrontation (and the possibility of unobstructed communication) between the terrorist and the victim (e.g., kidnappings, hostage-taking, skyjacking) and terrorist acts where there is neither face-to-face confrontation nor direct communication with the victim (e.g., bombings, letter bombs, sabotage, arson, sniping). Furthermore, we can distinguish between incidents where a single victim is collectively victimized, such as a political figure or a diplomat kidnapped by a group of terrorists or a prison guard taken hostage by a group of inmates, and cases where several persons are victimized by a solitary terrorist or by a small group of terrorists. This is often the case of aircraft hijacking where the passengers and the crew are held by one or two hijackers. It is also the case of hostage-taking in banks, prisons, or residences where a group of employees, prison officials, or a whole family are held by one or two individuals.

It is reasonable to assume that the psychological effects on the victims in such cases are likely to vary in direct relation to the number of terrorists involved and in conjunction with the number of persons being simultaneously victimized. Numerical superiority or inferiority of the victims vis-a-vis the terrorists can lead, together with other factors, to differential reactions and varying responses of the victim(s) and can affect the intensity of the traumatic effects resulting from the victimization experience. Research might reveal significant differences in personality traits, psychological make-up, and social and cultural history between terrorists who act in a group against a single victim and those who act alone against a group of victims. Differences may also be found between terrorists who opt for a form of terror involving face-to-face confrontation with the victim(s) and terrorists who prefer to use methods in which any personal contact and any direct confrontation or communication with the victim(s) are avoided. Face-to-face terrorism requires more psychological courage and a stronger effort to neutralize one's inhibitions and to legitimize the act than terrorism at a distance.

Assassinations and bombings both require not only
the physical courage to commit the act but also the
moral or psychological courage necessary to justify
the act before it is committed and to rationalize it
afterward. There is a greater need for courage in
the case of assassination than in bombing in that
there is direct contact and a face-to-face confrontation between the victim and the terrorist, which
necessitates a considerable amount of psychological
preparation, of society as well as of the terrorist
(Qureshi 1976, p. 165).

Comparisons between victims of face-to-face terrorism and
victims of terrorism at a distance are also nonexistent. We
simply do not know the possible variations in victims' reactions
and victims' responses. To what extent are the traumatic
effects of victimization in the first category different from the
effects in the second category? This and many other questions remain unanswered.
Comparisons of terrorism victims who were subjected to
actual physical violence with victims who were merely subjected
to oral or written threats might also prove useful. Whatever
differences might be found between the attitude, behavior, and
response of the first category of victims and of those of the
second category could be helpful in reaching a better understanding of the phenomenon and for elaboration of policies for
control and prevention of terrorism, and for the treatment of
its victims.

A TYPOLOGY OF TERRORIST TARGETS

The term "terrorism" embraces a broad range of activity
directed against a wide variety of targets. Some terrorist acts
are directed exclusively against human targets, others are
aimed predominantly at material targets. A third category
which includes bombing and air piracy involves mixed targets
(objects and persons). There are reasons to believe that
terrorists make distinctions between appropriate and inappropriate, accessible and inaccessible targets; between personalized and generalized, specific and non-specific targets.
Terrorists may concentrate their attacks on real or symbolic
targets or both. They may choose for their aggression an
immediate victim while aiming at pressuring and terrorizing a
more significant secondary target. The targets are likely to
vary according to the type and aims of the terrorist group,
and only research can determine which group chooses which
targets. To facilitate the systematic study of terrorism and its
victims, it is necessary to develop a typology or typologies of

targets. Such typologies would allow the characterization and differentiation of specific types; the assessment of the accessibility, vulnerability, and visibility of each type, and a better understanding of terrorists' preference for, and selection of, particular targets. This information can be very useful in identifying potential targets for terrorist attacks and in elaborating a preventive strategy aimed at hardening those targets.

Immediate and Secondary Targets

In his <u>Blueprint of Revolution</u>, Momboisse (1970) distinguishes between immediate and secondary targets. The immediate target is that which sustains the physical assault, while the secondary target, of more significance in most instances, is the group that identifies itself with the actual victim and will automatically feel itself exposed to danger.

> Thus if the victim is a peace officer or an occupying soldier, others belonging to that class will identify themselves as members of a marked group. This group will probably be both "terrorized" and subjected to disorientation effects. But a much larger group, the people, also notice the act and are affected by it. To this end, the terrorist chooses persons or objects as targets which will help him to gain the sympathy of the majority of the population. Thus his victim should be the leader that is least liked by the people. In addition, if the victim is a symbolically significant target, the failure of the government to protect him will be considered a demonstration of government weakness and the party's power.

The distinction between immediate and secondary targets applies to many forms of terrorism. In kidnapping or hostage-taking, those who are abducted or seized are the immediate targets while their families, employers, or governments are the secondary targets. Even in cases where the immediate victim is assassinated, the terrorists may have nothing personal against him but may be aiming at the government or organization he represents. As immediate targets, terrorists usually pick visible and important individuals: prominent public figures, persons who are at the top of industrial, governmental, judicial, military or police organizations - corporate executives, politicians, judges, chiefs of police, or military commanders. But the immediate target need not be human. It may be an object which has symbolic significance or which represents something hated or despised by the terrorists. In

disruptive terrorism, the terrorists may choose as a primary
target one of the vital systems whose destruction can have a
significant impact: transportation, electrical system, or water
supply.

A similar distinction is the one between direct and
indirect targets. Direct targets are the ones raided or hit by
the terrorists (the hijacked aircraft, the kidnapped diplomat,
etc.) while indirect targets are those the terrorists want to
pressure, force, or undermine. The category of direct or
immediate targets lends itself to numerous subgroupings, and a
preventive policy aimed at hardening the targets will have to
focus on the prediction and protection of those immediate
targets to be identified through a thorough analysis of terrorist behavioral patterns.

Appropriate and Inappropriate Targets

Indiscriminate terror and mass destruction terrorism are, by
definition, directed against random targets. Disruptive
terrorism and selective terrorism, on the other hand, are
usually aimed at carefully selected targets. In making their
selection, terrorists seem to make subtle distinctions between
appropriate and inappropriate targets. Needless to say, some
targets are more attractive and more accessible than others.
Moreover, an appropriate target is one whose destruction or
victimization would help best the cause of the terrorists and
would assist them in achieving their goals. For example, in
disruptive terrorism, the appropriate target is one that can
have an optimum potential impact. Russell, Banker, and Miller
(1977) describe how the appropriate target is chosen in the
cases of disruptive terrorism:

> Terrorists (or pseudo-terrorists) must ask what
> existing targets, or those in the research and/or
> development phase, could be attacked to bring about
> the desired degree of disruption, chaos, incon-
> venience, and frustration. On one level, the ter-
> rorist would consider systems in terms of criticality
> of impact. Quite simply, what are the aspects of
> life which, if disrupted, would most quickly and
> demonstrably affect many human lives? Food, water,
> air, means of communication, modes of transporta-
> tion, management of the flow of goods and services,
> financial systems, health and emergency services all
> immediately spring to mind. While a temporary
> disruption of such services will not of necessity
> cause a great number of casualties, it will generate
> great concern among those directly affected, among
> those responsible for insuring the integrity of these

systems and among those who otherwise could have
been potential victims.

In cases of political kidnapping, the victim is usually chosen
with great care. As the primary objective is often to exert
pressure and to coerce the secondary targets into agreeing to
certain demands, the person to be kidnapped has to be an
individual whose life and safety are terribly important to those
who are to be coerced. Naturally, less appropriate targets
may eventually be victimized, either because the most appropriate ones are well protected and inaccessible or because
of other technical difficulties. However, the degree of pressure will always be proportional to the importance of the
immediate target to those who are being pressured.
    If terrorism takes the form of sabotage, arson, or
vandalism, the objects to be destroyed have to be of such
strategic importance or material value that their loss would
constitute a heavy blow to the victims. Objects of less or of
no material value may also be appropriate targets if they have
symbolic significance. The choice of symbolic targets was
quite evident in the assaults of the FLQ (Front de Libération
du Quebec) during the early 1960s. On March 29, 1963, the
FLQ destroyed one of the symbols of colonialism: the monu-
ment to General Wolfe on the Plains of Abraham in Quebec
City. On the 20th of April, Jacques Giroux (19) and Yves
Labonte (18) set out to blow up the statue of Sir John A.
MacDonald in Montreal's Dominion Square. The sight of several
policemen, on normal duty on that busy thoroughfare, scared
them away. They still had their bomb, so they dumped it into
a garbage can behind the Canadian Army recruiting center on
Sherbrooke Street. When, some time later, the night watchman
at the Center, Wilfred Vincent O'Neil, threw some waste into
the garbage can, the bomb exploded; O'Neil was killed in-
stantly (see Gellner 1974, p. 65). During the following
weeks, federal mailboxes were bombed in the predominantly
English city of Westmount (see Szabo 1970, p. 710).
    In cases of political terrorism, the appropriateness of the
target is usually proportional to the potential importance of the
victim: "Why do they want to kill you?" someone asked Malcolm
X. "Why can't you see? It's because I am me." Rapoport
(1971) notes that Malcolm X was irreplaceable. When he was
slain, all threats to Elijah Muhammad's dominance ceased.
    In organized terror (such as revolution, rebellion, or
guerilla warfare) the appropriate targets can change over time
and may vary during the different phases of the revolution or
rebellion. Leites and Wolf (1970) note that:

In general, an efficient Rebellion is likely to start
by picking, as targets for violent attack, resented,

low-performing officials and landlords. In any set of officials or landlords, some must obviously be less good and more resented than others. . . . Choosing the low performers for attack enhances the probability of acceptance or endorsement by the population and minimizes the probability of denunciation. . . . As Rebellion grows from small to large, and from weak to strong, the level and the quality of targets may rise. Executing a good official, or a generous landlord, may then evoke reactions of acceptance and non-denunciation from the population. . . . And execution of "good" targets later further strengthens R's claim to irresistible power and inevitable victory. . . . As R grows, it may thus move from the "bad" to the "good" targets, and from the low and relatively inconspicuous to the high and conspicuous targets.

The distinctions terrorists make between appropriate and inappropriate targets for victimization can be observed in the Irish case. In his study of sectarian assassination in Belfast, Lebow (1976) found that the majority of the victims were relatively young men. In his interviews with members of paramilitary organizations, most of them expressed revulsion at the killing of young children or the aged. Elderly people are not seen to be politically involved, whereas men in their prime of life are perceived as more legitimate targets for victimization as they may well be members or supporters of paramilitary bodies.

Accessible and Inaccessible Targets

Criminological research has shown that many crimes are, to a large extent, dependent upon, and functional of, the opportunities to commit them. Easy targets are more prone to victimization than hard targets. Such findings led to a new approach which emphasizes the hardening of criminal targets as an effective means of crime prevention.

In their search for appropriate targets, the terrorists have to look for those which are readily or easily accessible. A certain target may be highly appropriate for the terrorists' purposes and still be abandoned or ignored because of its inaccessibility. The inaccessibility of specific targets may lead to the use of indiscriminate or random terror. Because the success of the terrorist operation is vital to the terrorist(s), the accessibility of the target is extremely important as it is a safeguard against running the risk of a clear defeat. Thus, if the intended kidnap or assassination victim is constantly guarded by police, body guards, or a friendly crowd, either he/she has to be replaced by a more accessible target (if this is at all possible) or an assassin who is willing to risk or sacrifice his life has to be found.

In most cases, the choice of a certain target is prompted by its accessibility and its specific vulnerability. In some cases, however, the terrorists may select a target and try to discover its most vulnerable points. This is particularly the case in disruptive terrorism where the choice of target is often made on the basis of its appropriateness and independently of its accessibility or vulnerability.

> Having selected a target system, the terrorist must then determine the most vulnerable points within the system, i.e., identify the weak link in terms of vulnerability to external attack or the Key element upon which the entire system depends. Obviously, the optimum or ideal case would be for those two target characteristics to coincide at the same locus (Russell, Banker, and Miller 1977).

In his study of Irish terrorism, Lebow (1976) explains the high rate of victimization of young males in the sectarian assassination in Belfast by their availability as readily accessible targets. He notes that assassinations are generally carried out at night under the cover of darkness and neither the very young nor the very old are likely to be on the street at that time.

A specific target is usually more vulnerable and more accessible in certain situations than in others. The analysis of several cases of political kidnappings including those of Sir Geoffrey Jackson in Uruguay and Aldo Moro in Italy clearly shows that diplomats, government officials, and business executives are more vulnerable and more easily accessible while in the car during the journey from home to work or the reverse.

Clutterbuck (1975) reports that, in an analysis of 35 major political kidnappings between January 1968 and June 1973, the Committee on Internal Security of the U.S. House of Representatives found that more than half (20) had been of officials or executives in their cars on the way between home and work, or while driving to, or returning from, official functions. Of the remainder, 11 were kidnapped from home and only 2 from their place of work. Two fell into none of these categories (e.g., one was an attache arriving for his customary 6:00 a.m. calisthenics on the polo field in Santo Domingo).

Chiefs of State and Heads of Government are also more vulnerable when in their cars than when they are at their offices or in their official residences where they are usually well protected. President Kennedy was assassinated while in a

car driving through the streets of Dallas, Texas. Several
attacks have been made on Heads of States while in their cars.
This is particularly true of countries governed by totalitarian
regimes where the Head of State rarely, if ever, comes into
direct contact with the people, and is rarely physically exposed to them.

Personalized and Generalized Targets

Totally random, indiscriminate terror seems to be the exception
rather than the rule. In most cases, targets for victimization
are not chosen in a haphazard fashion but are carefully
selected according to specific criteria and because they are
appropriate targets for aggression. In certain types of
terrorism, the personal characteristics of the victim are not of
particular importance. The victim is chosen as a target
according to a more global criteria, that of belonging to a
certain race, a specific ethnic group, being a member of a
particular religious faith, being a representative of a certain
government, or having an affiliation with a certain political
party. This pattern is particularly clear in Ireland. Lebow
(1976) noted:

> The conventional wisdom in Belfast assumes that most
> assassinations in that city are random sectarian
> killings. The available evidence does not support
> this conclusion. Nearly half of the murders of
> civilians in Belfast appear to be planned executions
> of specific persons. Many of those killed are sus-
> pected informers or victims of leadership struggles
> in paramilitary organizations. Such people are
> generally killed by members of their own communal
> group. Even those murders which are truly sec-
> tarian are less random than might be supposed.

"Target generalization" or "object generalization" are concepts
well known to students of violence and aggression. Miller and
Berkowitz, among others, have used these concepts in their
attempts to explain the choice of certain targets and the
displacement of aggression. Berkowitz (1962) carried out
experiments which suggest that hostility tends to generalize
from a frustrator to previously disliked individuals or groups.
The same generalization and displacement take place in many
terrorist activities and the result is a more generalized type of
terrorism. There seems to be a growing tendency to replace
the traditional, highly personalized targets of the past by more
generalized ones, and to move from the assassination of chiefs
of state and other men in positions of power to more generalized targets. Personalized targets remain, of course, popular

in tactical terror used by the ruled against the rulers, the oppressed against the oppressors. Terrorism in these cases tends to be directed, whenever possible, against those regarded as really responsible for the tyranny or oppression. On the other hand, terror aimed at weakening the government, erosion of institutions, and intimidation of decision makers is often directed against a generalized target and the popular technique is to place bombs or other explosives in places where people congregate.

In cases of hijacking, kidnapping, hostage-taking, and assassinations, targets are usually specific and highly personalized, whereas target generalization is more characteristic of riots, revolts, and civil disturbances. Discussing the types of violence employed in riots, Momboisse (1967) remarks that, when the mob violence "gets into high gear," the objects against which the violence is directed become more generalized.

> Whereas the violence may originally have been directed solely against members of another race, against management, or against school authorities, to name a few, the emotionally driven, nonlogical destruction may now spread to include other persons or property which, no matter how remotely, represent to the mob members symbols of the conditions producing the initial frustration. They may see the policeman or the other authorities as symbols for their hatred. The statehouse, police station, churches, grocery stores, pawn shops, liquor stores, and all sorts of establishments become "fair game" once the violence gets out of control.

Gurr (1968) gives several examples of object generalization in civil violence and quotes studies which demonstrated positive relationships between poor economic conditions and lynchings of Negroes in the American South. Another example is the initial reaction of urban white colonialists to African rural uprisings in Madagascar in 1947 and Angola in 1961 which was vigilante-style execution of urban Africans who had no connection with the rebellions. Gurr believes that object generalization is a crucial variable in determining who will be attacked by the initiators of particular acts of civil violence. He refers to psychological evidence regarding response generalization as a tool helpful in understanding why certain targets are victimized:

> Experimental evidence suggests that only a narrow range of objects provides satisfying targets for men's aggressive responses, but that almost any form of aggression can be satisfying so long as the angry person believes that he has in some way injured his supposed frustrator (p. 49).

The ultimate form of "response generalization" and "target generalization" is war, when terrorist acts are directed toward the entire people or toward a whole nation. Terror exercised during war is general and indiscriminate. Yet, in lesser forms, terror is used less indiscriminately and is usually conducted against definite objectives, with the aim of impressing on the masses that the terrorist methods can be used "next time" against other members of the group (see Roucek 1962, p. 169).

CONCLUSION

Effective action against terrorism requires better comprehension of the terrorists' aims and strategy and adequate understanding of their behavioral patterns and their targeting policies. To achieve such understanding, it is necessary to go beyond the study of the terrorist's motivation and personality to a careful analysis of his actions and his tactics: what techniques he uses, what targets he attacks, how he selects his victims. Target-hardening has proven to be one of the most effective strategies in crime prevention, and there is every reason to believe that it can be equally effective in combatting terrorism. A strategy of target-hardening should have as its goal the identification and protection of likely potential targets. It should aim at reducing the accessibility and vulnerability of the most popular victims or the most appropriate targets. Typologies of terrorist activities and of terrorist targets are useful tools in understanding terrorist behaviors, their selection of targets, and the criteria they use in such selection. Typologies make it possible to link certain types of terrorists (or terrorist groups) to specific types of targets and to find out what type of terrorist uses which techniques against which targets. Only then could terrorist strategies be countered and terrorist attempts be foiled because, as Fromkin (1975) pointed out, terrorist success is almost always the result of misunderstandings or misconceptions of the terrorist strategy.

Prevention of terrorism will further require a great improvement in the social conditions that produce, beget, or trigger terrorist acts, and the correction of the political and socio-economic injustices that breed the terrorist. Only a radical change in those conditions would substantially reduce the incidence of terrorism. Terror by governments (repressive terror) which claims many more victims and causes much more sufferings than individual terrorism (or terrorism by groups) has to be dealt with more effectively through the world's international organizations. It is only through the efforts of such bodies that the use of violence as an instrument of power or as a means of mass destruction can be stopped.

REFERENCES

Alexander, Y., Ed. International Terrorism. National, Regional and Global Perspectives. New York: Praeger, 1976.

Bassiouni, M.C. International Terrorism and Political Crimes. Springfield, Illinois: Charles C. Thomas, 1975.

Bell, Bowyer, J. Transnational Terror. Washington, D.C.: American Enterprise Institute for Public Policy Research, 1975.

Clutterbuck, R. Living With Terrorism. London: Faber & Faber, 1975.

_____. Protest and the Urban Guerrilla. London: Cassell, 1973.

Fromkin, D. "The Strategy of Terrorism," Foreign Affairs. July 1975.

Gellner, J. Bayonets in the Streets. Ontario: Collier-Macmillan Canada, 1974.

Gurr, T.R. "Psychological Factors in Civil Violence," World Politics XX, January 1972, pp. 245-278. Reprinted in Feierabend, I.K., Feierabend, R.L., and Gurr, T.R. Anger, Violence and Politics. Englewood Cliffs, N.J.: Prentice-Hall, 1972.

Hyams, E. Terrorists and Terrorism. New York: St. Martin's Press, 1974.

Jenkins, B.M. International Terrorism: A New Kind of Warfare. Rand Publications. P-5261, June 1974, p. 4.

Lebow, R.N. "The Origins of Sectarian Assassination: The Case of Belfast." Unpublished manuscript. 1976.

Leites, N., and Wolf, C., Jr. Rebellion and Authority. Chicago: Markham 1970, pp. 54-55.

Miller, N.E. "Theory and experiment relating psychoanalytic displacement to stimulus-response generalization," Journal of Abnormal and Social Psychology XLIII, April 1948, pp. 155-178.

Momboisse, R.M. Blueprint of Revolution. Springfield, Ill.: Charles C. Thomas, 1970, pp. 265-267.

Momboisse, R.M. Riots, Revolts and Insurrections. Spring-field, Ill.: Charles C. Thomas, 1967, p. 20.

Moss, R. Urban Guerillas. London: Maurice Temple Smith, 1972.

Pourcelet, M. "Hijacking: The Limitations of the International Treaty Approach." In Aerial Piracy and International Law edited by E. McWhinney. Leiden: A.W. Sijthoff, 1971.

Qureshi, S. "Political Violence in the South Asian Subcontinent." In International Terrorism: National, Regional and Global Perspectives edited by Y. Alexander. New York: Praeger, 1976, pp. 151-86.

Rapoport, D.C. Assassination and Terrorism. Toronto: T.H. Best, 1971.

Roucek, J.S. "Sociological Elements of a Theory of Terror and Violence," American Journal of Economics and Sociology 21 (Spring 1962): 165-72.

Russell, C.A.; Banker Jr., L.J.; Miller, B.H. "Outinventing the Terrorist." Paper presented at an International Conference on Terrorism. Evian, France, May 1977, pp. 19-20.

Szabo, D. "Assasination and political violence in Canada." In Assasination and Political Violence, a staff report to the National Commission on the causes and prevention of violence. Prepared by J.F. Kirkham; S.G. Levy; and W.J. Crotty. New York: New York Times, 1970, pp. 700-714.

II

Psychological Perspectives

3 The Psychodynamics of Terrorism
Abraham Kaplan

INTRODUCTION

This is a chapter on some causes of terrorism, not on the reasons for its occurrence. The causes of an action, as of any other event, are the distinctive conditions which bring it about (or which invariably precede that kind of event). The reasons for an action are the purposes it is meant to serve, as the actor sees them, or as he would see them if he were fully aware of his purposes. Something may be a causal agency even if it is not the cause (not strictly invariant); and more than one reason may be at work, as in a move at chess. There may be no reason at all, as in the expression of a whim; there is always a cause.

Causes and reasons may coincide. Theft may be caused by poverty, and getting rich quick may be its reason. But causes and reasons may also differ significantly. An act may be caused by posthypnotic suggestion or by operant conditioning, while its reason is conveyed in the hypnotist's cue for the action, or in the theme of the advertising by which the buyer was conditioned.

In terrorism, the reasons usually offered are far from causes. The assassin of President McKinley, Leon Czolgosz, gave the reasons of an anarchist egalitarian. "It is not right," he declared, "that the President should have every-

---

*This chapter was published originally in Terrorism: An International Journal, Vol. 1 (numbers 3 and 4), 1978, pp. 237–258. We acknowledge with thanks a special permission granted by Crane Russak, New York to reprint the chapter.

thing and we (sic) should have nothing." The reason for the assassination might lie with the President, but its causes must be sought in the psychopathology of the assassin. Arab terrorists may offer reasons which refer to "the just rights of the Palestinians," while the causes of their acts of terror may be traced back to circumstances preceding the emergence of any Palestinian identity.

Distinguishing between causes and reasons is not an attempt to penetrate rationalizations. To call a reason a rationalization is to say that it is only a purported reason, not the reason actually at work; it is not to say that it is a reason rather than a cause. A rationalization may be a good reason though it is not the real reason; and it may illuminate the cause though it obscures the reason. This chapter is not about reasons for terror (a fortiori not about its rationalizations), except as reasons suggest operative causes.

Among the reasons for terror, one frequently offered (usually a rationalization) is that it is the only recourse available in the struggle against overwhelming power. This cannot be a cause for terror. Terror has often been used by the superior power rather than by those struggling against it - as in the regimes of Mussolini, Hitler, and Franco. The chief spokesman of the French Reign of Terror, Robespierre, characterized terror as "nothing else than justice, prompt, secure and inflexible," and in a speech before the Convention stated that "the first maxim of our policy should be to conduct the people by reason, and the enemies of the people by terror."

Conversely, many revolutionary and resistance movements, though facing vastly superior power, nevertheless repudiated acts of terror. This was true of most Marxist revolutionaries, of Gandhi, of the French Resistance, and of the Haganah (decision of the Zionist Council, 1946). The use of terror either to strengthen a new regime or to overthrow an old one is not explained merely by reference to political struggle.

What is terror? The term functions as a political symbol, as well as a category of political science. Israel, for instance, was accused of terror when it raided so-called "refugee camps" which the subsequent civil war in Lebanon revealed to be armed bases. Maintaining security in the West Bank brings forth recurrent accusations of terror, accusations whose substance is no more than the circumstance that the area is under military administration. As a political symbol, "terror" is often applied to any use of force which those applying the symbol regard as unjust, illegitimate, or excessive. In this application, it means little more than violence disapproved by the speaker. Such loose usage may be politically effective, but contributes little to understanding.

I mean by terror the use of force primarily to produce a certain fearful state of mind - terror, in fact. Some element of fear is evoked by every exercise of power; in terror, this element looms large, whether as cause or as reason. Moreover, the fear is to be evoked in someone other than those to whom the force is applied. Terror is the use of force in a context which differentiates the victim of the violence employed from the target of the action.

Since victim and target may be related in various ways, the distinction between them may be unclear or debatable. Machine-gunning school children or bombing a civilian airliner are unmistakable acts of terror, since the victims are not involved in whatever motivated the acts, and so cannot be the targets. On the other hand, in an attack on a military base, victim and target coincide, although there may be a secondary effect on other military units, or on the civilian authorities making use of the military. The killing of an isolated soldier in a barroom may be an act of terror even though he is not only victim but part of the target.

Related to the distinction between target and victim is that between the demands made by the terrorist and the aim of his act of terror. The demands are the conditions he sets - for minimizing the effect on victims - conditions for releasing hostages, for example. The aims relate to the target, terrorizing him so as to produce a change in policy - for example, Kreisky's closing the transit center in Vienna for refugees from the Soviet Union.

The terrorist may deny that he has any aims other than those set forth in his demands. He may even deny that he is engaged in an act of terror, repudiating the distinction between victim and target by arguing that "there are no innocents" - as though the victims have identified themselves with the target simply be being where they are. Presumably, the pilgrims killed in the Lod airport massacre should not have been visiting the Holy Land while it was being occupied by "the Zionist entity."

Often the demands amount to little more than amnesty (safe conduct, etc.) for the act which provided the setting for the demands to start with. The closed circle appears to be empty only when the demands are dissociated from the aims, which are operative whether or not the demands are met, and which may even be better fulfilled when the demands are denied. A topical cartoon shows two policemen at a scene of recent violence; one is saying to the other, "It was an old-fashioned crime - it had a motive." Terror appears to be lacking a motive when it is only demands that are lacking; the aim - to terrorize - may be apparent just because the victims cannot in any way be mistaken for targets.

Acts of terror are often associated with other acts of violence, in which victim and target coincide. Such linked violence is illustrated by a bank robbery carried out (for instance, by the Symbionese Liberation Army) to finance subsequent acts of terror; by a battle (as by the PLO against the Jordanian army regulars) to secure a base of operations for a terrorist group; or by an act of revenge (for example, the assassination of the official responsible for the capture and death of Che Guevara). The linked violence has a conditional rationale; its causes are subsidiary to those for the planned or past terror from which it derives.

In addition to the terrorist, his victim, and his target, there is a fourth participant: the audience, the spectators viewing the action from the sidelines. The victim is destroyed (or threatened); the target is terrorized; the audience is impressed. Producing the impression is another aim of the act of terror; sometimes it is more important than terrorizing the target.

Two audiences can be distinguished. The general audience is usually referred to as "public opinion," on a national or international scale. In fact, what matters may be the opinion, not of any identifiable public, but of governments, or of certain officials. An act of terror may evoke widespread revulsion, yet succeed in its aims of producing an impression of strength and determination on those responsible for government decisions. What is the general audience for an act of terror may depend less on the media coverage of the act than on the political patterns by which the response will be structured.

The special audience consists of potential rivals or allies of the terrorist. An act of terror may aim chiefly at impressing the special audience with the capacity of that terrorist group for carrying out the major attack against the target which is presumed to be a basic goal shared with the special audience. The terrorist may "claim" responsibility for a certain outrage - "claim" it, not "admit" it - so as to make an impression on the special audience.

For the general audience, there may be at the same time a disclaimer of responsibility, even a declaration of intention to bring to justice those who are responsible. Distinct organisations, or at least symbols of identification, may be developed so that the one may claim responsibility while the other denies it. The terrorist who actually carries out the operation is an agent for a principal who may preserve a certain apparent dissociation from the act. States like Syria and Lybia, which; provide training and refuge for terrorist agents (whose target might be Jordan, Lebanon, or Egypt, as well as Israel), can properly be described as terrorist principals.

The empirical content of the distinctions drawn can be illustratively specified by reference to Arab terror in recent years. Violence, as distinct from terror, has been widely used in the Arab world in the course of power struggles.

Since 1948, there have been 60 attempted coups or revolts in the Arab states, about half of them successful; 22 top leaders - kings, presidents, prime ministers, and generals - have been assassinated. By and large, the victims of this violence were themselves the targets; aims were attained by the mere fact of their removal from the scene.

In contrast, acts of terror, with Israel or the "the Zionists" as their target, claimed such victims as 29 students injured in the bombing of the Hebrew University cafeteria; 47 passengers and crew killed on a Swissair plane in Zurich; 8 children killed and 20 wounded on a school bus in Galileo; 25 killed (mostly Puerto Rican pilgrims) and 72 injured at the Lod airport; 11 Olympic athletes killed in Munich; 18 residents of an apartment building killed in Kiryat Shemona; 23 children killed and 72 wounded in Ma'alot; a woman and two children killed in Nahariya; dozens of pedestrians injured in various bombings in Zion Square and elsewhere in downtown Jerusalem; dozens of supermarket customers injured, and more than 100 passengers injured in commercial airliners belonging to the United States, Belgium, Germany, Greece, Switzerland, England, France, Yugoslavia, and Italy.

The importance of the audience for acts of terror, particularly the special audience, is shown by the large number of casualties sustained by members of the audience rather than by the target or by victims whose fate might terrorize the target. (Many of these casualties result from linked violence rather than from acts of terror themselves.) Thus, in the course of the Algerian terror, the ratio of Algerians killed to Europeans, victims of violence carried out by Algerians themselves, was about 8 to 1. In Gaza, the ratio of Arab to Jewish casualties, produced by Arab terror and linked violence, is more than 15 to 1. The Lebanese civil war, to a significant degree violence linked with the demands by the Palestine Liberation Army for an autonomous base of operations, claimed more Arab casualties than all the wars against Israel put together.

It is intrinsic to terror that the victims are so loosely identified with the target, if at all. Moreover, the scene of violence cannot usually be given the remotest military significance: a school bus, a supermarket, an athletic competition, a hotel lobby, a theatre, or that favored locale for Irish terrorism: a bar. The terror is intensified by the innocence of the victim and the setting.

Lasswell speaks in this connection of the "symbolic enhancement" of violence - for instance, the Borgias attacking their victims in church. A modern instance of symbolic enhancement of violence is provided by the outbreak of the Yom Kippur war. Some of the reasons for a surprise attack were inoperative because it was Yom Kippur: mobilization was rapid because soldiers were easily located (in the synagogues),

and roads were completely free of traffic. Had the attach
been mounted on a festival like Rosh Hashanah (New Year)
some ten days earlier, soldiers would have been scattered in
parks, beaches, and resorts, and the roads clogged with
vacationers. The symbolic enhancement of attacking just when
all Israel was at prayer must have been judged to be worth
the loss of a certain tactical advantage.

Perceived immorality is intrinsic to the act of terror.
What makes it terrifying is not the sheer amount of violence
displayed (as an earthquake or atomic explosion is terrifying),
but the demonstrated readiness to sacrifice any victim, to use
any means in order to achieve an end. The loud cries of the
Japanese warrior are effective not only because they startle
but also because they simulate animality, and animals fight
with no restraints whatever.

There is likely to be a difference in moral judgment
between the terrorist and the special audience on the one
hand, and the victim, target, and general audience on the
other. The terrorist's thinking must be able to bridge this
difference, so that he can anticipate reactions. He must
choose acts which will be seen as sufficiently immoral to be
terrifying, but no so abhorrent as to evoke condemnation by
the general audience.

Terror becomes acceptable when the ends it is meant to
serve are seen as <u>absolutes</u>. If goals have an unconditional
value, they are nonnegotiable and, hence, may need violence
for their attainment. If their worth is incommensurable with
any other values, they justify violence which would otherwise
be immoral. Like virtue which, if compromised, is already
lost, an absolute end demands unqualified devotion, whatever
means it calls for.

Pursuit of the absolute end is the standard of morality.
The principle was formulated by the anarchist Mikhail Bakunin
who said that whatever aids the revolution is ethical and all
that hinders it is unethical and criminal. Today, in place of
"revolution" we are likely to find "national liberation." The
pattern of causal agency is the same: terror has a place on
the agenda whenever means are being assessed for absolute
ends.

The assessment presupposes a break between means and
ends, in holding that the quality of the end remains unaffected
by the means used to attain it. It is assumed that whatever
acts of terror are written into the first page of the new
nation's history, the second page will record justice, freedom,
equality, or whatever other values present themselves as
absolutes. Unless this assumption is made, terror loses its
rationale. The absoluteness of the end is both a necessary
and a sufficient condition for justifying acts of terror.

The terrorist must, therefore, be certain that the value
of his end <u>is</u> absolute. The <u>certitude</u> of the terrorist is a

repudiation of fallibility of politics. By contrast, Benjamin Franklin's aphorism that nothing's sure but death and taxes was framed in the context of debates on the proposed Constitution for the United States. Commitments can be made which are total in scope - pledging "our lives, our fortunes, and our sacred honor", in the closing words of the American Declaration of Independence - even though they are not based on certitude; but such commitments do not recognize any ends as being so absolute as to exempt their means from moral assessment.

Terrorist absolutism is also <u>doctrinaire</u>: the terrorist is certain <u>which</u> end is absolutely worthy. The goal to be attained and what stands in the way of its attainment is already known: we need only terrorize the target and all will be well. The new order which is to replace the old may be specified only vaguely, if at all, so long as the target is definite enough to provide a setting for the act of terror.

Terrorist doctrine does not require a detailed and coherent ideology. On the contrary; ideological explicitness might cast doubt on the supposed connection between the act of terror and the absolute end. How exactly will "imperialism" be defeated or "capitalism" overthrown by sporadic bombings of corporate offices, banks, or department stores in Palo Alto or Tokyo? In the state of mind which produces terrorism, such questions simply do not arise.

The illogic of absolutism is most blatant in the notion, not that the end justifies the means, but that the means justify the end. The inference likely to be made explicitly by the general audience and implicitly by the terrorist is that action so desperate testifies to the justice of the cause. How great a value the end must have if the terrorist attempts to attain it with such questionable means. A Zen master suddenly split a kitten in two in order to galvanize the assembled monks; another cut off his own arm to demonstrate the earnestness of his pursuit of <u>satori.</u>

Terrorism exhibits a self-righteousness which may conceal the terrorist's insecurities, and which evokes identification from audiences because of their own insecurities. If the battle is between the Children of Light and the Children of Darkness, we need no longer be anxious about our sins: it is <u>they</u> who are the sinners. The demonization of the target is important because it rationalizes destroying him, and even more important because it allows a corresponding heroization of the terrorist and of those in the audience who identify with him. Enough anxiety stifles guilt.

A need to pursue absolute ends, whether or not the need is rooted in anxiety, is characteristic of the terrorist. Personal need can determine social goals, as Lasswell long ago pointed out. Acts of terror on behalf of "the just rights of the Palestinians" may be committed by terrorists who are not

Palestinians, not even Arabs who might be thought to identify with the Palestinians, but Japanese, Germans, or Bolivians. The important thing is not <u>who</u> they are but <u>what</u> they are. An international network of terror is less an organizational reality than the pervasiveness of a psychopathology.

To the degree that terrorism is caused by absolutism, it can be lessened by reinstating the link between means and ends which absolutism breaks, especially with regard to the consequences <u>to the terrorist</u> of his actions. Though the general audience often "deplores" acts of terror, it does little beyond making the pious pronouncements. Undeniable crimes are committed (as distinct from legitimate acts of war) but punishment is far from swift and sure. On the contrary, it is virtually sure that punishment will be delayed or dispensed with altogether. Punishment of terrorists is, on the whole, lighter and less frequent than punishment of traffic offenders.

The causal efficacy of absolutism can be weakened by unwavering refusals to release arrested terrorist for "trial" by others, whether paralegal groups or bonafide states, since such proceedings invariably result in no punishment (as illustrated by the fate of the Khartoum terrorists). Rejection of all terrorist demands for the release of those imprisoned for previous terrorist acts maintains the connection between terror and consequences not desired by the terrorist. For the same reasons, full recognition must be given and appropriate steps taken with regard to the crime of accessory before or after the fact (for instance, canceling air transportation to countries harboring terrorists). The supposedly absolute end must be shown to be subject, in reality, to such intolerable conditions as no longer to invite terrorist means for its attainment.

Terrorism is a response to a lack of self-esteem. The terrorist is not simply fighting for a cause, the cause fights for him. He may have suffered a severe blow to his self-esteem - from a crushing military defeat, for example; or he may gradually have become aware of the lack of something he never had, a firm basis of self-respect. There may be a need to counter an impulse to self-contempt, an introjection of humiliations imposed by others - the mechanism familiar as identifying with the aggressor. The terrorist sees himself as occupying some secondary status. The end of colonialism in our time is the result more of an insistence on the autonomy essential to self-respect than of a rejection of foreign exploitation for the sake of purely economic gains.

Struggles for national independence share this content with egalitarian movements of all sorts, such as those directed against sexism and racism. The liberation to be achieved is essentially a liberation from what has come to be perceived as intolerable degradation. (Among young American blacks between the ages of 18 and 24, the chief cause of death is suicide.)

Embarking on terrorism is an alternative. Thereby, the terrorist acquires a sense of purpose; instead of drifting, he can prepare for, plan, and carry out a meaningful program of action. Any accomplishment, to say nothing of heroic achievement, will overcome the feeling of futility. He is at last the architect of his own fate, the creator of his life-circumstances, rather than their creature. Above all, from now on, he must be reckoned with, taken into account. In short, he is somebody, no longer a nonperson.

One component of the self-esteem afforded by terrorism is a renewed sense of masculinity. The "chivalric courtesy" of skyjackers has been widely noted. Of similar relevance is the observation that the pilot's attempts to deal with the situation only escalate the danger, since his intervention is perceived by the skyjacker as a challenge. The stewardess is likely to be more effective with the skyjacker than male passengers or members of the crew; for her to take the skyjacker seriously is already a significant fulfillment of his aspirations.

The response with an act of terror to a threat to masculine self-esteem is reinforced by the general tendency in many cultures to perceive "manliness" in terms of skills in the use of violence and a readiness to exercise them, rather than, say, in terms of the capacity for love. The sexual symbolism of sword, dagger, rifle, pistol, and bomb does not involve any Freudian subtleties, but is culturally defined as an expression of machismo. There is an unmistakable pornography of violence in our time, linked with classical sadomasochistic perversions. An analysis of the image and self-image of the female terrorist might be especially illuminating. Leila Khalid, Ulrike Meinhof, and Patty Hearst exemplify three types.

Whatever the role of sexual identity, there is no doubt that self-esteem demands self-determination. This is what it means to outgrow childish dependencies. Student and black unrest in the 1960s often evoked the unperceptive comment, "No matter what you give them, they're never satisfied." The satisfaction sought was from the capacity to take something, not to be given it. "Every decent man of our age must be a coward and a slave," wrote Dostoevsky in his Notes from Underground; in that case, to transcend cowardice and slavery, we must abandon decency. If I choose what is indecent, improper, condemned by all the right-thinking element in society, I demonstrate unequivocally that is is my own choice, not a contemptible conformism.

It is well known that revolutions are not made by the hopelessly downtrodden but by the upwardly mobile. Resources are needed with which to carry on the struggle. On the psychological side, the most important resources are self-reliance, self-confidence, and self-esteem. Such a state of mind is both a means and an end of revolutionary action. Every revolution, Lasswell has said, is a rupture of conscience; by the same token, it is a new birth of self-respect. On one level, the terrorist does not feel guilt for what he has done but pride. He "claims" responsibility not just to impress the special audience but to convey how much he himself has been impressed.

The frequency of attempted skyjackings rises sharply in the periods immediately following space spectaculars. The astronaut apparently serves as an ego-ideal to be emulated by a display of courage, resourcefulness and determination "up there." To the degree that terrorism is caused by the search for self-esteem, it can be lessened by negating its purported heroism.

Positive reinforcement of terrorist action is provided by the hero's welcome accorded its perpetrators (for instance, Gaddafi's treatment of the Munich Olympic Games terrorists). Less dramatic, but cumulatively more significant reinforcement results from labeling terrorists "freedom-fighters," in total disregard of the fact that no fighting is involved in attacking unarmed civilians, children, and other such victims. The less heroizing label "guerilla" also disregards the essential feature of terrorism, that the victim is not the target - in contrast to genuine guerilla action, which is carried out against military forces or their supply lines and communications, and not against civilian populations.

The role of the media is especailly important here. The self-restraint displayed by the media in other contexts (reporting of juvenile offenders, rape victims, and the like) contrasts markedly with the full coverage given terrorist actions, even while they are in progress. The publicity glamorizes the events, whatever perspective they are put in. The extent of the coverage is a measure which cannot be fudged of the importance being attached to the action. The terrorist is a celebrity no matter what.

Care should be taken that the punishment fits the crime, as the terrorist sees the punishment. If it is to serve as a deterrent, it should be labor which he will perceive as degrading, especially as unmanly - some act that has no relish of salvation in it. There is less deterrence in a sentence to hard labor than to what he sees as some sort of "woman's work," like being kitchen aide or hospital orderly.

Terrorism can not only shore up a weakened ego, it can also shatter its walls altogether, freeing the self from what has come to be felt as a prison. "Happiness is taking part in the struggle where there is no borderline between one's own personal world and the world in general" - this is a declaration of the assassin of John Kennedy, Lee Harvey Oswald. There is in terrorism a regression to what Freud called the "oceanic feeling" common to mysticism and to the infantile state in which self and other are not yet differentiated.

The connection with mysticism is manifested at another point. The terrorist is "twice-born," as William James put it in his analysis of the religious experience. Admission to the terrorist band may be marked by a symbolic rite of initiation. Subsequent discipline is less a training in the skills of violence than a continual reaffirmation of the divorce from the ordinary life which belongs to the departed individuality. The new identity is likely to be expressed in a new name, as happens in religious conversions, when Saul of Tarsus became Paul, or, mutatis mutandis, Cassius Clay became Mohammed Ali. The "code names" commonly employed by terrorists do not have a security function, being regularly reported in the public press; they express, rather, the negation of the conventionally recognized individuality. The act of terror is usually performed in the name of a group; the terrorist feels himself to be significant only as a member of the group, not as an individual. This is explicitly conveyed by the anonymity in such names as "Malcolm X."

That the ordinary self has been transcended is proved to the terrorist by the inhumanity of his terrorism. Another man might say, "I was beside myself when I did that"; the terrorist lives beside himself. The word "assassin" derives from the medieval band of terrorist who committed their murders while under the influence of hashish; dissociations of personality need not be drug-induced.

The loss of individuality is adequately compensated for if there are special needs to be met. A sense of impotence is overcome by merging individuality in the larger, far more powerful, group: however weak I was, we are strong, and I am now we. Moreover, new-found power accrues to whoever abandons old constraints - for instance, those of conventional morality. In that case, whatever he can do he may do. Furthermore, he can do it without assuming responsibility, for this belongs to the group. The search of refuge in collective responsibility motivates the individual's escape from freedom.

To the degree that terrorism is caused by the repudiation of individuality, it can be lessened by an emphasis on personal responsibility. The terrorist must be brought to account as an individual, not as a member of a group or movement, though other individuals can be tried as accomplices or co-conspirators. Moreover, as in the case of a soldier guilty of atrocities, the plea of "merely carrying out orders" must be strictly disallowed. Above all, demands for the release of other terrorists already convicted must never be granted, for this would reinforce the sense of a merged collective identity.

The terrorist performs on the stage of history. If single acts of terror do not have historic consequences - as compared, say with a coup d'etat - they, nevertheless, bring the terrorist into relation with the great ones of the earth. An act which creates "consternation and sleeplessness at the White

House" is no trivial affair. The whole world knows what the terrorist is doing, and breathlessly awaits his next move; kings and ministers speed at his bidding.

He has not only achieved self-determination; now it is he who compels others. Precisely those with power and prestige are the ones compelled, and they respond with humility: "Tell us what you want us to do." The target is being manipulated. Control over the victim is absolute – his fate lies entirely in the terrorist's hands. Once it was the terrorist who was victimized (he feels); now the tables have been turned. The victim of terror is usually anonymous, a nobody in the terrorist's eyes, such as the terrorist himself once was. The victim may also be, on the contrary, a notable, deliberately selected to symbolize the terrorist's ruthlessness and power. We might call him the glamorous victim. Occasionally, a personage is accidentally among the victims, such as the scientist brother of the president of Israel killed at Lod, or terrorist propaganda may subsequently exploit an accidental victim as glamorous.

Recent glamorous victims of Arab terror are exemplified by the Belgian and American diplomats killed at the Saudi embassy in Khartoum; the Anglo-Jewish magnate shot in his home in London; and the OPEC oil ministers kidnapped from their international headquarters in Vienna. Assassinated presidents such as Garfield and McKinley were, in their day, as glamorous as Lincoln and Kennedy; in any case, glamour attaches to the office, whatever the image of the man. It is the glamor which makes an assassination terroristic rather than purely political. The aim of terror is not by itself to replace a ruler (or ruling group), but to "teach them all a lesson."

If the anonymous victim represents the terrorist's past, the glamorous victim may serve as his ego-ideal for the future. Like imitation, violence, too, may be a form of flattery. That each man kills the thing he loves is romanticist moonshine, but psychopathology gives it substance. Sirhan Sirhan, the assassin of Robert Kennedy, said, "I loved that man." Violence as reaction-formation to positive feelings is well-known in childhood. Webster's nostalgic cartoon of the schoolboy and the girl in the cloakroom making faces at one another is labeled "Love at first sight." Linus speaks for the present generation: "She asked if I wanted to be friends, and I didn't know what to say – so I slugged her!" Terrorism may provide for the terrorist a sense of intimacy with both target and victim.

To the degree that terrorism is caused by the aspiration to such intimacy, it can be lessened by maximizing the psychic distance with which the terrorist is responded to. The victim may be helpless here, but target and audience have options. The terroristic act must be treated at as low a level as practicable; the steps taken are to be directed, not by the Prime Minister, Secretary of Defense, or Commander of Security Forces, but by the Deputy Assistant Inspector for the Northern Region, or some such local official. The response should not be presented as a negotiation (which implies a certain equality between the parties) but as a more or less routine police action in which nothing can be offered to the criminal, save avoiding the inevitable consequences of prolonging resistance to arrest.

Throughout, a low key should be maintained; terrorism is reinforced by the emotional excitement it can produce. Heightened suspense, anxiety, horror, moral outrage, and the like contribute to what the terrorist experiences as consummation, just as do approval and admiration. What the terrorist wants to be able to say is, "I didn't know you cared." He is disheartened only when he can no longer mistake for emotional involvement with him what is only our concern about the victim.

Terrorism is magic: it is thought to produce its effect no matter what, and all by itself. There are no causal linkages to be traced, as in the case of genuine military operations.

Terror is first of all a kind of symbol-magic. Reciting the magic formula or pronouncing the magic name puts irresistible powers at our disposal. The act of terror is symbolic; it has been called "propaganda of the deed." As such, it takes its place among other forms of symbol-magic widespread in our time - propaganda and promotion; advertising and "public relations"; slogans and emblems on bumperstickers and lapel buttons; demonstrations, manifestos, and formal resolutions.

Terror also embodies another form of magic, the magic of violence. We may try to open the door by calling out, "Open, Sesame!" Another familiar response is to kick the door. Belief in the magic of violence is the notion that enough violence will accomplish anything - banging the TV set, saturation bombing, shock therapy, or repeated acts of terror. Regardless of whether the audience is impressed or the target terrorized, destroying the victim has its own magical efficacy.

Without this belief, the act of terror is meaningless, for its effectiveness would then depend on a causal connection between victim and target, and the act would be reduced to a canonical use of force. Attacking a military installation or blowing up a bridge or troop train are not terroristic, even though they affect the will of the target as well as his capacity to continue a certain exercise of power. Kidnapping is not an act of terror unless the victim is truly a hostage: someone essentially irrelevant to the kidnapper's aims except by way of psychological effect. In the eyes of the terrorist, this effect is irresistable, because it is, at bottom, magical.

For the terrorist, the meaning of his action is localized in the violence. This is why the outcome of the violence is left so unstructured, as contrasted with the detailed and careful

planning of the steps leading up to the violence. There are
unanticipated developments in every operation; but, in terror,
even matters that can be anticipated are not prepared for, if
they come after what in another enactment of violence, the
bullfight, is revealingly called the moment of truth, the actual
killing. Downright blunders are not infrequent – for example,
demanding from negotiators passwords which have never been
communicated to them, or asking to be flown to destinations
which refuse to admit the terrorists.

The moment of truth is so called because it reveals the
character of the matador: his own life is also at stake. In the
act of terror, it does not matter who the victim is, but the
magical effect is greatest when the terrorist himself is among
the victims. In some cultures, as in traditional China and
Japan, suicide is a recognized tactic of disconcerting an
enemy. The folklore is that the enemy will thereafter be
haunted by the homeless ghost; realistically, the death will lie
at his door in the familiar sense of moral responsibility.

On a deeper level, self-destruction may be an expiation of
guilt. Terror thereby becomes a self-sustaining process: each
act of terror imposes a burden of guilt, to be expiated by
self-destruction in a subsequent act. The chain reaction does
not require repetition by the individual terrorist; it is the
group identity which is the locus both of sin and of atone-
ment.

The magic of violence is thus transformed into a sacrament of violence. The victim is a sacrifice, and the ultimate
sacrifice is of oneself. By sacrifice, the gods are compelled to
our service; our cause is made holy by the spilling of blood.
The sacred oath must be signed in blood, the covenant must
be sealed with our own flesh. Terrorists have complained at
the immorality of having armed guards on planes. Such
complaints are not as preposterous as they seem; the sacrificial
animal should not interfere with the ritual. That the victims
of terror are indiscriminately destroyed (as in the "Zebra"
killings in San Francisco) means only that the gods themselves
have chosen their victims; to be of the chosen people is a fatal
destiny.

The sacrament of violence shades off into Satanism; the
line between religion and idolatry is blurred. The modern
terrorist is a descendant of the historical Bluebeard and Dra-
cula, a kin to the high priests of the cult of cruelty. The
Baader-Meinhof group is not very different in the causes and
consequences of their actions, whatever their reasons, from
the Manson family. That the terrorist is conscious of a
sadistic thrill is doubtful; what is indubitable is that he finds
fulfillment in destruction, whether of the self or others.
Muggers often beat their victims after robbing them. In 1976,
a terrorist in Frankfurt who was demanding a large sum of
money and a plane to Cuba refused to leave even when his

demands were agreed to. The surviving Lod terrorist muti-
lated himself while in prison.

To the degree that terrorism is caused by a belief in the
magic of violence and is performed as a sacrament, it can be
lessened by avoiding responses which reinforce the image of
sacred violence. To "honor" agreements with a terrorist is to
recognize the sacrament as holy. If a prison term is imposed,
the prison must not be seen as a place where the blood of
sacrificial victims is spilled; maximum security is not to be
equated with the greatest display of force.

Above all, capital punishment is inappropriate, even
though it is recurrently called for. The fact is that it is called for by the terrorists themselves. The leader of an abortive
coup in Iraq in May 1973, facing a firing squad, acknowledged,
that anyone who undertakes such an adventure must pay that
kind of price. One of the Moluccan terrorists, at his trial in
March 1976, confessed that it worried him that he came out of
it alive. It is not for us to relieve him of his worries.

Not all the causes presented are of equal weight; not all
of them operate simultaneously. Correspondingly, not all the
tactics called for to lessen terrorism can be applied in given
circumstances. Some of them may even be incompatible with
one another. To cut off air travel to any nation harboring
terrorists may weaken the emphasis on the terrorist's personal
responsibility and contribute to his sense of performing deeds
of international significance. (The dilemma may not arise,
however; so far, the only resolution of the International Air
Transport Association relating to terrorism was one condemning
Israel.)

In broad outline, the implications for practice are clear.
Whenever seized, terrorists should be promptly brought to
trial, and the crimes with which they are charged not excused
or even mitigated by the political reasons offered for them.
They should be tried and, if convicted, punished by the
countries where the offenses were committed; and countries
training or harboring them should be treated as accessories.
There must be no negotiation of terrorist demands (except as a
delaying tactic), and no yielding to demands (except as
spurious agreements not subsequently fulfilled). Media
coverage must be minimized during the episode itself, and
subsequent coverage subjected to a code of self-restraint.
Response should be on a low level, and carried out in a low
key. No capital punishment should be inflicted; and, so far
as security permits, sentences must be served in penal institutions where violence has a low profile.

Additional recommendations for dealing with acts of terror
can be derived from the treatment of crimes of violence in
general, stemming from quite different causes. For instance,
counteraction should be taken as quickly as possible, while the
criminal - terrorist, would-be rapist, or whatever - is still on

unfamiliar ground, relatively disoriented, and uncertain of his own next steps. On the other hand, if the response is not immediate, protracting events as long as possible takes advantage of the criminal's fatigue, discouragement, and weakening of resolve.

No doubt, the most direct counter to terrorism is to deal, not with its causes, but with its reasons, about which nothing has been said here. It is tempting to think, "If only the British would get out of Ireland and Jews out of Palestine!" But terrorists in America, Bolivia, Germany, or Japan have their own nations as targets, and there will be something to protest against in every regime. Moreover, causes have a way of finding reasons, or of ignoring reasons altogether. Planes continued to be hijacked to Cuba even after the offer was made to provide free transportation to anyone wishing to go there. Counterfeiters have been known who worked hard enough on their counterfeits to have earned more - and in real money - than employees of the Bureau of Engraving.

It is likely that terrorism will continue and even increase. Psychic mechanisms are repetitive, and the social matrix in —which the causes of terrorism are generated shows little sign of changing. Absolute values and faith in violence to secure them, alienation, a sense of helplessness and of a lack of purpose and personal worth - these are pervasive features of modern society, by no means confined to the "decadent West." Such signs of change as there are presage greater temptations to resort to terrorism, and far greater loss of life from it, as sophisticated weapons systems and nuclear devices proliferate, and some of them sooner or later fall into private hands.

Just because of the increasing danger, there is a modicum of hope. As terror becomes more widespread, more audiences will identify with the victims rather than with the terrorists, and more will see themselves as targets. Until now, the United Nations has refused even to pass resolutions against terrorism, and only a very few international bodies, e.g., Interpol, have taken any action at all. Self-interest may eventually dictate concerted action against terrorism, just as other uses of violence - piracy, genocide, slavery - have at last become intolerable almost everywhere.

There seems to be no limit to how much can be destroyed by hatred before hatred destroys itself. As a fire spreads it does not necessarily burn itself out, but it may arouse a wider determination to stamp it out. Until this determination takes hold, we can at least continue the effort to understand the conflagration.

4 Psychological Sequelae of Terrorization

Rona M. Fields

The stress of sudden captivity and the physical and psychological trauma of indeterminate imprisonment under degrading conditions with the constant threat of death was the focal condition for studies of concentration camp survivors and POWs. In the laboratory, attempts have been made to emulate these circumstances through various modifications of sensory/perceptual stimulation and simulation/dissemblance kinds of experiments.

Yet, during the past two decades, there has been a proliferation of circumstances for such experiences in which the victims, unlike POWs or even concentration camp inmates, are almost randomly incorporated into traumatic captivity. Hostages and, in many instances, political prisoners who have been subjected to detention without charge or trial and depth interrogation experience many of the features of the laboratory stress experiment in combination with the uncertainty and physical debilitation of the POW or concentration camp inmate and, thus, comprise a new category of victims.

Hostage taking has become one of the major concerns for law enforcement systems throughout the Western world and the Middle East. While the actual circumstances of their captivity seem to vary in accordance with the objectives and character of their captors, nonetheless, there may be some common denominators and sequelae of the traumatic stress undergone by all of the victims. Obviously, there may well be differences in accordance with the level of preparedness of individual victims and of occupational groups. For example, one might expect that prison guards and guerrilla soldiers would be psychologically and perhaps physically prepared to cope with capture and hostility. This does not seem to always be the case, but it's not easy to ascertain from the relatively meager data available. Some of the contrasts and contradic-

51

tions among the studies and observations seem derivative from
such variables as whether the victim is an individual kidnap
victim or part of a group. Another variable that seems
relevant is whether the hostages had, prior to captivity, an
identity and a high level of interaction as a group. And, of
course, we have to consider the "Stockholm Syndrome" in
which the captives become sympathetic and even enamored of
their captors as is reported in at least one classic case of
hostage taking by bank robbers in Stockholm, Sweden. The
other captives (the political prisoners who may have never
functioned as part of a psuedo or paramilitary group and might
even be completely independent of the targeted political group
only or marginally related) are entirely isolated from ideological
or social support. Such a "hostage" is far less likely to
identify with his or her captors and is, in fact, a likely
prospect for membership in the targeted group if he or she
survives the torture and incarceration. There are even contradictions in studies of ex-POWs when the issues concern
psychopathological   and   physical   morbidity   consequences.

Lifton (1963) tells us that there are pathological consequences suffered by those who survive a general disaster in
which others perceived to be like themselves have perished.
Certainly, in major incidents of hostage taking, there have
been deaths and injuries and, according to Ochberg (1977) and
Baastians (1977), the Dutch train survivors or the two South
Moluccan terrorizations have seemed to recognize in themselves
behavioral consequences and major life changes.

In considering the prospect for such effects and especially for designing intervention and treatment programs for
victims of stressful, traumatic captivity, we need to concern
ourselves with the hypotheses and methodologies from the
existing literature on stress, on POWs and concentration camp
survivors, on prolonged threat, and on forced behaviors.

Finally, the accumulated and contradictory data are the
result of studies lacking empirical calibration, performed on a
case or clinical basis, devoid of base line data, inconsistent
with regard to follow up and longitudinal study. It is rare
indeed that base line data can be obtained on victims of
stressful captivity, and it is costly and difficult to plan
longitudinal and systematic follow up studies that accumulate
empirical measures. It is even more difficult to obtain the
requisite funding quickly enough to initiate immediate study.
My own experience in this domain has been a notable failure.
Nonetheless, I have managed to obtain some data on hostage
victims and tortured political prisoners that may add to the
argument for such studies while it serves to further compound
the debate on psychological consequences.

This chapter is a summary of my findings of the psychological sequelae experienced by the B'nai B'rith hostages
(who were held captive by the Hanafi Muslim group between

March 9 and 11, 1977) and political prisoners who suffered depth interrogation during captivity in Northern Ireland during the last months of 1976 and early 1977. In order to provide for comparability of data, the same psychological measures were used on each subject and the same bio-demographic information was elicited during an hour-long interview with each subject. Each subject was also asked to provide base line medical and psychiatric information that would indicate their condition prior to captivity. As we shall see, such information was made available for 80 percent of the sample of B'nai B'rith hostages while the only information obtainable on the Northern Ireland victims was through their own reports.

THE SUBJECTS

The sample under consideration here includes 24 subjects - 12 each of the B'nai B'rith hostages and Northern Ireland victims of torture at Castlereagh Barracks. For convenience, we will refer to the former group as hostages and the latter as victims. Six of the victims suffered their trauma in 1977 and within six months of examination. The other six had been interrogated the previous year and were also examined within six months of their experience. The hostages were examined one year after their release from captivity. Each individual was given an open-ended, nondirective, clinical interview through which the usual demographic information was elicited along with accounts of their subjective experience, prior medical history, and subsequent medical and psychological anomalies. The two samples differed in their distribution of men and women: the hostages included ten women and two men - roughly the same proportion of women to men as were held hostage; the victims included five women and seven men. All the individuals in both samples are urban dwellers and are between the ages of 18 and 65. Two of the B'nai B'rith hostages are black, the Northern Irish sample is all white, Catholic. The hostages included eight who were Jewish and four Protestants. One of the B'nai B'rith hostages was born in Europe.

Several persons in each sample had previous medical histories of some kind of anomalies. Of the hostages, one had a previously diagnosed heart condition, one woman was two months pregnant, two others had hiatus hernias, and yet another two had been diagnosed as having morbid obesity. One of the victims had a previous history of central nervous system disorders and another had a history of gastrointestinal problems. Otherwise, as a group, the victims reported themselves with less pathology prior to incarceration.

Only one of the hostages had never been married, while four of the victims had never been married. Four of the hostage women were either widowed or divorced, and the remaining seven were married. The victims were slightly younger, and less likely to be married. The mean age of the hostages is 39 while the victims average out at 33 years.

Although this sample is not of sufficient scope numerically, to deal with such important issues as the relative influences on stress reaction of such factors as age, duration, ethnicity, family status, and other demographic variables, they will be alluded to when the data suggests that such a consideration should bear further investigation. Unfortunately, the size of the sample of the hostages is too small for statistical significance in finer kinds of comparison.

Hostages share with political prisoners the fact that they are civilians and that they are neither sentenced to serve a particular amount of time in prison nor are they imprisoned for any criminal action. The situation differs, however, in that hostages are totally unsuspecting of the possibility of capture, while political prisoners may have been active dissidents in a totalitarian regime who recognized that they might face incarceration or worse.

Nonetheless, the literature on the effects of trauma-induced stress (often systematic torture) on political prisoners in several countries suggests some similarity with the reported condition of hostages. Longitudinal studies of concentration camp survivors who, as civilians, endured prolonged indeterminate and stressful periods of incarceration indicate some symptoms and pathological behaviors similar to those described by the clinicians attending the hostages (Belz, Parker, Sank, Shaffer, Sharpiro, and Shriber, 1977). After six months of treating some of the hostage victims, their clinicians reported that the hostages suffered from a syndrome similar to the skyjacking victims and the earlier studies of victims of incarceration and torture. It remains to be seen, however, whether these hostages, all of whom were adults, suffered any long-term effects or whether their symptoms were transitory and amenable to the prompt treatment initiated by the George Washington University Health Maintenance team.

METHODS USED

The psychological measures applied to these and other stress victims studied by this investigator included the Bender Gestalt (a test of psychomotor coordination and perceptual functioning that is sensitive to and standardized for diagnosing central nervous system damage and dysfunction); the Thematic Apperception Test, Story Sequence Analysis (this is a pro-

jective personality devise that was further developed by Magda
B. Arnold to yield an empirically derived motivation index
score that reflects a variety of motivational and personality
dynamics); the Memory for Designs Test (another test of
psychomotor function, but this test also indicates problems in
memory function and some of the higher level cognitive processes involved in conceptualization); and the Word Association
Test (another personality projective that is useful for examining commonly held associations for groups and categories
of populations). These tests were also selected orginally for
studies of torture victims on the basis that they are very
portable, readily administered, not likely to evoke behavioral
or thought disorders as a consequence of taking them, and
altogether relatively culture free having been standardized on
broadly constituted international samples of Europeans and
North and South Americans. Notably, the Bender Gestalt has
also been used in studies of concentration camp survivors
conducted by Eitinger and Strøm in Norway. Ideally, the
investigator would have hoped to utilize instruments of equivalent relevance throughout; but, as we shall see, few if any
empirical psychological measures have ever been employed in
studies of victims.

RESULTS OF THE TESTS

On the Bender Gestalt, 8 of the 12 victims scored measureable
brain damage. One of these, a woman aged 21, had a previous history of central nervous system damage; the others,
including five of the seven men in the sample, had work
experience that would have required a higher level of eye-
hand coordination than would have been possible for them at
the time they were tested. The other woman had been trained
as a hairdresser and was sometimes employed in that capacity
prior to her incarceration. There is little likelihood that she
could perform psychomotor tasks now that are more complicated
than shampooing. She admitted that she did not think she
would be able to cut hair now. Of the group, only two
Bender protocols were within the normal range. The other two
subjects scored as Psychoneurotic. With this latter diagnosis,
it is harder to determine onset or etiology of the pathological
symptoms. Table 4.1 describes the scores of the victims of
interrogation torture.
     In contrast with the Northern Irish sample, the B'nai
B'rith hostages contained a high proportion of normal or
borderline Bender protocols (6) and only two that looked as
though these subjects had suffered some organic damage to the
brain and central nervous system (see table 4.2). The
proportions were almost directly reversed, and this is sta-

Table 4.1. Test Scores of Northern Ireland Victims

Subject Code	Bender Gestalt	Motivation Index	Kent-Rosanoff Significant Words
Male A	Organic	85	Memory, religion, sleep, trouble, body, thief, deep, marriage, sweet, police, justice, social worker
Male B	Organic	60	Deep, soft, head, cold, dream, justice, health, bible, bad, quiet, love
Male C	Organic	90	Afraid, man, marriage, house, black, memory, love
Male D	Organic	75	Trouble, afraid, loud, comfort, hand, police, memory, justice
Male E	Organic	70	Sex, bible, man, marriage, comfort, police, justice, love
Male F	Normal	90	Religion, justice, cold, body
Male G	Normal	95	Memory, marriage, hand, police, justice
Female A	Psychoneurotic	90	Sex, deep, dark, trouble, command, police, justice, man, dream
Female B	Psychoneurotic	85	Fruit, bread, afraid, sex, religion, dark, deep, eating, marriage, comfort
Female C	(previous injury) Organic	80	House, heavy, religion, spider, sleep
Female D	Organic	95	Religion, justice, police, memory
Female E	Organic	105	Fruit, dream, bible, justice, memory, marriage

Mean M.I.   = 85   Significant Words for all Subjects together:
Organic   = 8
Psychoneurotic = 2   Memory = 6   Justice = 9
Normal   = 2   Police   = 6   Religion = 5
                                   Sex   = 3

Test Scores of B'nai B'rith Hostages

Subject Code	Bender Gestalt	Motivation Index	Kent-Rosanoff Significant Words
Female A	Normal Sexual Anxiety	110	Afraid, comfort, police, dream, bread, justice, religion, body, stomach, child, heavy, baby
Female B	Organic borderline	105	Table, love, marriage, comfort, fruit, sweet, low, bread, justice, girl
Female C	Neurotic borderline	100	Eating, wish, white, high, street
Female D	Psychoneurotic	110	Deep, dream, head, religion, white, stomach, street, afraid
Female E	Borderline	115	Afraid, street, quiet, baby, heavy, sex, whiskey, spider, working, summer, stomach, body, hard, trouble, pregnancy, thief, sickness, comfort, slow, bread, memory
Female F	Organic	80	Sex, religion, social worker, justice, bread
Female G	Borderline	115	Fruit, wish, bible, memory, white
Female H	Normal	100	Man, hand, head, sex, wish, rough, anger, working, pregnancy
Female I	Normal	115	Religion, anger, heavy, love, social worker
Female J	Organic	90	Joy, afraid, social worker, pregnancy, working, spider, religion, sex, marriage, comfort, dream, bible, memory
Male A	Neurotic	105	Comfort, dream, justice, wish, trouble, body, afraid
Male B	Neurotic	90	Afraid, street, pregnancy, hammer, stomach, trouble, working, wish, sex, bath, sickness, woman, dream

Mean M.I.   = 103
Organic   = 2
Psychoneurotic   = 2
Normal or
  Borderline   = 6

Significant Words for all Subjects together:

Justice = 7	Sex = 5	Afraid = 6
Memory = 4	Working = 3	Religion = 5
Police = 1		

tistically significant at the .001 level. In their word associations, the victims were more homogeneous. Nine of them
blocked on the word "justice" while only four of the hostages
blocked on that word. The word "afraid" was emotionally
significant for only two of the victims, while it elicited reactions from six of the hostages as the most consistently loaded
stimulus word. "Police" was another significant word for half
the victims and elicited only one emotionally loaded response
from a hostage. "Sex" and "religion" were about equally
emotionally loaded for the victim and hostage samples.

As for the Motivation Index scores, there is an important
difference between the two groups. The hostages' mean score
indicates average achievement motivation, while the victims (at
M.I. mean 85) are not likely as a group to achieve even an
average measure of success in social relations or by any
sociopsychoeconomic standards in Western society. These
scores reflect a consistently pessimistic, unrealistic, nega-
tivistic, inactive, and non-goal or achievement-oriented value
system, and attitudinal set among the victims.

There are other, less quantifiable variables differentiating
the two populations and relevant to interpreting the scores.
Nine of the 12 hostages received some kind of professional
mental health service following their traumatic experience. At
the time of testing, none of the victims had sought or received
such help. Of the hostages, two or possibly three might be
considered to have had experience of poverty and violence
before this trauma. All of the victims have, if not earlier,
experienced at least eight years of ongoing violence in their
home city. It is also likely that the victims, who had all been
born and raised in poverty and as members of a discriminated
against minority group, achieved a greater degree of cohesion
and homogeneity apart from their traumatic experience than
could the hostages whose experiential backgrounds and socio-
economic origins are considerably more varied. Furthermore,
the victims experienced their trauma as individuals in isolation,
while the hostages did not.

There is considerable evidence from laboratory and
medical and epidemiological studies that prolonged exposure to
stressful conditions can alter the activities of the cardio-
vascular system in such ways as to result in pathology and
premature mortality. So also, does continual gastrointestinal
reaction to stress produce an overabundance of enzymes
ultimately destructive to the system's functioning. Eitinger
points out that, when adaptive reactions fail, the victim
becomes frightened and the consequent anxiety syndrome can
persist over several years, even if the stress has been
relatively brief. He suggests this is due to the loss of trust
in one's integrity and in the capacity of protective agencies
and the stability of the milieu. Furthermore, as Symonds
points out (1975, pp. 19-20):

> Society has strange attitudes towards victims.
> There seems to be a marked reluctance and resis-
> tance to accept the innocence or accidental nature
> of victim behavior. . . . This general early re-
> sponse to victims stems from a basic need for all
> individuals to find a rational explanation for violent
> . . . crimes. Exposure to senseless, irrational,
> brutal behavior makes one feel vulnerable and
> helpless. . . . The community has other attitudes
> that block sympathetic response. One is the primi-
> tive fear of contamination by the unlucky victim.
> The result of this primitive response of fear is to
> isolate or exclude the victim.

Given these circumstances and corollaries to stress and victimization, it would seem altogether likely that the effect of
their traumatic stress under brutal interrogation procedures
would have resulted in greater damage to the victims who,
upon their release, also suffered from social stigmatization,
isolation, and the fear of the majority of people in their
community. Their reports of alienation from spouses and
lovers and their experience of stigmatization in the work force
which had already rejected many of them on account of their
Catholicism combined to extend their anxiety and prolong the
stress.

The hostages, too, despite the overwhelming media descriptions of them as "innocent victims," reported experiencing
a kind of social isolation and "guilt." Their experiences
ranged from being told by spouses and siblings to "stop
talking about it already, I don't want to hear anymore" to
finding themselves the subject of curiosity and uncomfortably
chagrinned at unexpected times.

The hostages suffered a combination of psychological and
physiological stress, as that term has been defined by Lazarus
(1971, pp. 54-55):

> Stress refers then to a very broad class of prob-
> lems, differentiated from other problem areas because
> it deals with any demands which tax the system,
> whether it is, a physiological system, a social
> system, or a psychological system. . . . The key
> feature distinguishing psychological stress from
> physiological stress is that in the former the reaction
> depends on how the person interprets or acquires
> (consciously or unconsciously), the significance of a
> harmful, threatening or challenging event, while in
> the latter it is the condition of the tissues which
> directly determines noxiousness. If the event is
> appraised as irrelevant to the person's welfare,
> there is no arousal of emotion or behavioral mo-

bilization . . . neither the stimulus event nor the reaction falls under the rubric of psychological stress. To understand psychological stress requires study of the mediating cognitive processes . . . determining the stress reaction, including the behavioral and subjective adjustments. . . . We know relatively little about the coping processes . . . and the short-and-long range consequences of their use. . . .

In a 1971 symposium on "Society, Stress, and Disease," Dr. Valentina Myager (1971, p. 258) pointed out that:

The material substrates of emotions are subcortical structures, including hypathalmic formations. These structures are closely related to the cerebral cortex, which controls the whole conscious activity of man, including his emotional attitudes.

There would seem to be no question in the literature that relentless accumulation of stresses day after day lowers a person's stress tolerance to the point where he or she begins to react to every minor stress as though it is a serious threat. In chronic threat situations (chronic may be interpreted to mean a continued or prolonged situation of hours' or days' duration) individuals experience excessive personal vulnerability; their mood is colored by depression and apathy along with anxiety symptoms, sense of abandonment or neglect, and feelings that no one cares or can be trusted. These experiences of anxiety result in behaviors that are inappropriate and often damaging to interpersonal relationships, as well as triggering somatic disorders. As described by May (1975):

Anxiety is the apprehension cued off by a threat to values the individual holds essential to his existence as a personality. These values form the "core" of his sense of worth and competence as a personality. The threat may be to physical or psychological life (death, loss of freedom), or it may be to some other value which the individual identifies with his existence.

Of the twelve victims, seven had endured previous interrogations and/or imprisonment, and three of the women had husbands who were already imprisoned or had been imprisoned (prior to the specific incident of confinement at Castlereagh Barracks). Even without their prior experiences with interrogation, these victims were well aware of the threat represented by the law enforcement agencies throughout their lives but most specifically since 1971 when the first cases of officially sanctioned torture became known. Therefore, there was an anticipatory stress reaction as well as the specific experiences of sleep deprivation, sound conditioning, beatings, accusations, and humiliation, and, in some cases, hooding and stress positioning. These particular experiences further modify (at least transitorily and it is unclear as to duration) the ability of the person to think and act. Activation levels which have been experimentally altered by threats of electric shock, sleep deprivation, and continuous loud noise result in lowered perceptual discrimination, motor coordination, and awareness. Living with this kind of continual or intermittent stress and threat of stress decreases the individual's motor efficiency and cognitive functioning. The latter is primarily affected in recall or memory functions.

Lazarus reported on a study of stress reactions both physical and psychological as a function of the anticipatory behavior engaged in by the subject - be it active or passive. His research suggested the importance of evaluating the individual's subjective interpretation (cognitive appraisal) of the significance of the stressful event. Others' work in the experimental psychology of stress reactions supports Lazarus' contention that it is the cognitive appraisal of the stressor that determines somatic responses. The physical condition of the individual contributes greatly to this response. In reviewing the evidence on increased morbidity and mortality as sequelae to stress, Levi (1972, pp. 3-11) summarizes the findings as follows:

Psychosocial stimuli lasting some hours increase stress. . . . This is reflected in increases in, e.g., adrenalin and non-adrenalin excretion, and in plasma 17-hydroxycortucosteroids, free fatty acids and triglycerides. . . . Psychosocial stimuli lasting several days increase stress. . . . This is reflected in, e.g., adrenalin excretion, in plasma free fatty acids, tri-glycerides, cholesterol, protein-bound iodine and fibrinolysis and in ST and T depressions in the EEG pattern. . . . Increased levels of triglycerides and cholesterol do predict an increased risk not only for subsequent degenerative heart disease (C.F. Keys 1970) but also for a variety of other diseases, as found by Tibblin. . . . It has further been shown that subjects exposed to frequent and dramatic environmental changes run a higher risk of developing myocardial infarction within the next six months (Theorell, 1970). Similar relationships have been demonstrated for other diseases including psychiatric disorders. . . . Finally it has been found that high triglyceride and cholesterol levels in a non-selected population are positively related to a subsequent increase in mortality, not only in myocardial infarction but in other diseases as well.

It is clear that, of the hostages, the two who appear to have suffered the greatest deleterious effects after one year are a 55 year old widow who lost her husband to cancer a year and a half earlier, had borne and raised seven children, was having problems with one of her children at the time of her captivity, has had various illnesses, accidents, and a history of high blood pressure, hiatus hernia, depression, and introversion; and a 30 year old black male. The latter was raised in Harlem, lost his mother when he was seven, served as point on army patrols in Vietnam, has been unemployed and suffered from numerous health problems including having received a medical discharge from the service in 1971. Interestingly enough, this man endured less than two hours of captivity. He has had psychological and psychiatric evaluation and some treatment during the year, but suffered further fear and trauma when he was required to testify at the trial of the terrorists. This young man was unable to return to work as a security guard without suffering disabling somatic complaints. He did go for counseling, but found himself at odds with his counselor and did not pursue it on any consistent basis. Examined again two years after his trauma, he demonstrated organic dysfunctions that were not apparent in the first examination one year following his ordeal. This "soft sign" could be a product of the wearing away effects of on-going stress and escalating, untreated anxiety. If these two people were included with the Northern Ireland sample of persons who had experienced repeated and continuous threat and stress, their scores and behavior would not be extraordinary (Female F and Male B on table 4.2).

As a group, the hostages are characterized by anxiety syndromes and psychoneurotic tendencies related to the anxiety. They evidence problems in sexuality, sleep/dreams, memory, and working. Thus, indications are not only derived from their interview self-appraisals, but are also evidenced in their TAT, Bender, and Word Association protocols. Most of them have experienced problems with spouses since their captivity and several who had initially denied any ill effects experienced anxiety reactions at the time of the first year post-anniversary (some of them having had nightmares the night before their appointments with this investigator).

All of the Jewish hostages and one of the Christians experienced at least one condition of their captivity as reminiscent of the Holocaust. The Jewish hostages demonstrated in their TAT stories similar kinds of identity conflicts as were prevalent in the victims. (In victims' TAT stories, the verbal threats and humiliation revolved around the attribution of IRA membership to the victims because they were Catholic.) The Jewish hostages had attributed to them conspiratorial and other negative traits on the basis of their being, as Khalis called them, "Yehudis." At the same time, the two black hostages felt particularly exposed and afraid to make any kind of public identification or accusation against their captors. As they expressed it, they lived "in the community themselves" and retaliation would be comparatively easy since they feel they lack the protection their white colleagues would have from the authorities.

Lazarus (1974, p. 281) describes subtypes of intrapsychic coping: "attention deployment, reappraisal and wish fulfilling fantasy." It might be useful to consider the reactions of the hostages, as revealed in the interviews and through the TAT in these three categories. The two hostages who seem to have suffered the most extensive aftereffects (who also have more extensive histories of stress) both employed attention deployment. They focused somewhat on the fact that each of them, for different reasons, had withdrawn large sums of money that day and had these funds on their person. They concerned themselves with hiding the money and with containing themselves and not being conspicuous. Both of them experienced physical pain reactions to one or another aspect of their situation. Both suffered illnesses afterwards. The woman suffered from shingles and the man from mononucleosis. These disease reactions support the hypothesis that stress lowers resistance to infection. Neither of these individuals related to others in the hostage group during their captivity. One of the significant TAT story imports for this kind of coping was "... if a sad thing happens you look away and become very defensive." This was the import from one of the Male B's stories.

Examples of the reappraisal reaction among the hostages were some women who focused their attention on helping those who were wounded. One of these women, Female A (an asthmatic who has in the past suffered from a spastic colon), is surprised because she suffered none of these problems during her captivity. She has not had therapy but is continuing to experience various aftereffects, both psychological and somatic. A typical import from such copers is: "You are grief-stricken about the loss of a loved one but you go on and find someone else." It is worth noting that the majority of the hostages tended to utilize reappraisal and fantasy. However, in describing their reactions one year later, they could be classified in two groups - those who experienced the events as observers, and those who recognized their own participation status.

This polarity was not particularly remarked upon by the torture victims. They tended to orient appropriately to the reality of their victimization, but often afterwards experienced a sense of alienation from themselves as they had been during that stress. Their comments about it are to the effect: "That wasn't like me to act that way," or "I didn't know myself," or, the classic response of "I was so numb, I couldn't feel and I wondered if I was still alive and I hit my head on a pipe to see if I could still hurt."

Sleep deprivation and other sensory manipulation characterized the capitivity of each group. It is possible that the psychological and physiological aftermath as well as the subjective stress reactions were a direct consequence of sleep deprivation or sensory stimulation.

The secondary effects of environmental or traumatically induced stress are frequently as organically damaging as the immediate effects. Sleep deprivation, in the case of the hostages, was both a primary and secondary stress condition. Persons who go without sleep for long periods of time show a marked loss in mental efficiency, poor judgment, and disorganized thinking. They can become functionally psychotic as a result of the physiological changes in the brain. Sleeplessness and other physiological and biological reactions induced by psychosocial stimuli were the subject of a review by Froberg, Karlsson, Levi, and Lidberg presented in symposium in Stockholm in 1970. Besides reporting on calibrations of physiological reactions to experimentally induced stress, this Stockholm group presents a very cogent thesis on the inter-relationship of psychological stress with organic concomitants. They note:

> We all know that homeostatic neuroendocrine regulation in man is affected by psychic stimuli. . . . Man reacts not only to the actual existence of danger, but to threats and symbols of danger experienced in the past. . . . This created a situation in which homeostasis is adjusted not only to the needs of the organism . . . the pattern of response involves physiological as well as psychic processes. . . . The inter-relation between these two types of processes has attracted considerable attention, some laboratories studying the physiological reactions accompanying normal and pathological emotional processes, while others have centered on the opposite problem. . . . Of these two sets of variables, the physiological has usually been easier to objectify . . . the physiological variable might be used for the objective measurement of psychological processes in cases where these processes are not readily accessible to direct psychological measurement. . . . The constellations of stressors . . . are, however, very complex as a rule and it is, therefore, difficult from clinical data alone to dis-

tinguish between cause and effect in the medical
chain of events (Froberg, Karisson, Levi, and
Lidberg 1970, p. 280).

The psychodynamics are further complicated by the physiological consequences of basic needs deprivation. Imposed
sleeplessness, restricted movement, limited diet, and intense,
on-going anxiety states inhibit circulation and produce various
gastrointestinal and metabolic disturbances. The individual's
subjective experience of stress combined with physical symptoms contributes to cognitive and affective impairment that may
be long-lived. The variety of mistreatment of political prisoners in Northern Ireland combined with the commonality of
their post incarceration pathologies and the similarity of these
syndromes with those of Chilean refugees whose treatment
differed from the former in duration and kind suggests that
the physical and mental stimuli imposed on the prisoners were
not in themselves the significant instruments of damage, but
were, for the victims, the repeated reminders of their own
helplessness and hence their vulnerability.

Among the hostages there was a wide range of experience
in relation to the Hanafis. Some of the hostages had no
personal interchanges and seemed not to have perceived as
insults to themselves their captors diatribes against Jews (some
of those who were not Jewish did not even recall hearing these
tirades as anti-Jewish). Two of the non-Jewish captives
recognized the anti-Jewish insults as such, but distinguished
themselves from the targets. There appears to be a quantifiable relationship between experience of personal humiliation
and the extent of stress pathology. This is, again, distinct
from actual physical abuse. The Irish victims emphasized as
stressful their experience of insult and humiliation as individuals whose lives past and present seemed well known to
their interrogators. One aspect of the interrogation in
Northern Ireland during the past several years has been the
captors' divulgence of information about the captive that was
obtained through electronic surveillance of his or her home and
neighborhood as well as through admissions or confessions
made by colleagues or neighbors or even spouses.

Given the suggestability of victims, their lowered threshold for subjectivity, and, apparently, even their lowered
susceptability to implicit stressors, threat is readily perceived
and magnified. This fact in itself would make persons who are
aware of vulnerability, by virtue of their race or religion,
even more stressed.

In studies of correctional officers held hostage, Wolk
found that the duration of their captivity was unrelated to
their post-hostage symptoms (Wolk, 1977). This is apparent
also in the Vasquez and Reczynczki sample of Chilean refugees
(1976) and was reported by Fields of Irish internees (1973).

The depression and anger experienced by the hostages are a product of the threat and denigration of the hostages' ego state by the captor, thus, not only underscoring the individual's vulnerability, but actively defusing any prospect of group morale or support by group members of each other. Being a captive is a regressive experience in that dependency needs are enhanced and exaggerated by the limited alternatives and restriction of movement imposed by the captor(s).

Both groups suffered from social ostracism. For some of the hostages the experience was more prolonged but, generally, and with the exception of the week of their one year anniversary, this ended after a couple of months. Two of the hostages experienced prolonged alienation from their closest kin. For the Irish victims, social isolation is more extensive and long-lived. Work itself and returning to their jobs had a salutary effect on the hostages (with the exception of the one who had been the security guard and didn't find himself able to cope in that role afterwards). The Irish victims, nine of this sample, had no jobs to which to return. Furthermore, the organic damages suffered by the Irish victims left them unqualified for the kinds of skilled and semiskilled, blue collar type jobs they had previously handled. It is interesting to note that of the hostage victims, the single blue collar worker examined was also least able to deal with the demands for physical coordination intrinsic to his job.

CONCLUSIONS

The data of this study support the hypothesis that stress effects are subjective consequences. The two groups contain within them a variety of individuals and a variety of combinations of coping strategies. Despite the relatively small size of the sample, it is a larger sample than any previous study has incorporated with the exception of the classic studies of concentration camp survivors who demonstrated similar patterns on the same psychological measurements. Yet, in contrast with the concentration camp survivors, these trauma victims display more variety in both the aftereffects and conditions of imprisonment. From an evaluation of the aftereffects, it would seem that the physical conditions of their incarceration had less differentiating impact than did two other factors. First, their experience of trauma and stress prior to this specific one; and second, the kind of treatment or lack of treatment in the year following the trauma. The Northern Irish sample had, for the most part, experienced more intense and repetitive trauma and had no access to psychotherapy. They have remained in the same stressful environment and were subjected to additional stress in the form of harassment.

The hostages feared reprisals, experienced traumatic effects when they were required to testify in court and face their tormentors again, but, otherwise, returned to a supportive environment.

Eitinger's studies in Israel (1964) suggested that some of the victims who received prompt attention upon their arrival fared better than others. Vasquez and Rezcynczki (1976), having treated some of the Chilean victims over a period of two years, report that there has been some recovery of affective and cognitive functions, but hesitate to consider this anything more than a tentative possibility at this time. Plunkett (1976), a psychiatrist in Northern Ireland, has treated more than twenty of the victims of torture in that country and found that none have made a complete recovery and that psychiatric therapy has not been sufficient to prevent repeated hospitalization for four of his cases. Of the fourteen victims of the "hooding tortore" whose case was brought to the European court by the government of the Irish Republic, two have died; four others are certifiably mentally ill, and the other eight continue to suffer physical and psychological effects. In a study done by Parreira (1976), Portuguese naval men forced to serve in antiguerrilla campaigns in southern Africa suffered aftereffects to stress similar to concentration camp survivors. However, clinical treatment of the psychological disorders has resulted in decreased symptomatology.

Ochberg reported a case study of a Dutchman who had been held hostage by the South Moluccans and had experienced what has come to be regarded as a classic syndrome of reactive depression: feelings of vulnerability, internalized anger, and alienation from even the most intimate relationships (Ochberg 1977). This provides an intensive clinical perspective with which some parallels may be drawn, but no empirical data.

The Stockholm syndrome, a condition in which the hostages come to identify with their captors and vicariously share their antipathy for the rescue forces, seems not to have been evidenced in the Ochberg study nor is it reported by Wolk (1977) in his preliminary study of prison guards who were held hostage during an inmates' uprising.

An extensive study of Israeli concentration camp survivors and their offspring reported by Dor-Shav (1975) found measureable personality and cognitive effects 30 years after the experience and those differences also exist in the cognitive and personality functions of the children of these survivors.

The K-Z syndrome described by Lømmun (1961), the long-term effects on concentration camp survivors and their children described by Dor-Shav (1975), the Chilean victims (Vasquez & Reczynczki 1976), and the Northern Ireland hooding torture victims (Fields 1973, 1976) all share increased rates of morbidity and mortality associated with suffering acute anxiety and stress.

Incarceration in a concentration camp and systematic application of psychological and physical techniques designed to break the will of an individual (torture) may, at first glance, appear to be a different, and perhaps more extreme circumstance than that of the hostage.

It is worth noting that one year after their trauma, the hostages who did not undergo some kind of psychotherapy have begun to experience psychic distress and are planning to seek some professional help. To date, no treatment plan has been arranged for the Irish victims. If the implications of the data of this study are being accurately interpreted, there is every reason to believe that the majority of the Irish victims will suffer premature morbidity and mortality, and that their psychological and physical conditions will worsen as their harassment continues. Among the hostages, careful monitoring will probably serve to avert some of the most severe effects, but several of them are likely, if they do not receive psychotherapy, to suffer psychic and organic ill effects.

The earlier studies, as well as the contemporary ones, clearly indicate that the long-term effects of such stress as well as the functional anomalies which follow immediately afterwards present on-going problems for the individual and his or her entire social surroundings. Eitinger and Strøm (1973) found that such factors as paranoid personality syndromes, family alienation, education levels, age, and conditions of internment contributed in various measures to the post-imprisonment effects. Specific pathological and organic scarring effects have been noted in studies by Kluge (1961), Lømmun (1961), and Helveg Larson (1962). Studies by Chodoff (1966), David (1962), and by Trautmann (1964) ascertained that the effects of such treatment have been destructive as long as fifteen and twenty years after it was inflicted.

IMPLICATIONS

There are obvious methodological and sampling problems in this study that emphasize the need for further study. Additional funding will be required if we are to understand and, thereby, develop appropriate treatment procedures for persons who have been victims of indeterminate captivity. If such studies are undertaken epidemiologically rather than (as they are) episodically, an empirical data bank could provide the clues and direction.

Taken together it is apparent that the victims of indeterminate captivity suffer a stress syndrome similar to that of other trauma-stress victims. It is also evident that the subjective experience is the major determinant of physiological and psychological sequelae. It would be valuable to compare data for victims who have experienced bullet wounds and other invasive shock with those who are less overtly physically impaired. It is conceivable that, even in such a comparison, the subjective interpretation of the experience would be the crucial factor in understanding the severity of psychological consequences and organic impairment.

As for the other implications of these findings, we can assert that persons who have experienced positive and less stressful environments, particularly in their earlier years and in the years immediately preceding the stressful experience, have greater coping capacity for enduring and overcoming stress effects. It is also apparent that persons who are able to effect a social orientation during the experience – one of concern and some kind of contact with another person in a sympathetic fashion – are able to reappraise the situation and organize it into a personal and purposeful meaning and are less likely to endure the most severe psychological sequelae.

Finally, psychotherapy, when made available to and utilized by the victims, seems to have benefits in facilitating integration of the experience within a shorter time frame. In this, again, a social or group therapy experience seems particularly productive especially in view of the severe problems suffered by these victims in their return to their social milieu.

There are many unanswered questions that arise out of this data. For example, what happens to the aggressive response of the victim to the agression against him or her? How much of the consequence is a product of that aggression turned inward as has been hypothesized about concentration camp survivors? Is it probable that the Northern Ireland torture victims are going to mobilize their aggressive reaction into terrorization of their tormentors? Much of the data on that conflict would support this hypothesis. Certainly, the data of behavioral psychology would suggest that at least the younger victims of such aggression would adopt this as a model for their own retribution.

Perhaps this study can stimulate more effort to understand and intervene in behalf of the victims of terrorism. Despite all the effort expended in analyzing and countering terrorism, the victim remains a blurred image on yesterday's front page.

REFERENCES

ADAMHA News, Vol. 111, No. 9, May 10, 1977. "Mental Health Program Geared for Aid to Terrorist Victims and Families."

Albuquerque, Alfonso, and Fields, Rona. "Portuguese Torture Victims," Unpublished paper, 1974.

Armati, Silvia. "Some Thoughts on Torture to Introduce a Psychoanalytical Discussion", Paper presented at Brussels Conference on Violence, November 1977.

Arnold, Magda. Story Sequence Analysis. N.Y.: Columbia University Press, 1963.

Belz, Mary; Ellen Z. Parker; Lawrence I. Sank; Caroly-Shaffer; Joan Sharpiro; and Linda Shriber. "Is There a Treatment for Terror?" Psychology Today, October 1977.

Chodoff, P. "Effects of Extreme Coercive and Oppressive Forces: Brainwash and Concentration Camps," in American Handbook of Psychiatry 111, New York: Basic Books, 1966.

Daly, Robert J. "Psychiatric Effects of Counterinsurgency Operations," Paper presented at American Psychiatric Association Annual Meeting, Miami, Fla., May 10-14, 1976.

David, J. Pathology of the Captivity of the Prisoners of World War II, Works of the International Medical Conference, Brussels, 1962; published in Paris, 1963, as Ex-Prisoners of War.

Dor-Shav, Netta Kohn. "On the Long Range Effects of Concentration Camp Internment on Nazi Victims and their Children," Paper presented at the International Conference on Psychological Stress and Adjustment in War, Tel Aviv, Israel, January 1975.

Eitinger, Leo. Concentration Camp Survivors in Norway and Israel. Oslo, Norway: Universities Press, 1964.

Eitinger, Leo, and Alex Strøm. Mortality and Morbidity after Excessive Stress. New York: Humanities Press, 1973.

Fields, Rona M. A Society on the Run: A Psychology of Northern Ireland. Hammondsworth, England: Penguin, 1973.

Fields, Rona M. Society Under Siege. Philadelphia, Pa.: Temple University Press, 1976.

Fields, Rona M. "Torture and Institutional Coercion." Paper presented at ASA and APA meetings, September 1976.

Froberg, Jan, Class-Goran Karlsson, Lennart Levi, and Lars Lidberg. "Physiological and Biochemical Stress Reactions Induced by Psychosocial Stimuli," Society, Stress and Disease: The Psychosocial Environment and Psychosomatic Diseases, edited by Lennart Levi, New York: Oxford University Press, 1971.

Hacker, Frederick. Crusaders, Criminals, Crazies: Terror and Terrorism in Our Time. New York: Norton, 1976.

Helveg-Larson, P. "Famine Distress in German Concentration Camps," Acta Psychiat. Scand., Suppl. 83, 1962.

Hinkle, L.E., Jr., and Wolff, H.G. "Communist Interrogation and Indoctrination of the Enemies of the State." Archives of Neurological Psychiatry: 115-74, 1956; see also Robert Jay Lifton. Thought Reform and the Psychology of Totalism. A Study of "Brainwashing" in China. New York: W.W. Norton, 1963.

Jacobson, S. "Leadership Patterns and Stress Adaptations Among Hostages in Three Terrorist Captured Planes," Paper presented at the International Conference on Psychological Stress and Adjustment in Time of War and Peace, Tel Aviv, Israel, January 1975.

Kluge, E. "Uber die Felgen schwerer Hafstein," Nervenratz 29, (1961): 462-65.

Lazarus, R. "The Concepts of Stress and Disease," in Society, Stress and Disease, Edited by Lennart Levi. New York, London: Oxford University Press, 1971.

Levi, Lennart. "A Synopsis of Ecology and Psychiatry: Some Theoretical Psychosomatic Considerations: Review of Some Studies," Report from the Laboratory for Clinical Stress Research, Karolinskasjkhuset, Stockholm, Sweden, 1972.

_____. Society, Stress, and Disease. London: Oxford University Press, 1971.

Lifton, Robert J. Thought Reform and the Psychology of Totalism: A Study of Brainwashing in China. New York: W.W. Norton, 1963.

Lømmun, A. "An Analytical Survey of the Literature Published of Internment in Concentration Camps," translation, Experts meetings, Oslo, Norway, 1960, Vet. Feder, Paris, 1961.

May, Rollo. "Anxiety and Values," Paper presented at the International Conference on Psychological Stress and Adjustment in Time of War and Peace, Tel Aviv, Israel, January 1975.

Nathan, T.S.; Eitenger, L.; and Winsik, H.L. "A Psychiatric Study of Survivors of the Nazi Holocaust. A study in Hospitalized Patients," Israel Annals of Psychiatry and Related Disciplines 2 (1), April 1964.

Ochberg, Frank. "The Victim of Terrorism: Psychiatric Considerations," Paper presented at meeting in Evian, France, May 1977; and Personal Communications.

Parreira, Orlindo G. "Psychological Effects of Counterguerilla and Port Revolution," Paper presented in symposium at APA Convention, 1976.

Plunkett, Gerrard. "The Psychiatric Effects of Imprisonment in Northern Ireland," paper presented in symposium at APA Convention, 1976.

Schein, Edgar H. "Man Against Man: Brainwashing," Corrective Psychiatry and Journal of Social Therapy 8 (2), (1962): 90-97.

Stressman, H.D.; Thaler, Margaret; and Schein, E.H. "A Prisoner of War Syndrome: Apathy as a Reaction to Severe Stress," American Journal of Psychiatry 112 (1956): 908-1003.

Strøm, Axel. Norwegian Concentration Camp Survivors. Oslo: University Press, 1973.

Symonds, M. "Victims of Violence." The American Journal of Psychoanalysis 35, 1975, 19-26.

Trautman, E.C. "Fear and Panic in Nazi Concentration Camps," International Journal of Social Psychiatry 10 (1964): 134-41.

Vasquez, Anna, and Katia Reczynzki. "Ethical Questions Submitted to Psychologists on Torture Techniques used in Chile," Paper presented in symposium at APA convention, Washington, D.C. 1976.

Wolk, Robert. "Psychoanalytic Conceptualization of Hostage Symptoms and Their Treatment," 1977, Unpublished paper.

5 Contagion and Attraction of Terror and Terrorism
Frederick J. Hacker

VIOLENCE AND TERRORISM

The model situation of aggressive or violently aggressive acts is a diadic relationship requiring and often demanding only two parties: the aggressor and the victim. In contrast, terror and terrorism (the attempt to influence by intimidation) is triadic, needing, in addition to a perpetrator and a victim, an observer, an audience for whose benefit the terroristic action is performed in the expectation of producing behavioral consequences. Terroristic actions are demonstrative, spectacular, and theatrical, akin to show business in trying to bring about calculated effects on the audience, i.e., the victim's family, friends, nations, and identity groups.(1) Terrorists intentionally manufacture, direct, and perfect the sensations they need to captivate their fascinated audiences. Mass media-oriented terrorism and terrorism-oriented mass media thrive on sensational, surprising, and exceptional events that occupy total audience attention for periods of time.

The victims are often condemned to a purely passive role, are merely pawns in the terroristic game, and are "extras" in the terrorists' dramatic production. They are used only as instruments to help the terrorists obtain their goals which may be to alarm, arouse, disturb, confuse, insult, horrify, or blackmail the audience or gain sympathy and support. Terror and terrorism very rarely represent senseless, explosive outbursts, symptomatically signifying loss of control; they are predominantly instances of strategic, well-planned, deliberate, purposeful aggression carefully timed and figured out to produce optimal results, that is, maximum audience reaction and participation. Hence, terrorism, more than any other form of aggression, stems from and depends in its motivation, its

73

perpetration, and its short and long-range effects on the
general social context, on the political situation, the choice
and "value" of victims, time and place of the deed, the
anticipated actual audience reaction, and many other such
factors. To ignore or deny the crucial psychological dimension
of terrorism would be folly. The attempt to explain terrorism
merely by the personality structures and psychodynamics of
terrorists, or to "treat" terrorism as if it were an illness
would be psychological reductionism which, behind its scientific
sounding nosology, conceals and distorts the realistic impact of
terrorism and its essential transactions with victims, audience,
the terrorists' organization, and the world at large that are
the distinguishing characteristics of any form of terrorism.

TERROR FROM ABOVE AND TERRORISM FROM BELOW

When in the Western world today there is talk about terrorism
(usually accompanied by the expected disapproval and indignation), terrorism from below is meant, i.e., the manufacture
and spread of fear by rebels, revolutionaries, and protestors.
Dialectically opposed to this type of terrorism from below -
exemplified by the attempts of the so far powerless (or would
be powerful) to attract attention, to gain influence, or to
exert control through intimidation - is the terror from above -
the manufacture and spread of fear by dictators, governments,
and bosses, to coerce, guide, and influence the behavior of
those under their control. Terror and terrorism are twins.
They hate and despise each other, yet they are very much
alike. They originate from the same family background of
violence with a clean conscience. They resemble and copy
each other and they depend and thrive on each other as each
claims to be necessary and caused by the other's existence.
Terror from above forever justifies itself by claiming to be the
only available remedy for and safeguard against terrorism from
below which, in turn, claims to be the only available means to
effectively break and fight the terror from above.
    Terrorists from below have no difficulty in continuing to
operate in the same old style in an entirely new position when
their group gains power; the former terrorists from below then
assume high functions in government, in the army, or in the
security forces. (Stalin was an ideologically inspired bank
robber before he became a high functionary of the Bolshevist
regime; many German National Socialist bomb throwers wound
up as generals or police chiefs, as expert fighters against
terrorism from below which they themselves had practiced
successfully for a long period of time.) Terrorists from below
often operate in organizations that are internally structured
according to the principles of terror from above; the Mafia

pattern of organization dominated by a single, omnipotent ruler or a ruling clique, clearly demonstrates that the terrorizing terrorists can, in a different context and at the same time, be terrorized, intimidated pawns and instruments of a terror regime from above.

Terror from above and terrorism from below are not the same but they belong together, indissolubly linked by the shared belief that fear is the strongest if not the only effective human motivation and that violence is the best if not the only method to produce and maintain fear.(2)

FASHIONS

Terroristic assaults from below often occur in clusters. Longitudinal studies disclose patterns of waves that rise, peak, fade away, and disappear, to be followed by other forms of terrorism claiming full public attention. The modus operandi of modern terrorism uses and repeats the same dramatic formulas that once have proven effective; the serialization of crime dramas with similar story lines continues until, through habit and fatigue of the audience, the elements of stimulation and surprise have worn off, and a new, entirely different series has to be invented in order to captivate the attention of the public. Ideologically and presumably idealistically inspired terrorists, like their spiritual ancestors the Crusaders, form the vanguard of terrorism. They are the inventors of changing themes and scenarios, and the widely visible, glamorous examples to be copied by the emotionally disturbed and the criminals. The models and designs of the fanatics are adopted by the disturbed and the greedy who join and imitate but do not start their own trends. Extravagantly publicized and glamorized violence is as catching as an infectious disease which can reach epidemic proportions; but this kind of violence also catches on like a popular tune, an illuminating aphorism, or a successful political ploy to be repeated over and over again for its entertainment value. Bomb throwing, skyjacking, seizure of buildings, and hostage taking have all occurred in rashes; the frequency and intensity of repeated episodes copying each other waxes and wanes. These trends are comparable to fashions seemingly originating from nowhere, although they are usually carefully calculated, reaching climactic highs that spread through copycat imitations, then decline due to tiring repetition, only to reappear again in other places or at other times. Modern skyjacking is one example of an activity often employed for terroristic purposes that was invented by crusaders motivated by political or ideological goals which later on was copied and adopted by the disturbed and the criminals.

Following the group escapes from countries behind the Iron Curtain, the airlift to Berlin in 1953, and the mass exodus of anti-Castro Cubans to the United States (by all means of available transportation, including skyjacked planes) enforced detours in the opposite direction, the coerced change of destination from a point in the United States to Cuba became and remained fashionable for many years.(3)   This same operational pattern was repeated over and over again until, in 1971, a 26 year-old Canadian, Paul Joseph Cini, claiming to be a member of the Irish Republican Party, demanded a parachute and $1.5 million with the threat to blow up the Canadian aircraft if his demands were not met.   Cini was clumsy and obviously mentally disturbed; he confused the safety belt with a parachute and was promptly overwhelmed without any difficulties.   Yet his exploit was widely publicized and sensationally reported by the mass media.   Two weeks later, a man calling himself D.B. Cooper duplicated the deed with professional perfection.   With a similar threat, he demanded and obtained $200 thousand and four parachutes, suggesting that he might force some of the passengers to accompany him.   Eventually, he jumped off the plane alone with his loot, disappeared and, in spite of intensive searches, has not been discovered.   This novel style of skyjacking, never practiced before, quickly became the vogue.   During the week following Cooper's act, skyjackings featuring the taking of hostages, extortion of ransom, and parachute jumps were imitated dozens of times in subsequent months.   A new fashion had been created; extortionist skyjacking was "in" at that moment, other forms of terrorism were temporarily "out."(4)

In just seven days in early February 1977, the United States was stunned by five highly publicized attacks by gunmen on individuals: on February 8, in Indianapolis, a mortgage company executive was held for 63 hours by a man with a shotgun; on February 9, in Silver Springs, Maryland, bank employees were held hostage by a young man; in Cincinnati, February 11, a couple held eight hostages at gunpoint in a home for unwed mothers; in Wheaton, Maryland, a man held his six-year-old son hostage for five hours on February 12; and in New Rochelle, New York, on February 14, a man with a rifle killed five men and wounded five others.

The recurring fashion of kidnapping important personages for terroristic purposes of blackmail or of sheer intimidation to demonstrate irresistibility, developed in South America, spread to Europe, created the odd American variation in the bizarre "work" of the Symbionese Liberation Army that abducted and converted the millionaire heiress Patty Hearst, and culminated in late 1977 and in 1978 with the kidnapping and killing of leading German industrialist Schleyer and the copycat "execution" of abducted top politician and Italian presidential candidate Aldo Moro.   All these and many similar acts were

carried out by desperate terrorists from below, fanatic individuals organized in small groups called gangs or bands,
that, in contrast to guerrillas, had to battle against the
increasing and indominable hostility of the overwhelming
majority of the population. Yet, in spite, or because of the
unprecedented, inhuman (dehumanizing and dehumanized)
cruelty of these deeds, performed with a curious mixture of
sophisticated technological calculation and primitive fury (a
kind of dispassionate passion), an amazingly large portion of
discontended establishment critics everyplace, openly or
clandestinely, sympathized with the terrorists, although, intellectually, they neither approved of their ruthless means nor
did they share their alleged goals.

ENTERTAINMENT AND "SHOWIFICATION"

The terroristic contagion no doubt is also a product of mass
media influence. The mass media willingly or unwittingly are
the spokesmen of the terrorists, the transmitters of the
terroristic message, the instrument through which terroristic
deeds with all their excitement, drama and significance in-
stantaneously become known to a world audience. Voracious
print and electronic media eagerly lap up the sensational fare
provided by terrorism as prime time entertainment. Packaging
dramatic stimulation as news has the additional titillation value
of being real and authentic. Research amply demonstrates
that particularly the "showification" of terroristic acts, the
simultaneous reporting of ongoing terroristic events, influences their outcome in at least two predictable ways: to make
a short, violent "solution" more likely; and to increase the
likelihood of copycat repetitions and imitations of violence
regardless of whether this violence is employed by terrorists
or the representatives of law and order.(5)
      The intrinsic mutual dependency of terrorism and mass
media on each other (they would have to invent each other if
they did not already exist independently) certainly is an
important factor in making terrorism a fast-spreading growth
industry since, without the possibility (or likelihood and even
certainty) of notoriety and hence contagion, terrorism could
not flourish. But it is not sufficient to point out over and
over again that terroristic actions have a seductive appeal for
predisposed individuals with a character structure and personality organization similar to that of the terrorists; nor to
complain that as long as terrorism is rewarded by the virtual
certainty of widespread publicity, the expectation of such
terroristic "success" will remain an important motivation for
future terroristic acts. Society will continue to have to pay a
high price in violence for its insistence on being entertained

by violence, but making media the sole scapegoats confuses the dangerous transmission and reinforcement of a psychosocial evil (often covered up by hypocritical explanations about the duty to inform or by rationalization of commercial competitiveness) with the sources and the significance of the phenomena itself. Terrorism from below, in its self-understanding and self-interpretation, tries to signal, alarm, awaken; the more indifferent society is in regard to remediable injustice, the greater the likelihood of terrorism attempting to violently draw attention to actual or alleged injustices ignored by a deaf and blind environment which, according to the terrorists' argument, has to be aroused, forced to see and hear by violence because nothing else will interrupt its slumber of smug complacency.

THE ACTION "HIGH"

Many intelligent and well-informed terrorists acknowledge that their deeds, no matter how desperate and spectacular, probably won't change very much either now or in the long run. However, some terrorists are quite reconciled (though by no means resigned) to the role of martyrs who, unlike heroes, don't succeed but fail honorably. At least they know that they tried: the unshakable belief that they work, fight, and die for purposes transcending their own narrow interests gives them the fanatic self-righteousness which makes their often self-destructive acts so destructive, dangerous, and contagious. The deed performed for seemingly nonegotistical reasons, for an ulterior purpose, becomes violent without restraint when the seeming display of individual courage is but slavish obedience to orders from above, a manifestation of relief from the curse of individuation. In this grandiose identification with a sacred cause and its representatives, the terrorist, by giving up his individual will, individual responsibility, and individual interest, experiences the "high" of "liberation" from his individual problems, guilts, and anxieties. The cruel act, stylized as morally superior to mere thinking or talking, mystically and realistically confirms the belonging to the identity group in a self-sacrificial mood which distracts from all personal problems, the act of super-Macho, now also available to females, radically removes all doubt and permits full aggressive gratification without self-punitive guilt, shame, doubt, or anxiety, in the name and for the sake of the higher cause.

ACTION ADDICTS AND FANATICS OF SIMPLICITY

In the subjective, although collectively manipulated illusion of certainty (of doing more than one's own thing, namely, the right thing), the certainty of the illusion that nothing but spectacular violence will influence reality becomes a firm conviction which transforms ordinarily self-protective individuals into fanatics, indifferent to personal danger, ready and even eager to sacrifice their own lives. The sacred cause (usually represented by an organization of terror from above) gives the promise of unity, of wholeness, of cohesion, and unanimity. The National Socialists expressed it in the slogan "one people - one empire - one leader." By insisting on a fully united "in" group that is one intact whole, supposed to give all adherents the feeling of family, shelter, and security, the enemy image is also simplified and unified. One definite enemy is provided in whom all the evil in the world is condensed and manifested. This one enemy appears in many guises and different manifestations in many different places, but he is, nevertheless, always the same, the principal and sole manifestation of all the evil in the world. If the one enemy can be totally eradicated, the principle of the good, healthy, and valuable (all represented by one's own identity group), will have been totally triumphant; by instant salvation, all problems will disappear. The constantly emphasized and celebrated unity of the identity group(6) also provides the projective screen and projective images with prefabricated content of such projections for selective use facilitating the fantasy of a radical, sudden, and total resolution of all conflicts and all difficulties if only the conventional, legal, and humane inhibitions against unrestrained violence can be overcome. As soldiers, heroes, martyrs (or instruments, puppets, marionettes) of the sacred cause, every gratification that can be rationalized to serve one's own cause and to destroy the enemy is permissible and even required. The fanatic representatives of the cause (in contrast to the "as if" personalities described by psychoanalysis) are indeed "as characters." They act and soon feel and think, not individually, but only as representatives, as parts of a larger whole, carrying out their assigned missions to serve a higher design. The presumably lofty morality of the group, indifferent to all human suffering, transcends the narrow boundaries of individual egotism, but only in order to confirm and strengthen the more powerful group egotism that satisfies the hunger for the unlimited exercise of power and satisfies the thirst for dependent submission.

The unifying identity conferring worth, belonging, and meaning is the group, institution, and symbol under the cover of which the individual can gratify his most elementary, infantile, and grandiose desires for omnipotence, omniscience, narcissistic satisfaction, and aggressive release. The all deciding and all justifying group is often only the concrete product of the members' need to belong; the group ideal to which the members are sworn to obedience reflects only their own hopes and fears. This seems to serve a cause but, in fact, the cause serves them and their own wishes. They often die in its service, victims of self-deception and puppets of their own delusions. Barbarization performed and condoned in the name of a higher purpose constitutes regression to infantile states of automatic obedience and ecstatic emotionalism. Brutalized children of all ages thus invest their "direct actions" and the propaganda of the deed with historic significance.(7) (Ralph Waldo Emerson wrote that "Terrorism feels and never reasons and therefore is always right.")

In the terroristic strategy, all the disturbing complexity of inner and outer conflicts is crudely simplified and moralistically reduced to one; the conflict between good and evil, between us and them. Terrorism (and, incidentally, also war or war-like escalated confrontation situations) is attractive to the impatient, the disturbed, the searchers and seekers, the mistreated and the injured due to its radical simplification, the reduction of complexity, and moralistic polarization with the inbuilt certainty of being on the right side. The implicit promise of instant liberation and salvation (because of the enemy's destruction) irresistibly lures the bored and the desperate, not just by providing ready-made projective images of inner conflict resolution and new more dignified political rationalization for personal conflicts, but also by supplying subculturally approved defense systems which can be internalized and serve as introjected superego and behavioral guides in all conceivable situations. The action appeal fascinates and hypnotizes; the fanatics of either/or simplicity become action addicts, who need the kicks and highs of the spiritual deed to experience their identity which they have, in fact, surrendered to the drug-like need to belong.

EGO IN THE SERVICE OF REGRESSION

The degree of functional rationality (choice of appropriate means to bring about certain ends) is no measure of substantive rationality (choice of "reasonable" ends). Desirable ends may never be reached due to the deficient means chosen or used and, conversely, excellent functioning means may promote an unworthy (irrational, infantile destructive, regressive) goal. Even conventional wisdom finally had to acknowledge that crusading terrorists are not necessarily either cowards or fools. Ernst Kris described in psychoanalytic terms the process of Controlled Regression (regression in the service of the ego) observable in artistic activity, psychoanalysis, creative activity, etc., many terrorists demonstrate the paradigm of "ego in the service of regression."(8)   Under certain conditions, the archaic primitivism (for instance, of terrorists' aims and terrorists' organizations) may employ the sophistication of technology and justification for its crude simplistic ends, and engage the seemingly voluntary services of committed, well-functioning, intelligent (and hence, particularly dangerous) individuals.

The terroristic deed is intended to alarm and to illuminate; in the glaring searchlight of explosive action, imperfect society is shown to be totally evil, perverted, and hopeless. The unembellished face of opression is relieved by terrorism's shortcut to "real reality" which tears off every hypocritical disguise; hence, the deed can be experienced as a moment of truth, an extraordinary, memorable, unique event which elevates from the dreary repetitiveness of everyday, profane, and trivial routines to the height of a sacred game with rich, symbolic significance.   To have participated in such a hallowed ritual means, for the terrorist, to have acquired lasting importance and to have established and reaffirmed the mystical bond to his community.(9)   By having acquired lasting eternal life within the community, he has overcome the dread and transcended the reality of his own individual death.

ANTITERRORISM

In this chapter, we have attempted to show what terrorism has to offer and for what reason it can (and only too often has) become contagious and attractive.   A more complete understanding of terrorism in all its dimensions is urged not in order to excuse or glamorize terrorism but to give a theoretical underpinning for urgently needed practical measures to successfully meet the terroristic challenge.   There is a large literature on terrorism and how to mobilize behavioral science and psychiatric resources in the fight against terrorism from below and hopefully also against terror from above.   The perfection of interview and negotiation techniques, the acceptance of the principle that talking is better than shooting and negotiations are, therefore, always preferable to violent confrontations (because negotiating is not equivalent to yielding), the establishment of special psychologically trained action groups within law enforcement, the improvement of intelligence and detection methods, the conclusion of bilateral and multilateral treaties between countries to combat international terrorism, and several other such developments can be cited as evidence for some, even though modest, progress in

the battle against terrorism based on clearer understanding of
terrorism.(10)

        Soberly and realistically, it must be admitted that one of
the most highly advertised and probably most popular, seemingly easiest ways to eliminate terrorism from below is the
introduction of terror from above. There is no terrorism from
below under totalitarian regimes when the regime has pre-
empted and monopolized all terroristic activities which are
organized and government justified from above. The ruling
circles practice what they prohibit; gaining and maintaining
influence and power through universal intimidation and indiscriminate arousal of fear. Police state measures in small
dosages tend to stimulate and increase terrorism from below
which is then crushed by energetic, total terror from above.
But under "ideal" conditions of totalitarian control, terrorism
blanketed in silence and condemned to anonymity by nonre-
porting media can be eliminated by radical measures including
population transfers, torture, and deprivation of civil rights.
Justification for police state measures (easily provided by a
number of totalitarian, nationalistic or religious ideologies) can
always count on support by the widespread belief that a
terrible end is a lesser evil than terrorism without end, and
that order, any order, is better than chaotic disorder.

        In the United States, with its relatively flexible social
institutions, its inviolable constitution, and its tradition of
liberty, the introduction of a totalitarian police state regime
does not appear to be an imminent danger, although some local
developments (the summon for vigilante groups, the call to
suspend constitutional safeguards for the trial of terrorists, or
the demand to free the police from all constitutional restraints
in their investigation and prosecution of terorists) indicate
that now, more than ever, eternal vigilance is the price of
freedom. At present, a majority of Americans still seem
convinced that the suggested cure (terror from above) is as
bad or worse than the disease (terrorism from below); yet the
greatest terroristic threat consists of the possibility that, in
the name of the sacred cause called "fight against terrorism,"
terroristic methods and terroristic brutality might become
widely used by antiterrorists and be generally tolerated and
accepted as lawful.

SPECIFIC PSYCHIATRIC TASKS

Intensive study and possible rehabilitation of terrorists might
not be impossible if it were ever tried; psychiatric help for
the conduct of negotiations and active participation in such
negotiations (the author was privileged to actively take part in
the negotiations with Arab kidnappers on behalf of the Au-

strian government during an ongoing terroristic attack)
certainly are worthwhile psychiatric tasks. But a new, more
important use to which the specific psychiatric, human,
clinical, and therapeutic experience could be put is not just
emergency intervention, but patient, persistant, ongoing work
with the authorities responsible for safety and security, with
media representatives and with representatives of the people.
The provocative, often mocking and taunting, insulting and
ridiculing terrorists frequently bring out the worst in the
terror fighters; namely, the hidden terrorist in the antiterrorists. This is where the psychiatrist is particularly needed.

Mere enlightenment about essentially unconscious psychosocial processes will not in and by itself modify their course,
but the psychiatrist may have some credibility, some prestige
and authority with those who use him or her as advisor and
consultant, and also may have some independent, legitimate
access to news media and to educational institutions of all
kinds. Therefore, the psychiatrist may be able to point out
with all the professional skill at his disposal that particularly
those engaged in fighting terrorism are not necessarily immune
to its contagion and attraction. Law enforcement officers often
also lead unexciting lives and may wish for instant fame and
for a moment of glory through which they can gain status
among their group, and a feeling of having meaningfully
participated in an extraordinary event. Policemen and chiefs,
officials and politicians up to the very top, are not, as a rule,
totally impervious to the lure of publicity nor averse to the
public display of apparent decisiveness and seemingly contagious Macho determination. They, the framers and representatives of law and order, are also known to stress their
self-sacrificial service for higher goals, and only the most
responsible among them will refuse to ever simplify a complex
problem or to advertise themselves and their methods as the
only safeguard against some kind of alleged or actual danger.
Provoked by unrestrained aggression, the temptation is great
to reply in kind and to retaliate for indiscriminate violence
with indignation and equally indiscriminate counterviolence.
Everybody who, in whatever function with whatever responsibility, has ever participated in a crisis staff called to meet a
terroristic emergency knows that; he remembers how hard it
was to sustain the necessary patience and attention to every
trivial detail that may become the cue for successful intervention under mounting tension and pressure for a quick,
decisive "solution." He recalls the extreme difficulties of
resisting the ever more insistent urgings of the advocates of
the military option accompanied by the innuendo that the
refusal to act decisively and immediately indicates cowardice.
He relives the agony of not permitting himself to regress to
the same infantile level as the terrorist did and not to retaliate
in kind; he knows the temptation of terrorism because he has

experienced it. This is certainly not to say that we are all
terrorists at heart to different degrees, but only that the
conscious, deliberate, and frequently effective strategy of
terrorism appears to touch upon and mobilize universal,
unconscious strivings. Due to our fearful experiences and our
education through fear, violent impulses (drive derivatives,
defenses against drives, or habituated responses) can become
manifest as they have in the terrorists and then lead to the
escalation of violence and counterviolence in the terroristic
antiterrorism that has become indistinguishable from terrorism.
This is where psychiatric knowledge, psychiatric counsel and
psychiatric help can be of benefit.

To fully understand and appreciate the attraction of
terrorism in order to prevent its contagion and imitation, the
phony ritual of the terroristic act has to be demythologized;
violence which is not uplifting and liberating but mean and
trivial has to be deglamorized. The terrorist, who more often
is a misguided terrorized poor devil than a devil, has to be
desatanized, not just for his sake, but for that of the victims
and all those who know that there are better, more lasting,
and more humane methods of conflict resolution and regulation
than terroristic confrontation and violence.(11)

Terror and terrorism are not exclusively psychological let
alone psychopathological phenomena; hence, they have to be
dealt with (or preferably avoided) on different levels and
with different methods than psychiatric skills. What is essential is the prompt relief from remediable injustice, the
availability of credible nonviolent conflict resolution, the
possibility for voicing of grievances, and international agreements that prevent the irrational cult of sovereignty through
which each and every arbitrary act and injustice (including
the support of terrorism by proxy) is removed from scrutiny
or interference by being declared an internal affair. All
behavioral scientists should contribute to innovative social
planning and intuitive social experimentation to the best of
their ability. The specific psychiatric contribution could be
the prevention of the terroristic contagion and the creation of
conditions under which terror from above and terrorism from
below may still not have lost their menacing characteristics but
at least have been deprived of their present exciting entertainment value, imitation potential, and seductive attractive-
ness.

NOTES

1. See, for example, Frederick J. Hacker, Crusaders,
Criminals, Crazies - Terror and Terrorism in Our Time   (New
York: W.W. Norton, 1976); Abraham Kaplan, In Pursuit of

Wisdom - The Scope of Philosophy (Beverly Hills, Calif.:
Glencoe Press, Benzinger Bruce & Blencoe, London: Collier
Macmillan, 1977); and Brian Jenkins, "Soldier Versus Gunman:
The Challenge of Urban Guerrilla Warfare," Rand Paper Series,
1974.
    2. Hacker, Crusaders, Criminals, Crazies.
    3. David Hubbard, The Skyjacker (New York: Mac-
millan, 1971).
    4. Hacker, Crusaders, Criminals, Crazies.
    5. U.S., Congress, House of Representatives, Terror-
ism, parts 1-4. Hearings before the Committee on Internal
Security (Washington, D.C.: Government Printing Office,
1974).
    6. Jillian Becker, Hitler's Children (Philadelphia: J.B.
Lippincott, 1977).
    7. Jurgen Habermas, Towards a Rational Society (Bos-
ton: Beacon Press, 1971).
    8. Ernst Kris, Selected Papers of Ernst Kris (New
Haven: Yale University Press, 1975).
    9. Robert J. Lifton, Death in Life/Survivors of Hiro-
shima (New York: Simon and Schuster, Touchstone Book,
1967).
    10. Hacker, Crusaders, Criminals, Crazies.
    11. Ibid.; Frank Ochberg, "The Victim of Terrorism:
Psychiatric Considerations," Terrorism 1 (2) (1978).

6 The Terrorist Organizational Profile: A Psychological Role Model

Thomas Strentz

One of the most spectacular police shootouts in recent years occurred on May 17, 1974, when a rather odd mixture of young people calling themselves the Symbionese Liberation Army (SLA) decided to make a desperate stand against the Los Angeles Police Department and the Federal Bureau of Investigation. Their ill-chosen fortress was a rather dilapidated frame house in a seedy section of Los Angeles. Their fate was predictable; all six perished in the flames of the burning house, steadfastly refusing to surrender, and firing their weapons defiantly at police until the end. All but one of these who died in this incident were educated young people from comfortable middle class backgrounds; most had been loved by their parents and nurtured on a dream of the perfect world. As a comrade, these young people had chosen an escaped convict with a long criminal record. All of them died together, having made a vow the previous day to fight to the death against the "oppressive establishment." They planned to defeat the Los Angeles Police Department and continue to "fight for the rights of needy people." Their goal was to "kill the fascist insect who preys upon the life of the people."(1)

It is essential for law enforcement to try to understand something of the dynamics of the terrorist personality as it functions within certain roles in the group. The SLA appears to differ only slightly from other terrorist organizations that also operate within and against democracies. If some insight can be gained through an examination of the role model of the SLA, this knowledge could be applicable to terrorist groups in general.

PROFILE OF THE TERRORIST: A THEORETICAL DESIGN

The Symbionese Liberation Army exemplified the various roles, the personalities attracted to these roles, and each role's function in terrorist organizations. Three distinct roles are discernible in the SLA prototype:

1. The Leader: a person of total dedication, a trained theoretician with a strong personality;
2. The Activist-Operator: a person with an antisocial personality, frequently an ex-convict, an opportunist;
3. The Idealist: usually the university dropout with a life pattern of searching for the truth, the minor functionary.(2)

These three roles and personality types frequently emerge in terrorist groups found in democratic nations.(3)

The Leader

In leftist groups, the leader is frequently female, e.g., Nancy Ling Perry in the SLA, Ulrike Meinhof of the German leftist Baader-Meinhof terrorist gang,(4) and Fusako Shigenobu of the Japanese Red Army.(5) These are cynical yet dedicated personalities.(6) Of the three roles, the leader shows the fewest signs of self-interest. This personality is rigid, dedicated, overly-suspicious, and highly motivated. She or he projects personal faults and inadequacies onto others and ascribes evil motives to those who disagree. The leader is convinced of her righteousness and the underlying evil of those who oppose her. The development of the leader's thought patterns is gradual and culminates in an intricate, complex, and elaborate belief system. The leader sees herself as unique, with superior ability and knowledge.(7)
  The leader's primary defense mechanism is projection, and, to a lesser extent, she uses denial and rationalization. She uses these mechanisms and other means to overcompensate for basic feelings of inadequacy.(8) She "specializes," i.e., knows a lot about a very little. When conversing, she is generally rational; however, she will ultimately steer the conversation and, to a point, control others' parts in it. She is the perfectionist; she is too insecure to tolerate error. Her life is planned down to the last detail lest she leave room for failure. She is persuasive and totally dedicated to molding men's minds.

Psychological development of the leader

The leader is as dedicated, but not nearly as delusional as the paranoid personality. However, the development of similar reasoning processes are probably parallel. Paranoia is a gradually developed delusional system sustained by perceptions of events which are interpreted to support the basic thought patterns. The paranoid individual refuses to be confused by the facts. Like the leader, only his interpretation of events is correct: he is O.K. and others, unless they totally agree with him, are not O.K. "Basically they are bitter and hostile against the world with a tendency to be suspicious of the motives of everyone."(9) "Paranoia is a poison of suspicion that infuses the total psychic life of its victim."(10)

The paranoid state begins early in life and is agitated by the normal perils of living.(11) People who are normal develop a basic trust in others and consider the world to be a safe place in which they can freely interact with their fellow man.(12)

The terrorist leader is irrationally dedicated to a set of beliefs that are not generally supported by most members of the democracy. Although the evidence the leader presents to justify her beliefs may be inconclusive, she is unwilling to accept any other explanation. Argument and logic are futile. She is insulated from the beliefs of others. In fact, any serious questioning that challenges the authenticity of her explanation convinces her that the interrogator has sold out to the enemy.(13)

"Many paranoiacs become attached to extremist political movements and are tireless and fanatical crusaders. . . .(14) Frequently, the leader develops her belief or beliefs around a grain of truth, but her fallacious and perverted logic brings her to invalid conclusions no longer resembling that truth.

It is important to note that, though the leader of a terrorist group has certain personality traits most commonly associated with the paranoid personality, she or he is not mentally ill. She is more dedicated, single-minded, intelligent, and theoretically-oriented than most people. She is more suspicious and, like the blindly prejudiced individual, inclined to selectively interpret events, but not to the degree found in true mental illness. The leader is, on the surface, self-confident; she has all the answers to the problems of life.

The leader's role in group

The leader can read people well and appeal to their needs. The leader uses her followers in comfortable, fulfilling roles. She allows them to have their fantasies; she understands, tolerates, and satisfies their needs for recognition, achievement, and self-fulfillment. The leader allows each follower to be a self-appointed general. She allows the criminal element his "Jesse James" fantasy as she uses each in his role to achieve her purpose and his pleasure.

SLA prototype of a leader

The leader, Nancy Ling Perry, was the "brains" of the SLA organization. She wrote and/or edited the many pronouncements of the group.(15) Ms. Perry, called Fahizah by the SLA, was an intelligent young woman, a graduate of the University of California with a degree in English Literature. When engaged in graduate work in chemistry, she became involved in the Black Cultural Association at the California Adult Authority facilities at Vacaville and Folsom. Typical of the terrorist leader, she was intelligent, a college graduate, single, had no children, and was underemployed.(16) She became involved in radical political activity which predated her criminal endeavors.

The leader and law enforcement

Police involvement with this person is infrequent as the leader is behind the scenes, i.e., a policy developer. She or he may occasionally venture out with the group to show it how to accomplish a particular task. If apprehended, the leader is generally bright enough to maintain her silence. However, should she begin to talk, the general superior attitude and the assured discussion of the "conspiracy theory of history" will begin to evolve. This is especially true if the leader thinks the interrogator is a possible convert. She is not an easy mark for the interrogator; the interview will probably be a political, economic, and psychological education for the police.

The Opportunist

This is generally a male role, held by one whose criminal activity predates his political involvement. Psychologically, the classification that most closely approximates his life-style is that of the antisocial personality, also known as the sociopath or the psychopath. Terrorist groups that operate against democracies appear to embrace this person, the muscle of the organization. Some of the more infamous include Donald David DeFreeze of the SLA, Gregg Daniel AdoRnetto of the Emiliano Zapata Unit (EZU),(17) Andreas Baader and Hans Joachim Klein of the Baader-Meinhof Gang,(18) and Akira Nihei of the Japanese Red Army.(19) On our eastern seaboard, Stanley Bord and William Gilday, inmates engaged in a work release program, teamed up with Katherine Ann Power and Susan Edith Saxe, college students from Brandeis University, to rob a bank and murder a Boston police officer. Similarly, the Johnathan Jackson-Sam Melville organization and the Fred Hampton Unit were groups of reform-minded college students that deteriorated into criminal gangs.

The opportunist is not mentally ill or crazy; he is oblivious to the needs of others and unencumbered by the capacity to feel guilt or empathy.(20)

> To sum up his personality, he is basically unsocialized, and his behavior pattern brings him repeatedly into conflict with society. He is incapable of significant loyalty to individuals, groups or social values. He is grossly selfish, callous, irresponsible, impulsive and unable to feel guilt or to learn from experience and punishment. Frustration tolerance is low. He tends to blame others or offer plausible rationalizations for his behavior.(21)

He is O.K., the world is out of step. One outstanding criminal psychologist discusses the problem of the sociopath as follows:

> A major concern and interest of mine over the years has been the study of the psychopathic offender. It seems evident to me that there is an increasing number of offenders coming into our institutions with definite sociopathic or psychopathic traits. Of the many kinds of offenders that might be identified, in my opinion, this is the most dangerous, the most damaging, and the most difficult to identify and treat. Of the psychopathic offenders who commit offenses, we are faced with a kind of disorder whereby the individual is not psychotic, is not neurotic, is not mentally retarded, and frequently appears not only normal, but hyper normal. While these individuals often commit crimes of the most despicable nature, they frequently are not transferable to the Department of Mental Health, and the best minds in the country have attempted to put together a treatment program for this kind of behavior problem without notable success.
>
> Some of the essential traits of this kind of mentally disturbed offender are a lack of concern, anxiety, remorse or guilt feelings relative to the crimes that they may have committed. The inability to learn from experience, the superficial charm, the intelligence, and the almost total lack of concern about what their actions will bring about dictates that this particular kind of offender should be scrutinized and perhaps is deserving of a classification unique in itself.(22)

Psychological development of the opportunist

There is considerable disagreement in psychiatric circles on how this antisocial personality develops, and the causation theories are numerous. The traditional psychiatric theory holds that early childhood and family experiences shape the personality toward deviant or nondeviant behavior, and behavior after these early childhood years is merely acting out tendencies formed at that time.(23) One study reports a high incidence of psychopathic personalities - particularly fathers - in families of children who later manifest psychopathic behavior.(24) Another authority suggests the psychopath was rejected or cruelly treated or may have suffered early brain damage. He strikes back at the world with aggressive, unrestrained, attention-drawing behavior. Since conscience is instilled by early love, faith in the adults close by and the desire to hold their affection by being good, the child unrewarded with love grows up experiencing no conscience. Uncared for, he doesn't care, can't really worry about whether he's good or bad, and literally has no idea of guilt.(25)

There are many models. Sigmund Freud, the father of modern psychiatry, conceived a three-part human personality consisting of the id, ego, and superego. The functions of these components, as conceived by Freud, are as follows:

> The id is man's expression of instinctual drive without regard to reality or morality. It contains the drive for preservation and destruction, as well as the appetite for pleasure.

> The ego functions to satisfy the basic forces of the id in practical ways or tolerates the id drive until such times as these drives can find realistic expression.

> The superego dictates to the ego how the demands of the id are to be satisfied. It is, in effect, the conscience usually developed by parental ideals and prohibitions formed during early childhood.(26)

Criminal activity, according to the psychoanalyst, is the result of the conflict between the id, ego, and superego. The drives of the primitive id are not sufficiently balanced by the superego and come into conflict with the rules of society. The proper interactions of these three components are usually learned prior to the child's fifth year. Every woman and man, according to Freud, is born with criminal potential in the sense that he is selfish, hateful, spiteful, and mean because he is under the control of the id. His early experiences must be loving, kind, and sympathetic in order to develop the proper superego structure. If this is not accomplished in early childhood, antisocial behavior is a common result.(27)

More recently, there is evidence that early organic brain damage may be a causative factor. Dr. George L. Thompson, former Chief of the Neuro-Psychiatric Unit of the Los Angeles County Hospital, is convinced that a form of childhood encephalitis is a cause of sociopathic behavior.(28) This disease leaves the victim - the future sociopath - with minimal organic brain damage. Other authorities report an 80 and 90 percent incidence of irregular, abnormal brain waves reflected in EEG (electroencephalogram) tests administered to individuals previously diagnosed as sociopaths.(29)

Recruitment of the opportunist

The opportunist is generally recruited from the prison population by the leader or the third functionary in the organization, the idealist. The intelligence of the opportunist varies; the brighter he is, the more of a threat he could pose to the leader. There is a possibility of the opportunist taking over the group; therefore, to maintain control, the leader may become paranoid. This relationship between leader and opportunist is extremely sensitive - internecine war is a threat.(30)

An intelligent leader will function in the shadow, if her personality will allow this, and be the power behind the throne. Thus, the opportunist can take his ego trip and emerge as the seeming leader. This was the situation in the SLA with Perry as the thinker and DeFreeze as the actor.(31)

Recruitment of the opportunist is relatively easy, especially today with the influx of volunteers active in various prison rehabilitation programs. The opportunist is seeking "easy time." He is to be found in every prison in great numbers; by some estimates, he represents 40 percent of all criminals who commit 80 percent of all crimes.(32)

As he "does time," he must sooner or later face the issue that he may not be "O.K."; he was wrong, stupid, or something else that is less than his self-concept will allow, otherwise he would not be here, incarcerated with the "common" criminal. The mind set of the psychopath is such that he is always O.K. He always has some rationale for his seeming failure, i.e., life mistreats him, or people do not recognize his latent ability. The student volunteer, politically-oriented toward the left, offers the perfect rationale. He tells the inmate, "Mr. Convict, you are innocent; you are O.K.; you are not a criminal; you are a political prisoner. You are right. The system is wrong. You were framed." This idea of being a victim of an oppressive, discriminatory political system fits perfectly in his mind scheme. Now he can add political rhetoric to his vocabulary, excuse his predicament, and impress his fellow inmates, who, for the most part, are

politically ignorant. A mutually supportive relationship develops; each gives and takes; each needs the other. The
convict needs the rationale to justify his incarceration. The
movement needs his muscle.(33)

The opportunist's role in group

The middle-class student tells the convict his misdeeds were
political and he is really O.K., thus directly and indirectly
admiring his masculinity, his "machismo." Gradually, the
opportunist is brought into the political fold as the strong-arm
type. The prisoner, in turn, is playing the game by engaging
in political rhetoric and sees the opportunity, upon release or
escape, to live a hedonistic life with support from an organization he views as naive and within his control.(34) The
organization will provide his needs, e.g., physical needs,
shelter, sexual activity, and, in some instances, drugs,(35) in
exchange for his criminal knowledge and daring. He is not
frightened by violence; in fact, he is intrigued by its excitement.(36) Contrary to his middle-class associates, his
lifelong focal concerns are trouble, toughness, smartness, and
excitement, not law-abiding behavior, hard work, and delayed
gratification.(37)

Given his penchant for aggressive behavior, his criminal
experience, and his antisocial orientation, the opportunist is
well-suited for the responsibilities of a terrorist group field
commander. He can serve the function of transforming a
rhetoric-oriented political group into a criminally-oriented
terrorist group. The opportunist provides the needed technical skills. He may also force the verbalizing leader to
demonstrate her dedication by participating in physical criminal
activity. The terrorist organization, under the careful manipulation of the leader, becomes the opportunist's gang. The
leader allows the opportunist to act out his fantasy of leading
the group. The leader manipulates the opportunist and uses
his criminal skill to further political goals.

SLA prototype of an opportunist

The SLA example of this role type was Donald David DeFreeze.
DeFreeze was a school dropout at age sixteen. After his
fifteenth felony arrest at age seventeen, he provided information in an attempt to plea bargain his sentence. After his
last conviction, he bargained himself into a soft, trustee-type
assignment and walked away from the California Correctional
Training Facility at Soledad on March 5, 1973, not to be heard
from again until mid-February 1974, when he surfaced as
General Field Marshal Cinque. He was to become the field
commander of the SLA and the strong arm of Nancy Ling
Perry.

The SLA tapes featuring DeFreeze as General Field Marshal Cinque(38) exemplify his nonpolitical, nonleadership role. In those tapes, he read words he did not understand. On one tape, he read the word coup (as in coup d'etat) as coop (as in chicken coop). He was intellectually over his head when he listed on another tape "some Pacific factors" and plans to alleviate the "current suffering they are now under." Later, in April 1974, one of his tapes set out the battle plan of the SLA, saying that, "No prisoners will be taken prisoner." Psycholinguistic evaluation of Donald David DeFreeze showed him to be merely parroting words and phrases outlined by a more intelligent white female.(39)

Cinque manifested a need for significance, power, and acceptance. He was the action focus of the group; he was the doer, not the thinker. He was intellectually inferior to Jalena (Angela Atwood), who was second in the group's pecking order. His ability to conceptualize was sparse. He had difficulty comprehending complex political theory and had a rather single-dimensional outlook. Clearly, he looked to Jalena, who was the scribe for Nancy Ling Perry, for his intellectual support.(40) His function in the group was to provide the terror that the others only talked about.

Before DeFreeze, the SLA only spoke of revolution. His presence and expertise provided the group with its action arm. He had the experience and willingness to demonstrate that actions speak louder than words. This is evidenced by the killings, kidnappings, and robbery the group engaged in with his assistance. When SLA members ventured into criminal activity without him, they could not even succeed in shoplifting. The death of DeFreeze, the opportunist, reduced the SLA to rhetoric until another opportunist was recruited in 1975.

The opportunist and law enforcement

Without the opportunist, a group is radical only in rhetoric. He provides the terror to the terrorist group.(41)

The opportunist is familiar to the police officer. Even the officer who has limited experience has met someone with this personality disorder many times - the vicious con artist or the good informant, the individual who is meek as a kitten when cornered yet vicious when he has the upper hand.(42)

The law enforcement officer should be aware of the opportunist's sociopathic personality and his criminal potential. Some methods of identification are complicated, such as the Galvanic Skin Response (GSR),(43) a measure of stress. The experienced polygraph operator will certainly recognize the sociopath because of his flat reaction and lack of anxiety while being tested.

Most police, parole, or probation officers may be able to tentatively classify an individual as a sociopath by reviewing his arrest record. The record of the sociopath reflects a variety of antisocial, impulsive acts which frequently include rape. The variety of offenses is perhaps the best indication. The best key to identification for the officer on the street is the ability to recognize the glib, con artist style of conversation, coupled with the inability to follow through or engage in any behavior that is not self-serving. The opportunist is quite different from the leader; he is less educated though equally glib - an actor rather than a thinker. Most significantly, he is entirely self-serving.

The opportunist will be an old, familiar face to the police officer. His act will be the same; only his rhetoric will have changed. He will turn under pressure as he is out only for himself. On some occasions, the opportunist's role has been played by an individual who had been an informant prior to his involvement with the terrorist group. He is the key; his removal will deactivate the terrorist group, and his glib tongue will and has identified other members. This member of the group is the key for law enforcement intervention. His politics are superficial; he is a member of this group only because it is meeting certain physical or psychosocial needs.

The leader of the group lured the opportunist into the organization by making him a compellingly attractive offer. This process can be and has been used by law enforcement agencies to develop the opportunist as an informant defector or informant in place. Law enforcement can encourage his defection by making him a better offer. He is a realist and is willing to deal if he must to better his personal circumstances. He will sell the lives of others without a second thought. This was demonstrated by Gregg Adornetto when he was arrested with other members of the EZU in February 1976, in Richmond, California.

The Idealist

The last personality in the group is almost normal. The most charitable diagnosis for the idealist, i.e., the "idealist" role player in terrorist groups, would be a victim of political naivete, the spoiled child, or perennial sophomore. Most adolescents rebel; some turn toward delinquency; very few join terrorist groups. The idealist is initially an innocent person dedicated to a better world. His innocence is exploited and radicalized by the strong personality of the leader, subverted by rhetoric that sounds so perfect. In extreme cases, the idealist borders on the inadequate personality classification.(44) Between the points of political naivete and inadequate personality is the personality described in Eric Hoffer's book, The True Believer:

He's a guilt ridden hitchhiker who thumbs a ride on every cause from Christianity to Communism. He's a fanatic, needing a Stalin (or a Christ) to worship and die for. He's the mortal enemy of things as they are, and he insists on sacrificing himself for a dream impossible to attain.(45)

This "true believer" is the terrorist group's "idealist."

As a college student from a middle class family, the idealist feigns poverty in his life-style, perhaps as an expression of guilt. A few generations ago he was called the "Aginner." He is against whoever is in power - the terminal malcontent. The world never seems to be the perfect place he thinks possible.

Psychological development of an idealist

There are many explanations for the development of the idealist personality. A current explanation is set forth in Midge Decter's book, Liberal Parents, Radical Children.(46) She discusses the misdirected youthful idealism that seeks to achieve, yet falls short of the mark. These "idealists" are taught from youth that everything that frustrates them is an injustice that must be altered.(47) Others contend that this rise of "radical children" is an international phenomenon.(48)

The frustration-aggression theory of revolution developed by Berkowitz and set forth by Gurr also provides an explanation for the violence of the middle-class student.(49) In his futile attempt to remake the world as a land of milk and honey, the idealist meets with frustration at every turn. Certainly, the vast majority redirect their efforts toward more realistic goals and make part of the world a better place in which to live. However, for those few who cannot redirect, the frustration mounts and, in some cases, finds expression in political violence orchestrated by the opportunist. Anarchy and revolution are fulfillment of his needs, born from the impatience of youth. As one matures, time seems to fly; to the young, time drags. He cannot wait. He can see no other course of action but to strike out.

The terrorist group gives these individuals the answers they seek to the problems of the world. Such phrases as, "Everything must go; the system is so corrupt we must start from scratch"; "Death to the fascist insect that preys upon the life of the people"; or their call for "participatory Democracy," exemplify the type of sophomoric political rhetoric which might be heard.

The idealist's role in the group

The idealist's role in the group is the soldier; the idealistic follower who reconnoiters buildings prior to bombings, follows the opportunist into the bank, carries the messages, and is generally the cannon fodder for the revolution. He is the desperate, dependent youth who is seeking the truth and has fallen victim to the leader's rhetoric and the opportunist's deceit. He accepts the dictates of the leader and disciplines himself well beyond the point his parents or former associates thought possible. He is a dedicated follower who works at capacity for the leader's goals. He is determined to learn all the tactics the opportunist teaches. The idealist is short-lived in his altruism and inclined to drift from group to group as he drifted from his family. Most mature and outgrow the role of misguided idealist. He is expendable and is expended, as the SLA demonstrated.

SLA prototypes of idealists

Angela Atwood, a former schoolteacher who worked in San Francisco as a waitress, was a young, idealistic divorcee who engaged in political activity prior to her criminal involvement. Camilla Hall, from the Midwest, was a college graduate and former social worker who worked as a gardener and park attendant in San Francisco. She was another true believer who hitched her wagon to the wrong group and paid for this decision with her life. William Wolfe, the most intelligent of the SLA idealists, was an early leader of the organization until a stronger personality, Nancy Ling Perry, took over the reins. She put the group together using her close associate, Donald David DeFreeze, as the muscle to forge this association. Wolfe, the son of a professional family, was involved in programs for the betterment of his fellowman but lost his patience and then his life in his quest for a quick solution.

The SLA, with its many generals, played a fanciful game with self-made intrigue and persistent paranoia. They made vain attempts to give meaning to their empty lives and status to their weak egos. They claimed positions they would not be qualified to hold in any moderately well-functioning society. The problem was, of course, that they played their immature games with dynamite, gasoline bombs, automatic weapons, and human lives. Smart, skilled, and sane revolutionaries do exist. However, within a dynamic democracy, peaceful change can be achieved. In democracies, the terrorist is involved more because of his psychosocial needs than because of his desire to achieve political-social betterment for the masses.

The idealist and law enforcement

The idealist's rhetoric is heavy with statements calling for protracted wars of national liberation. He looks with pride upon the Chinese example of the Long March and reflects a martyr intellect. Perhaps this element of the terrorist groups is a personification of Freud's death wish.(50)

Those dealing with the idealist will recognize the lack of depth in his rhetoric. He parrots pet phrases: "If only everyone will love, then the world will be wonderful" is an example of his answer to international problems.

He is the group member most likely to become committed to new ideologies; however, he is unlikely to become an informant. Under pressure he may become, in his eyes, a martyr and thus elevate his status among his peers, the only people he trusts and cares for. When in custody, he will not, at least initially, turn on those who have given his empty life purpose and provided recognition and status to his weak ego. If he can be persuaded that the group has deserted him, or is actually counterrevolutionary and hypocritical, then the idealist is left with little security and may be ripe for conversion to another cause that offers him the warmth and recognition that he has just lost. His dependency needs must be met; as long as the terrorist group does this adequately, he is loyal. Some idealists, the pure type, would be most opposed to law enforcement. They follow the rules of the revolution; whereas the leaders make the rules, therefore, only the leaders may bend them.

The extreme idealist or "true believer" is not a successful person in the usual sense. His self-concept is poor. He views his life only as a member of the group. Without the emotional support and recognition of the group, he is a loser. Only they, not his parents or our society, can give his life meaning.

Of the three role types in terrorist groups, the idealist is the most salvageable. Given time, he may outgrow his revolutionary role. It is a phase through which he passes. One need only look at the many professional, responsible people of today who were the idealists of the 1960s, the cannon fodder of the various groups that played their game for headlines a few years ago, to see that this is so.

OTHER GROUPS

This chapter has dealt with the SLA as a prototype. Through them, a role model for terrorist groups in a democracy has been hypothesized. Foreign groups and another domestic organization fit this profile as well. In contrast, some groups differ from the profile and, consequently, differ from the SLA in their method of operation. Both will be mentioned.

A study of the Emiliano Zapata Unit of the Red Guerrilla Family, arrested by the FBI in Richmond, California, on February 21, 1976, reflects a table of organization similar to the SLA. They proclaimed their revolutionary rhetoric in the Berkeley Barb and placed one-half dozen bombs in the Bay area. They claimed credit for explosions beginning March 27, 1975, and, subsequent to their arrest one year later, were finally convicted of bombings in the San Francisco area. Laurence Allen Kisinger, their leader,(51) was the oldest, although not the most educated, of the group. The opportunist was Gregg Daniel Adornetto, a criminal with many arrests for narcotics violations; the others were the idealists.(52) On the east coast, the Fred Hampton Unit was responsible for at least five bombings. Their reign of terror ended on July 4, 1976, when they were arrested after planting a bomb at the Massachusetts State Police barracks.

In Northern Ireland, we see a similar pattern in the Irish Republican Army. New Scotland Yard has long labeled the IRA functionaries as Grand Counsel (Leader), Godfathers (Opportunists), and Bullyboys (Idealists).(53) Other foreign examples that follow this model more closely include the Japanese Red Army, Baader-Meinhof and the various South American groups identified by Brooks McClure.(54)

The Japanese Red Army, perhaps the most professional terrorist group with roots in a democratic country, reflects a similar profile. Two women, Fusako Shigenobu and Tsutoma Shirosaki, appear to hold leadership positions. Convicted criminal Akira Nihei, or one of the other prisoners released in the Fall of 1977, is the opportunist. Others in the group, Ehita, Bondo, and Tohira, appear to be the idealists.(55)

Within the Baader-Meinhof group, Ulrike Meinhof replaced Horst Mahler as the leader and Andreas Baader functioned as the opportunist.(56)

In contrast to these terrorist groups reflecting the role prototype, right wing groups in the United States generally lack the opportunist. Therefore, they also lack his criminal expertise and activity. The American Nazi Party, the Minutemen, and the California Rangers, to name a few, are right wing and generally function with the leader and idealist spreading their propaganda and engaging in less violent deeds of revolution. These groups, though they may possess firearms which they generally secrete away, are content with spreading propaganda, picketing, parades, and long-winded speeches. The absence of the opportunist precludes overt violence. They do not kill, kidnap, or bomb as do the other groups who place the opportunist in the role of field commander.

Right-wing groups have been the personal militia of their leader. There is no second in command because the leader's personality will not tolerate any competition. Therefore, when the leader is killed or incarcerated, as the leader of the American Nazi Party, George Lincoln Rockwell, was in 1967,(57) or the leader of the Minutemen, Robert Bolivar DePugh, was in 1969,(58) the groups fold.(59) Generally, they remain inactive or disappear until a new leader, their charismatic fuehrer, arrives on the scene.

The idealists in these groups tend to be middle class, with the Nazi organization attracting younger people than the Minutemen. The idealists in the Nazi organization are usually former military enlistees who have less-than-honorable discharges.(60) Perhaps they sense a lack of masculinity in themselves, as evidenced by their inability to adjust to the military as their fathers did, and now seek to establish their manhood by activity in right-wing groups. One also notices a lack of female involvement in such groups; they are reactionary and certainly "anti-lib."

Over the years we have seen radical groups alter their complexion from nonviolent to violent. An examination of the change in leadership personalities frequently sheds light onto the reason for this policy change. Two groups clearly exemplify this change.

In the early 1960s, on the campus of any large university in the United States, one heard of the Student Nonviolent Coordinating Committee (SNCC). This group was large, dedicated to peace through nonviolence, and followed the teaching and practices of the great Hindu leader, Mohandas Karamchand Gandhi. The leadership of SNCC and many of the followers were Quakers or other religious people of good character. In the late 1960s, this pacific character changed. The militants and the opportunists took over and publicly suggested that the group's name be changed to the Student Violent Coordinating Committee.

A similar change is seen when one examines the American Indian Movement (AIM). In the 1960s, AIM was established in Minneapolis-St. Paul, to assist the American Indian who chose to leave the reservation and try a new urban life. By its charter, the Bureau of Indian Affairs was unable to assist an Indian once he left the reservation. Local agencies could not meet the need; therefore, a need existed and AIM was created. Initially, AIM was a middle-class, self-help, altruistically-oriented group that took as its name the Concerned Indians of America. However, as time passed, the more militant, criminal minority in the American Indian population gained influence, and altered the name, goals, and functions of the group.(61)

The 1950s and 1960s gave rise to many legitimate civil rights groups within the United States. Most of these groups retained their middle-class values and leadership. They have avoided the opportunist or neutralized him if he joined. By effectively dealing with the opportunist, these civic-minded groups effectively contributed to a better world for us all – the better world the terrorist group talks about but destroys by the influence and activity of the opportunist. ". . . Terrorists feed on problems without solving them."(62)

SUMMARY

Three separate elements (leader, opportunist, and idealist) are identified in current terrorist groups. These roles seem to attract specific personality types who complement each other.

Terrorist groups are fluid, task-oriented gatherings of individuals. Individuals change; roles remain. When two leaders appear in a group, one must go. The displaced leader may become an idealist or start his own group. These three roles are seen in many terrorist groups that operate in democratic nations throughout the world. The hostage (particularly in a kidnap-imprisonment situation) is likely to encounter all three types of terrorists. The activist operator (opportunist) seizes him; he is interrogated by the training leader, and finally encounters the idealists who guard and feed him.(63)

Though the SLA and other domestic and some foreign groups(64) that operate in democratic societies fit the Terrorist Organizational Profile, a question yet to be answered is, does this model of terrorist roles fit other groups? This is presently the subject of continuing research.

Knowledge of the roles of various functionaries in terrorist groups will not prevent terrorism. However, it does give us a better picture of our adversaries. We can better judge their capacity for violence, better interview them when they are in custody, and more effectively defuse the group by knowing who the activist members of each organization are by determining who is functioning in which capacity.

The message for law enforcement is clear. Do not focus efforts on the arrest, incarceration, and interrogation of the idealist. He knows little and is reluctant to discuss the group, as the organization is his cherished family. The group has given his empty life its first purpose. The leader is equally resistant to conversion. However, the opportunist is loyal only to himself and is seeking personal satisfaction and comfort. If arrested and faced with a stiff prison sentence, he will seek to plea bargain for his personal satisfaction and safety. He is nobody's friend; he wants what is best for himself and will provide information on others to achieve personal well-being. Additionally, without his criminal expertise, the terrorist group is reduced to a hate group.

If terrorism is a new form of warfare, then new police counterstrategies will be needed to effectively meet this threat. The Terrorist Organizational Profile may be one form of a beginning in understanding and defusing our adversaries' ability to disrupt our democracies.

NOTES

1. Los Angeles Times, May 18, 1974, p. 1.
2. U.S. Congress. Senate. Committee on the Judiciary, Terrorist Activity: Hostage Defense Measures, Part Five, before a subcommittee to investigate the Administration of the Internal Security Act and Other Internal Security Laws, Senate, 94th Congress, 1st Session, 1975, pp. 263-64.
3. Ibid.
4. "Year of Terror," Newsweek Magazine, January 1976, pp. 27-28.
5. Ibid.
6. James C. Coleman, Abnormal Psychology and Modern Life, 5th ed. (Glenview, Ill.: Scott, Foresman, 1976), p. 331.
7. American Psychiatric Association, Diagnostic and Statistical Manual of Mental Disorders, 2nd ed. (Washington, D.C.: APA, 1968), p. 38.
8. Elton B. McNeil, The Psychoses (Englewood Cliffs, N.J.: Prentice-Hall, 1970), p. 106.
9. O. Spurgeon-English, M.D., and Gerald H.J. Pearson, M.D., Emotional Problems of Living (New York: W.W. Norton, 1963).
10. McNeil, The Psychoses, p. 103.
11. Elton B. McNeil, The Quiet Furies (Englewood Cliffs, N.J.: Prentice-Hall, 1967), p. 163.
12. Erik H. Erikson, Childhood and Society (New York: W.W. Norton, 1963).
13. Coleman, Abnormal Psychology and Modern Life, p. 331.
14. Ibid.
15. Murray S. Miron, "Psycholinguistic Analysis of the Symbionese Liberation Army," Assets Protection Journal 1 (4) (1976):17.
16. Charles A. Russell and Bowman H. Miller, "Profile of a Terrorist," Terrorism 1 (1) (Spring 1977): 17-34.
17. Times (Los Angeles), February 29, 1976, Part I, pp. 9-10.
18. Lillian Becker, Hitler's Children (Philadelphia: J.B. Lippincott, 1977), pp. 73-77.
19. Mainichi Shimbun (Tokyo), October 1, 1977, p. 1.
20. Gail Sheehy, Passages: Predictable Crises of Adult Life, (New York: E.P. Dutton, 1976), p. 193.

21. Diagnostic and Statistical Manual of Mental Disorders, p. 43.

22. Robert E. Hardin, The Rapist and the Victim (Indianapolis: Indianapolis Women United Against Rape, 1976), pp. 1-2.

23. Marshall B. Clinard, Sociology of Deviant Behavior, 3rd ed. (New York: Holt, Rinehart and Winston, 1975), p. 175.

24. Coleman, Abnormal Psychology and Modern Life, p. 380.

25. Alan Harrington, Psychopaths (New York: Simon and Schuster, 1972), p. 15.

26. Calvin S. Hall, Freudian Psychology (Cleveland: World Publishing Co., 1954), pp. 34-36.

27. Ben Karpman, The Individual Criminal: Studies in the Psychogenetics of Crime (Washington, D.C.: Nervous and Mental Diseases Publishing Co., 1935), p. ix.

28. James M. Reinhardt, The Psychology of Strange Killers (Springfield, Ill.: Charles C. Thomas, 1953), p. 193.

29. Harrington, Psychopaths, pp. 10, 11; Coleman, Abnormal Psychology and Modern Life, p. 372; Harvey Cleckley, The Mask of Sanity (St. Louis: C.V. Mosby Co., 1964), p. 453.

30. Hendrick van Dalen, "Terror as a Political Weapon," Military Police Law Enforcement Journal III (Spring, 1975).

31. Miron, "Psycholinguistic Analysis of the Symbionese Liberation Army."

32. Planning and Research Section, Dallas Police Department, The Dallas Repeat Offender Study (Dallas, January 1973), pp. 10-11.

33. van Dalen, "Terror as a Political Weapon."

34. Ibid.

35. Coleman, Abornmal Psychology and Modern Life, p. 107.

36. Harry E. Allen, Ph.D., Simon Dinitz, Ph.D., Thomas W. Foster, Ph.D., Harold Goldman, Ph.D., Lewis Linder, M.D., "Sociopathy: An Experiment in International Environmental Control." Paper presented at the annual convention of the American Society of Criminology, Toronto, Canada, October 30-November 2, 1975.

37. Walter B. Miller, "Lower Class Culture as a Generating Milieu of Gang Delinquency," The Journal of Social Issues 14 (September 1958).

38. Miron, "Psycholinguistic Analysis of the Symbionese Liberation Army."

39. Ibid.

40. Ibid.

41. van Dalen, "Terror as a Political Weapon," p. 25.

42. Coleman, Abnormal Psychology and Modern Life, p. 582.

43. The Dallas Repeat Offender Study, p. 11.
44. Diagnostic and Statistical Manual of Mental Disorders,
p. 46.
45. Eric Hoffer, The True Believer (New York: Harper
& Row, 1951), cover.
46. Midge Decter, Liberal Parents, Radical Children (New
York: Coward, McCann and Geoghegan, 1975).
47. Ibid.
48. Patricia G. Steinhoff, "Portrait of a Terrorist: An
Interview with Kozo Okamoto," Asian Survey 16 (9) (September
1976): 835.
49. Barbara   Salert,   Revolutions and Revolutionaries;
Four Theories (New York: Elsevier, 1976), p. 57.
50. Patrick   Mullahy,   Oedipus Myth and Complex   (New
York: Grove Press, 1955), p. 35.
51. Times (Los Angeles), February 29, 1976, Part I,
pp. 9-10.
52. Ibid.
53. Personal Interview, Commander James F. Nevill,
Commander Anti-Terrorist Squad, New Scotland Yard, at Los
Angeles, California, October 1, 1976.
54. Terrorist Activity, pp. 263-64.
55. Mainichi Shimbun (Tokyo), October 1, 1977, p. 1.
56. Jillian Becker, Hitler's Children (Philadelphia: J.B.
Lippincott, 1977), pp. 73-77.
57. Washington Post, August 25, 1967, p. 1.
58. Times Journal (New York), July 14, 1969, p. 25.
59. Ibid., May 1, 1973, p. 53.
60. CBS, "60 Minutes," February 20, 1977.
61. The American Indian Movement Hearing.
62. Albert Parry, Terrorism: From Robespierre to Arafat
(New York: Vanguard Press, 1976), p. XII.
63. Terrorist Activity, p. 264.
64. Ibid. p. 263.

7 Social and Psychodynamic Pressures Toward a Negative Identity: The Case of an American Revolutionary Terrorist

Jeanne N. Knutson

The subject of terrorism has an immense power to engage us intellectually and emotionally, with both fascination and revulsion. In many disquieting ways, the terroristic act confronts and challenges our basic beliefs about order - both political order and inner, psychological order. We have reacted to terrorism largely on the basis of our aroused fears: the literature abounds in works focusing on either description of the phenomenon through time or elucidation of methods for the control and eradication of terrorism today.

Few writers have responded to the challenge of terrorism by seeing it, additionally, as a confrontation of established political assumptions - assumptions about legitimacy, order, and the receptivity of political systems to objective and subjective pain: the pain of being devalued, rejected, unheard, and victimized. Indeed, consideration of the perspective of the terrorist has generally been seen as condoning his behavior, as if understanding is synonymous with advocacy (Watson 1976, p. 24). There has been only a meager attempt to consider the terrorist event as evidence of failure of a political system, as due to its inability or unwillingness to meet the challenges of socialization, of receptivity to variance, of the social roots of psychic disorder, of initially nonviolent rejections of its monopolistic demands.

There has been even less interest in objective consideration of the psychodynamic and social factors which impel individuals to commit acts of terrorism. The horror of their acts and the affront of their deviance disallow our concern with terrorists as individuals and, therefore, as driven by universal and comprehensible psychological pressures - pressures to understand the world that they perceive, to obtain and maintain a coherent and positive sense of self, to achieve an emotional balance between inner and outer reality, between ideals and actions.

The literature on terrorism repetitively echoes the lacunae in our knowledge of the terrorist, of which the two following statements illustrate common concerns: "It is this writer's view that the psychology and beliefs of terrorists have been inadequately explored to date, although such a study could be a valuable aid to advance in the subject" (Wilkinson 1974, p. 133). "In-depth data from clinical experiences with crusading terrorists are rare and not likely to become more available in the near future" (Hacker 1976, p. 105).

There are a number of reasons for this knowledge gap. There is, of course, the general inaccessibility of terrorists to evaluation. There is our own abhorrence which promotes an out-of-hand rejection and emotional dismissal of people capable of so terrorizing us and of so totally rejecting a moral code in which human life alone is an absolute value. There is also an implicit political conservatism which unquestioningly rejects demands for major changes in the political order as being invalid, irresponsible, impossible, or insane. Terrorists are inaccurately dismissed as absolutist and, therefore, as requiring an absolutist response. A statement from a recent book focused on improving "protective services" is typical:

> The protective services, with which this text is concerned, have as their objective the safeguarding of the individual and the community against enterprises which, though criminal in character and execution, are also of a political or ideological character implying a total rejection of the established legal, political, social, or economic systems so as to require their overthrow in the power struggle (Kobetz and Cooper 1978, p. 4; also see the Foreword to Watson 1976).

This chapter represents an effort to help fill this void in our knowledge of the terrorist and his motivations. The data presented here are derived from an ongoing project in which an attempt is being made to evaluate all prisoners in United States federal prisons who have been convicted of committing a crime for a political purpose.(1) A control sample will, hopefully, be gathered through arrangements now being made with prison authorities in two other countries.

As is readily apparent, gaining access to such unique and valuable data has been a most difficult process. The prison systems must be assured that the researcher will adhere closely to the guidelines of the Federal Privacy Act regarding confidentiality and protection of human subjects, to the orderly administration of prison routine, and to the canons of scientific objectivity. On its part, The Federal Bureau of Prisons must provide the additional staff needed to locate files and individuals and, initially, to develop a list of possible subjects for

evaluation. The reticence of the subjects is an equally difficult obstacle to continuously overcome - requiring the establishment of scholarly and objective credibility, of an accepting
attitude toward them as individuals, and of binding legal
protection for such privileged research to ensure that no
person is put at risk by agreeing to become a subject in this
project.(2)

As the subject population is exhausted in each prison
facility, the next facility's warden is contacted and arrangements are made for someone on his staff to serve as liaison for
this project. That person, in turn, asks each case manager at
the facility to submit a list of possible subjects, based on
personal knowledge of the cases in his or her respective units.
Such a procedure is necessary, as politically motivated crime
is not a legal or penal category. Thus, a good deal of staff
time is essential in order for this project to go forth. Such a
list, however, is only a beginning. As each subject is interviewed, he or she often suggests other possible subjects
who should be contacted. Personal contacts with staff at the
prison facility lead to further suggestions.

Approximately 90 percent of those inmates who have been
contacted have been willing to be interviewed, in spite of the
very natural suspicion that the purposes of the study might be
other than as stated. Those very few individuals who have
refused to be interviewed were either, (a) told by their
group's leader not to talk with any psychologist or psychiatrist; (b) openly psychotic, with a highly likely diagnosis
of paranoid schizophrenic, and thus extremely frightened;
(c) considered themselves legally at risk, in that their stated
offense represented only a part of their illegal activities and,
thus, they were not free to talk openly. (It should be noted
that this third status generally is not a deterrent.)

The almost universal cooperation of the inmates is at
considerable variance with what prison authorities had predicted. Considering the constraints of the prison atmosphere,
it is noteworthy that these subjects are joining with interest in
this project. Several reasons seem important: first, the
usually unannounced request for an interview avoids the
development of a negative set toward this project on the part
of the inmate, and provides an opportunity for some open
exchange of concerns; second, clinical skills promote the
development of necessary rapport and, further, clinically
based insights over the course of the interview are perceived
as useful and rewarding by most subjects. Before the taped
interview is begun, one or more hours may elapse in discussing the study and in answering all questions of interest to
the subject. After the interview is completed and the tape is
turned off, the discussion often continues for some time and
an attempt is made to offer some psychological insights to
assist the person to deal more adequately with his prison

experience and his life in general. Often, the comments are made in a very confronting manner. The caring on which they are based is generally recognized and appreciated.

Moreover, all individuals have a need to justify their behavior. For people who frequently are serving one or more life sentences, such pressure is intense. These subjects, almost uniformly, comment on the frustration which they have felt that no one - judge, jury, press, or attorney - cared to know why their terroristic act was committed; interest was expressed only in what was done. At last, the person finds someone truly interested in his or her perceptions of the social and political system, in the rationale for the offense, and in him or her as a person.

The amount of interest in this project on the part of the subjects can be attested by their subsequent behavior, which at times has included: requesting a further interview on the next visit to the facility (to discuss other features of their lives that might be of interest); having the Director of Psychological Services (or other liaison person) place a telephone call so that they could immediately relay some additional information; after reflection, taping answers to additional questions left with them; arranging for anonymous interviews with members of their group who are not in prison. The subject on whose life and act this chapter is based reviewed the original draft and furnished a detailed commentary, clarifying some historical events of interest.

Each interview lasts from four to eight or more hours with, as discussed, additional time before and after the interview. Further, during breaks in the interview, the often voluminous information in the subject's prison records (or "jacket") - both his or her general file and the medical and psychological file if any - are carefully reviewed. These records generate other questions about aspects of the person's life which had not yet been discussed (for example, a bad military experience, a traumatic childhood event, opportunities utilized in prison to obtain further education).

The interviews follow a standardized group of interest areas (see Appendix), although the interview itself is free flowing and proceeds in very open fashion. In addition to the interview, each subject is given two standardized psychological assessment tools: the Rorschach test and the Political Thematic Apperception Measure (Knutson 1973a, 1974a, 1974b). This evaluation procedure generates an extremely rich data base for each subject, with the transcripts running from 60 to over 100 single-spaced typed pages, including a detailed psychological and political evaluation which is written for each case after all the data has been transcribed and analyzed (including formal scoring of the Rorschach by the system of Exner [1974]).

Each case is assigned a research number by which all data are kept. In two cases to date, the subjects have insisted that they would participate only if they were identified. In a third case (to be presented here), on a reinterview, the subject was asked to consider waiving his anonymity. First, it was felt that he would not be at risk in so doing. Further, as he is an extremely bright and articulate person, he well represents a type of American terrorist (although he himself is not American) who is Left-oriented, humanitarian,and extremely tortured by the use of political violence, so that his personal history illumines the characteristics of this group of actors. He agreed to do so, on the basis that he could read any ensuing manuscript before publication, to assure an accurate presentation of the facts, understanding however, that the interpretations would not necessarily reflect his own views. In addition, his attorney's assurance was sought and received that his waives of anonymity would not, in any way, put him at risk.

There are two areas of discomfort which all these subjects share. First, except for one psychopathic killer, none of the subjects in the project accepts the designation of "terrorist." Indeed, this appellation is a source of considerable discomfort. As is well known, "one person's terrorist is another person's freedom fighter." Yet, when questioning each subject about the intended and actual effect of his or her action, each agrees that one intended effect was fear, and pressure through fear, although many other effects are seen as more important, such as demonstrating, through personal sacrifice, both the importance of his cause and his personal dedication to it.

Second, it is difficult for subjects (and readers) to at times remain cognizant of the fact that an evaluation of personal factors which led to a political behavior does not obviate the importance of objective, political conditions which demand change. To the subject, it is generally the political conditions which are of overwhelming importance, and it is these conditions which he or she wishes to elucidate. After discussing his perceptions of political conditions and details of his personal life history, however, each subject is asked the same question toward the end of the interview:

There are many people who felt [or feel] as you do about this political situation. But very, very few people would be willing to risk their lives in a total commitment to such political goals by actions such as yours. Why you? What aspects of yourself made such activity possible?

This question arouses puzzlement and considerable interest and is often the stimulus for the followup letters, tapes, reinterviews, and conversations. Hopefully, the subject on whose actions this chapter is based will continue to feel that interest in the psychodynamics of his behavior does not disallow the importance of the political, social, and economic factors which led to his actions.

SOME THEORETICAL PERSPECTIVES

The study of the social and intrapsychic pressures toward terrorist behavior is so underdeveloped, and the data which are being gathered are so rich that it is difficult to select which aspects should be formally discussed here. As data are being gathered, there are developing clearly distinguishable subtypes of actors, divisible by personality dynamics and their congruence with political issues. The subject of this chapter, as stated above, is well representative of one such type - the tortured liberal responsible for violence because of his dedi- cation to humanitarian goals.

Myriad dimensions of equal interest are also developing as areas which require intensive future study. For example, there is the tantalizing question of the self-limiting behavior of terrorists, who could easily (as government publications repeatedly announce) do so much more damage than they do. There is the question of the extent to which terrorists' demands are truly political - that is, demands to which (even if willing) the political system could be responsive.

The question with which this chapter deals has been suggested frequently in the interviews which are being gathered. It deals with the inner and outer pressures often experienced in the life of a person toward assuming the socially negative identity of "terrorist." The data presented here illustrate how various life experiences often selectively and continuously disallow the successful fulfillment of life goals based on the person's own constraints, values, and needs, while - at the same time - there is a growing pressure to assume a new, initially rejected, and even abhorrent, identity in a total acceptance of the role of a revolutionary who en- gages in acts of violence. Except possibly in nationalistic wars of attrition, it appears likely that only schizophrenics, psychopaths, and brain damaged subjects - those with truly diminished capacity - comfortably and without apparent anxiety embrace the identity of revolutionary terrorist. For the rest - the great majority - the assumption of such an identity involves the considerable psychic stress which accompanies the renunciation of dreams, of values, of family ties past and future, perhaps of life itself.

Awareness of the weighty sacrifice required by this jealously insatiable calling makes it harder emotionally to become a revolutionary terrorist than for the proverbial camel to pass through the eye of a needle. Once through that narrow aperture, there are a host of additional areas which bear analysis - foremost being the immense success with which peer pressure is exercised; and, secondly, the dynamics by which a revolutionary may decide eventually to take his political goals intact (leaving violence and revolution for an evolutionary viewpoint) and make the long journey back through that narrow aperture (Steinhoff 1974).

The concept of "negative identity" is useful in elucidating the narrowing psycho-social process which eventuates in terroristic behavior. It is a term employed by Erikson (1968) to illumine one avenue by which conflicted individuals may confirm a sense of self. It represents a growing interest in psychology in understanding the pathways by which a stable compromise is reached between inner needs and outer realities. To illustrate the formation of negative identity, consider the child who reminds his mother of his devalued father, and who, thereby, may find the roots of a positive identity weak or nonexistent as his mother constantly accuses him of "badness." The child may, at some point, come to embrace the only identity in which he feels he can truly succeed, that of being a "bad" boy.

As Erikson notes, such a negative identity is "an identity perversely based on all those identifications and roles which, at critical stages of development, had been presented to them as most undesirable or dangerous and yet also as most real" (Erikson 1968, p. 174). He adds:

> Such vindictive choices of a negative identity represent, of course, a desperate attempt at regaining some mastery in a situation in which the available positive identity elements cancel each other out. . . . At any rate, many a sick or desperate late adolescent, if faced with continuing conflict, would rather be nobody or somebody totally bad or, indeed, dead - and this by free choice - than be not-quite-somebody (Erikson 1968, p. 176).

On a macro-level, society mirrors parents in facilitating or denying access to the roots of positive identities, and in labeling certain identities as "bad" and others as "good" (Steinhoff 1978). Erikson notes the critical role which societal agents play in this labeling process through their power to "identify" - and thus "recognize" and "confirm" - a developing identity in a young person who, "for reasons of personal or social marginality, is close to choosing a negative identity, [so that] that young person may well put his energy into becoming exactly what the careless and fearful community expects him to be - and make a total job of it" (Erikson 1968, p. 196). It is critical to the argument here to note that the development of an identity (and here, of a negative, i.e., socially devalued, identity) is an <u>interactive process</u> between a person's inner needs and the outer constraints and realities with which he must deal. (See the statement by Lussier in Morf 1970, p. 15.)

Whether an identity is socially defined as negative or positive, what is critical for each individual - indeed, vital in a very basic sense - is to avoid inner fragmentation and, for youth, this is of particular importance (Erikson 1968, p. 88), thus accounting for the frequent alternating embrace of competing ideologies as youth seeks a sense of distinctive wholeness (Hoffer 1951). In order to avoid personal disintegration and psychic (if not physical) death, it is necessary to establish a sense of oneness where one's inner perceptions of self are validated by outer acceptance. (See Hubbard 1971, for examples of skyjacking as a means to establish identity and avoid fragmentation.)

Life experiences may selectively cut off access to the establishment of a positive identity, as defined by the person's own familial and cultural values, thus leaving the individual stripped of a firm sense of self. Such vulnerability then interacts with authoritative action. Authorities - familial and societal - function as partial gate-keepers of identities and, by their dramatic sanctions when a negative identity is approached, may both shore up a person psychologically and stem the tide of his or her disintegration, as well as further acceptance of that negative identity.

If access to the desired positive identity is denied, there are two avenues open to an individual: acceptance of a sense of failed identity and the consequent devalued self-image <u>or</u> the search for an alternative identity in which he or she <u>can</u> comfortably succeed. The ultimately selected, alternate identity <u>may</u> be one which is socially (and personally) defined as "negative". When this negative identity is selected over an alternate positive identity, it is the thesis here that authorities have played an active part in its assumption over a considerable period in the person's development.

What does this process offer to the theoretical analysis of the pathways to revolutionary terrorism? The personal pressure to confirm a comfortable identity (and with it, meaning, goals, and personal values) must be seen in the context of the total field of forces which interact to produce political behavior. The model offered here is one that has been employed in the analysis of other types of political behavior (Knutson 1972, 1974c, 1977). It posits the target behavior - here, the assumption of a terrorist identity - as resulting from three <u>equally important</u> factors. First are socialization experiences which inculcate basic beliefs, attitudes, and perspectives about the world. Each subject in this

study acted in concert with pre-established socialization, both
critical experiences and learned values, that were taught in
the home, by the village elders, and by example of valued
individuals.

For example, Kozo Okamoto - the sole survivor of the
terrorist group responsible for the Lod Airport massacre in
1972 - was the product of a family strongly (and for Japanese
society, most unusually) committed to social concerns and the
welfare of others.   Indeed, his father had become a social
worker following his retirement as an elementary school principal.   Further, Okamoto's slightly older brothers were deeply
involved in radical student movements during their university
years and one brother, Takeshi, was an early member in the
student Red Army faction.   This same brother, in protest of
various aspects of Japanese official policy, was one of the
participants in the hijacking of a domestic Japanese airplane to
North Korea, where he apparently remained (Steinhoff 1976).

One can also consider the example of Ulrike Meinhof, a
leading member of the Baader-Meinhof group that so terrorized
West German society.   This revolutionary terrorist was raised
by a well-known Leftist professor, Renate Reimeck, a brillant
and unconventional woman who took charge of Ulrike and her
younger sister, Wienke, when their mother died of cancer (her
father had died earlier of cancer).   But even before that
second loss, Reimeck was a close associate and confidante of
the family - an idolized friend whose radical views were well
known and comfortable to them (Becker 1977).

From the life histories available for terrorists (see
especially Morf 1970), it is clear that these individuals are
acting upon values into which they have been comfortably
socialized - both directly by teaching, and indirectly by life
experiences of themselves and important others.   However,
these social-cultural-political values which are sanguine to a
revolutionary terrorist identity are a necessary but not sufficient ingredient in the formation of the terrorist.   They are
obviously not able, by themselves, to distinguish this small
group of political actors who choose to divorce themselves from
conventional morality and conventional political action from the
much wider group of similarly socialized actors who can find a
comfortable adjustment within the given political order.

Equally important to the acceptance of a revolutionary-
terrorist identity are psychological needs intensively pressing
for actualization through behavior and commitment.   As discussed above, these needs can be the inner pressure toward
the assumption of a clearcut identity in which one may achieve
a feeling of wholeness and of success, and an end to frustration and continual defeat in the unsuccessful pursuit of
other identities as traditionally and personally defined.

To give another example, a need of not infrequent importance in pressuring a given individual to join a terrorist

group (as opposed to becoming the individual actor) appears to
be the need for belonging and affection (Davies 1963; Knutson
1972; Maslow 1954). In spite of a generally disparaging
portrayal, Becker's presentation of the life of Ulrike Meinhof
gives a classic and poignant example of how this intrapsychic
need resulted in Meinhof's assumption of the identity of
terrorist. As mentioned above, her parents both died of
cancer - her father when she was six; her mother when she
was fifteen. As Becker notes:

> Ulrike did not have the self-confidence that her
> youthful ability to impress others would seem to
> imply. By temperament and circumstance she needed
> to please: to win approval, to be accepted, to
> belong. She was not, and never became, a daring
> loner. Her later oppositionism, like her even later
> "radicalism," resulted from an urge to be part of a
> dedicated elite rather than from critical independent
> thinking (1977, p. 117).

She married a fellow radical - a man continuously unfaithful.
When she became pregnant, she had a rare opportunity to
demonstrate the importance to her life of the need for belonging. She began to have severe headaches and trouble
with her vision and was told to choose between having the
child and having brain surgery. Her symptoms worsened, but
Ulrike choose the child:

> One of her eyes moved erratically, and one eyelid
> would suddenly and uncontrollably flop down. She
> could not open her mouth wide, and she smiled
> lopsidedly. It became unsafe for her to drive a car.
> She began to have a continuous headache (Ibid., p.
> 142).

At seven and a half months, twin girls were delivered by
cesarean section and, four weeks later, Ulrike had brain
surgery to correct what turned out to be a swollen blood
vessel, despite her agonizing fears that, like her parents, she
was suffering from cancer.
    Then, at her thirty-third birthday party, her husband
appeared with his current mistress, and then, in the middle of
the party, left with the woman. Following this traumatic
event, Ulrike decided on divorce and, in this process, shifted
from a bitter depression to a violent hatred for the establishment. Yet, the need for affection and belonging appears
dominant in her ensuing years as well. She spoke frequently
of the pressure to be part of a collective (p. 161). She also
did research and wrote a television play on the fate of illegitimate and orphaned girls, living unwanted in welfare homes
and angry over their improper care (pp. 171-72). In helping

Andreas Baader to escape from prison, Becker clearly describes Meinhof's leap from her despair over her old, failed identity to a new identity - that of terrorist. In both old and new identities, affiliative needs appear to shape her behavior. (She even attempted to sacrifice her young daughters to her new affiliation, by sending them to a P.L.O. camp for training and education. Fortunately, their father located them in transit in Italy - for the designated camp was shortly thereafter demolished by an Israeli attack.)

Thus, to socialization into congruent values, beliefs, and attitudes must be added pressing and painfully experienced unmet personality needs. However, just as the vast majority of persons socialized into radical beliefs do not become terrorist revolutionaries, so the overwhelming preponderance of those with painfully unmet personality needs do not seek their fulfillment through political activity, which is a rare phenomenon statistically, even in accepted behaviors, apart from voting (Campbell, Converse, Miller, and Stokes 1960; Woodward and Roper 1950).

But neither social-culture-political values that are sanguine to revolutionary activity nor personality needs such as identity, belongingness, or a suitable expression of violent impulses unaccepted directly alone or together are sufficient to lead to a revolutionary-terrorist identity. There is a third factor which the available evidence strongly suggests to be the catalyst: a severe life disappointment (or series of disappoint‑ ments) which dramatically shifts the balance of expectations away from other available identities.(3) For Meinhof, it was the humiliating and unmistakable evidence of her husband's disregard for her. For Okamoto, it was likely his failure of the entrance examinations at the prestigious Kyoto University - the University which his two older brothers were successfully attending.

This chapter will focus on the process by which socialization, personal needs, and severe life disappointments eventuate in one person's assumption of the identity of a revolutionary terrorist. While the search for a comfortable identity - and the interactive process through which a negative identity is finally assumed - represents only one possible aspect of the individual-level etiology of terrorism; its importance makes it a valuable dimension for our examination.

ONE JOURNEY TO VIOLENCE

The subject whose life story will be related below was interviewed in a United States maximum security penitentiary, where he is serving a life sentence for "Air Piracy Resulting in an Officer's Death." While it was originally ten years

before he would be eligible for parole, a modification of his
sentence on April 3, 1979, made him and his codefendants
eligible for parole beginning December 31, 1979. (Whether and
when parole will be granted in a case of such severity is quite
another matter.)

He is a slender, handsome, bearded man, with a non-
tracking left eye, which indicates its artificiality. He appeared calm and reflective through many hours of interviewing,
and exhibited a warm sense of humor and a good ability to
relate. But the notable sweat under his armpits, the chain-
smoked cigarettes used to an incredibly short length, and the
constant "uh-uh" which peppered his words, together suggest
an enormous inner tension - similar to that of a coiled spring
of tightly wound wire.

His name is Zvonko Busic, but all who know him well call
him Taik. His cause is that of Croatian nationalism - the
freedom of Croatia from its domination within Serbian-controlled
Yugoslavia and its establishment as an independent national
entity.

The event which placed him in prison (with only a minor
prior record for any kind of illegal activity) was the hijacking
(along with his wife and three Croatian companions) of a
Chicago-bound Trans World Airlines plane in New York and the
placement of a bomb in Grand Central Station (along with a
note telling the police where it was and how to dismantle it),
thus demonstrating his power to harm if his demands were not
met. His demands were partially met: his manifesto was
published in five leading newspapers, but the 100,000 leaflets
which were on board the plane were only partially distributed - over Montreal and Paris, but not over Croatia. Furthermore, the bomb was not successfully dismantled, and the
resulting explosion killed one policeman and seriously wounded
three others. Busic and his wife, along with their three
Croatian colleagues, were taken into custody in Paris and
transported back to the United States where they have been in
custody ever since.

The following essay attempts to elucidate those factors in
Busic's history which led to that fatal, political event, examining his life in terms of the theoretical issues discussed
previously. It is written with the firm conviction that understanding the multiple causes of such a tragedy is an
essential precondition to the eventual elimination of violence as
a valued means to accomplish political ends.

Zvonko Busic was born in a small village near the borders
of what used to be Croatia, an area which is now within the
state of Yugoslavia. The village was and is very poor, with
medical aid a rarity, as is literacy among his parents' generation. Neither Croatian history nor Croatian language is
permitted in the schools, but the village is alive with stories
of Croatian history and of Croatian patriots. Particularly

impressive were the stories about the great Croatian patriot, Stephan Radic, a brillant man who fought with words alone and was murdered by the Serbians after addressing their parliament. As Busic states:

> I knew the Croatian . . . I dug into Croatian history and I went all through the centuries of Croatian people fighting for their survival, independence or being on the border between Western and . . . and Eastern . . . Eastern . . . strength . . . and . . .Turkish empire and Western civilization and so on . . . and so . . . I investigated and learned more and more about it and that was refreshed by everyday presence of the police, and then in schools, when I went to the schools, I discovered how Croatian language even was suppressed and was not permitted . . . we were not . . . admitted . . . or allowed to be . . . to say that we were Croatians at all . . .

Thus, Croatia was not only oppressed; historically, it had also been torn between Eastern (Turkish) strength and Western (Christian) civilization.

Busic's father was not a patriot in activity, but it is critical to his perception of his father that he was only saved from being hung after the war because he was hospitalized for a kidney removal which took him out of the last part of the war. Busic sees his father as having been in special jeopardy as his brother (Busic's uncle) was "very close" to the Croatian government during the war. However, his father's nationalistic beliefs have always had to be inferred. When asked if his father talked about Croatian feelings, Busic replied:

> Very, very little. Almost none. My father's very simple and . . . God fearing man . . . was raised as a Christian and . . . and believes in . . . God very, very uh blindly and is Croatian, has feelings for it and . . . as everybody else.

He describes his mother as "same, same way" - barely literate with:

> very narrow . . . views or knowledge. Very little knowledge about the whole Croatian history and . . . they are very simple farmers who . . . who are . . . very religious, like I said, and . . . that's the kind of family . . . very conservative family that I was raised in.

In other words, engaging in political violence to further the Croatian cause was <u>not</u> a familial value, although devotion to the Croatian culture existed minimally in the home and, more generally, in the village.

As in most peasant families, education was the supreme value - ensuring a better life away from the marginal existence which the village offered. Because he was always a very good student, Busic received "a little more respect" from his parents than did some of his siblings. It was perceived as conditional distinction based upon an identity of a <u>successful</u> scholar.

Busic's oldest brother is now a technical engineer in Zagreb, the capital of Croatia. He completed his university education, is married, and has two children. He is described as:

> nationalist as I am . . . would love to see Croatia free and independent as I would; however, . . . did not take . . .so much concern and . . . was not that much involved as I was.

This disengagement bothers Busic; it is obviously an issue over which he has pondered. When asked about this disparity in commitment, he answered:

> I don't know . . . is that a lack of courage or lack of information or . . . his own selfish reasons or have . . . again we come to that hard question and even harder answer?

Because his first brother had such excellent grades, Busic's second brother was taken out of school after only four years' attendance, because he only had "very good, but not excellent grades" and someone had to stay home and help on the farm. This brother also helped to support Taik because "I had again excellent grades and they put me farther in the school." The second brother helped to support the two family scholars in the university as well, went to Austria, and sent back money to help the family. He is now working in Germany is married and has five children.

There is a youngest brother who went to "some kind of a business school" and worked in Croatia, but is now also working in Germany, is married, and has one child. Taik has a sister who immigrated after he did and also lives in the United States. She is married and has children. There is also a younger sister who stayed in Croatia.

What effect, Busic was asked, did his terrorist deed have on the family? Correspondence is poor as he is afraid of further harrassment for his family, but he has a general impression of their feelings:

> Well, they . . . were she - quite shocked and
> surprised that I . . . did what I did, not completely
> surprised, you know. They knew me; they knew
> that I was dedicated; they . . . and . . . in . . .
> some strange way they are proud of me. I believe
> that . . . and . . . even. . . .

He was asked whether they had actually voiced their pride
and, after a pause, he said "Yeah" very softly but went on to
make a distinction which was expressed several times in the
interviews:

> Yeah, if I, for example, did, something, for my own
> personal, prosperity or something, or, for God's
> sakes, stole something, for example, from somebody,
> or - my family would reject me, completely. They
> would just forget me, they . . . they would be so
> saddened and so surprised and. . . .

But, he was asked, acts for Croatian nationalism do not fall in
the category of crime, as they would see it?

> No . . . no, no, they know that the act itself was
> out of love, and, I believe even they, themselves, in
> some way, feel proud . . . of it.

It should be noted that this self-bolstering perception is an
inference of Busic's.

It is critical to Busic's history that his activities for
Croatian nationalism have been carried out against a backdrop
of constant threats to his parents by the Yugoslav Secret
Service - threats that he would be killed or that something
would happen to them unless his nationalistic activities ceased.
These threats are experienced as very real: Busic has had
five good friends in the movement murdered and, the month
before the initial interview, his hero-cousin was assassinated
in Paris.

This cousin, along with Stephan Radic, is a major figure
in Busic's life, the quintessence of what an ideal should be:

> Yeah, as a matter of fact, he was one of the . . .
> of, . . . people I looked for as some kind of an
> ideal of Croatian nationalism and patriotism. He was
> . . . he was well-known dissident in Croatia. He
> was a journalist and a writer and a scientist . . .
> very, very intelligent person and he was loved, in,
> throughout Croatia.

Taik explained that his cousin, whose name was Bruno Busic,
had never engaged in illegal violence. Asked, "So why was he

assassinated? Why him?", he responded: "Because sometimes
the . . . (clears throat) writing seems more dangerous than
arms."

This combination of education and nationalism, of patriotic
warfare - but always with words, never with violence - is the
ideal on which Taik modeled his own life. It was the life-style
of the two men whom he most greatly admires, Stephan Radic
and Bruno Busic. This life-style was played out against the
background of government terror, what Hacker (1976) calls
"terror from above."

Taik began his university studies in Yugoslavia, clearly
seeking a primary identity of an educated man, and a man who
used his education to speak and write for Croatian nationalism.
At the university, where he majored in literature, the situation
was tense. Friends in nationalist work had been jailed and,
after he joined other Croatian intellectuals in support of a
"Declaration for the Preservation of the Croatian Literary
Language," Taik was tipped off that his turn was approaching.

It was not the experience of jail per se of which he was
afraid: "I knew and had friends who came from jail and I saw
them, how they looked and what they did to them in jail,
so. . . . " One example was particularly vivid:

> Well, a friend of mine in Cleveland . . . is living
> now in Cleveland. He is about seven . . . almost
> six and a half feet tall. When he came out of jail,
> he had about hundred and five pounds and didn't
> have any of his teeth, was scared, so paranoid,
> unbelievable, and imagined all kinds of things: how
> they were following, how the . . . just . . . he was
> excellent student. He was at the third year of
> economy when they took him to jail. He . . . he
> came back; he was just, a vegetable, a living
> vegetable . . . nothing. Dead. . . .

Busic left Croatia, in fear and terror, and went to Austria
where he worked hard at learning German for approximately
eight months and then entered the University of Vienna. He
wanted to finish his schooling and was majoring in comparative
literature and Slavic languages. At this point, he was still in
no major way a deviant political actor; his goal was to become
an educated man. However, in Austria as well, the barriers
became insuperable:

> However, I couldn't continue my schooling because, I
> didn't have enough money to support myself and to
> study in Vienna. Life became pretty expensive and
> I couldn't be anymore . . . I didn't feel comfortable
> being . . . sitting on shoulders of my father and
> brother. So, I had to stop schooling and I came to

> this country later. Of course there were some again
> some ideas. I . . . I met and was starting to be
> organized with other Croatians, in . . . Western
> Europe, and. . . .

This was the traumatic disappointment, the turning point at
which Busic's energies became redirected. The first point at
which his options had been limited was when it was not possible for him to obtain a university education in Yugoslavia.
However, at that point, his drive and determination and need
to become an educated man overrode the crisis. He became
fluent in a second language and reentered university life in a
second country.

This time, however, the degree to which the options
were closed was immense and successfully blocked his movement in the direction which, according to his own values and
needs, he had been striving. As a foreign student, he did
not have the funds to stay at the University of Vienna.
Constantly, he was aware that his education was burdensome
to his father and brother. Further, at this critical juncture –
when barriers of an insurmountable nature were being raised
to his ambition – he was finding a needed role, a sense of
belonging, and a valued identity by joining with other students active in the cause of Croatian nationalism.

Immediately after having to leave the University of
Vienna, Busic found another barrier existed which he also was
not able to circumvent. The Austrian visa which he possessed
was a student visa. When he had to drop out of the University, he also lost his legal right to remain in Austria. He
applied for a visa to come to the United States and, when it
was granted, "I just forgot my schooling . . . and came
here." Here, however, his access to the identity of an
educated man was again denied. "I worked. I couldn't go to
school because I couldn't speak one single word of English."
He worked in a tool factory, trying to save some money in
order to reenter a university. After fourteen months, a
number of workers, including Busic, were laid off from the
factory.

> I lived on this unemployment checks for about
> another four months and I got sick of it and I
> returned to Europe again, I lived in . . . in
> Austria. I saved some money and I thought, well, I
> can probably finish my schooling in Austria now. So
> I came in Austria . . . I lived there for couple of
> weeks, went again to the school, was . . . at that
> time, I was already known in some kind of a
> Croatian, . . . person, who was doing all these,
> . . . meetings . . . and I came into eye of . . .
> different kind of police forces and I believe C.I.A.
> and Interpol and so on and. . . .

Busic went on to explain that there had been an incident in
Cleveland in which he had been involved in anti-Yugoslav
activity and had ended up in jail. This incident, as his
records show, had firmly placed him in police awareness. The
incident?   He and four others threw raw eggs at a Yugoslav
singer. The outcome?

> I was beaten up too, because there were . . . this
> Yugoslav government supporters over there and
> this, . . . from consulate people were there, so
> they beat me pretty bad up. I . . . so I end up in
> jail (after a trip to the hospital).

He was released that night. While in the United States, Busic
had also begun to receive telephone calls "so that I should
stop these Croatian activities and . . . and everything else,
otherwise I would be . . . killed or something." He began to
carry a gun.

Then a second incident occurred. A girl brought him to
a bar where he was hit from behind with an iron stick. He
pulled his gun and told the people to back off, escaped out
the kitchen door, and went home. "I didn't want to hurt
anyone . . . anybody - just to save my life." He was later
arrested and, after a trial, fined $59. Now however, he had a
record of carrying a gun and of threatening violence. (While
it was agreed in his trial not to mention this incident and thus
prejudice the jury, the U.S. Attorney mentioned it anyway.)
As Busic noted:

> And the judge later on told us as usual disregard,
> but that's if something slips in jury's mind, they
> won't - figure out. They even suspect it even
> more. Even something worse. . . .

Obtaining a police record - no matter how minor the offense -
can change the life of a young political activist in a quali-
tatively important manner, especially if he is not a citizen. If
the offense involves <u>anything</u> that suggests the potential for
violence, in a very serious degree, life options are dramatically narrowed. From this time forward, the activist's records
will include such phrases as "history of violence," "potential
for violence," or "known to carry a weapon." Such historic
encoding radicalizes the government's further treatment of the
person and can even lead to the person's death in a confrontation with the police - who are warned by such phrases
to be defensive, threatened, and to experience the person as a
nonhuman and potentially lethal object. Such phrases deny
the basis for negotiation.

Tired of unemployment checks, as noted previously, Busic
then returned to Europe. Possessing a police record and a

solidifying identity as a Croatian revolutionary, he was con-
fronted with radically different options and different constraints in his life. He relates that there was "a trap" set in
Munich which threatened his life. Shortly thereafter, he
moved to Salzburg, where agents identified as Austrian Secret
Police approached him with a job offer. They pointed out
Busic's valuable qualities – "I know many Croatians: I have
been in America . . . I have . . . many friends . . . and
. . . have influence in Croatian organization." They told him
that acceptance of their offer would end any problems with the
police or with his student visa. They also knew of the Munich
incident which had occurred a short time before.

Taik pointed out to them that, while he had positive
feelings toward Austria, his commitment to the independence of
Croatia was diametrically opposed to their desire to maintain
the status quo there; in short, the answer was no. The next
day, he was expelled from the university and told to leave the
country within one hour. The reasons given were "politically
active and, as such, potentially dangerous."

> So I did. I told them that, they . . . they . . .
> gave most criminals twenty-four hours to leave the
> country, and to me, who never committed anything
> wrong as . . . per . . . in Austria in particular,
> nothing, . . . just a person and student over there,
> and, never did anything . . . never org. . . .

And his reaction?

> Well, I felt that they were doing me a great in-
> justice, again. I . . . I was used to those kind
> of . . . things and feelings. I was . . .

And his feelings?

> As a person who didn't have any rights whatsoever
> . . . who didn't have uh any place he was welcomed
> to . . .

Neither as a nationalist-revolutionary nor as an unavailable
counteragent could Busic feel acceptance by government
authorities any longer. He was a pariah – an outcast who was
treated, in his own perception, with the same injustice as
Croatia had been treated historically. This was 1971.

In 1969, Taik had met a charming, warm, and intelligent
girl from Oregon who was tutoring English in Vienna. Julie
had accepted Taik and the importance of Croatian nationalism
and, at the time of his expulsion, they were living together,
with plans to settle in Austria permanently. Forced to
abruptly leave Austria (even having to leave a suitcase of

personal belongings behind in their apartment), Julie and Taik
went to Berlin to stay with his second older brother.   "I was
just thinking and organizing myself what to do again."   They
stayed four months in Berlin, working - as on each stop of
their hegira - at whatever they could obtain to support
themselves.   Generally, Julie could obtain a white collar job;
in Berlin, Taik worked for a Croatian printer and then in a
wine cellar.

     After four months in Berlin, Busic was sent by some
Croatian groups on a mission to Ireland, to meet with some
I.R.A. leaders.   He felt that there was a good deal of similarity between Croatian and Irish history and that there was a
possibility that each could help the other's cause.   He believes
that he was followed; the I.R.A. leader with whom he met was
interned immediately afterward.   One can only speculate the
degree to which this contact solidified, in government perceptions, the seriousness of Busic's revolutionary role and of
his dangerous potential.

     Taik and Julie returned to Germany and lived six months
in Frankfurt-am-Main.   Julie worked in a travel agency, but
Taik could not obtain a job as he had no legal status in
Germany.   It was at this time that they were married.   It was
also at this time that their lives began to assume a quality of
terror.

>   I had . . . difficulties with . . . all kinds of, all
>   sorts of things and happenings . . . some friends of
>   mine were assassinated and I got pretty scared,
>   myself and . . . there were traps and traps and
>   . . . attempts and . . . in Berlin, we had a . . .
>   me and Julie together, we had a . . . attempt to -
>   we were shot at.

Busic believes that the Yugoslav Secret Service was behind the
assassination attempt.   His Croatian friends previously had
warned him several times that there would be such an attempt
on his life.

     This attempt on his life and the atmosphere of growing
tension led to a further move in what was becoming a nomadic,
rootless existence, stablized only by his connections with "The
Cause" and with Julie.

>   Well, then I saw the . . . the time was running out
>   pretty much and they were pretty hot on me, then
>   I . . . I picked up the last solution I had . . .
>   come to . . . return to this country because that
>   was . . . still the safest place . . . because in
>   Germany, see, I feel and believe that . . . German
>   Secret Service . . . cooperates quite widely . . .
>   not all of them, I would say . . . probably not the

> headquarters or something, but cooperates with
> Yugoslav . . . Secret Service and Yugoslav agents.

Like Croatia, Busic felt that he too was isolated, threatened,
and without any support anywhere. In August 1972, he and
Julie returned to the United States, stopping with his sister in
Cleveland and then going to Oregon. The couple stayed in
Oregon for approximately two and a half years while Julie
completed her college work and obtained her Bachelor of Arts
degree. Taik became acquainted with Julie's parents and with
her father, who is a university professor.

Their lives were so disparate. Julie and her parents
lived in a university atmosphere; Taik did menial work of all
kinds. Sometimes, he would sit in on Julie's European history
classes:

> And there were some professors from Czechoslovakia
> and Rumania and so . . . I know that the history
> because I took that courses in uh at University of
> Vienna in January, so it was interesting for me how
> these professors were explaining this history to
> American students, so I learned and I took some-
> times . . . parts in discussions and stuff. I gave
> even a lecture on . . . on current happenings in
> Yugoslavia at the Portland State University which
> was supported by . . . by a German-born professor
> who has this . . . this particular quarter.

The pride and more – the life-sustaining sustenance which
Taik received from these opportunities to be the educated
man – shine through his account of an otherwise drab life,
enlivened only by some Croatian activity and two speeches to
Croatian groups in Vancouver, Canada. There is little opportunity for Croatian revolutionary activity in a place like
Portland, Oregon.

With Julie's education completed in the summer of 1975,
Julie and Taik moved to New York City where she took a
teaching job (English as a second language) and he took
another menial job. Now, however, he was in the center of
Croatian activity and in a politicized multiethnic city. His
evolving identity had solidified into that of a revolutionary. It
was an identity about which police in several countries now
would concur. Still, by personal choice, this identity was that
of a nonviolent actor who fought with words. (According to
Busic, the records show that he was under C.I.A. surveillance
since 1970.)

At this point in the interview, Busic was asked to talk
about the way in which the idea of hijacking an airplane
developed at that time. His answer confirms the power of the
identity crisis which he was experiencing:

So, it's not . . . feeling of . . . of . . . I didn't
feel my responsibility to do such extreme . . . a
thing. I didn't. And I don't think . . . anybody
or any cause deserves that, but . . . hijacking of
an airplane, it was . . . some . . . some kind of
. . . _escape_ for me personally, of the difficulty,
and miserable situation I was . . . I was living in.

The emotional state in which Busic was during those months
before the hijacking took place was shaped by the growing
terror which surrounded his new, socially negative, but
personally acceptable identity, of nonviolent revolutionary:

As I mentioned to you before, this . . . that I lost
. . . about five close friends in Germany, who were
working . . . more or less legally . . . and . . .
on Croatian . . . cause. . . . It relates . . . very
good to the stories of my youth I was telling you
about . . . like . . . a good friend of mine was
. . . found after he was missing for about six
months. . . . He was found . . . in the Rhine
River in Germany and when the police pulled him
out . . . he was in some sort of plastic sack. . . .
he . . . he didn't have eyes, nose, ears. He was
tortured and killed in torture . . . through torture.

In a clear expression of his nonacceptance of violent, destructive impulses, Busic stated that the man _must_ have had
vital information which the killers badly wanted. "I _believe_
that there's no human that enjoys that much of torturing
people and . . . or another human so they obviously had
a . . . reason . . . in doing this."

Busic also told of planning to go by train to meet a
Croatian friend in a southern German town at this time. He
bought a newspaper to read on the train.

On the train I read that he was assassinated that
night at two o'clock in the morning in the hotel. He
arrived from Sweden and in his hotel room, he . . .
he was . . . killed with two bullets in the mouth.

More important than events is the interpretation of events
which an individual uses to guide his behavior. Busic's
interpretation of the terror around him is critical:

So . . . and those . . . happenings, you know,
when you have . . . those experiences . . . in life.
Somehow life becomes . . . pretty miserable and
worthless and only what keeps you going is the
love for the cause you have and you support . . .

actually every individual supports his ideas . . .
and believes they are justified, so . . . to back off
wouldn't be . . . wouldn't be fair towards the
victims who paid their lives already or it wouldn't be
fair to your own self . . . I would personally lose
all my identity, all my . . . feelings and I would
feel . . . very low . . . to . . . to agree with
something I fought practically all my life against.

Busic goes on to explain that never, in all the frightening
times in Germany and America, had he thought about reprisal
or other "extreme actions." "It never occurred to me in my
mind that I could, for example, take the life of another
person."

Busic went on to declare his belief in the eventual
freedom of Croatia and to discuss the purpose of the hijacking:

The hijacking was to brighten up those ideas, to,
like I said, keep hopes alive, to calm down people
and . . . make them aware, most - because most -
of these Croatian people in the United States,
Canada and these countries are quite simple and
uneducated people, not with that great schooling.
They have difficulties with the language here. They
cannot read . . . newspapers of these countries.
They cannot . . . follow the happenings and developments or anything. They're just, it's pretty
. . . desperate life they're living and very few
people even try to understand that. You know, but
I felt that on my own skin, when I came into Germany, when I came into the United States, when I
met this difficulties, for example, with the language,
with society you came in, to adjust the societies, it
is extremely hard.

In the above declaration, Busic relates that he had made a
firm emotional identification in his mind between his own
plight, that of Croatian immigrants generally and - equally
important - the plight of Croatia: powerless, friendless, and
with an identity that will be extinguished unless it is constantly defended. To Busic, passivity - for himself or for
Croatia - is the equivalent of death. (This theme will be
elaborated below).

Yet there must be a catalyst to precipitate such radical
action as the hijacking of an airplane and the manufacture and
placement of a powerful bomb - a powerful catalyst to lead to
a final identification. Two of the precipitants were the atmosphere of terror and the closed access to an educated life,
both of which led Busic to desire to escape from the "dif-

ficulty, and miserable situation." Another reason was the need
to confirm his identification with the Croatian people and the
Croatian cause, to finalize his revolutionary identity.

A further precipitant was the frustration (generally
shared by revolutionary terrorists) that the media were know-
ingly slanted and inaccurate in reporting his cause:

> Well, one of the reasons is dishonesty and unac-
> curacy and false things of American news media, and
> not only of American news media but of news media
> of uh Western European countries too, so-called free
> press which are whenever articles appear about
> Yugoslavia they are just articles which were inspired
> and the sources is from the Belgrade officials and
> from the country itself and does not present the
> true situation at all and Croatians are called all
> kinds of names through the history and now es-
> pecially as as as fascists, as terrorists and as
> everything else.

Similar in intensity to the feelings of Job, the urge for justification and a fair hearing is an intense dynamic fueling
modern-day terrorism. The oft-repeated statements that
terrorists operate within political situations where other,
nonviolent options are viable (Watson, 1976, forward) from the
terrorist's viewpoint, is simply inaccurate.

In addition to all the reasons listed so far, Busic was
driven to his act of terrorism by another, overwhelming
precipitant, which - as he realizes - was experienced in the
context of terror: "I feared for my life quite a bit . . . I was
some kind of a paranoid." It is a common act of government
intelligence services to spread false information about individuals in revolutionary groups, and thus to create an atmosphere of distrust which erodes their effectiveness. In
1972, a small band of Croatian nationalists had gone into
Yugoslavia as guerrilla warriors, all had been captured.

> Now some of the American agents, I don't know if
> they believed that or or they just were misled
> themselves or or they spread that kind of infor-
> mation on purpose. . . . they told some of my close
> associates that I was the one who led this group into
> Croatia, but I survived and I came back so that led
> this particular person, my associate, to - to suspect
> me as one who is - how can I take nineteen people
> down there and be the only one who . . . who gets
> away with it?

Thus, at this time of great terror for him, even his identity
as a Croatian revolutionary was being eroded. Only an ex-

treme, dramatic act which ran counter to his valued identities would solidify his personal connection with Croatian nationalism. Failing to become an educated man, this was the only valued identity worth struggling to achieve.

Busic recognizes that the critical point, however, was his isolated and threatened condition:

> Uh, the main thing was that, as I feel it, as I look at it now, that is, that at that point when I - before I decided, at the time I decided to do this thing, this hijacking, I was very paranoid - which is very unusual for my personality. Usually I'm not I . . . I . . . I do not <u>fear</u>, because somehow I was always ready and I was always looking to death and I was always ready to die if my moment comes.

Busic accurately notes that it is his normal psychological state not to be afraid and, further, to continue activities that would overwhelm most people with anxiety about their frightening consequences. (This is an interesting point of his personal psychology to which we will return below.) His state of fear was a clue to Busic that his physchological condition was abnormal, but he was not able to surmount this condition.

He was asked, "So, by paranoid, you mean you were really afraid?"

> I was afraid, yeah. I got information even from my own mother that a <u>cousin</u>, in fact, of mine was paid by . . . (who was <u>just</u> a gambler or an alcoholic) and that he was sent between others to to get me or to kill me or something. And I was very paranoid. At that particular time, I used to - my wife was very suspicious about me and how I handled the situation, like, like when I came to to our apartment, for example, I would go all over the place - <u>look</u> into every corner and see, and and barricade the doors. For example, when I entered the the house, I would look around. I would look always around me and so, it's it was just a very strange situation. . . .

Busic tells of placing threads across the door when leaving his apartment, to learn if someone had entered when he was gone, of spending hours against a wall at night if he heard footsteps outside, and of otherwise being controlled and controlling Julie by his fears. But he concluded, "So, I didn't let them scare me but I was, as I say, I was quite paranoid."

Busic's thinking at this point brings together all the precipitating factors in an identity crisis that had become truly life-enveloping:

At that time I said how, what's what's escape of this
situation? I see justice, unjustice there, unjustice
there and I believe in myself, I believed in all human values. I was raised as a Christian. Now I am
here in the situation - in the situation facing the
death and - which is even more mysterious and desperate for me and difficult is, after I'm killed, they
are going to spread, to spread some stories that I
was really some kind of a doubl-double agent and
that would not please anybody, me at least. Uh and
that would bring even more conflicts into Croatian
groups. One would support one story. The other one
would support the other story. And so in in that
situation, the Yugoslavian Secret Service, UDBA,
would successfully plant in the story that my my life
was as a as priz - as a - as a results of Croatian
complex which are, they are some conflicts. . . .

But why hijack an airplane? Why decide on that particular
type of activity? Busic has two answers. First, hijacking an
airplane is a very efficient and dramatic way of making a
statement. But equally important, "I also felt that would, that
would be extremely human showing human way of handling
something radical." By "human," Busic means humane and
protective of human life - warfare that is not violent or
sadistic, a revolutionary terrorist act in which the perpetrator
is loved and respected by all whom he loves and respects.
The people on the plane could not be jeopardized: there would
be no weapons, only false bombs. The possibility of violence
would be removed, split off from the act, for the bomb - along
with manifestos and demands - would be left in New York
City, along with explicit instructions to the police. The
purposes of the instructions were two-fold: to frighten, by
threatening to detonate similar bombs on the hijacked airplane
(an empty threat; there were no real bombs) and to protect
lives (by making the device extremely simple and the instructions explicit). Thus, Busic accepted the negative identification with violence, but tentatively, and out of desperation
that all other identities were eroding beyond repair.

At this point in the interview, logic and freely offered
introspection give way each time to a rigid protection against
guilt. If a policeman was killed and three others were maimed
by Taik's bomb, someone other than Taik wanted them dead.
The someone was probably Yugoslav Secret Service agents,
wishing to spoil, by violence, the triumph of Taik's message
to the world and the impact of his personal sacrifice. There
is a palpable barrier here against reflection, a barrier which
disallows discussion of Busic's ultimate responsibility for the
tragedy. The barrier is permeable, however, and his personal, unending terror for arranging such an inhuman act
breaks through in various ways, as will be discussed below.

The original plan had been to distribute the 100,000 leaflets brought on the plane to people massed outside an old church in Croatia in celebration of an ancient religious event. In addition, declarations of the Croatian cause, written in English and French, were to be dropped over Montreal, New York, and London, and printed in five major American newspapers. With Busic went Julie and three Croatian friends who believed, when they boarded the plane in New York, that Chicago was indeed their destination (although the knowledge which Julie had is a matter of legal debate). It is clear that the plan was Taik's and his alone and thus can be examined from the perspective of his own personal psychology.

Once airborne, Busic strapped a fake bomb on himself and took control of the plane. The others were ordered to hold the switch on other bombs - bombs which only Taik (and perhaps Julie) knew to be fake. He explains:

> See I couldn't . . . the behavior of people in different situations is . . . very unpredictable so, I wouldn't risk at all having real explosives with the people, even with my closest friends and people I trust completely and people who, who are following my orders. I wouldn't trust them because I care so much about a human life that I wouldn't put that - in that particular situation, for example, I would put - human life of these passengers into another person, into into into another person's hands and I couldn't do that, I couldn't do that to - it's against my principles. In this desperate situation, I was lived, I took responsibility and blame for myself to play so or to endanger temporarily the live, the lives of people, but but and I believed after the danger would be over and after they would discover that there was really not danger - however, they did experience fear and danger, but I thought and believed, after I explained myself to them either on the plane later on or later in the court they would somehow forgive me, at least partially - if not forgive me, then understand me, because I do not ask much patience of people, but I do ask and expect understanding.

To frighten and intimidate, to recognize and play out his inner potential for violence and harm, was a repugnant, conflicted role to contemplate and, then, to assume. The action was only possible by elaborate ideological, physical, and emotional preparations to ward off the actuality of assuming the responsibility for harming others. An essential part of the psychological protection was the pleasurable contemplation of the time when he would be unmasked in front of his victims as a harm-

less benefactor of others and be accepted and forgiven by
those on the hijacked plane. (Such fantasies are frequent
with this type of perpetrator. For example, one antiwar
protestor who hijacked a plane, hoping to take it to North
Vietnam, held the thought that, after showing the bombed
hospitals and terrible destruction to his passengers, they
would return united with him as activists in the antiwar
movement, with anger toward him deflected to the "real
target.") But the anxious guilt seeps in:

> Well I, I don't know how they think; however, it is
> very hard to forgive anybody who scares you to
> death, you know, and but I feel, to tell you the
> truth, I feel a little in res - inresponsible and guilty
> about that. Otherwise, as far as the death of a
> police officer, I have no . . . bother my conscience
> of - or anything, because I feel that it's not my
> fault at all. . . .

The guilt is mostly subconscious, but the tortured emotions
are real. A special agony arises from the fact that he was not
able to explain his cause at his trial to ensure that "the jury
would at least look me as a human being, not as animal."
    Busic again returned to the contrast between his outcast
position - labeled variously a terrorist, a murderer, and a
Croatian national hero - and the outcome which he had im-
agined possible:

> I thought if everything went smoothly, we would
> return from from Croatia and land up again some-
> where in Europe and on the way, right there and
> then I would give up and tell the passengers and
> Captain and everybody else that these things are not
> real and they - and I would stand then on the way
> back - that's what I had in my mind. I would be
> then at their mercy and I would try to give my
> message across to them, now, without their fearing
> me. And - to tell you the truth, I I pictured that
> return to the United States as somehow . . . happy
> ending of that dramatic situation because they
> wouldn't be a - scared any - anymore. Now they
> would discover that I wasn't really such animal and
> or willing or or being capable to harm them or kill
> them because I couldn't possibly do anything with
> those things I had on the plane. It's just, it's
> just - not explosive but kit-plat-kit kits you play on
> making all different kinds of. . . .

The hijacked plane was first ordered to Paris. When it land-
ed, the French police took a firm nonnegotiating stance.

However, inside the plane, there had been a dramatic change
in the terrorist commander, for Busic had learned about the
bomb explosion in New York City. "It changed my idea of uh
going uh down to uh Yugoslavia - just took off my strength
completely." Indeed, Busic could not believe the news when it
was telephoned to him on the plane by the United States
Ambassador. When he sent Julie off the plane to confirm the
publication of his manifesto by a telephone call to a friend in
New York, she also heard and relayed to Taik a confirmation
of the tragic news. When the reality of the tragedy could no
longer be denied, "I couldn't stop crying and they were no
false tears."

Yet, in spite of Busic's emotional and intellectual awareness of this tradedy, he is unable consciously to accept
feelings of anger or revenge in others or of guilt in himself.
He is bewildered and disturbed by the anger expressed by the
maimed officers during his trial.

> I expected them as human beings to understand that
> I did not intend to hur - to hurt them and . . . I
> know they were. . . . No one can give the blind
> sight again or this one bad injuries I - but that was
> just somehow my and their fate and they should not
> be that angered with me because I did not intend to
> hurt anyone. If anybody was . . . besides them
> was hurt, it was me and my wife at the most.

The hurtfulness of these firmly held negative opinions is clear.
"I expect humans to behave better even in that situation
because I would." He is particularly upset by the anger of
one injured officer who stated on television that he was sorry
that the Busics would be eligible for parole in just ten years.

> That's just, that's a pure revenge and revenge -
> unjustified revenge and . . . civilized people don't
> do that and . . . and now, to tell you the truth,
> I . . . have learned my lesson and I would, in my
> life, I would take much more precautions and re-
> sponsibilities and . . . but because my conscience is
> is is clear. I just, I feel sorry for them, and I feel
> sorry that they cannot understand me and probably
> never forgive me for what I have done. Uh but I
> do not feel sorry for myself, in any case.

At the end of this first interview, Taik was thanked for being
willing to share his life and his political views. He responded:

> Well, to tell you the truth, I never was afraid to
> . . . to show myself as I am because I don't think I
> should feel guilty about anything. I did my best all

the time in life and . . . and . . . I did what I
could, humanly could, and, as I said, . . . that was
<u>only me</u> and . . . only escape from that miserable
situation and I <u>felt</u> that something like it had to be
done, once and <u>for</u> all.

DISCUSSION

The life of Zvonko Busic well illustrates the complex, multivariate pathway which eventuates in political behavior and the
specific causal nexus which can lead to the assumption of
a negative political identity - over personal and familiar values
and, in the case of this type of actor, never comfortably or
fully assumed. First of all, there was a consistent socialization into the Croatian cause and an identification of that
cause with both righteousness and helplessness. The heroes
of his life are Stephan Radic and Bruno Busic, fighters for
the cause of Croatian independence whose skill with words was
no defense against the weapons of their Serbian opponents.
    Second, there were personal psychological factors to
cause this Croatian youth to dedicate his life to Croatian
freedom. Many are socialized, but very few hear the Siren's
call to revolution. The personal factors in Taik's life were
unclear at this point, but there are three important clues to
dynamic issues which shape his behavior. The first is his
obvious discomfort with violent or sadistic impulses, his
<u>reaction formation</u>(4) against such violence which shows in his
inability to recognize or accept such impulses in himself or
others, and his need to devise a terroristic act where the
violence was split off and independent from the control (and
the responsibility) of the nonviolent terrorist. Second, there
is his nonawareness of fear and his counterphobic behavior in
which he repeatedly places himself in fearful situations. In
spite of being aware since childhood of the mental and physical
risks in being a revolutionary, in spite of being offered the
chance to remove himself from the terror and remain in
Oregon, in spite of growing feelings of panic, on a conscious
level Busic was not afraid - and he carefully distinguishes his
paranoia as a <u>different</u> state than fear. He wonders if the
reason his oldest brother is not also a revolutionary is due to
<u>lack of courage</u>. Not being afraid is critically important to
Busic.
    Third, in discussion continued after the taped interview
was over, Busic told - with pain and considerable difficulty -
how he had lost his left eye. He was eighteen and playing
with other boys in a field, when an object was driven into his
eye. After several days of increasing pain and difficulty with
the eye, the family finally took him from their poor village to a

doctor in Zagreb, who removed the eye and noted that it <u>could have been saved</u> if he had prompt medical attention. He also mentioned, in passing, that he had almost died of typhoid when he was six years old.

One further inner dynamic is available to us. Busic's Rorschach protocol and his Political Thematic Apperception Measure stories offer rich insights into his present psychological state, his personal dynamics, and his perceptions of power, of human relationships, and of efficacy and hope. One particular phenomenon is of note for discussion here: these novel tasks are met with considerable discomfort and difficulty and are handled badly. On the Rorschach, Busic's need to be incorporative, to develop "grand schemes," to almost disappear in a haze of intellectuality, cause him again and again to cross the borderline of reality, to be unable to deal creatively with material in front of him, to rationally perceive alternatives, to flexibly change cognitive sets.

It is likely that this <u>personal style</u> and an individual psychodynamics interacted with his reaction-formation to his own potential for violence to eventuate in the tragic bombing. It is a style fueled by over-intellectualization that produces plans divorced from reality considerations and serious investigation of alternatives. It is related to another characteristic common in this sub-set of political actors: feelings of omnipotence, of ability to control outcomes by one's own will, and to consider untoward consequences as the result of fate – historical, social, religious. (In retrospect, a number of these subjects are amazed by the degree to which they felt omnipotent in controlling untoward consequences before and during their acts.)

In addition to his identification with the Croatian cause and his personal dynamic factors (yet unclear), there were clear precipitating circumstances where sharp disappointments successively limited his life chances and redirected his psychic energies from his original goal of becoming an educated man who would further the Croatian cause by preserving and enlarging its literature. First in Zagreb, when he had joined other university students in signing a manifesto, and later in Vienna, when his funds had run out, the doors to a university education had been shut against this bright and sensitive youth from a subsistance level peasant family. Becoming a revolutionary who fought only with words was also denied when questions were planted about that identity.

When life options are closed, it is not all given that a person's energies are redirected into negative roles, which are rejected both by society and one's family. Most people possess an array of possible identities; when energies are deflected from one, they are able to make an adjustment in another – still congruent with personality needs and the familial, cultural, and social constraints into which they were socialized.

In some rare cases, however, the narrowing access to a chosen identity is accompanied by <u>an interactive process</u> in which the <u>push</u> away from a socially and personally valued identity is accompanied by a <u>pull</u> toward a socially sanctioned identity.

In the case of the identity of a revolutionary terrorist, it is unfortunately a well-established historical phenomenon for government surveillance to blend over into deviant labeling and <u>identity control</u>, enforced by the power of government sanctions, both covert and overt (Loftland, 1969; Steinhoff, 1978). This powerful process then interacts with the person's inner dynamics and internalized values. The identification with violence of Salah Khalef, the leader of the Black September group, mirrors the path traveled by Busic - Khalef is described as turning from moderate nationalism to terrorism when his revolutionary identity was called into question. This occurred when he made an address to his comrades to lay down their arms, at the urging of the Jordanian army that had captured him (Dobson, 1974, pp. 43-47).

After reflecting on the above data, a number of questions remained about Busic's personal dynamics. Most Croatians are imbued with a love for their homeland and their culture, but very, very few are willing to risk their lives for its cause. No one else in Busic's family took such a radical position; how could he? Further, how could he, over and over again, put himself at jeopardy - and not conclude that the game was not worth the candle? There also were questions about the mechanism which a bright, thoughtful, and humane man could use to insulate himself from fearful responsibility for possible future tragedy and, thus, be able to make and place a powerful bomb. Finally, there were questions about how he maintained the split between his perceived self and his violent self. A second interview was arranged.

FURTHER QUESTIONS AND CRITICAL ANSWERS

The second interview, which took place six weeks later, began with a question about how Busic handled fear. He acknowledged his uniqueness in this area by saying: "Oh, it's - sometimes when I - when I am a, when I feel right, I would tell God straight ahead whatever I think." He went on to talk again of his martyred cousin, Bruno Busic, who - with four others - had been taken out of school to a prison car before his very eyes. Taik was eleven; Bruno was seventeen. The other four were so frightened by their prison experience that they stopped all nationalistic activity - but not Bruno. The story rang with admiration as Taik told of subsequently learning from his hero cousin much of the long and tortured history of Croatia.

The subject of fear continued to be discussed. Taik made it very clear that he was willing to risk his life, but <u>not</u> when there was no chance of success: "No, I'm not that kind of fanatic." Urged again and again to consider the uniqueness of his ability to risk his life, Busic also found it a difficult phenomenon to understand. In trying to explain his behavior, he noted:

> Well, I believe - first of all, I believe . . . I believe in Croatia freedom and I believe also to to regain that freedom and independence, somebody has to fight for it and I believe if nobody would fight for it, Croatian nation would die.

For the Croatian nation, struggle is essential to life; passitivity is synonymous with death. Possibly, it occurs at this point, this is experienced as true for Busic, himself, in a personalized, existential sense.

At this juncture, Busic was asked to retell on tape the experience when, as a child, he had almost died of typhoid. He was "seven and a half or eight years old." He was told that he was in bed 29 days, eating and drinking nothing. Although the family was very poor, they had managed to procure some honey, "but I couldn't take that either."

> So uh, when I was lying in bed, I remember uh seeing all kinds of visions. Uh that was probably part of the weakness, I felt. And that last week, I don't remember anything and, as my parents told me later, I was pronounced dead by the priest and some kind of a fellow who is a doctor in another city and he, at that particular time, he was on vacation at home or something and he came to see me and he said that I was dead(5) and my father told me later on that he prepared even the coffin for me, you know. That's - it shouldn't be big funeral, you know. When the kids die, they usually just kids from the class go on the funeral and father and mother . . . that's a tradition in our village.

Suddenly, Taik began to recover and, two weeks later, to move from his bed "but I couldn't walk. See, I was just like a baby, just born." Eventually, he returned to school where he was "one of the best pupils." The first day back in school is clearly remembered; he had found out that all the students were to learn a poem and he had memorized it. However, most of the other pupils did not know the poem when they were asked to recite. The teacher became angry at them as Taik, sick for two months, had done his work. As Busic remembers, the result of his academic glory was that the other pupils were beaten by the teacher.

The emotional experience of near death and resurrection, of being "just born," sets in motion powerful inner dynamics. Before the effect of this experience is discussed, there are two other themes of great importance which arose in the second interview. One of these deals with guilt. The associated theme is sadism and violence. Taik was asked to talk about any experiences he could remember when he hurt or was hurt by someone. He began with his parents, explaining that, as he was not a "big problem," he was not beaten much at home. His father, "who was not much uh uh participating in upbringing up the kids," was forgiving and nonpunitive. However, his mother "was pretty strict person and uh sometimes I felt that she was exaggerating this . . . things, especially when she beat my younger brother or my sister."

And outside the family? Taik loved to wrestle, "but not actually fight." When a certain, other boy wanted to fight with Taik, he followed a certain ritual:

> And he used to hit me quite good, but I used to wrestle him and I used to put him on the on the uh the and on the ground and spread his hands, in order to prove to other people that I am stronger. But I - I remember I would not hit him once and he cannot move. I was so much stronger than he is and then I let him go and he jumps up and hits me with a stone.

His adversary's father was a violent man who drank a lot and beat his wife. If Taik hit his son, he was tremendously afraid of what the father would to to him. "I had a fear that I that might continue not as a game - just a fist fight or anything - but I might I might suffer a lot for it. Like I might be beaten or stabbed or something . . . else." Busic gives one other reason why he was not a fighter: "I believe my some my nature that I don't like to hit people at all, no matter uh what kind of fight that is." Indeed, in all his battles:

> Personally, I was in fight many times, but I never hit with my bare fist, person in in in his face, because I think that could that would be too dangerous. I have been hit but I think if I would hit somebody with my bare fist that would be very very . . . harmful and dangerous for the person.

He was asked, "Dangerous in that then they might really want to kill you?" He responded: "No, no, no, no. It it would hurt them so much."

Busic was asked about fighting among his many brothers and sisters. In his memory, there was little. However, he then remembered a psychologically very important event, which

occurred when he was thirteen or fourteen. He was alone in
the house with his sister, who is five years younger. Feeling
like the "boss of the house," Taik wanted to impress his
parents and told his sister that she had to clean the house.

> And she refused and refused and kept refusing and
> and I started uh slapping her and and she still
> refused and she was - she told me that she would
> tell to mother and so I said, "Go ahead and tell her"
> and I wanted to force her really to do it, and so I
> didn't slap her in order to hurt her really, but I
> remember [he said, laughing] when she started
> doing it and crying, you know. And I said, "How
> about to sing now. I really doesn't hurt you - go
> ahead and sing" and she [he said, still laughing]
> was and she was. She still remembers that.

Taik was surprised at himself then and is still surprised today
that he acted in such a fashion. It was suggested to him that
this event allowed him to be angry in a safe way, a way that
was not dangerous. He agreed: "Yeah, or I knew that I
wouldn't beat her in order to hurt her and nobody else was
there." Taik ended by noting that this sister "loves me very
much" and expressed the view that he has helped her to
develop and change to better attitudes about housework.
        The incident illumines some important features of Busic's
psychology. First of all, it illustrates that he does indeed
possess violent, even sadistic impulses. Second, these impulses which are so carefully kept in check can be released
only "for free" - that is, when they cannot harm another
seriously or, in turn, bring the threat of great harm to him.
Third, when these rarely used aggressive impulses are employed, they can be tinged with sadism - at least, in the case
of anger toward a woman.
        Busic noted that, as with the boy in his village, in
prison it is necessary to monitor constantly any firm stands by
continuous assessments of the danger of the situation. He
then related an event which allows further understanding of
the dynamics fueling both violence and guilt for this man.
The event occurred the morning after he had spent a sleepless
night because he had just learned about his cousin's murder in
Paris. As is routine in prisons, that morning the lieutenant
went from cell to cell, telling the inmates to, "Get up, get up
and make your bed and uh clean your cell."

> I was pretty - after two months on the road and I
> was pretty desperate and after that news, it's
> - I was - I was tired an sleepy and I said, "No,
> I'm tired and sleepy and I will not get up," I told
> him.

The officer told Busic that he must do as ordered and Busic replied that the officer was wasting his time. Busic was left to sleep, troubled that he had not followed the rules but feeling, "Well, I'm not a soldier and I have explanation."

The lieutenant returned about two o'clock. Busic was up and had made his bed. The officer now told him to pick up and put away a locker that was on the floor. The locker had been down since Busic arrived as he used it as a desk - a use which he explained to the officer. He was ordered twice to pick it up, and twice he refused.

> So he came and again now - like he was by himself and now there are three of 'em - so if anything happens. I said, "I'm not trying to fight or anything. I won't touch you if you don't touch me. And but no matter how many people you get, I won't pick that up because I said so and do to - anything to me."

The officer retired and then returned with a captain who said "Mr. Busic, I'm captain so-and-so, and I want you to pick up that locker." Again Busic refused. The captain then said that he would be locked down in disciplinary segregation. Busic replied:

> No, you won't put me. I am going to go over there. You can order me there, but if you touch me, I don't know what might happen, so please keep you hands off me and order me where to go.

On the way, Busic said to the lieutenant:

> I know you came and pick up the locker because of my refusal this morning and I have very good and humane explanation for it.

The officer replied: "I don't want to listen to it" and slammed the door.

> And I yell - I remember I was yelling at him, "You might be someday sorry for this what you have done. Have you ever been sorry what - for things you have done?"

It was suggested that "being sorry" was obviously a very painful place for Busic to be. For what, in addition to the incident with his sister, was he sorry?

Busic then described a second incident, which involved his breaking off from the only other woman of importance in his life except his wife. It occurred before he had met Julie.

The girl was young and Croatian - 19 years old to his 22 or 23 years. Her brother was a priest and she was staying with some nuns in Vienna in order to learn German. Taik decided that he wanted to break with her. He knew that "she was deeply in love with me" but realized that he did not love her in return. Taik and some friends had organized a party in a bar. The girl heard of the affair and showed up. Taik was a bit drunk when the girl arrived and ignored her, going instead to sit with some other girls. The girl just sat crying as he and his friends drank and talked.

> And... she never drank anything and she was just drinking apple juice or something and when I returned from that table, I just wanted to provoke her. I know, just wanted to hurt her because I didn't feel any love in her and I wanted know her - to let her know openly.

As Taik states, "I'm aware that I was playing a role for myself, but somehow I was playing role in order to succeed in something, you know. She will hate me now."

> And so on and so on and I was pretty drunk and called her all kind of names in front in front of other people and I was very sorry for. . . .

Taik is still sorry and only wishes that he had the opportunity to express his sorrow and to "explain myself" to her.

> and at least less in - with my example, probably I might help that some other people who will have chance to save their nation uh using my example, they will.

AN ATTEMPT AT SYNTHESIS

In this last statement, Busic clearly states his need to fight - even if the cause is lost. This need to struggle is closely connected with a fear of passivity and a rejection of his passive, noninvolved father's style of relating to life. Pride and positive self-regard are connected with struggling. The need to fight is also related to his close encounter with death, an event which he experienced as actually having occurred. To Busic, death is the opposite of struggle and, in this conflicted area, Croatia has come to stand for his own inner stress so that he has been specially able to act out Croatian needs to survive as a culture.

The need to fight - and thus to survive and not die - must, however, be arranged in a way that neither is he in danger for his life nor is there the equal danger that Busic's sadistic-aggressive impulses will break through. This conflict underlies the unusual plan for the hijacked airplane: the weapon of destruction was split off, both physically and emotionally, from the perpetrator of the act. As in the fights in his village, he held down his adversary but would not use his terrible destructive force to bring danger to either one of them. He would only make his adversary aware of his power, so that he himself would not harm or be harmed. With the history of bomb detonation in New York City, this was indeed a plausible outcome which would not only have been politically efficacious but also would have allowed Busic's violence to remain isolated - a valued goal in itself. For every time he has had to fully accept his ability to harm as a part of his own self, he has been tortured by remorse. Thus, his present denial is truly life-saving.

There is an additional theme which relates to very personalized distaste for injustice. This theme is connected with the dichotomy he sees between those who are weak and righteous and educated, against those who are strong and brutal and unfeeling. It is mirrored in his view of the historic struggle between East and West over Croatia. In this connection, Julie's comments about her visit to Taik's parents in their Croatian village are of interest. The father was described as quiet, accepting, and a bit withdrawn. The mother (who disciplined by beating the children too much) is described as outgoing, a person who gossips all day long.

> I don't really think I can say this from my own experience, but his father is a lot better person than his mother. Uh his mother - she's a very good person too, but she has certain weaknesses that he doesn't think his father has.

> Uh, she waivers in her principles at times, he feels, and I'm not really sure what he's talking about specifically, but his father's a totally good person and he never he never wishes evil on other people. . . .

> But his mother is is . . .she's mean and nasty and catty at times and she's getting into other people's business, but she's basically very good-hearted and very generous but, you know, these are qualities that he feels that his father doesn't have at all and his father would never be involved in things like that.

In the second interview, elements in Busic's personal psychology allow a more complete understanding of the intrapsychic factors which eventuated in revolutionary terroristic activity and, equally important, which shaped the plan and outcome of his individualized terroristic act. If Busic's inner conflicts had allowed him to be armed and threatening - that is, to assume a complete identification with violence for the period on board the airplane - his basically humane instincts likely would have disallowed any possibility of acting violently to harm another. However, the necessity of experiencing himself as nonviolent - though in a violent role - and of being seen in this light by his captives made it essential for him to place a powerful weapon where he could not control it. No matter what precautions he took - and they were legion - he, in the end, could not predict or direct the outcome because he could not fully identify himself with violence. The negative identity which he reluctantly assumed to shore up his fragmenting sense of self was thus fraught with failure.

Before the event, he also could not control his fear, as the various government forces moved to frighten him out of revolutionary activity. His fear is reminiscent of his equally terrifying fears of his village adversary's father. Then, too, the threat and the response became divorced from rational considerations and passed the borderline of reality. To fear, Busic is free to offer only one response: denial of fear in activity he defines as courageous. He is not able to rationally assess great fear. Nor is he able to move away from fear or to reduce its threat by passivity and conciliation. As Erikson (1964, p. 138) notes, "whenever, for whatever reason, a later crisis is severe, earlier crises are revived." The terror preceding the hijacking reawakened the terror stalking his village which made children's funerals so unremarkable that only parents and school friends attended. It is in the light of this personal reign of terror that the active but conflicted move toward a negative identity through hijacking a plane by violence can be seen, in Eriksonian terms, as an attempt to regain mastery and a firm sense of self.

In order to understand the psychology of the terrorist at the moment before the event, it is important to realize that he perceives himself as having no other alternative. (At times, as in Busic's case, this perception occurs in a period of diminished reality testing; in other cases, it does not.) The many published views by government and academia listing alternative political options and the openness of our (and other democratic) societies to societal demands simply miss the meaning of the terroristic act. The terroristic act is perceived as the end of the options, the final statement after all alternatives have been exhausted. It is often (though not always) enacted with a degree of futility which acknowledges it as only that - a statement - not a means to achieve a concrete political end. It is critical for those who wish to reduce the threat of terroristic acts to understand this feeling of having no other place to go, psychologically or politically. Professor Richard Lowenthal recently stated:

> Those radicals who remain disaffected need not necessarily turn into terrorists: whether they do, will depend - apart from factors of individual psychology - on the willingness and ability of the society to prevent their total isolation and to maintain a form of communication or dialogue with them. This requires an effort at an attitude of tolerance toward non-criminal, non-terrorist but otherwise radically disaffected critics of our society and government - tolerance not in the sense of ignoring them in "tolerant" neglect, nor of pretending sympathy for their views, but of a constant willingness to maintain serious argument with them, to get them out of their ghetto into discussion without branding them as "terrorist sympathizers" (which may end by turning them into such). A democracy that does not wish to increase the ranks of its terrorists must learn to live, and to argue, with disaffected radicals - however fruitless such arguments may often be, at least in the short run (1978).

The willingness of society to engage in such a dialogue must be undertaken with the knowledge of the psychological place from which many terrorists operate: experiencing for years constantly narrowing life options, lack of flexibility and understanding by authorities personal and impersonal; in not infrequent cases, to be able to say with Charlie Manson: "I don't think like you people. You people put importance on your lives. Well, my life has never been important to anyone. . . ." (Bugliosi, 1974, p. 391).

In the end, it is necessary to reinstate the original premise. Personal dynamics color and shape activities; alone, they are insufficient to eventuate in political behavior. Busic's personal dynamics are coupled with socialization into revolutionary values shared by a much wider group of people who do not engage in deviant political behavior. In turn, both values and personality are shaped by social and political events which successively limit opportunities for assuming other, positive identities - either as an educated man or a fighter with words alone. Only in extended political struggles do perpetrators grow up comfortably adopting roles employing political violence.

Thus, the pathway by which Busic arrived at a terrorist act shares those elements - socialization, personal needs, and precipitating circumstances - that shape other, normal political behaviors. Unfortunately, the specific interactive pathway leading to his assumption of the socially and personally negative identity of a violent revolutionary terrorist is also not uncommon, as this particular subtype of political actor's personal needs and values interact so powerfully with the needs and values of government security, as presently defined.

In the end, however, Busic's activity cannot merely be reduced to common and ordinary pathways. Today, he is an acknowledged leader among Croatian nationalists who have raised an immense international defense fund for him and his codefendants. Busic is not only a solitary individual working to resolve his personal conflicts; he is preeminently a man whose personal needs and values interact with those of this wider group so that his actions confirm their group identity and his words speak for their own desires and hopes.

As Erikson once noted, in the case of another national leader:

> This, then, is the difference between a case history and a life-history: patients, great or small, are increasingly debilitated by their inner conflicts, but in historical actuality inner coflict only adds an indispensable momentum to all superhuman effort (1969, p. 363).

Busic's needs must be understood in the context of providing the momentum through which national aspirations and national identity, in addition to a solution of his own inner conflicts, were sought, and - for a moment as he headed out over the Atlantic - appeared to have been won.

NOTES

1. I wish to express my deep gratitude to Mr. Norman Carlson, Director of the United States Federal Bureau of Prisons, and to his staff throughout this large system, who have been uniformly cooperative with my research requirements and supportive of the needs for confidentiality and protection of my subjects' rights of privacy in talking with me. I would also like to express appreciation to Nathan Leites, John Mack, and Lawrence Z. Freedman for their helpful critiques of this paper.

Financial support for this research project was partially provided through Dr. David Hubbard of the Aberrant Behavior Center in Dallas, Texas and Dr. Louis J. West, Chairman of the Department of Psychiatry of the University of California, Los Angeles.

Finally, I would like to offer special appreciation to Gail Hellstein and Sally Vamdiver, whose patient editing of the research transcripts has ensured their accuracy and preserved their sense of immediacy.

2. I would like to acknowledge the assistance and interest of Mr. Ira Kirschbaum, Assistant General Counsel for the U.S. Prison System, and Mr. Paul Nejelski, former Assistant Deputy Attorney General, in locating those Federal Regulations which protect this project's data and its subjects' legal security (50.10 of the Code of Federal Regulations, extended by The Attorney General in 1975 to cover researchers' rights and privileges). (See also Nejelski 1978; Nejelski and Finsterbusch 1973.)

3. I would like to express appreciation to Professor Franco Ferracuti of the University of Rome for offering this valuable insight.

4. According to the Modern Synopsis of Psychiatry (1972, p. 789) a reaction formation is defined as follows: "An unconscious defense mechanism in which a person develops a socialized attitude or interest that is the direct antithesis of some infantile wish or impulse in the unconscious. One of the earliest and most unstable defense mechanisms, it is closely related to repression; both are defenses against impulses or urges that are unacceptable to the ego." The operation here of this defense was suggested by Professor Nathan Leites, to whom I wish to express appreciation for helping to clarify the function of aggression in this subject's life. Interesting confirmation of this point comes from an interview on April 17, 1979, with one of the passenger-hostages, Mr. Rudy Bretz. Mr. Bretz described Zvonko Busic as wearing large purple and pink tinted sunglasses during the hijacking, which prevented anyone from seeing his eyes, and notes that he "didn't seem to be enjoying his power."

5. This was said in an incredulous tone.

REFERENCES

Becker, J. Hitler's Children. Philadelphia: J.B. Lippincott, 1977.

Bugliosi, Vincent. Helter Skelter. New York: W.W. Norton, 1974.

Campbell, A., P. E. Converse, W. E. Miller, and D. E. Stokes. The American Voter. New York: John Wiley & Sons, 1960.

Davies, James C. Human Nature in Politics. New York: John Wiley and Sons, 1963.

Dobson, Christopher. Black September. New York: Mac-
    millan, 1974.

Erikson, Erik H. Insight and Responsibility. New York:
    W. W. Norton, 1964.

_____. Identity: Youth and Crisis. New York: W. W.
    Norton, 1968.

_____. Gandhi's Truth. New York: W. W. Norton,
    1969.

Exner, John E., Jr., The Rorschach: A Comprehensive
    System. New York: John Wiley & Sons, 1974.

Freedman, A. M., Kaplan, H. I. and B. J. Sadock. Modern
    Synopsis of Psychiatry. Baltimore: The Williams &
    Wilkins Co., 1972.

Gaylin, W. In The Service of Their Country. New York:
    Grosset & Dunlap, 1970.

Hacker, F. J. Crusaders, Criminals, Crazies. New York:
    Bantam Books, 1976.

Hoffer, Eric. The True Believer. New York: Harper & Row,
    1951.

Hubbard, D. G. The Skyjacker. New York: Macmillan, 1971.

Knutson, Jeanne. The Human Basis of the Polity. Chicago:
    Aldine, 1972.

_____. "The New Frontier of Projective Techniques," in
    The Handbook of Political Psychology, edited by J.
    Knutson. San Francisco: Jossey-Bass, 1973a.

_____. "Personality in the Study of Politics," in The
    Handbook of Political Psychology. 1973b.

_____. Constraints on Political Learning: Pre-Political
    Ideology in Black and White Children. Berkeley: The
    Wright Institute, 1974a.

_____. "Prepolitical Ideologies: The Basis of Political
    Learning," in The Politics of Future Citizens, edited by
    R. Niemi. San Francisco: Jossey-Bass, 1974b.

_____. Psychological Variables in Political Recruitment:
    An Analysis of Party Activists. Berkeley: The Wright
    Institute, 1974c.

_____. "Human Needs Constraining Political Activity."
    Human Needs and Politics, edited by R. Fitzgerald.
    Sydney, Australia: Pergamon Press, 1977.

Kobetz, Richard W., and H. H. A. Cooper. Target Terror-
    ism. Gaithersburg, Maryland: Bureau of Operations and

Research, International Association of Chiefs of Police, 1978.

Loftland, John. Deviance and Identity. Englewood Cliffs, N.J.: Prentice-Hall, 1969.

Lowenthal, Richard. Statement at the International Scientific Conference on Terrorism, Berlin, Federal Republic of Germany, November 12, 1978.

Maslow, A. H. Motivation and Personality. New York: Harper & Row, 1954.

Morf, G. Terror in Quebec. Toronto: Clarke, Irwin, 1970.

Nejelski, Paul. "The Rule of Law and Social Research." Address before the Conference on Solutions to Ethical and Legal Dilemmas in Social Research, Washington, D. C., February 23, 1978.

Nejelski, Paul, and Kurt Finsterbusch. "The Prosecutor and The Researcher: Present and Prospective Variations on the Supreme Court's Branzburg Decision," Social Problems, 21 (Summer 1973): 3-21.

_____. "Tenko and Thought Control." Paper presented at the Annual Meeting of the Association for Asian Studies, Boston, April 1-3, 1974.

_____. "Portrait of a Terrorist: An Interview with Kozo Okamoto," Asian Survey 16 (9) (1976): 830-45.

Steinhoff, Patricia G. "Political Dissent and Psycho-Social Conflict," Paper presented at the Annual Meeting of the Association for Asian Studies, Chicago, 1978.

Watson, F. M. Political Terrorism: The Threat and the Response. Washington: Robert B. Luce, 1976.

Wilkinson, Paul. Political Terrorism. London: The Macmillan Press, 1974.

Woodward, J. L., and E. Roper. "Political Activity of American Citizens," The American Political Science Review 44 (4) (December 1950): 872-85.

APPENDIX

Interview Questions Research Project on Political Terrorism

NAME (to be converted to a code number after interview and
    associated data collection are completed)
DATE(S) OF INTERVIEW
LOCATION AND CONDITIONS OF INTERVIEW (translation
    necessary, degree of privacy, etc.)

I. IDENTIFICATION OF SUBJECT

   A. Sex, race, age, physical description, nationality
   B. Reason for present imprisonment, legal conditions of
      imprisonment, perception of time remaining in prison

II. PERSONAL HISTORY

   A. Social, educational, vocational, medical, and psy-
      chiatric
   B. Emphasis on areas of functioning and levels of
      coping; personal resources and deficits
   C. Critical life disappointments
   D. Personal, familial, and cultural values

III. POLITICAL HISTORY

   A. Understanding of the working of the political system:
      the available inputs; the viability and degree of
      efficacy associated with various inputs; the causality
      of political outputs; degree of trust in this or any
      organized political system, in terms of specific system
      parameters
   B. Understanding of working of the social system and
      place of subject within that system; belief in the
      existence of in- and out-groups; belief in social
      mobility and rigidity
   C. Beliefs concerning human nature (e.g., the possiblity
      of tolerance for and trust in others and in cooper-
      ation for mutual goals); beliefs in the nature of
      causality of personal events
   D. Development of focused political viewpoint: significant
      events, antecedents (familial, cultural, social),
      rationale; whether viewpoint is isolated or tied to a
      personalized or established ideology
   E. Politically relevant behaviors committed to support
      political viewpoint
   F. Any significant changes in political viewpoint over
      time to present date

APPENDIX (Continued)

IV. THE EVENT LEADING TO PRESENT IMPRISONMENT

A. Rationale for behavior leading to present imprisonment
B. Structuring of personal and political situation and reality at the time of event
C. Exploration of alternative behaviors, if any [other life choices]
D. Precipitating events
E. Role of affiliates and social supports
F. Definition and description of role of media
G. Defined political and personal goals and relation between this event and those goals
H. Perception and fantasies about life after this imprisonment
I. Understanding of congruence between political activity and personal needs

V. MENTAL STATUS

A. General appearance, manner, and attitude, including reasons for cooperating in research project
B. Demonstration of effective conscience (superego controls)
C. Affectivity and mood
D. Thought processes, thought content, perception, memory, judgment, and insight
E. Ability to abstract and reason and to flexibly change cognitive sets
F. Personality maturity
G. Estimate of intelligence
H. Evidence of organicity
I. Degree of aggressiveness; defenses against it (if any); direction (intra- or extra-psychic)

III

Data Bases, Quantitative Analyses and Case Studies

8 Iterate: Monitoring Transnational Terrorism

Edward Mickolus
Edward Heyman

Much blood has been shed in the past decade as a result of the depredations of terrorists. Researchers have spilled a comparable quantity of ink in attempting to analyze the spread of this phenomenon, how we can deal with it, and what the future holds in store for us. While many hypotheses have been put forward, depressingly little attention has been paid to the rigorous testing of what passes for conventional wisdom in this field.(1)

One of the ways to fill this gap is to create a widely-available body of data on the topic, subject to the critical scrutiny of representatives of all disciplines. One must begin this endeavor by tackling the thorny problem of definitions. To paraphrase Mr. Justice Potter Stewart's observations on obscenity, "I can't define it, but I know it when I see it." To many, terrorism is precisely a matter of perception, subject to a choice of values. We have attempted to transcend this issue of evaluation by combining the elements of some oft-cited definitions to arrive at a scientific, operational definition of terrorism, which we find to be "the use, or threat of use, of anxiety-inducing extranormal violence for political purposes by any individual or group, whether acting for or in opposition to established governmental authority, when such action is intended to influence the attitudes and behavior of a target group wider than the immediate victims."(2)

The concept can be further refined by creating a 2 x 2 table, using as our axes the degree of governmental sponsor-

---

*Originally presented to the Joint National Meeting of the Operations Research Society of America and The Institute for Management Sciences, New York, May 1-3, 1978.

ship, and the number of nationalities involved. Transnational terrorism, our subject of inquiry, is terrorist action carried out by basically autonomous nonstate actors, whether or not they enjoy some degree of moral and/or material support from sympathetic governments. Furthermore, the action's ramifications may transcend national boundaries through the nationality or foreign ties of its perpetrators, its location, the nature of its institutional or human victims, or the mechanics of its resolution.

The next task is to survey the literature on terrorism, noting which variables theorists find crucial in describing, explaining, and predicting terrorist activity. Our search for concepts led us to opt for a longitudinal crossnational study of terrorism, while maintaining a respect for the academic division of labor and for rigorous examinations of specific cases.

The literature search resulted in a set of categories believed to describe the structure of any given transnational terrorist incident. (Appendix B gives a listing of the general types of variables of interest, as well as the specific items for which data was sought.) To test the utility of these categories, the Rand Corporation's chronology of international terrorism from 1968 through the beginning of 1974 was used to generate 539 cases. Gaps in the Rand compilation were filled with descriptions of incidents given in the American press. Checks were made of item discrimination, and the results of simple one-way frequency distributions and crosstabulations of the data were compared with the findings of more traditional studies. This pilot dataset was then made available to other researchers.(3)

The reception of the pilot dataset within the academic and governmental communities was heartening, although several problems in its conception and implementation became apparent. Of greatest importance is the issue of what the National Bureau of Standards refers to as "critically-evaluated data," more popularly known to computer specialists as "garbage in, garbage out." Political scientists who employ events data in their studies of trends in international interactions have discovered that the use of a single source (such as the New York Times) or a certain genre of sources (such as governmental reports) can lead to biases regarding what is reported and how the events are described. Secondly, data for many of the variables simply was not available. Thirdly, some of the incident descriptors were inapplicable to several kinds of incidents. (For example, "Number of Hostages" is irrelevant in a discussion of a bombing.) Finally, as with most datasets, it was impossible for other researchers to employ different selection criteria without a textual description of the incident.

The present version of the dataset has been designed to solve these problems. The data base has been expanded to include material from the United States and foreign media (including television, radio, and press commentaries), foreign governmental descriptions, descriptions of events by academics, and a host of official American chronologies, including material from the Departments of State, Defense, Commerce, Justice, USIA, CIA, FAA, and their contractor/consultants. A textual chronology now accompanies the numerical compendium. The original 107 incident descriptors have been separated into four different datasets which describe, respectively, all types of incidents, hostage situations, aerial hijackings, and the disposition of the offenders. Finally, we have deleted some of the variables for which data was unavailable, freeing a significant amount of computer core storage. (See Appendixes A and B for a comparison of the two datasets.)

GENERAL FINDINGS

Most of our time has been spent in collecting data, correcting errors, and otherwise cleaning the dataset. We are only now moving into the exploratory analysis of the material available. A few summary statistics are of interest in suggesting further research directions.

Between 1968 and 1977, there were 3,329 incidents of transnational terrorism. This works out to one a day, with Sundays but not holidays off. (Terrorists have been found to commemorate certain days, usually the feast day of one of their comrades, with followup attacks.) Damages have totaled at least $332,590,000, although this does not count ransoms paid, costs of protective services, opportunity costs, etc. Nor does it include the paper losses to Lufthansa stock as a result of the costliest terrorist threat in recent memory - the Red Army Faction's warning that it would shoot down Lufthansa jets with missiles. The costs of protective measures, loss of company goodwill, etc., conceivably compare with the dollar losses which would have accrued if the group had carried out their threat. Death has come to 1,695 people, including terrorists, and 4,772 have been wounded. Unfortunately, attacks have continued to be a low-risk proposition for terrorists, who have found that there is only a .061 chance that one of their members will be killed in the action, and a .033 chance that one of them will be wounded. In only 415 of the cases has at least one of the terrorists been arrested or killed at the scene. Only 1,747 arrests have been made in those 415 incidents, and most of those individuals have been freed.

In 316 cases of hostage-taking (including kidnapping, barricade-and-hostage situations, and terrorist hijackings), 6,042 hostages have been held. $182 million in ransom has been paid (although the total may surpass this, as families and

corporations are understandably wary of releasing such figures), while $335 million in ransom has been demanded (this
figure, by the way, does not include extortionate demands).
While revolutionary rhetoric would have us believe that terrorists are weak, and that their actions are designed to aid
"the people," portraying themselves as latter-day Robin Hoods,
only 6 percent of their ransom demands have been philan-
thropic in nature. The rest of the $300 million demanded has
been to fill their organizational coffers.

Since aerial hijacking began in 1931 with an attack in
Peru, there have been at least 618 attempted hijackings,
including one of a cropduster; 1,613 people have engaged in
this activity, resulting in 489 deaths and 334 injuries. The
most popular plane to divert has been the B-707, turning up
in 92 cases. In at least 70 cases (16 percent of the total), it
was later determined that the hijacker was carrying no weapon
whatsoever. And for those of you planning future flights,
July has been the worst month for flying, with 65 attempts,
while February has seen only 34 attempts.

Although traditional analysts of terrorism may be correct
in saying that most political violence occurs in less-developed
nations, this does not appear to hold true for transnational
attacks. In terms of numbers of attacks (with no weighting
for publicity or severity of attack), table 8.1A demonstrates
that industrialized nations are most often the scene of attacks.
This selection is due in part to better media coverage (although not all individuals who engage in terrorist actions are
seeking publicity), ease of operations in liberal democratic
societies, and perception by the offenders of suitability and
availability of targets.

Table 8.1B notes the groups which have engaged in the
largest number of incidents in the past decade. It becomes
readily apparent that leftist revolutionaries are not alone in
such activities. One cannot speak of a Terrorist International,
with common goals and sources of support. Individuals have
engaged in terrorist attacks for numerous reasons, and one
makes undifferentiated generalizations about their motivations
only at great peril. It becomes further apparent from the
table that those groups who have generated tremendous
publicity (such as the Baader-Meinhof Gang, the Japanese Red
Army, and Carlos' associates) have not felt it necessary to
engage in sustained campaigns, and have resorted instead to a
few spectaculars.

As shown in table 8.2, national involvement in specific
incidents ranges from being the victim or unwilling host of the
operation to entering into the episode's denouement, by
providing good offices in mediation or by granting safe haven.
Of note in this last regard is that, while Middle Eastern
nations have been criticized for being terrorist refuges, they
have refused asylum in more attacks than the rest of the world

Table 8.1
A. Location of Start of Transnational Terrorist Incidents*

Country	Number of Attacks, 1968-1977
United States	345
Argentina	327
United Kingdom	212
Italy	178
France	176
Israel	142
Lebanon	124
Greece	120
Netherlands	112
India	99
West Germany	99
Turkey	97

B. Group Claiming Responsibility for Incident

Group	Number of Attacks, 1968-1977
Irish Republican Army (IRA)	211
Black September Organization	137
Palestinians not noting affiliation	132
Popular Front for the Liberation of Palestine (PFLP)	79
People's Revolutionary Army - Argentina	57
Armed Forces of National Liberation - Puerto Rico	53
Montoneros-Argentina	36
Fatah	34
Croatian exiles	32
Jewish Defense League (JDL)	29
El Poder Cubano	27
Eritrean Liberation Front (ELF)	26
Peronist Armed Forces - Argentina	25
PFLP-General Command	23
Tupamaros	23

*Note: This table notes only the countries and groups for which the most incidents were reported. Numerous other nations and groups have been affected by transnational terrorism.

Table 8.2. Number of Incidents, by Region, of State Involvement in Terrorism

Region	Demand Target	Asylum Grantor	Asylum Denier	Ancillary	Victim	Terrorist	Starting Location	Ending Location
North America	14	–	–	8	1,471	165	390	395
Latin America	40	24	6	30	410	578	829	836
Western Europe	62	4	4	49	997	487	1,155	1,119
Eastern Europe	2	2	–	6	144	41	29	30
Africa	4	3	–	5	81	73	104	105
Middle East	49	37	25	84	758	631	494	553
Asia	18	2	4	18	136	146	292	220
Pacific	–	–	–	–	9	2	22	27

combined. Table 8.3 explores the relationships between these
types of national involvement. The first figure is the Pearson
correlation coefficient, with the eight regions as the cases.
The second figure in each cell is the Kendall rank-order
correlation, with corrections for ties, which avoids the variance dependency of Pearson's and is based upon roughly
equivalent variances for all variable pairs, allowing comparisons between cells. Interpretations are left to the reader.

RESEARCH APPLICATIONS

Tentative steps have also been taken to use ITERATE for more
than descriptive purposes. An earlier effort was reported by
the senior investigator to evaluate suggested hostage negotiation options.(4) This work was later replicated by Abraham
Miller at Cincinnati.(5) Milbank of CIA used the dataset in
two general surveys of global terrorism.(6) Researchers at
the Naval Postgraduate School studied the effect of the media
in spectacular incidents upon subsequent terrorist activity,
while others looked at the degree of threat to U.S. interests.(7)
    The dataset is frequently used as a simple data retrieval
device in preliminary searches for incidents of particular
interest to the researcher. (For example, a chronology can be
tailored to list all incidents reported between 1972 and 1975 of
attacks in selected nations by specific groups.) Such a
capability could, for example, allow one to engage in quasi-
experimental studies of the effects of penal policy changes.
The dataset can also be used to provide a history of previous
behavior by groups engaging in incidents similar to the one
faced by crisis managers.
    Finally, ITERATE has been used to study global diffusion
patterns of transnational terrorism over time. Our companion
piece(8) concentrates on the spatial patterns created by the
distribution of terrorist events within the international system
in the last decade. This research generates the hypothesis
that spontaneous generation of terrorism - that is, that it
occurs independently of parallel developments in other regions - is a random component or residual effect of a larger
diffusion process. A corollary is that terrorism diffuses by
means of imitation, through direct interpersonal contact
between terrorists and potential actors, and as a result of the
relocation or migration of terrorists to new locations. To
illustrate these points, the research introduces contiguity maps
which display longitudinal and spatial distributions, and
employs Markov chains to determine international systemic
stability, as well as the equilibrium states of terrorist activity
within certain geopolitical regions.

Table 8.3. Correlations Between Types of National Involvement

	Asylum Grantor	Asylum Denier	Ancillary	Victim	Terrorist	Starting Location	Ending Location
Target of Demands	.60 .59	.62 .70	.86 .86	.51 .57	.93 .79	.92 .86	.94 .86
Asylum Grantor		.91 .77	.82 .59	.13 .22	.83 .67	.36 .44	.42 .44
Asylum Denier			.92 .78	.21 .29	.75 .78	.29 .54	.34 .54
Ancillary				.38 .57	.88 .79	.60 .71	.64 .71
Victim					.44 .50	.56 .57	.58 .57
Terrorist						.81 .79	.85 .79
Starting Location							1.00 1.00

NOTES

1. The reasons for this arrested theoretical development are too numerous to mention here. See the remarks of J. Bowyer Bell to this conference, as well as Edward Mickolus "Reflections on the Study of Terrorism" in Complexity: A Challenge to the Adaptive Capacity of American Society, edited by Thomas Harries. Proceedings of a conference sponsored by the Society for General Systems Research, Columbia, Maryland, March 24-26, 1977.

2. Among the works we have found useful are Brian M. Jenkins and Janera Johnson, "International Terrorism: A Chronology, 1968-1974" (Santa Monica: The RAND Corporation, R-1597-DOS/ARPA, March 1975); David L. Milbank, International and Transnational Terrorism: Diagnosis and Prognosis (Washington, D.C.: Central Intelligence Agency, PR 76 10030, April 1976); Jordan J. Paust, "Terrorism and the International Law of War," Military Law Review 64 (1974): 1-36; and Martha Crenshaw Hutchinson, "The Concept of Revolutionary Terrorism" Journal of Conflict Resolution 16 (3) (September 1972): 383-96.

3. An extended discussion of this preliminary ITERATE (International Terrorism: Attributes of Terrorist Events) can be found in Edward Mickolus, "Statistical Approaches to the Study of Terrorism" in Terrorism: Interdisciplinary Perspectives edited by Yonah Alexander and Seymour Maxwell Finger (New York: John Jay Press, 1977), pp. 209-69. Those wishing copies of the pilot dataset should write the Inter-University Consortium for Political and Social Research, Box 1248, University of Michigan, Ann Arbor, Michigan.

4. Edward F. Mickolus, "Negotiating for Hostages: A Policy Dilemma," Orbis 19 (4) (Winter 1976): 1309-25.

5. Abraham H. Miller, "Negotiations for Hostages," paper presented to the 18th annual convention of the International Studies Association, St. Louis, March 16-20, 1977.

6. Milbank, International and Transnational Terrorism; and David L. Milbank, "International Terrorism in 1976" (Washington, D.C.: Central Intelligence Agency, RP 77-10034U, July 1977), 19 pp.

7. R.W. Peterson and W.G. Chrisman, International Terrorism Threat Analysis (Monterey, California: Naval Postgraduate School, Department of National Security Affairs, 1977).

8. A more extensive discussion can be found in chapter 9.

APPENDIX A: ITERATE VARIABLES

ITERATE includes data on 3,329 incidents of international terrorism from 1968 to 1977, as well as 528 nonterrorist hijackings from 1931-1977.   The COMMON file gives descriptions of all of the terrorist incidents.   The HOSTAGE file includes data on incidents of terrorist seizure of hostages. The FATE file notes the disposition of terrorists after the conclusion of the incident.   The SKYJACK file describes all hijackings, both terrorist and nonterrorist.   All entries, save where noted in SKYJACK, are coded numerically, although output can be either numeric or textual, depending upon the SPSS format requested by the user.   The four files are linked to each other through use of a four-digit identification code unique to each incident.

Filename: COMMON

General Category of Variable		Variable	Level of Measurement *
General Description	C	Quarter in which incident occurred	I
		Month	I
		Day	I
		Year	I
		Type of Event	N
		National Location of Start of Incident	N
	C	Regional Location of Start of Incident	N
		National Location of End of Incident	N
	C	Regional Location of End of Incident	N
		Physical Scene of Incident	N
		Total Nationalities Involved	R
		Logistic Error by Terrorists	D
		Success	O
		Weapons	O
Terrorist Characteristics		Number of Groups	R
		Name of Group (2 possible)	N
		Number of Nationalities of Terrorists	R
		Nationality of Terrorists (3 possible)	N
		Regional Nationality of Terrorists (3 possible)	N
		Number of Terrorists in Attack Force	R
Victim Characteristics		Number of Victim Nationalities	R
		Nationality of Victims (3 possible)	N
	C	Regional Nationality of Victims (3 possible)	N
		Type of U.S. Victim	N
		Type of Victim	N
		Physical Nature of Victim	N

(continued)

APPENDIX A (Continued)

Filename: COMMON (continued)

General Category of Variable		Variable	Level of Measurement *
Casualties and Damage		Total Wounded	R
		Terrorists Wounded	R
		Foreign Wounded	R
	C	Domestic Wounded	R
		Total Dead	R
		Terrorists Dead	R
		Foreign Dead	R
	C	Domestic Dead	R
	C	Total Casualties	R
	C	Terrorist Casualties	R
	C	Foreign Casualties	R
	C	Domestic Casualties	R
	C	Existence of Deaths	D
	C	Existence of Casualties	D
	C	Existence of Injuries	D
		Existence of Damage	D
		Dollar Damage due to Losses or Theft	R

Filename: HOSTAGE

	Variable	Level of Measurement
Characteristics of Demand Targets	Number of Governments Upon Which Demands Were Made	R
	Nation Upon Which Demands Were Made (3 possible)	N
	Regional Location of Nation Upon Which Demands Were Made (3 possible)	N
	Number of Nongovernmental Actors Upon Which Demands Were Made	R
	Nongovernmental Actor Upon Which Demands Were Made (2 possible)	N
	Demands Against Host Nation	D
General Characteristics of Demands	Prisoner Release	D
	Political Changes	D
	Safe Passage	D
	Publication	D
	Other Nonlogistic Demands	D
	Terrorist Ability to Forward Demands	N
Specific Characteristics of Demands	Number of Prisoners Released	R
	Number of Prisoners Whose Release was Demanded	R
	Destination of Released Prisoners	N
	Code Number of Incident in Which Prisoner Had Engaged	N
	Dollar Amount of Ransom Paid	R

(continued)

APPENDIX A (Continued)

Filename: HOSTAGE (continued)

General Category of Variable	Variable	Level of Measurement *
Specific Characteristics of Demands (continued)	Dollar Amount of Ransom Demanded	R
	Dollar Amount of Philanthropic Ransom Paid	R
	Dollar Amount of Philanthropic Ransom Demanded	R
	Dollar Amount of Organizational Coffers Ransom Paid	R
	Dollar Amount of Organizational Coffers Ransom Demanded	R
	Type of Ransom Demanded	N
Negotiation Characteristics	Terrorist Negotiation Behavior Regarding Demands	N
	Sequential Hostage Release	D
	Substitution of Hostages	D
	Deadline Adherence	N
	Type of Negotiators	N
	Number of Negotiators	R
	Response of Target of Demands	N
	Source of Ransom Payment	N
Victim Fate	Number of Hostages	R
	Fate of Victims (2 possible)	N
	Hours of Hostage Detention	R
	Month of End of Incident	I
	Day of End of Incident	I
	Year of End of Incident	I
Terrorist Fate	Number of Asylum Deniers	R
	Nation Denying Asylum (2 possible)	N
	C Regional Location of Nation Denying Asylum (2 possible)	N
	Number of Asylum Grantors	R
	Nation Granting Asylum (2 possible)	N
	C Regional Location of Nation Granting Asylum (2 possible)	N
	Number of Nations with Ancillary Involvement	R
	Nation with Ancillary Involvement (2 possible)	N
	C Regional Location of Nation with Ancillary Involvement (2 possible)	N

Filename: SKYJACK

General Description	Month in Which Hijacking Occurred	I
	Day	I
	Year	I
	Plane Transfer	N

(continued)

APPENDIX A (Continued)

Filename: SKYJACK (continued)

General Category of Variable	Variable	Level of Measurement *
General Description (continued)	Number of Crewmen	R
	Number of Individuals on Plane	R
	Number of Hijackers	R
	Number of Refuelings and Other Stopovers	R
	Number Wounded	R
	Number Dead	R
	Success	O
	Weapons	O
Characteristics of Those Involved	US Aircraft Involved	D
	Carrier	N
	Type of Plane	N
	FAA Profile Applicability	N
Location	Initial Embarkation Point	A
	Hijacker Embarkation Point	A
	Scheduled Landing Point	A
	Hijacking Ending Point	A

Filename: FATE

Offender Disposition	Penal Fate (4 possible)	N
	Number Receiving Fate (4 possible)	R
	Months Served (2 possible)	R
Extradition Characteristics	Extradition Requested	D
	Extradition Requestor	N
	Extradition Granted	D
	Extradition Grantor	N

---

*Level of Measurement refers to the type of information conveyed by the numerical coding. The level determines the applicability of certain statistical techniques available in the SPSS ITERATE dataset. A C appearing before a variable name means that the item was computed from other values in the dataset, and does not itself appear on the input records. The absence of a C indicates a variable which is input into the system by the user.

A Alphanumeric (textual) characters not retrievable via SPSS but residing in ITERATE dataset.

D Dichotomy

N Nominal

O Ordinal

I Interval

R Ratio

APPENDIX B: PILOT ITERATE VARIABLES

The Pilot version of ITERATE includes data on 539 incidents of transnational terrorism from 1968 to 1974. Only one data file is available.
All entries are coded numerically, although output can be either numeric
or textual, depending upon the SPSS format requested by the user.
Four-digit identification codes are used to identify each incident. Variables appearing with as asterisk (*) are pilot variables which were not
carried over into the present version of ITERATE.

General Category of Variable		Variable	Level of Measurement
General Description		Month in which incident began	I
		Day	I
		Year	I
		Type of Event	N
		National Location	N
	*	Urban Environ	N
		Physical Scene of Incident	N
	*	Warning	D
	*	Attributed Purpose of Attack	N
	*	Month in which incident ended	I
	*	Day on which incident ended	I
	*	Year in which incident ended	I
	*	Length in Days of Incident	R
American Involvement	*	US Citizens as Victims	D
	*	US Ships or Aircraft Involved	D
	*	US Official Installations Involved	D
	*	US Corporation Involved	D
	*	US Government as Demand Target	D
Victim Characteristics	*	Indiscriminate Victim Selection	D
		Victim Nationality (4 possible)	N
		Number of Victim Nationalities	R
		Number of Hostages	R
		Type of US Victim	N
	*	Hostage Rank	O
		Type of Victim	N
		Physical Nature of Victims	N
		Victim Fate	N
Terrorist Characteristics	*	Group Popularly Believed Responsible (4 possible)	N
		Group Claiming Credit (4 possible)	N
	*	Group Actually Responsible (4 possible)	N
	*	Group Denying Responsibility (4 possible)	N
		Number of Groups Involved	R
		Terrorist Nationality (4 possible)	N
		Number of Terrorist Nationalities	R
	*	Fedayeen	D
		Number of Terrorists	R
	*	Number of Male Terrorists	R
	*	Number of Female Terrorists	R
	*	Terrorist Leadership	D

(continued)

APPENDIX B (Continued)

General Category of Variable	Variable	Level of Measurement
Terrorist Characteristics (continued)	* Mean Age of Terrorists	R
	* Age Range of Terrorists	R
	* Mode Education of Terrorists	O
	* Group Views Toward Own Death	O
Casualties and Damage	Domestic Wounded	R
	Foreign Wounded	R
	Police Wounded	R
	Terrorists Wounded	R
	Domestic Dead	R
	Foreign Dead	R
	Police Dead	R
	Terrorists Dead	R
	Dollar Losses	R
Terrorist Fate	* Number Dead in Shootout with Police	R
	* Killed Selves at Scene	R
	* Dead via Death Penalty	R
	* Long Jail Term	R
	* Long Jail Term, Release Demanded in Subsequent Incident	R
	* Long Jail Term, Released due to Demands in Subsequent Incident	R
	* Short Jail Term	R
	* Short Jail Term, Release Demanded in Subsequent Incident	R
	* Short Jail Term, Released due to Demands in Subsequent Incident	R
	* Freed via Court Verdict	R
	* Escaped Captors	R
	* Granted Asylum	R
	* Not Tried by Courts	R
	* Ultimate Destination	N
Extradition Characteristics	Requested	D
	Requestor	N
	Granted	D
	Grantor	N
Characteristics of Demand Targets	* Type of Target	N
	Number of Governments upon which Demands were made	R
	Nation upon which Demands were made (4 possible)	N
	Number of Nongovernmental Actors upon which Demands were made	R
	Nongovernmental Actors upon which Demands were made (4 possible)	N
	Demands Against Host Nation	D

(continued)

APPENDIX B (Continued)

General Category of Variable	Variable	Level of Measurement
General Characteristics of Demands	Monetary	D
	* Arms	D
	* Release Members of Own Group	D
	* Release Other Prisoners	D
	* Independence	D
	Political Changes	D
	Safe Passage	D
	Publication	D
	* Change Sentences of Prisoners	D
	Other Nonlogistic Demands	D
	Terrorist Ability to Forward Demands	N
	* No Demands Made	D
Specific Characteristics of Demands	Number of Prisoners Released	R
	Number of Prisoners Whose Release Was Demanded	R
	Dollar Amount of Ransom Paid	R
	Dollar Amount of Ransom Demanded	R
	Dollar Amount of Philanthropic Ransom Demanded	R
	Dollar Amount of Philanthropic Ransom Paid	R
	Dollar Amount of Organizational Coffers Ransom Demanded	R
	Dollar Amount of Organizational Coffers Ransom Paid	R
	Type of Ransom Demanded	N
Negotiation Characteristics	Terrorist Negotiation Behavior Regarding Demands	N
	Type of Negotiators	N
	Response of Target of Demands	N
	* Objective of Pressure by Victim Government Upon Host Government	N
	Source of Ransom Payment	N
	* Number of Governments Spontaneously Denying Safe Haven	R
	* Governments Spontaneously Denying Safe Haven (4 possible)	N
	* Number of Governments Denying Safe Haven Request	R
	* Governments Denying Safe Haven Request (4 possible)	N
	* Number of Governments Spontaneously Granting Asylum	R
	* Governments Spontaneously Granting Asylum (4 possible)	N
	* Number of Governments Granting Asylum Request	R
	* Governments Granting Asylum Request (4 possible)	N

APPENDIX C: ITERATE DATA SOURCES

Analysis of the Terrorist Threat to the Commercial Nuclear Industry, report submitted to the Special Safeguards Study, Nuclear Regulatory Commission, Washington, D.C., in response to Contract No. AT (49-24)-0131 (Vienna, Virginia: The BDM Corporation, September 30, 1975, BDM/75-176-TR), 414 pp.

"Appendix A: Hijackings of Planes to Cuba and Frustrated Attempts to Hijack" in Air Piracy in the Caribbean Area, Report of the Subcommittee on Inter-American Affairs, Committee on Foreign Affairs, US House of Representatives (90th Congress, Second Session, December 10, 1968), pp. 9-11.

"The Arab Communist Organisation" IV-42, 350 Fiches du Monde Arabe (August 6, 1975).

Arey, James A. The Sky Pirates. New York: Scribner's, 1972, 360 pp.

Baumann, Carol Edler. The Diplomatic Kidnappings: A Revolutionary Tactic of Urban Terrorism. The Hague: Nijhoff, 1973, 182 pp.

Bell, J. Bowyer. The Myth of the Guerrilla: Revolutionary Theory and Malpractice. New York: Alfred A. Knopf, 1971, 285 pp.

Bell, J. Bowyer. "Assassination in International Politics: Lord Moyne, Count Bernadotte, and the Lehi," International Studies Quarterly 16 (1) (March 1972): 59-82.

Ben-Dor, Gabriel. "The Strategy of Terrorism in the Arab-Israeli Conflict: The Case of the Palestinian Guerrillas - Appendix: Arab Cross-National Terrorism 1968-1974." Israel: University of Haifa, 1976, mimeo, 52 pp.

Bilinsky, Yaroslav. "The Background of Contemporary Politics in the Baltic Republics and the Ukraine: Comparisons and Contrasts" in Problems of Mininations: Baltic Perspectives. Edited by Arvids Ziedonis, Jr., Rein Taagepera, and Mardi Valgemae. California State University, San Jose: Association for the Advancement of Baltic Studies, Inc., 1973.

"Bomb Summary: A Comprehensive Report of Incidents Involving Explosive and Incendiary Devices in the Nation." Washington, D.C.: U.S. Department of Justice, FBI Uniform Crime Reports, (1972), 27 pp.; (1973), 28 pp.; (1974), 32 pp.; (1975), 35 pp.

"Bombing Incidents, Mob Action and Harassment Against US Installations Overseas, July 1, 1969-June 30, 1970." Washington, D.C.: U.S. Information Agency, September 4, 1970, 51 pp.

Bowden, Tom. "The IRA and the Changing Tactics of Terrorism," The Political Quarterly (London) 47 (4) (October-December 1976): 425-38.

"Briefing Packet." Washington, D.C.: U.S. Information Agency Seminar on International Terrorism, August 11, 1975.

"Chronology of Attacks upon Non-Official American Citizens, 1971-1975." Washington, D.C.: U.S. Department of State, Cabinet Committee to Combat Terrorism Working Group, January 20, 1976, 6 pp.

"Chronology of Hijackings 1968 through 1975." Washington, D.C.: U.S. Department of State, Cabinet Committee to Combat Terrorism Working Group, 1976, 16 pp.

"Chronology of Hijackings of US Registered Aircraft and Current Legal Status of Hijackers, as of January 1, 1976." Washington, D.C.: Federal Aviation Administration, Civil Aviation Security Service (1976), 46 pp.; (1977), 48 pp.

"Chronology of Major Events in Domestic and International Terrorism," Counterforce (issues since January 1977).

"Chronology of Sabotage and Terrorism Against Cuba: 1973-1976." Paper distributed by Venceremos at Latin American Studies conference, Pittsburgh, Fall 1976.

"Chronology of Significant Terrorist Incidents Involving US Diplomatic/Official Personnel, 1963-1975." Washington, D.C.: U.S. Department of State, January 20, 1976, 7 pp.

"Chronology of Terrorist Attacks in Lima, Peru in 1974," Caretas, November 11, 1974.

"Chronology of Unlawful Interference with Civil Aviation." Montreal: International Civil Aviation Organization (1969), 12 pp.; (1970), 14 pp.; (1971), 11 pp.; (1972), 18 pp.; (1973), 8 pp.; (1974), 6 pp.; (1975), 6 pp.; (1976), 5 pp.

Clutterbuck, Richard. Living With Terrorism. London: Faber and Faber, 1975, 160 pp.

Clyne, Peter. An Anatomy of Skyjacking. London: Abelard-Schumann, 1973, 200 pp.

Cooley, John K. Green March, Black September: The Story of the Palestinian Arabs. London: Frank Cass, 1973, 263 pp.

Crozier, Brian. Annual of Power and Conflict 1974-1975. London: Institute for the Study of Conflict, 1975; 1975-1976 (1976), 1976-1977 (1977).

Cutter, Curtis. Interview with the author, February 1976.

Dobson, Christopher. Black September: Its Short, Violent History. New York: Macmillan, 1974, 179 pp.

Dobson, Christopher. and Ronald Payne The Carlos Complex. New York: Putnam's, 1977, 254 pp.

"Domestic and Foreign Aircraft Hijackings, as of July 1, 1976." Washington, D.C.: Federal Aviation Administration, Civil Aviation Security Service, 1976, 61 pp.; January 1, 1977 update (1977), 63 pp.

Dortzbach, Karl and Debbie. Kidnapped. New York: Harper and Row, 1975, 179 pp.

Elliott, John D. "Action and Reaction: West Germany and the Baader-Meinhof Guerrillas," Strategic Review 4 (1) (Winter 1976): 60-67.

"Explosions Aboard Aircraft, as of January 1, 1976." Washington, D.C.: Federal Aviation Administration, Civil Aviation Security Service, 1976, 20 pp.; (1977), 19 pp.

Fly, Claude. No Hope But God. New York: Hawthorne, 1973, 220 pp.

Goldblatt, Messick, Hank Goldblatt, and Burt Goldblatt. Kidnapping: The Illustrated History. New York: Dial, 1974, 206 pp.

Hacker, Frederick. Crusaders, Criminals and Crazies. New York: Norton, 1976, 355 pp.

"Hijacking Statistics, US Registered Aircraft, 1961-Present, Updated January 1, 1977." Washington, D.C.: Federal Aviation Administration, Civil Aviation Security Service, 1977, 18 pp.

Jenkins, Brian Michael. "Hostage Survival: Some Preliminary Observations" (Santa Monica: The RAND Corporation, April 1975), presented to the US Information Agency's International Terrorism Seminar, Washington, D.C., August 11, 1975.

Jenkins, Brian Michael. "International Terrorism: A New Mode of Conflict." Santa Monica: California Arms Control and Foreign Policy Seminar Research Paper 48, published by Los Angeles: Crescent Publications, January 1975, 51 pp.

Jenkins, Brian Michael. "International Terrorism: A New Mode of Conflict" in International Terrorism and World Security edited by David Carlton and Carlo Schaerf. London: Croom Helm, 1975, pp. 13-49.

Jenkins, Brian Michael, and Janera Johnson. "International Terrorism: A Chronology, 1968-1974." Santa Monica: The RAND Corporation, R-1597-DOS/ARPA, March 1975, 58 pp.

Jenkins, Brian Michael, and Janera A. Johnson. "International Terrorism: A Chronology, 1974 Supplement." Santa Monica: The RAND Corporation, R-1909-1-ARPA, February 1976, 23 pp.

Kohl, James, and John Litt. Urban Guerrilla Warfare in Latin America. Cambridge, Mass.: MIT Press, 1974, 425 pp.

"Legal Status of Hijackers, Summarization, Updated January 1, 1976." Washington, D.C.: Federal Aviation Administration, Civil Aviation Security Service, 1976, 1977 update (1977), 6 pp.

Mallin, Jay, ed. Terror and Urban Guerrillas: A Study of Tactics and Documents. Coral Gables, Florida: University of Miami Press, 1971, 176 pp.

"Meir Kahane: A Candid Conversation with the Militant Leader of the Jewish Defense League," Playboy 19 (10) (October 1972): 69ff.

Moss, Robert. The War for the Cities. New York: Coward, McCann and Geoghegan, 1972, 288 pp.; published in England as Urban Guerrillas: The New Face of Political Violence. London: Temple Smith, 1971.

Nanes, Allan S. "International Terrorism." Washington, D.C.: Library of Congress, Congressional Research Service, Major Issues System, Issue Brief IB74042, May 11, 1977, 28 pp.

Parry, Albert. Terrorism from Robespierre to Arafat. New York: Vanguard, 1976, 538 pp.

Phillips, David. Skyjack: The Story of Air Piracy. London: Harrap, 1973, 288 pp.

"Report of the Task Force on Disorders and Terrorism." Washington, D.C.: National Advisory Committee on Criminal Justice Standards and Goals, 1976, 661 pp.

Rich, Elizabeth. Flying Scared. New York: Stein and Day; and Toronto: Saunders, 1972, 194 pp.

Russell, Charles A., James F. Schenkel, and James A. Miller. "Urban Guerrillas in Argentina: A Select Bibliography," Latin American Research Review 9 (3) (Fall 1974): 53-89.

"Significant Worldwide Criminal Acts Involving Civil Aviation 1976." Washington, D.C.: Federal Aviation Administration, Civil Aviation Security Service, 1977, 16 pp.

Smith, Colin. Carlos: Portrait of a Terrorist. London: Sphere, 1976, 304 pp.

Snow. Peter, and David Phillips. The Arab Hijack War. New York: Ballantine, 1970, 176 pp.

Sobel, Lester A. ed. Political Terrorism. New York: Facts on File, 1975, 309 pp.

Steinhoff, Patricia. "Portrait of a Terrorist: An Interview with Kozo Okamoto," Asia Survey 16 (9) (September 1976): 830-45.

Stevenson, William. 90 Minutes at Entebbe. New York: Bantam Books, 1976, 216 pp.

"Subject: Japanese Red Army." Washington, D.C.: Embassy of Japan, n.d., mimeo.

"Summary and Analysis of Security Incidents Overseas: August 1, 1953-May 20, 1959." Washington, D.C.: U.S. Information Agency, Office of Security, declassified by Richard Bond, IOS/P, June 7, 1976, 37 pp.

The Terrorist and Sabotage Threat to US Nuclear Programs: Phase One Final Report. Prepared for Sandia Laboratories under Contract No. 82-9139 by the Historical Evaluation and Research Organization, Dunn Loring, Virginia, August 1974.

"Threats of Violence and Acts of Violence to Licensed Nuclear Facilities, 1969-1975." Washington, D.C.: U.S. Nuclear Regulatory Commission, 1976, 3 pp.; 1976-February 23, 1977 update (1977), 6 pp.; August 22, 1976-March 3, 1977 update (1977), 1 p.

Tinnin, David B. "The Wrath of God," Playboy 23 (8) (August 1976): 70-74.

Tinnin, David B. with Dag Christensen. The Hit Team. Boston: Little, Brown, 1976, 240 pp.

U.S. Department of State Airgram A-066 (Unclassified) from American Embassy, Guatemala, June 14, 1976, Enclosure: "Major Terrorist Acts Attributable to the Extreme Left in Guatemala, January 1970-May 1976," 7 pp.

U.S. House of Representatives. Political Kidnappings 1963-73, a Staff Study prepared by the Committee on Internal Security (93rd Congress, 1st session, August 1, 1973), 54 pp.

U.S. Information Agency. "Dissident and Terrorist Acts Against US Installations and Personnel Overseas, July 1, 1965-June 30, 1967." Available through Office of Security, USIA, Washington, D.C., 26 pp. "July Through December 1971, with Analysis of Targetting Against USIS Installations and Personnel." 31 pp.; "January 1 through March 31, 1972." (May 19, 1972), 8 pp.; "April 1 through September 30, 1972." (January 11, 1973), 28 pp.; "October 1, 1972 through December 31, 1972." (March 19, 1973), 14 pp.

U.S. Information Agency. "Incidents Against US Installations Abroad July 1, 1967 - June 30, 1968." Memorandum to IOS, Mr. Paul J. McNichol from IOS/P Charles M. Dulin, July 22, 1968, 22 pp.

U.S. Information Agency. "Report of Bombing Incidents, Mob Action and Harassment Against US Installations Overseas July 1, 1968-June 30, 1969." Washington, D.C.: USIA, IOS 11997, July 31, 1969, 16 pp.

U.S. Information Agency. "Reports of Significant Security Incidents, Worldwide, 1976." Washington, D.C.: USIA IOS/P, 1977, 40 pp.

U.S. Information Agency. "Significant Security Incidents of Overseas Installations for Calendar Years 1973, 1974 and 1975." Washington, D.C.: USIA Office of Security, 1976, 34 pp.

U.S. Senate, Committee on the Judiciary, Subcommittee to Investigate the Administration of the Internal Security Act and Other Internal Security Laws. "Terroristic Activity: International Terrorism, Part 4, Hearings." 94th Congress, 1st session, May 14, 1975.

United Nations document A/c.1/L.872, November 20, 1972.

Watson, Frank. Political Terrorism. New York: McKay, 1976, 248 pp.

Whelton, Charles. Skyjack. New York: Tower, 1970.

Wilkinson, Paul. Political Terrorism. New York: Wiley, 1975, 160 pp.

Wilkinson, Paul. "Terrorism Versus Liberal Democracy: The Problems of Response," Conflict Studies 67 (January 1976).

Williams, Marilyn. "Chronology of Attacks Upon Non-Official American Citizens 1971-1976." Washington, D.C.: U.S. Department of State, Cabinet Committee to Combat Terrorism Working Group, 1976, 6 pp.

Williams, Marilyn. "Chronology of Significant Terrorist Incidents Involving US Diplomatic/Official Personnel and Installations 1963-1976." Washington, D.C.: U.S. Department of State, Cabinet Committee to Combat Terrorism Working Group, July 1976, 16 pp.

"Worldwide Criminal Acts Involving Civil Aviation 1974." Washington, D.C.: Federal Aviation Administration, Civil Aviation Security Service, 1975, 9 pp.; "1975", 8 pp.; "January-June 1976", 8 pp.

The aforementioned data sources have been supplemented by accounts given by the Associated Press, United Press International and Reuter Tickers, Foreign Broadcast Information Service, ABC FM Radio News, ABC, NBC, and CBS Evening News, the Detroit Free Press, New Haven Register, New York Times, Washington Post, and Washington Star. Chronologies from journalistic sources which have proven helpful include:

ABC News Olympic Special, 8 p.m., January 5, 1976.

Chicago Tribune (June 18, 1974).

Chronologies provided the author by Dr. Carol Edler Baumann.

The Economist (August 9, 1975).

New York Times (December 20, 1973), and (May 16, 1974).

"One Act of Guerrilla Violence After Another: Major Arab Terrorist Attacks in the Last 3½ Years," US News and World Report, May 27, 1974.

"Terrorists: Where are they now?" The Economist, March 9, 1974.

Washington Post-Parade, March 16, 1975, p. 7.

9

Imitation by Terrorists: Quantitative Approaches to the Study of Diffusion Patterns in Transnational Terrorism

Edward Heyman
Edward Mickolus

INTRODUCTION AND PURPOSE

Spatial diffusion refers to the spread of a particular phenomenon, or class of phenomena, within a given environment
over time. The topic of our discussion is the diffusion of
transnational terrorism within the international system.

Terrorism is by no means a new phenomenon. Individuals
and groups throughout history have used select acts of terror
to wrest political concessions from their foes, or to impose
control over them. What is new about terrorism is how it is
used, and the frequency with which it is used. The growing
complexity of the international system, and developments in the
technologies of travel, mass communication, and weapons, allow
this old tactic to take on new dimensions. Today, terrorism
spreads farther and faster, and affects more nations and
people, than ever before. The ramifications of terrorist acts
are no longer contained within individual countries, but spill
like so much oil into the international arena.

This chapter explores new analytical techniques for
understanding how and why terrorism diffuses in the international system. We infer, on the basis of our research, that
terrorism does, in fact, diffuse. The acts which confront us

---

*Originally presented to the Joint National Meeting of the
Operations Research Society of America and The Institute for
Management Sciences, New York City, May 1-3, 1978. The
institutional affiliation of the authors should in no way be
interpreted as a statement of the views or policy of the
United States Government or any of its agencies.

175

are not random occurrences arising out of spontaneous generation.   Our inference is bolstered with a discussion of
adjacency maps which illustrate the spatial distribution of
transnational terrorist incidents.   We will also explore a new
application of Markov chains to determine the stability of the
international system, and find the equilibrium states of terrorist activity within certain geopolitical regions of the world.

DIFFUSION RESEARCH

Some background on basic diffusion processes will be useful
before we discuss transnational terrorism.   In this section, we
will present the conceptual framework with which we will be
working.(1)
        The concept of diffusion has been implicit in a number of
popularly held notions in international relations.   The "domino
theory" underlying the policy of containment is an excellent
example of a conceptual structure built over an implied diffusion process.   The "no-bargaining" policy of the United
States in dealing with terrorist acts is another example.   The
belief that capitulation to terrorists will only encourage others
to make similar demands is based on a concept of diffusion
which sees ideas traveling within an environment over time.
        Conceptually, diffusion describes or "explains" changes in
the observed spatial distribution or location of a phenomenon
over time.   The task at hand is to account for the phenomenon
being in one place at time t+1 when it was observed elsewhere
at time t.   We can identify four types of diffusion processes:
relocation, expansion, contagion, and hierarchical.   The first
two deal with the pattern of movement, while the latter two
deal more with the mechanics of the diffusion process.
        Relocation diffusion refers to members of a population
moving from one place to another between times t and t+1.
The change may be the result of migration, or simple travel.
Population here refers to the classes of phenomena under
investigation, and may be anything from military bases, to
weaponry, individuals, religious groups, or terrorist cells.
        Expansion occurs when new members are added to the
population between time t and t+1, and are located in such a
way as to alter the spatial distribution of the population as a
whole.   It can also be used to describe cases in which an
event in one place gives rise to a similar occurrence elsewhere, or can be shown to correlate with it.
        The difference between relocation and expansion diffusion
lies in what leads to the change in the observed spatial
distribution of the phenomenon.   Change through relocation is
the result of the actual movement of the population from one
location to another.   Change by expansion, on the other hand,

is accounted for by the introduction of new members to the population. The original members need not move; indeed, in expansion diffusion they need never move. Another way to see the distinction is to note the size of the population. In relocation diffusion, the population size may remain constant over time, while in expansion diffusion, the population necessarily grows from one time period to the next.

The second set of diffusion processes deals more with the mechanics of diffusion. Contagious diffusion is the spread of the phenomenon through direct interpersonal contact between diffusers and adopters. According to this view, rumors, cultural traits, or terrorist tactics are passed from one individual to another. However, contagion is strongly influenced by the frictional effect of distance, as formalized by John Q. Stewart in the law which bears his name.(2) The possible number of interactions between two groups of individuals is a function of the intervening distance which separates them:

$$X = \frac{p_1 p_2}{d},$$

where p_1 and p_2 are the size of the respective populations or groups, d is the distance between them, and X is the number of interactions between them. The number of interactions (X) decreases as the distance (d) increases.

Hierarchical diffusion, on the other hand, applies where distance is not the strongest influence on interaction. Here, ideas and innovations tend to leapfrog over intervening people and space. Hierarchical diffusion describes the spread of news, innovations, or commands through a structured network. Large places and cities, or important people, receive the news first, and transmit it to others lower down in the hierarchy.

The relationship between the different types of diffusion can be seen in the figure 9.1. It should be noted that the diffusion processes are not necessarily one type or another. The categories in this figure are not mutually exclusive. In a multistage diffusion process, say the news of a terrorist incident, word might be sent over the news wires to major cities in a hierarchical pattern. Once received, however, the news might spread through the cities and towns in a manner more resembling contagion.

THE DIFFUSION OF TRANSNATIONAL TERRORISM

We will now use this conceptual framework to analyze the spread of transnational terrorism within the international system during the period from January 1, 1968 to December 31, 1977. The following discussion is based on certain ma-

	contagious	hierarchical
expansion	ideas and innovations at local levels: riots, diseases, mass action, regional wars	ideas, innovations at central places; elite actions; transnational phenomena
relocation	migration waves; refugees moving away from a spreading conflict	elite migration, i.e., patterns of exile; movement of corporations or the location of military bases

Fig. 9.1.   The Relationship Between Different Types of Diffusion.

nipulations of the ITERATE databank presented in chapter 8 of this volume.   ITERATE employs an events data approach to the study of terrorism, taking the individual incident as its unit of analysis.(3)   ITERATE fills a critical gap in terrorism research by providing a comprehensive and detailed data source on terrorist incidents.   The number of data points is sufficiently large not only to allow statistical manipulation, but to lend credence to the findings.

There are, of course, certain problems and limitations in using such an approach.   Altering the definition of terrorism and the types of events to be studied may affect some statistical findings and distributions.   However, this chapter is designed more to suggest the utility and implications for research of applying the concept of spatial diffusion to the study of terrorism, than to present concrete results.   The results presented here are subject to refinement and expansion.

THE ADJACENCY MAPS

For this study, ITERATE data were aggregated by country and year for the period from January 1, 1968 to December 31, 1977.   Crosstabulations were made which matched each country that experienced transnational terrorist incidents with the number of incidents it experienced for each of the ten years. The data were then plotted on adjacency maps to facilitate the observation of the spatial distribution of the data.

Political maps of the world are usually drawn to show a country's area or territory.   Each state in a conventional map spans a given area.   To display information about states, whether the quality of life, the level of literacy, the economic system, or the number of terrorist incidents experienced, each state is shaded or colored according to the assigned value. However, two problems arise. First, smaller countries are difficult to shade; and second, larger countries tend to distort the overall qualitative distribution of the data. The adjacency map attempts to remedy these problems in a way which enhances the display of spatial patterns.

The adjacency map, as designed by Claudio Cioffi-Revilla, is based on two criteria. (These maps are located in Appendix C.) First, each state, regardless of its size, is represented by a single point or node which indicates its location. Second, each node is linked to its neighbors by lines or edges which represent the borders.

When an adjacency map is used to plot data for states, the common regional qualities can be seen easily. The regional patterns which emerge are not distorted by territorial size. As regional patterns can change from year to year, maps are drawn for each time period for which we have data, allowing ready observation of the changes in the patterns of distribution. The maps are particularly useful for displaying diffusion patterns, represented on the maps as a series of contour lines.

Our findings are based on four sets of maps. One set shows the cumulative diffusion of transnational terrorism. Beginning with 1968, a map was drawn for each succeeding year showing the yearly accumulation of states affected by transnational terrorism. The contour lines indicate those countries that experienced incidents. The squares indicate states that experienced incidents for the first time during the time period of the map, while the triangles indicate those states that saw no activity for a period of two or more years. The second set of maps shows the diffusion of a specific type of incident, terrorist kidnappings, and follows the same guidelines as the cumulative diffusion maps. A third set was constructed showing the cumulative diffusion of terrorist skyjackings. The final set shows the annual location and intensity of terrorist activity. In this set, the contours indicate the number of incidents the country experienced during the year of the map, allowing a quick observation of the annual frequency and intensity of terrorism. We should note here that the maps do not distinguish or weight the various kinds of terrorist incidents. Bombings, kidnappings, assassinations, armed assaults, and barricade and hostage incidents are treated equally, except in those maps which focus on a single type of incident.

Careful inspection of the maps allows a number of conclusions. The cumulative diffusion maps indicate the extent to which geographical proximity is a factor in the diffusion of transnational terrorism. It is interesting to note not only the new countries which enter in each time period, but the pattern of countries which are removed from the distribution. African countries, in particular, have a tendency to "drop out" of the pattern soon after they enter.

Observation of the maps that display only terrorist sky-jackings and kidnappings show the rapidity with which incidents diffuse throughout Western Europe and Latin America. The maps indicating the annual intensity of terrorist activity show Western Europe, Latin America, the Middle East, and North America as the hardest hit regions. Sub-Saharan Africa and Asia experienced relatively few incidents. The intensity maps also indicate a marked shift in the location over time of the hardest hit regions. High intensity terrorism apparently moved from Latin America into the Middle East, and then into Western Europe. After 1972, Western Europe became a "sink" for high levels of terrorist activity.

THE MARKOV CHAINS

The observations of regional intensities are borne out by an investigation of the equilibrium states of the regions. First order Markov chains showing the transition rates between levels of terrorist activity were constructed for Western Europe, the Middle East, and Latin America on the basis of 40 three-month periods from January 1968 to December 1977. (These can be found in Appendix B).

Markov chains show the probable movement of a process between states. Markov chains consist of a set of undefined states, and a set of real numbers called transition probabilities. We generated two sets of Markov chains, each employing a different definition of "state." The first set shows the absolute increase or decrease over the last time period of the number of incidents occurring within each region. Here, "state" is defined as an increase, a decrease, or an absence of change in the level of activity. In the second set, each state represents a defined level of activity, and the Markov chains for each region show the probable movement of the process between the levels of activity.

ITERATE data was aggregated by region and three month periods to allow the construction of the Markov chains. The changes in the level of activity were plotted in NxN matrices to determine the initial transition probability matrices. To find the long-term or asymptotic behavior of the regions, we then raised the initial transition matrices to a higher power, generating the stationary state of the matrices.

The stationary state matrices show the long-term probability of movement between the "states." The row probability vectors indicate the equilibrium state of the process. While it would be possible to use these stationary states as a forecasting tool, the assumption of stationarity "requires that the parameters remain constant throughout the predictive period."(4)   We find the necessary imposition of the ceteris paribus overly restrictive, and will use the stationary state as a descriptive rather than a predictive tool.(5)

The time period for transition was three months, allowing 39 transitions between January 1968 and December 1977.   Table 9.1 shows the initial and stationary states of the Markov chains.   Inspection of the Markov chains indicating simple increases or decreases of activity shows that the overall tendency of the international system is to absorb increasing amounts of terrorist activity.   Each of the three regions investigated tends to oscillate between increasing and decreasing levels of activity.   The second set of Markov chains indicates that Western Europe gravitates toward the highest level of activity (i.e., more than 28 incidents per quarter), while the Middle East seems grounded in the first two levels (less than 19 incidents per quarter).   Much of Western Europe's high level of activity derives from massive letter-bombing campaigns, and the fact that Western Europe tends to be the location of activities perpetrated by terrorists from other regions.   Latin America is a curious case, with near equal probability of moving from any state to any other state.

The following observations can be made from the adjacency maps and the two sets of Markov chains:

1. The diffusion process is hierarchical between regions at first, and then becomes contagious within the regions.
2. The rate of contagion varies according to region, and according to the type of incident.
3. Incidents tend to diffuse most rapidly in Latin America. Western Europe tends to have the highest levels of activity.
4. Border contiguity appears to account for a large amount of diffusion.   In 78 of the 88 cases of new countries experiencing transnational terrorism after 1968, the country shared a border with a state which had previously experienced incidents.
5. Some regions seem immune to particular types of incidents. For instance, most of the Sub-Saharan region in Africa is unaffected by terrorism in general.   Asia and Africa were left relatively unaffected by terrorist skyjacking.   Kidnapping diffused little outside of Latin America, Western Europe, the Middle East, and Southern Africa.
6. Theoretically, the diffusion of any phenomenon within a finite population will reach a saturation point.   Transnational terrorism appears to have reached its saturation point at the end of 1973 or early 1974.   This does not refer to a reduction in the recorded number of incidents, but to a reduction in the rate with which terrorism spread to previously unaffected countries.

Table 9.1.

The first set of Markov chains defines "state" as follows:

state 1: an absolute increase in the level of activity over the preceding period.

state 2: an absolute decrease in the level of activity over the preceding period.

state 3: no change in the level of activity over the preceding period.

region*	initial state			stationary state**		
Latin	.35	.65.	0.0	.44	.55	0.0
America	.52	.48	0.0	.44	.55	0.0
	0.0	0.0	0.0	0.0	0.0	0.0
Western	.22	.72	.06	.48	.46	.06
Europe	.76	.18	.06	.48	.46.	.06
	.50	.50	0.0	.48	.46	.06
Middle	.37	.58	.05	.52	.43	.05
East	.65	.29	.06	.52	.43	.05
	1.0	0.0	0.0	.52	.43	.05
International	.45	.50	.05	.56	.41	.03
System	.75	.25	0.0	.56	.41	.03
(all regions)	0.0	1.0	0.0	.56	.41	.03

The second set of Markov chains defines "state" as follows:

state 1:   0 - 9 incidents
state 2:   10 - 18 incidents
state 3:   19 - 27 incidents
state 4:   28 or more incidents

region	initial state				stationary state			
Latin	.12	.25	.38	.25	.22	.24	.23	.30
America	.45	.45	.10	0.0	.22	.24	.23	.30
	.22	.22	.11	.45	.22	.24	.23	.30
	.09	.09	.36	.46	.22	.24	.23	.30
Western	.66	.17	0.0	.17	.10	.14	.20	.56
Europe	.25	.63	.12	0.0	.10	.14	.20	.56
	0.0	0.0	.29	.71	.10	.14	.20	.56
	0.0	.06	.23	.71	.10	.14	.20	.56
Middle	.56	.38	0.0	.06	.33	.51	.14	.02
East	.29	.47	.24	0.0	.33	.51	.14	.02
	0.0	1.0	0.0	0.0	.33	.51	.14	.02
	0.0	0.0	1.0	0.0	.33	.51	.14	.02

All figures are rounded to two decimal places.

Graphs of the Markov chains may be found in Appendix A.

*The definition of these regions may be found in Appendix B.

**The stationary state was found by raising the transition matrix to a power of 40.

7. The highest level of activity, aggregated by region, moved over time from Latin America, to the Middle East, and then to Western Europe.
8. The Markov chains show that Western Europe is prone to high levels of activity over the long run. The Middle East seems stationary at more moderate levels of activity.
9. The Markov chains also indicate a long-term tendency for the international system to absorb increasing numbers of transnational terrorist incidents. In other words, the overall tendency is for terrorism to increase rather than decrease.

HOW AND WHY TERRORISM DIFFUSES

Terrorism does appear to diffuse. Its spread throughout the international system is observable. The questions which now arise are how and why terrorism diffuses.(6) Recalling the conceptual framework discussed earlier, we can isolate four hypotheses to account for the diffusion of transnational terrorism:

1. Spontaneous generation: This explanation posits that there is no connection between the various incidents or location of terrorist incidents. It rejects the very assumption of diffusion. Each area or country which is affected develops a problem with terrorism independently, and in isolation from every other affected area. All activity is in response to purely indigenous factors. Accordingly, terrorism does not diffuse, but develops spontaneously to create the observed spatial patterns. Although the explanation rejects the assumption that terrorism diffuses, it may account for very early activity in the system which occurs before contagion can take hold. Or, it may be a random component or residual of an overall diffusion process.
2. Cooperation between groups (hierarchical expansion): The archetypical example of transnational terrorism is the Lod Airport "massacre" in which Japanese terrorists acting in the name of the Palestinian revolution made their way through Europe with the aid of Western European contacts, and used Czechoslovakian weapons to kill Puerto Rican pilgrims in an Israeli airport.
    This explanation focuses on the links between the various terrorist groups and cells, both within individual countries and throughout the world. The diffusion of terrorist tactics and strategies is accounted for by the free exchange of ideas, information, and assistance. For example, training centers are run by the PFLP and Al Fatah in the Middle East. The Cubans have allegedly been

involved in training urban guerrillas in Latin America. The Revolutionary Coordinating Junta (JCR) was founded in 1974 by the Argentine ERP, the Bolivian ELN, the Chilean MIR, and the vestiges of the Uruguayan Tupamaros (MLN) to serve as an umbrella organization. These links between groups provide a ready channel for the diffusion of tactics.

3. Actual transport (hierarchical relocation): Not all of the countries which have suffered terrorist incidents have spawned indigenous terrorist groups. Many of these countries are simply the victims of terrorists from other countries carrying their conflicts to new locations. Organizations or terrorist cells may move to new areas for a variety of reasons. They may be driven out of their original locations, as was the case with many Latin American groups which fled their native countries to other Latin American countries and Western Europe. They may attack a government which they feel is an ally of their enemy, as with the Palestinian attacks against the supporters of Israel. They may attack their own countrymen on foreign soil, as is the case with Armenian terrorist attacks against Turkish targets. Or, a group might decide to carry out an attack where they can best maximize the publicity and effect of the incident, for example, the Black September assault on the 1972 Munich Olympic Games.

   In terms of diffusion, this pattern is seen as hierarchical relocation. Terrorist cells move from place to place, with no necessary increase in the number of terrorists, yet "carrying" terrorism with them, thus altering the spatial distribution of the phenomenon as they travel.

4. Influence and imitation (contagious expansion): This explanation focuses on groups which pattern their activities after the incidents they see, read, or hear about. A classic example of imitation occurred in the early 1970s when, within weeks after the Argentine Montoneros "kidnapped" the corpse of General Pedro Aramburu for ransom, Burmese terrorists stole U Thant's body from its crypt to use as leverage in their own negotiations.

   A brief note on formal modeling is useful here. The basic assumptions of the Contagious Poisson distribution, a model which has been used in the study of diffusion,(7) state that, once an individual acts, the likelihood increases that he will act again; and one individual's action increases the probability that another will act in a similar fashion. Research is presently underway to determine whether the Contagious Poisson model fits the distribution of terrorist activity.

   The news and other communications media provide the essential link between the diffuser and the adopter, and are the channel for the diffusion of tactics and ideas. In this case, the media provide an alternative to direct interpersonal contact between groups.

SUMMARY

This chapter set out to show the utility and implications of applying the concept of spatial diffusion to the analysis of terrorism. We have explored adjacency maps and a new application of Markov chains as analytical techniques that may yield new insights into the diffusion of transnational terrorism. The lion's share of research remains to be conducted, but important questions have been asked, and some tentative answers offered.

Bringing the concept of spatial diffusion to the study of terrorism generates the following hypotheses. First, it suggests that spontaneous generation is a random component of the diffusion process. Second, it suggests that terrorism diffuses throughout the international system by means of imitation, by direct interpersonal contact, and by the relocation or movement of individual terrorists to new locations.

APPENDIX A: GRAPHIC REPRESENTATION OF THE MARKOV CHAINS IN TABLE 9.1

(Note: Markov chains may be represented in two forms: by matrix, as in table 9.1, or by graph. In matrix form, the value p of any element s_{ij} in the matrix indicates the probability of the process moving from state$_i$ to state$_j$ in one time period.

In graphs, the process is represented by a series of nodes representing the states, and directed edges showing possible paths of movement. The probability that during the next time period the process will move from any state$_i$ to state$_j$ is given by the numbers beside the particular edge or path.)

The definitions of the states in the two sets of Markov chains appear in table 9.1.

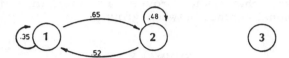

Latin America Initial State

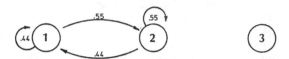

Latin America Stationary State

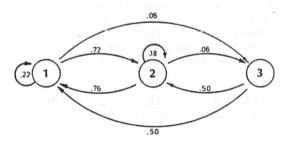

Western Europe Initial State

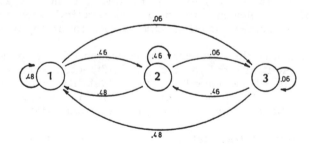

Western Europe Stationary State

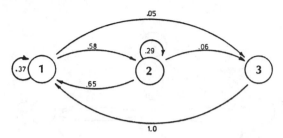

Middle East Initial State

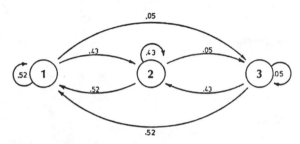

Middle East Stationary State

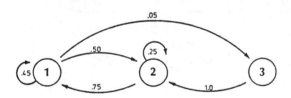

International System Initial State

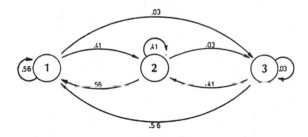

International System Stationary State

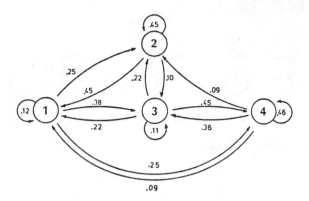

Latin America Initial State

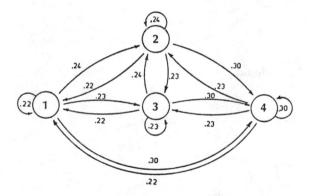

Latin America Stationary State

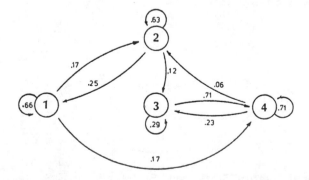

Western Europe Initial State

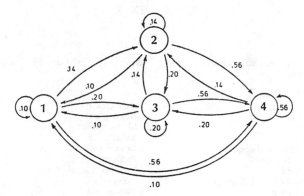

Western Europe Stationary State

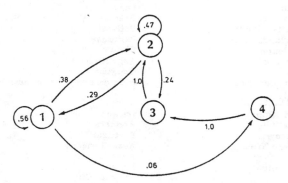

Middle East Initial State

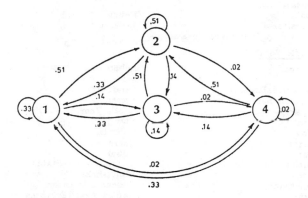

Middle East Stationary State

APPENDIX B

In the Markov chains, the political regions were defined as follows:

Latin America

Bermuda	Guatemala
Bahamas	Honduras
Cuba	El Salvador
Haiti	Nicaragua
Dominican Republic	Costa Rica
West Indies	Panama
Jamaica	Panama Canal Zone
Trinidad and Tobago	Colombia
Barbados	Venezuela
Dominica	Guyana
Grenada	Surinam
St. Lucia	French Guyana
St. Vincent	Ecuador
Antigua	Peru
Montserrat	Brazil
St. Kitts, Nevis, Anguila	Bolivia
Netherlands Antilles	Paraguay
Guadeloupe	Chile
Martinique	Argentina
Mexico	Uruguay
British Honduras	Indeterminate Latin American

Western Europe

United Kingdom	Ireland
Isle of Man	Andorra
Guernsey	Portugal
Northern Ireland	West Germany
Scotland	Austria
Netherlands	Italy
Belgium	Vatican City
Luxembourg	San Marino
Corsica	Malta
France	Greece
Monaco	Cyprus
Leichtenstein	Sweden
Switzerland	Norway
Spain	Denmark
Gibraltar	Iceland

Indeterminate Europe

Middle East

Morocco	Lebanon
Ifni	Jordan
Canary Islands	Saudi Arabia
Spanish Sahara	Yemen
Algeria	South Yemen (PRDY)
Tunisia	Kuwait
Libya	Bahrain
Sudan	Qatar
Iran	Dubai
Turkey	Trucial Oman States
Iraq	Abu Dhabi
Kurdistan	Muscat and Oman
Egypt	United Arab Emirates
Syria	Indeterminate Middle East

APPENDIX C: THE ADJACENCY MAPS [*]

This appendix is divided into four sections.

The maps in Section 1 show the cumulative diffusion of all transnational terrorist incidents according to the country in which they occurred. The squares indicate the countries in which incidents occurred by December 31 of the year indicated on the map. The triangles mark those countries, once active, that were inactive for a period of two or more years as of the date of the map.

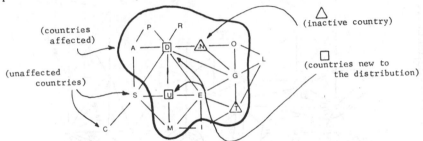

The maps in Section 2 show the cumulative diffusion of terrorist kidnappings, and follow the same graphic format as the maps in Section 1.

The maps in Section ·3 show the cumulative diffusion of terrorist skyjackings, and also follow the same graphic format.

The maps in Section 4 show the actual spatial location and intensity of all incidents for the specific year indicated on the map. The contours represent gradients of five incidents. Thus a country circled once experienced between one and five incidents during the year of the map; a country circled twice experienced between six and ten incidents that year. The maps allow for five gradients or contours.

Number of Contours	Number of Incidents Experienced
1	1-5
2	6-10
3	11-15
4	16-20
5	21 or more

* Adjacency Maps are used by permission of Professor Claudio Cioffi-Revilla, Department of Political Science, University of North Carolina, © C. Cioffi-Revilla. Source: ITERATE II

Appendix C, Section 1: Cumulative Diffusion of Transnational Terrorist Incidents of All Types

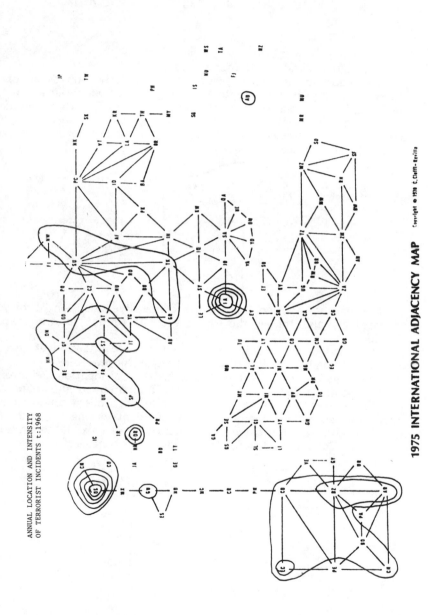

ANNUAL LOCATION AND INTENSITY
OF TERRORIST INCIDENTS t:1968

1975 INTERNATIONAL ADJACENCY MAP   Copyright © 1978 C.Cheff-Orville

Appendix C, Section 1: (continued)

ANNUAL LOCATION AND INTENSITY
OF TERRORIST INCIDENTS t:1969

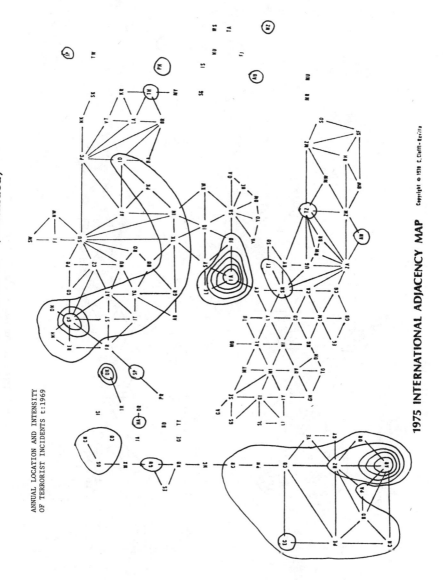

1975 INTERNATIONAL ADJACENCY MAP   Copyright © 1978 C. Cioffi-Revilla

193

Appendix C, Section 1: (continued)

ANNUAL LOCATION AND INTENSITY
OF TERRORIST INCIDENTS t:1970

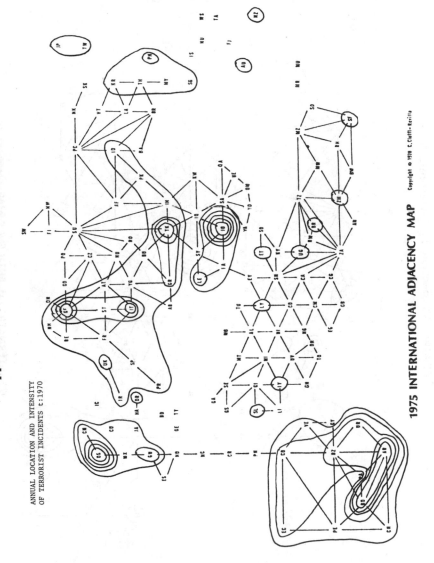

1975 INTERNATIONAL ADJACENCY MAP

Copyright © 1978 C.Cioffi-Revilla

194

Appendix C, Section 1: (continued)

ANNUAL LOCATION AND INTENSITY
OF TERRORIST INCIDENTS t:1971

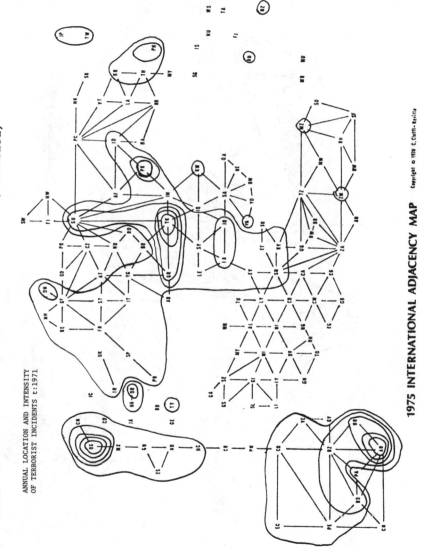

1975 INTERNATIONAL ADJACENCY MAP   Copyright © 1978 C. Cioffi-Revilla

195

Appendix C, Section 1: (continued)

ANNUAL LOCATION AND INTENSITY
OF TERRORIST INCIDENTS t:1972

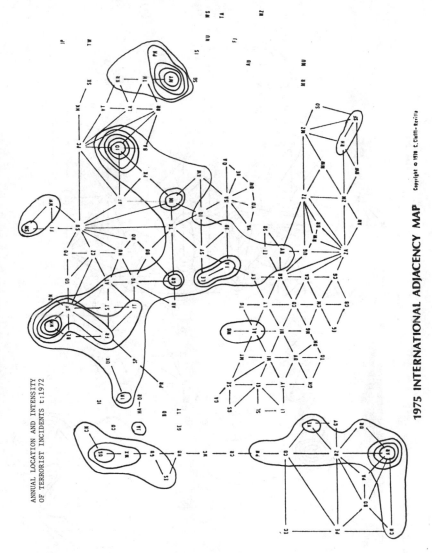

1975 INTERNATIONAL ADJACENCY MAP   Copyright © 1976 C.Claffin-Reville

Appendix C, Section 1: (continued)

ANNUAL LOCATION AND INTENSITY
OF TERRORIST INCIDENTS t:1973

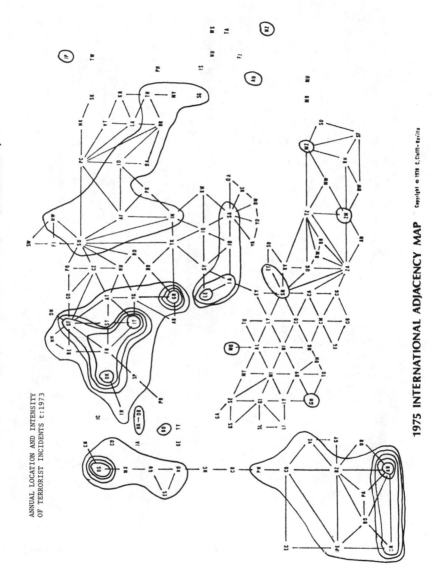

1975 INTERNATIONAL ADJACENCY MAP   Copyright © 1978 C.Cioffi-Revilla

197

Appendix C, Section 1: (continued)

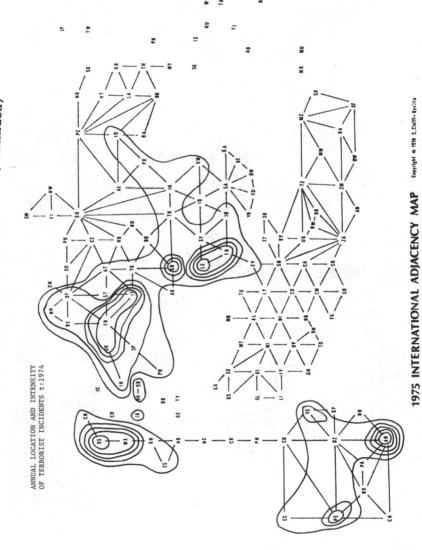

ANNUAL LOCATION AND INTENSITY
OF TERRORIST INCIDENTS t:1974

1975 INTERNATIONAL ADJACENCY MAP

Copyright © 1978 C.Cioffi-Revilla

Appendix C, Section 1: (continued)

ANNUAL LOCATION AND INTENSITY
OF TERRORIST INCIDENTS t:1975

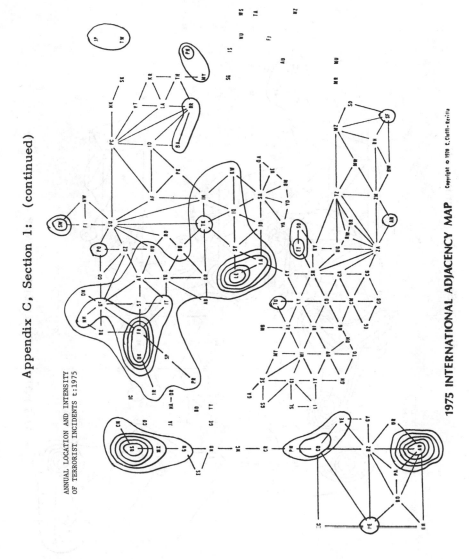

1975 INTERNATIONAL ADJACENCY MAP

Copyright © 1978 E. Choll-Revilla

199

Appendix C, Section 1: (continued)

ANNUAL LOCATION AND INTENSITY
OF TERRORIST INCIDENTS t:1976

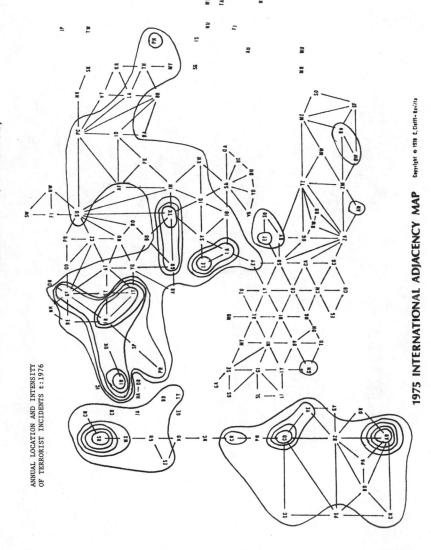

1975 INTERNATIONAL ADJACENCY MAP

Copyright © 1978 E. Cioffi-Revilla

Appendix C, Section 1: (continued)

ANNUAL LOCATION AND INTENSITY
OF TERRORIST INCIDENTS t:1977

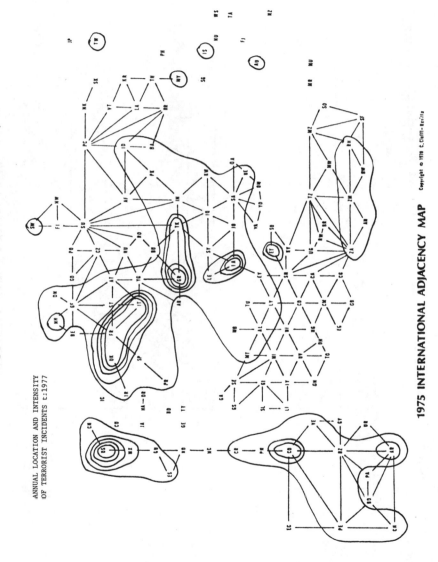

1975 INTERNATIONAL ADJACENCY MAP   Copyright © 1978 C.Cioffi-Revilla

201

Appendix C, Section 2: Cumulative Diffusion of Terrorist Kidnappings

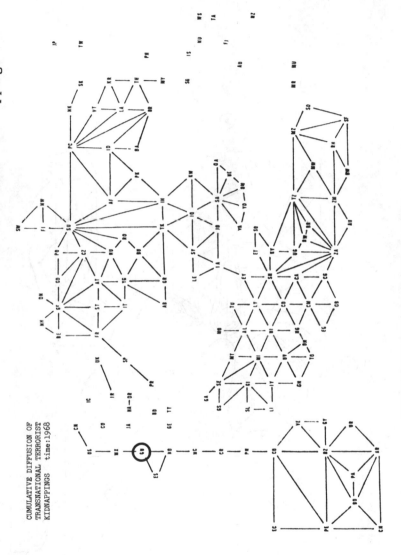

CUMULATIVE DIFFUSION OF
TRANSNATIONAL TERRORIST
KIDNAPPINGS   time:1968

1975 INTERNATIONAL ADJACENCY MAP   Copyright © 1976 C.Cioffi-Revilla

202

Appendix C, Section 2: (continued)

CUMULATIVE DIFFUSION OF
TRANSNATIONAL TERRORIST
KIDNAPPINGS   time:1969

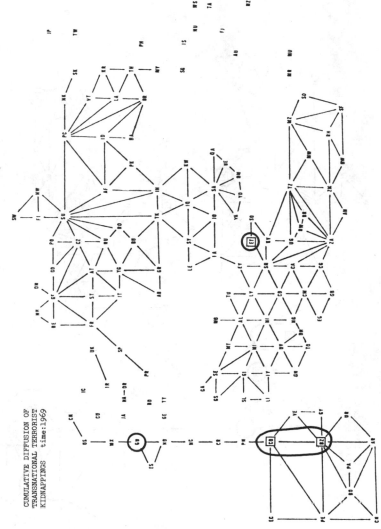

1975 INTERNATIONAL ADJACENCY MAP   Copyright © 1978 C.Ciuffi-Revilla

203

Appendix C, Section 2: (continued)

CUMULATIVE DIFFUSION OF
TRANSNATIONAL TERRORIST
KIDNAPPINGS   time:1970

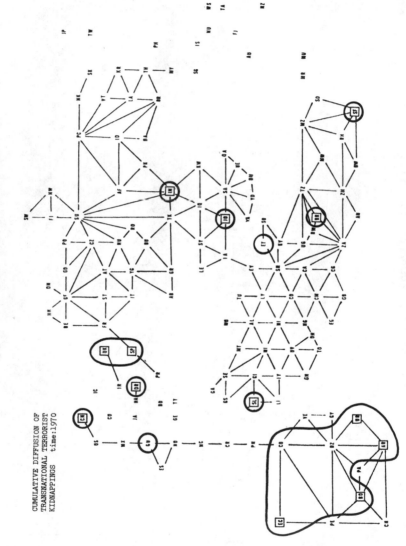

1975 INTERNATIONAL ADJACENCY MAP   Copyright © 1978 C.Cioffi-Revilla

204

Appendix C, Section 2: (continued)

CUMULATIVE DIFFUSION OF
TRANSNATIONAL TERRORIST
KIDNAPPINGS time:1971

1975 INTERNATIONAL ADJACENCY MAP   Copyright © 1976 C. Cioffi-Revilla

Appendix C, Section 2:   (continued)

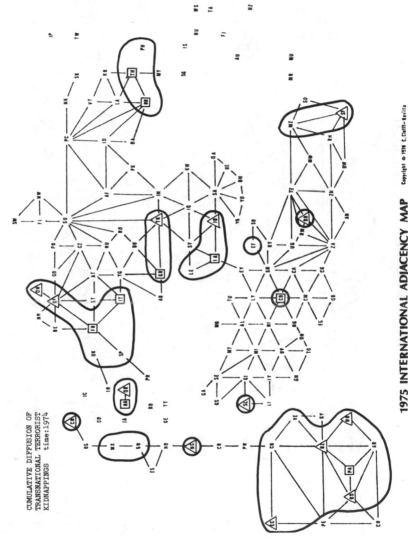

CUMULATIVE DIFFUSION OF
TRANSNATIONAL TERRORIST
KIDNAPPINGS   time:1974

1975 INTERNATIONAL ADJACENCY MAP   Copyright © 1976 C.Cioffi-Revilla

206

Appendix, C, Section 2: (continued)

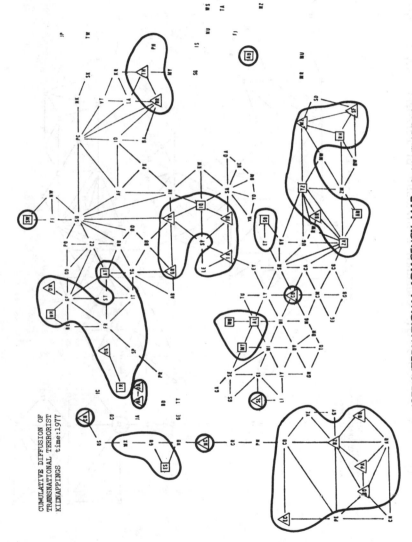

CUMLATIVE DIFFUSION OF
TRANSNATIONAL TERRORIST
KIDNAPPINGS   time:1977

1975 INTERNATIONAL ADJACENCY MAP   Copyright © 1976 C.Cioffi-Revilla

207

Appendix C, Section 3: Cumulative Diffusion of Terrorist Skyjackings

CUMULATIVE DIFFUSION OF
TRANSNATIONAL TERRORIST
SKYJACKINGS   time:1968

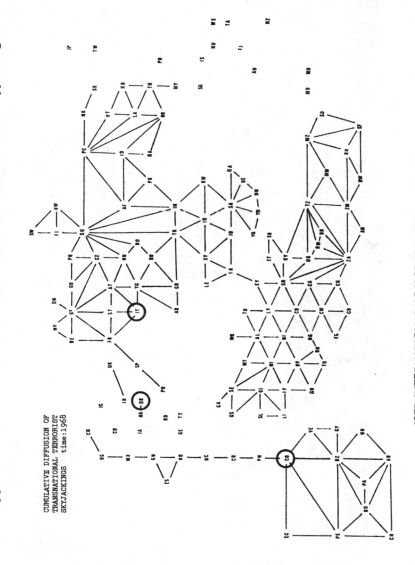

1975 INTERNATIONAL ADJACENCY MAP   Copyright © 1976 E. Claflin-Bonilla

208

Appendix C, Section 3: (continued)

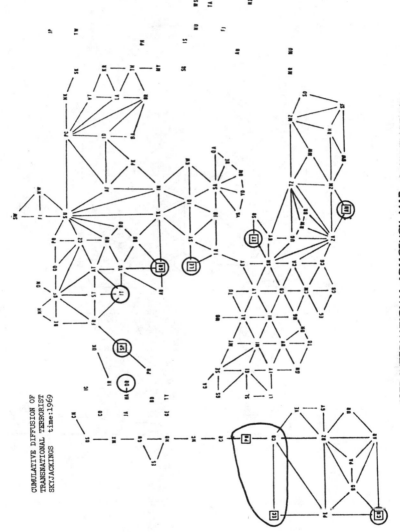

CUMULATIVE DIFFUSION OF
TRANSNATIONAL TERRORIST
SKYJACKINGS   time:1969

1975 INTERNATIONAL ADJACENCY MAP   Copyright © 1976 C. Cioffi-Revilla

209

Appendix C, Section 3: (continued)

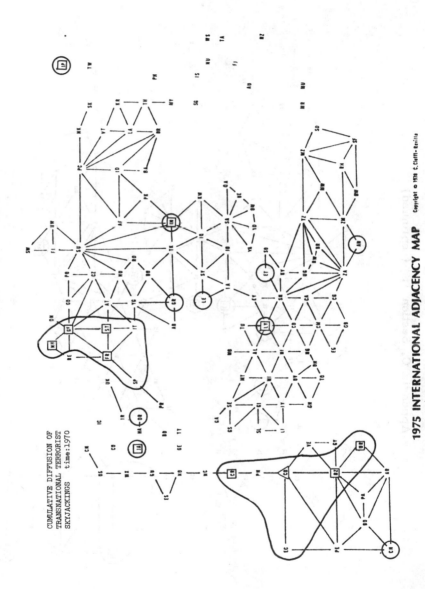

CUMULATIVE DIFFUSION OF
TRANSNATIONAL TERRORIST
SKYJACKINGS   time:1970

1975 INTERNATIONAL ADJACENCY MAP   Copyright © 1976 C.Cioffi-Revilla

210

Appendix C, Section 3: (continued)

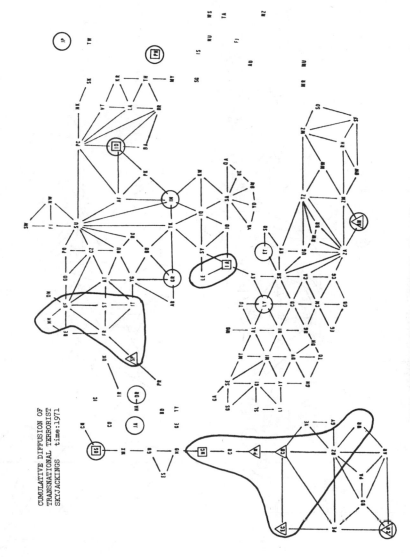

CUMULATIVE DIFFUSION OF
TRANSNATIONAL TERRORIST
SKYJACKINGS   time:1971

1975 INTERNATIONAL ADJACENCY MAP   Copyright © 1976 C.Cioffi-Revilla

Appendix C, Section 3: (continued)

CUMULATIVE DIFFUSION OF
TRANSNATIONAL TERRORIST
SKYJACKINGS   time:1972

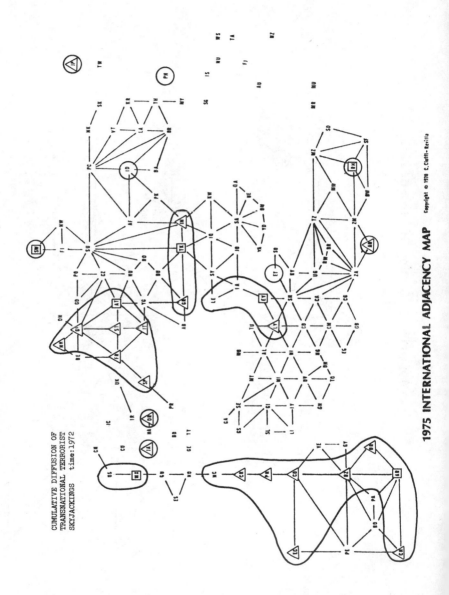

1975 INTERNATIONAL ADJACENCY MAP   Copyright © 1978 C.Cioffi-Revilla

212

Appendix C, Section 3: (continued)

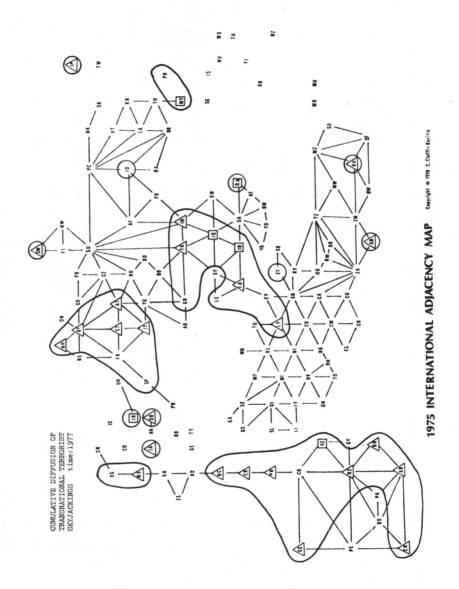

CUMULATIVE DIFFUSION OF
TRANSNATIONAL TERRORIST
SKYJACKINGS   time:1977

1975 INTERNATIONAL ADJACENCY MAP   Copyright © 1978 C.Cioffi-Revilla

213

Appendix C, Section 4: Location and Intensity of Transnational Terrorist Incidents

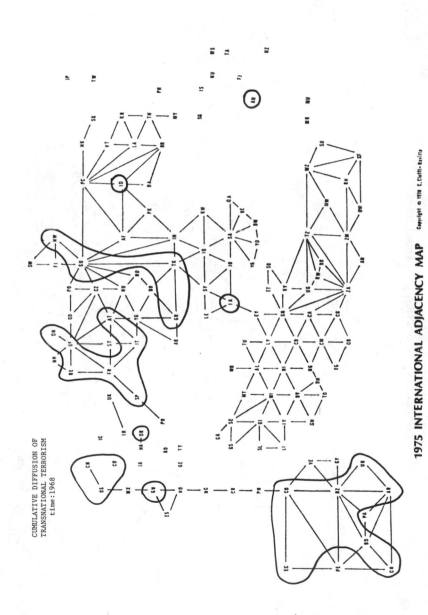

CUMULATIVE DIFFUSION OF
TRANSNATIONAL TERRORISM
time:1968

1975 INTERNATIONAL ADJACENCY MAP   Copyright © 1976 C.Cioffi-Revilla

Appendix C, Section 4: (continued)

CUMULATIVE DIFFUSION OF
TRANSNATIONAL TERRORISM
time:1969

1975 INTERNATIONAL ADJACENCY MAP   Copyright © 1978 C.Cioffi-Revilla

215

Appendix C, Section 4: (continued)

CUMULATIVE DIFFUSION OF
TRANSNATIONAL TERRORISM
time:1970

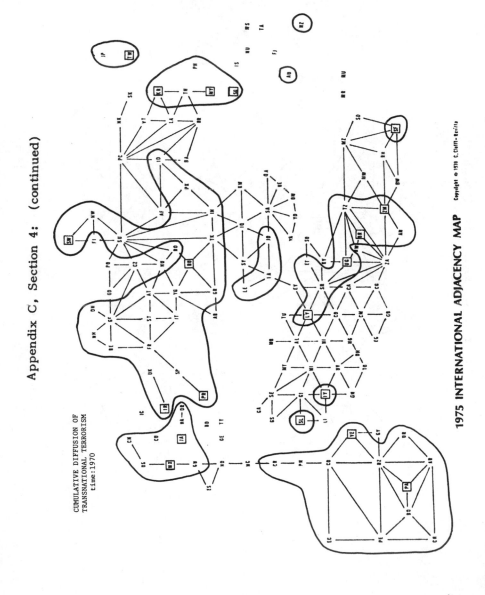

1975 INTERNATIONAL ADJACENCY MAP

Copyright © 1970 E.Chaffi-Revilla

216

Appendix C, Section 4: (continued)

CUMULATIVE DIFFUSION OF
TRANSNATIONAL TERRORISM
time:1971

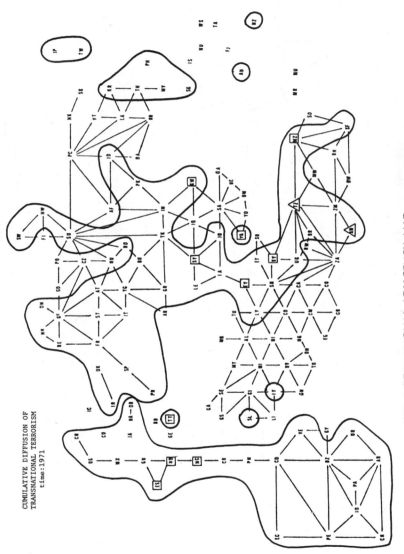

1975 INTERNATIONAL ADJACENCY MAP   Copyright © 1978 C.Cioffi-Revilla

217

Appendix C, Section 4: (continued)

CUMULATIVE DIFFUSION OF
TRANSNATIONAL TERRORISM
time:1972

1975 INTERNATIONAL ADJACENCY MAP   Copyright © 1978 E. Cioffi—Revilla

218

Appendix C, Section 4: (continued)

CUMULATIVE DIFFUSION OF
TRANSNATIONAL TERRORISM
time:1973

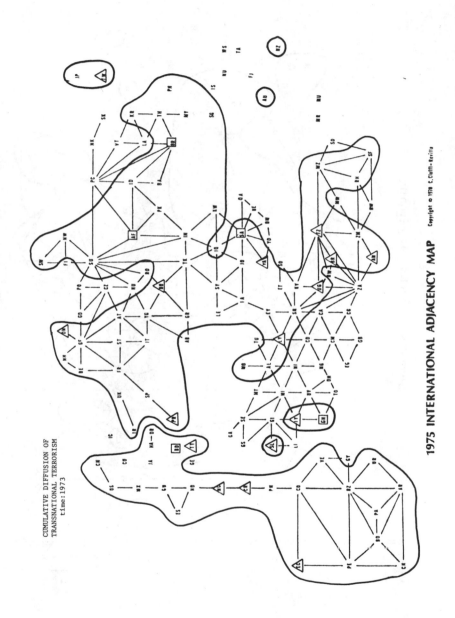

1975 INTERNATIONAL ADJACENCY MAP   Copyright © 1978 C. Cioffi-Revilla

219

Appendix C, Section 4: (continued)

CUMULATIVE DIFFUSION OF
TRANSNATIONAL TERRORISM
time:1974

1975 INTERNATIONAL ADJACENCY MAP

Copyright © 1976 C. Cioffi-Revilla

Appendix C, Section 4: (continued)

CUMULATIVE DIFFUSION OF
TRANSNATIONAL TERRORISM
time:1975

1975 INTERNATIONAL ADJACENCY MAP

Copyright © 1978 C.Cioffi-Revilla

221

Appendix C, Section 4: (continued)

CUMULATIVE DIFFUSION OF
TRANSNATIONAL TERRORISM
time:1976

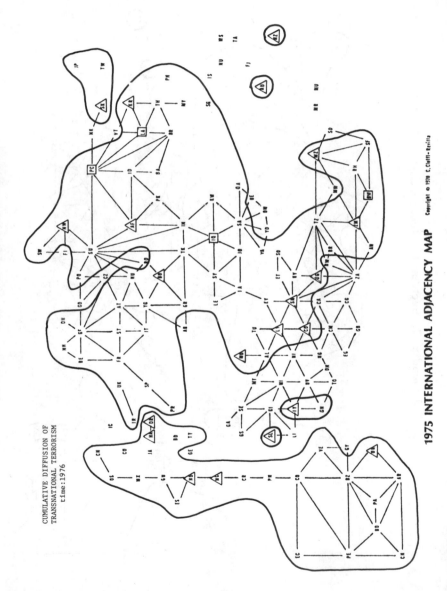

1975 INTERNATIONAL ADJACENCY MAP   Copyright © 1976 C.Cioffi-Revilla

222

Appendix C, Section 4: (continued)

CUMULATIVE DIFFUSION OF
TRANSNATIONAL TERRORISM
time:1977

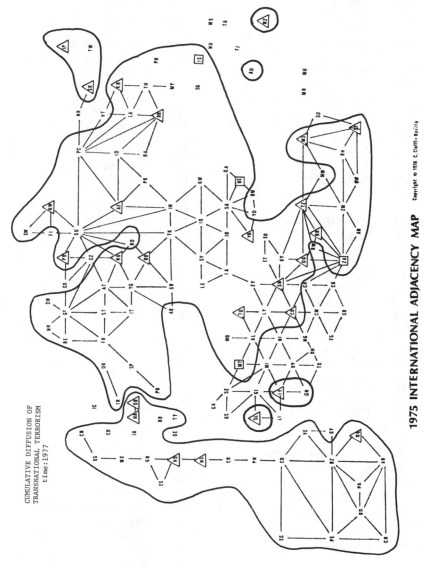

1975 INTERNATIONAL ADJACENCY MAP   Copyright © 1978 C.Cioffi-Revilla

223

APPENDIX D: ADJACENCY MAP COUNTRY CODES

AB	Albania	GD	East Germany
AF	Afghanistan	GE	Grenada
AL	Algeria	GF	West Germany
AN	Angola	GH	Ghana
AR	Argentina	GI	Guinea
AT	Austria	GR	Greece
AU	Australia	GS	Guinea Bissau
		GU	Guatemala
BA	Bangladesh	GY	Guyana
BD	Barbados		
BE	Belgium	HA	Haiti
BH	Bahrain	HO	Honduras
BN	Bhutan	HU	Hungary
BO	Bolivia		
BR	Burundi	IA	Israel
BU	Bulgaria	IC	Iceland
BW	Botswana	ID	India
BZ	Brazil	IN	Iran
		IQ	Iraq
CA	Central African Republic	IR	Ireland
CD	Chad	IS	Indonesia
CG	Congo	IT	Italy
CH	Chile	IY	Ivory Coast
CM	Cameroon		
CN	Canada	JA	Jamaica
CO	Colombia	JO	Jordan
CR	Costa Rica	JP	Japan
CU	Cuba		
CY	Cyprus	KR	Cambodia
CZ	Czechoslovakia	KW	Kuwait
		KY	Kenya
DH	Dahomey		
DN	Denmark	LA	Laos
DR	Dominican Republic	LE	Lebanon
		LI	Liberia
EC	Ecuador	LY	Libya
EG	Equatorial Guinea	LX	Luxembourg
ES	El Salvador		
ET	Ethiopia	MI	Mali
EY	Egypt (UAR)	MO	Morocco
		MR	Malagasy Republic
FI	Finland	MT	Mauritania
FJ	Fiji	MU	Mauritius
FR	France	MW	Malawi
		MX	Mexico
GA	Gambia	MY	Malaysia
GB	Gabon	MZ	Mozambique

NC	Nicaragua	SO	Somalia
NG	Nigeria	SP	Spain
NH	Netherlands	ST	Switzerland
NI	Niger	SU	Soviet Union
NK	North Korea	SW	Sweden
NU	Nauru	SY	Syria
NW	Norway		
NZ	New Zealand	TA	Tonga
		TH	Thailand
OM	Oman	TK	Turkey
		TO	Togo
PA	Paraguay	TT	Trinidad and Tobago
PC	People's Republic of China	TU	Tunisia
PE	Peru	TW	Taiwan
PH	Philippines	TZ	Tanzania
PK	Pakistan		
PN	Panama	UE	United Arab Emirates
PO	Poland	UG	Uganda
PR	Portugal	UK	United Kingdom
		UR	Uruguay
QA	Qatar	US	United States of America
		UV	Upper Volta
RO	Rumania		
RW	Rwanda	VE	Venezuela
		VT	Vietnam
SA	Saudi Arabia		
SD	Swaziland	WS	Western Samoa
SE	Senegal		
SF	Union of South Africa	YA	North Yemen
SG	Singapore	YD	South Yemen
SK	South Korea	YG	Yugoslavia
SL	Sierra Leone		
SN	Sudan	ZA	Zaire
		ZM	Zambia

NOTES

1. The following discussion draws on the work of Lawrence A. Brown, particularly his Diffusion Processes and Location: A Conceptual Framework and Bibliography (Philadelphia: Regional Science Research Institute, 1968).

2. See John Q. Stewart, "Concerning 'Social Physics,'" Scientific American 178 (May 1948): 20-23.

3. ITERATE closely follows the conventions suggested in Ted Robert Gurr's, Politimetrics (Englewood Cliffs, NJ: Prentice-Hall, 1972).

Definitions of terrorism vary widely, and it is not our purpose to contribute to what has so far been a sterile semantic debate. We have found it useful to employ a composite conceptualization of the problem, based on the work of a number of analysts. We view the transnational form of terrorism as "the use, or threat of use, of anxiety-inducing extranormal violence for political purposes by any individual or group, whether acting for or in opposition to established governmental authority, when such action is intended to influence the attitudes and behavior of a target group wider than the immediate victims and when, through the nationality or foreign ties of its perpetrators, its location, the nature of its institutional or human victims, or the mechanics of its resolution, its ramifications transcend national boundaries." Compare this formulation of the problem with that of Brian M. Jenkins and Janera Johnson, "International Terrorism: A Chronology, 1968-1974" (Santa Monica: The RAND Corporation, R-1597-DOS/ARPA, March 1975); David L. Milbank, International and Transnational Terrorism: Diagnosis and Prognosis (Washington D.C.: Central Intelligence Agency, April 1976); and Jordan J. Paust, "Terrorism and the International Law of War" Military Law Review (1974), pp. 1-36.

The statistics presented in this chapter exclude terrorist attacks on U.S. and allied personnel installations in the Vietnamese conflict, as well as most of the mutual assassination efforts and crossborder operations associated with the Arab-Israeli conflict. Exceptions are incidents which either victimized noncombatant nationals of states located outside the principal arena of conflict or were of such a nature that they became the subject of widespread international concern and controversy. On the other hand, related but separately targeted actions were counted as individual incidents, even when they were staged on the same day in close proximity to one another. No weighting is given to actions based upon the degree of publicity generated, casualties or damage caused, degree of logistic, tactical, or strategic success of the perpetrators, or type of attack.

As mentioned in chapter 8, the dataset is not based on only one source. An attempt has been made to collate descriptions provided by academic, journalistic, and official sources into a centralized collection. The effects of attempting a comprehensive survey of data sources, rather than reliance upon a single source, have been explored in the events data literature and will not be reviewed here. See especially Edward E. Azar, "The Problem of Source Coverage in the Use of Events Data," International Studies Quarterly 16 (December 1969); Phillip M. Burgess and Raymond W. Lawton, "Evaluating Events Data: Problems of Conception, Reliability, and Validity," in International Events and the Comparative Analysis of Foreign Policy edited by Charles W. Kegley, G. Raymond, R. Rood, and R. Skinner. (Columbia: South Carolina, 1975); Robert Burrowes, "Mirror, Mirror, on the Wall...A Comparison of Events Data Sources," in Comparing Foreign Policies edited by James N. Rosenau (New York: Wiley, 1974), pp. 383-406; Charles F. Doran et al., "A Test of Cross-National Event Reliability: Global Versus Regional Data Sources," International Studies Quarterly 17 (2) (June 1973):175-203; Russell Leng, "Problems in Events Data Availability and Analysis." (Paper presented to the New England Political Science Association Annual Convention, Kingston, April 1972); Patrick J. Mc-Gowann, "A Bayseian Approach to the Problem of Events Data Validity," in Rosenau, ed., Comparing Foreign Policies, pp. 407-33; and Hamid Mowland, "A Paradigm for Source Analysis in Events Data Research," International Interactions 2 (1) (1975).

A comparison of the pilot version of ITERATE and the updated dataset upon which this chapter is based is being conducted by Russell Osmond at Syracuse University.

4. Lyndhurst Collins, An Introduction to Markov Chain Analysis (East Anglia, Norwich: Geo-Abstracts, Ltd., 1975), p. 25.

5. Space limitations will not permit a formal investigation of the theory and structure of Markov chains. Excellent discussions of the formal structure of Markov chains and Markov processes may be found in Patrick Doreian, Mathematics and the Study of Social Relations (New York: Schocken Books, 1971); Daniel P. Maki and Maynard Thompson, Mathematical Models and Applications (Englewood Cliffs, N.J.: Prentice-Hall, 1973); and Emanuel Parzen, Stochastic Processes (San Francisco: Holden-Day, 1962).

6. Perhaps of equal interest is why terrorism does not diffuse in certain regions and with certain intensities. Regarding the latter, we tend to agree with Milbank, who points out that "the record suggests that no group can long sustain a high intensity campaign of terror without running up against some very serious practical problems in terms of (1) depletion of resources, (2) fractional divisions, (3) erosion of inter-

national sympathy or support, or (4) more vigorous counter-measures (at least at the national level). In short, while the internal dynamics of a campaign of terrorist violence tend to create pressures for escalation, the process would appear to be to some degree self-limiting." See International Terrorism in 1976 (Washington, D.C.: Central Intelligence Agency, RP 77 10034U July 1977). This hypothesis could also figure heavily in the explanation of the observed oscillation between in-creasing and decreasing numbers of terrorist incidents as experienced in the geopolitical regions noted in the first set of Markov chains (Table 9.1). As to the former, it is undoubt-edly bound up in the problem of the causes of terrorism per se, and the specific causes of its transnational variant.

7. See James S. Coleman, Introduction to Mathematical Sociology (London and New York: The Free Press of Glencoe, 1964), pp. 41-43, 288-314 for the derivation and use of the Poisson models in the study of diffusion. Other souces on the use of Poisson models in diffusion research are Richard Li and William Thompson, "The Coup Contagion Hypothesis," Journal of Conflict Resolution 19 (March 1975): 63-88; Manus Mid-larsky, "Mathematical Models of Instability and a Theory of Diffusion," International Studies Quarterly 14 (March 1970): 60-84; and Midlarsky, On War (New York: The Free Press, 1975), chapter VII.

10 Dynamics of Insurgent Violence: Preliminary Findings

Lawrence C. Hamilton

There are numerous types of insurgent violence, and almost as many typologies. This chapter reports on what began as research into the causes and effects of terrorism.(*) However, terrorism proved to be conceptually and statistically (i.e., factor analytically) difficult to distinguish from several other types of insurgent violence. I was forced to broaden my focus to include the related actions of political bombings, assassinations, and small-scale guerrilla warfare. In addition to their blurred conceptual boundaries and pattern of intercorrelations, these four types of violence share a common strategic rationale. That rationale is built upon assumptions about the dynamic process they can set in motion.

At the core of this rationale is the fact that terrorism and the rest are tactics born of weakness. In part, this weakness is military. Terrorists cannot realistically expect to do significant direct damage to the coercive powers of the modern state. Most states have at their disposal very much larger forces, and they can generally survive the occasional loss of personnel quite well. There is little reason to expect that states will topple at the detonation of a few bombs.

Another aspect of the weakness is political. If terrorism is a tactic of insurgents who cannot hope to defeat the state militarily, it is also a tactic of insurgents who cannot hope to defeat the state politically. Since much of modern terrorism takes place in the democracies, this often simply means that

---

*I am indebted to Ted Gurr for sharing his data with me, and to Otomar Bartos, Thomas Mayer, Elise Boulding, Frank Beer, Dick Williams, and Kathryn Guido for assistance throughout this research.

the insurgents lack popular support.   Terrorism is, by itself,
merely likely to increase the political isolation of its perpetrators.

Because they are unable either to seize territory or to
mobilize popular support, terrorists are cut off from the
classic insurgent programs outlined by Mao Tse-Tung (1960),
Che Guevara (1961), or Vo Nguyen Giap (1962).   Although lip
service is still paid to these worthies, modern terrorists have
developed an entirely different theory of how to gain power.
This theory relies on terrorism's most conspicuous effect: its
powers of provocation.   Terrorism is capable of provoking a
violent counterattack that may be so offensive as to drive the
populace into the arms of the insurgents.   David Fromkin
(1975:694) has made the point succinctly:

> The tiny FLN band of outlaws could have blown up
> every bus in all of Algeria and never won a single
> convert to their cause of independence.   Failing to
> understand the strategy of terrorism, the French did
> not see that it was not the FLN's move, but rather
> the French countermove, that would determine
> whether the FLN succeeded or failed.

The most influential statement of this rationale for terrorism is
found in Carlos Marighela's Minimanual of the Urban Guerrilla
(1971).   Marighela advocates terrorism (or, euphemistically,
"urban guerrilla war") as a means of transforming the political
situation in a country into a military situation.   The authorities are provoked into intensifying repression to Nazi-like
extremes until, finally, the population is so desperately
miserable it has no choice but to revolt.   In more formal
terms, Marighela's argument suggests two propositions: there
is a positive feedback relationship between terrorism and oppression, and this feedback operates to increase the ultimate
probability of revolution.   These propositions are illustrated in
fig. 10.1 as a causal theory.

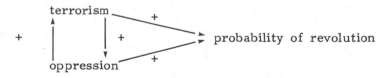

Fig. 10.1

A less sanguinary, though no less sympathetic, account
of terrorism's effects has been offered by Edward Hyams
(1975).   Hyams argues that terrorism improves the prospects
for moderate reform, and it thereby brings about a more just

and liberal society in which terrorism is no longer necessary. Thus, terrorism is "self-reducing" and productive of peaceful, nonrevolutionary reforms.   More formally, Hyams is describing a negative feedback loop as shown in fig. 10.2.

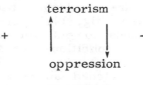

Fig. 10.2

In dynamic systems a positive feedback such as Marighela envisions (fig. 10.1) will amplify deviations.   The introduction of terrorism destabilizes the systems, setting them on a path of escalating violence which culminates in mass revolution. The process closely resembles Lewis Richardson's (1960) arms race model.   A negative feedback (fig. 10.2), on the other hand, operates to minimize deviations.   The introduction of terrorism leads to reforms which reduce the causes of future terrorism; society moves toward a happy and stable equilibrium.

A quite different kind of negative feedback is implicit in the writings of historian Walter Laqueur (1976, 1977), among others.   Laqueur agrees with Marighela that terrorism's immediate effect is usually to provoke repression.   However, he takes issue with Marighela's belief that such repression will benefit the insurgents and stimulate them to further attacks. According to Laqueur, this may have been true of "premodern" dictatorships or of liberal regimes whose powers of repression are strictly limited.   But many contemporary governments have learned that domestic insurgencies can be successfully suppressed by force, once the government loses any initial reluctance it may have had to do so.   The effect of regime reaction is, then, to crush terrorism, not to increase it. Furthermore, the population is likely to side with the government, tolerating whatever countermeasures seem necessary to root out the insurgents.

Laqueur's assertions are represented formally in fig. 10.3.

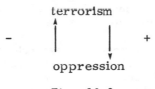

Fig. 10.3

As with figure 10.2, this is a negative or deviation-reducing feedback loop. However, the two loops move toward radically different equilibrium states. In Hyam's view (fig. 10.2), terrorism is the result of bad conditions, which it causes to improve. Stability is achieved when improvement is complete, i.e., when conditions are no longer bad enough to cause terrorism. Laqueur's view (fig. 10.3), in contrast, holds that terrorism causes conditions to get worse. Stability in this system is achieved when conditions are so bad that no one dares to rebel.

The three models sketched above are clearly not compatible. In addition, they directly address the strategic rationales often offered to justify or condemn terrorism today. Thus, the question of which of the models is more realistic is a question of some practical, as well as theoretical, interest. It seems well worth the effort to investigate the question empirically.

Several methods may be proposed for doing this. The most venerable such method is doubtless the historical case study, or (preferably) a number of historical case studies. A more recently fashionable approach would involve multivariate statistical analysis of cross-sectional data. With time series data and stochastic modeling techniques, quantitative analysis could be extended into the time domain. None of these methods is without serious drawbacks, for which reason it seems that they might profitably all be used together. The following sections look briefly at each method in turn.

HISTORICAL CASE STUDIES

The literature on terrorism is replete with historical case studies. Both Hyams and Laqueur, for example, build their work mainly upon such studies. The drawbacks of the method become conspicuous when we note that their use of it leads them to totally opposite conclusions. Such contradictions between case historians are found repeatedly in the literature, despite the finite pool of notable cases from which to draw examples.

Inconsistency is by no means the exclusive province of case historians, of course. Case histories do have a sensitivity to nuance, detail, and singularity which is often lost in more quantified approaches. They also present quantitative model builders with an important test of the realism of their models' assumptions.

My own modest historical research has inclined me to suspect that figure 10.3 represents the dynamic of much modern terrorism. There are, of course, exceptions to the pattern, but one searches in vain for recent instances of major strategic victories won by terrorists. In a number of cases (especially in Latin America), insurgent left-wing terrorism has appeared instrumental in bringing repressive right-wing regimes to power. Except in Argentina, such regimes have, in turn, proven fairly effective in suppressing terrorism, often at considerable human cost. The Tupamaros of Uruguay and the MR-8 of Brazil are two of the more notable casualties of these antiterror reactions.

CROSS-SECTION STATISTICS

Cross-sectional data are less than ideal for investigation of feedback in dynamic systems The disadvantages, however, are somewhat mitigated by the wide availability of good cross-national data sets. The well-developed techniques of path analyses provide analytical tools which have been widely used to study dynamic processes (Duncan 1975; Heise 1975; Kenny 1979).

A path model evaluated with crossnational data is shown in figure 10.4.

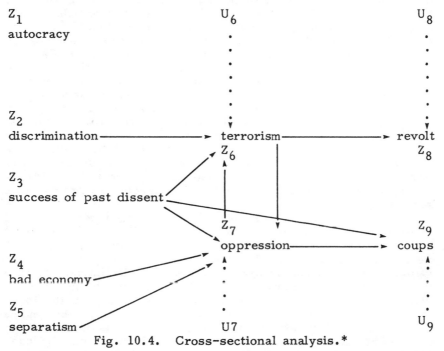

Fig. 10.4. Cross-sectional analysis.*

*Only paths with betas $\geq$ .15 shown; see Appendix A for variable definitions.

Definitions of variables are included in Appendix A. For visual simplicity, the path coefficients are omitted in fig. 10.4. Solid arrows indicate paths with coefficients (beta weights) greater than .15, i.e., substantial positive relationships. Dashed arrows indicate paths with coefficients less than -.15, i.e., substantial negative relationships. Unmeasured influences are indicated by dotted lines. The sources of data, analytical techniques, and findings have been described in detail elsewhere (Hamilton 1978). Briefly, the five exogenous variables were developed from variables in Ted Gurr's Conflict and Society data set, which contains information on 86 countries. This data set is on file with the Inter-University Consortium for Political and Social Research (#7452). The four endogenous variables measure degrees of strife obtained through logarithmic transformations of raw strife events counts. Principal components factor analysis was employed in constructing new measures; as shown in the Appendix A, most of the variables in figure 10.4 are actually factor scores. Path coefficients were estimated through ordinary least squares (OLS) and two-stage least squares (2SLS) regression.

The 2SLS technique allows estimation of the path coefficients in the hypothesized reciprocal relationship between terrorism, Z_6, and oppression, Z_7. As shown in figure 10.4, the mutual causality is positive. At first glance, this might appear to support Marighela's "positive feedback" view of terrorism (fig. 10.1). The fact that terrorism also has a positive influence on the occurrence of revolt or guerrilla war, Z_8, also seems to bear out the Marighela hypothesis. Caution is in order on several grounds, however. First, the "revolt" variable, Z_8 measures the occurrence of wider violence, not of successful revolution. Second, the simultaneous reciprocal causality shown in figure 10.4 cannot be directly interpreted in dynamic terms. The information given is insufficient, for example, to establish whether a disturbed system would move toward a stable equilibrium or diverge from an unstable one. Nor does it allow us to characterize the equilibrium level itself. Purely cross-sectional data cannot be expected to provide this sort of dynamic description.

Understanding of the relationship between terrorism and oppression over time may be improved somewhat by the use of lagged variables. Terrorism and oppression in figure 10.4 are measured simultaneously for the period 1960 to 1966. Earlier values of the same or similar variables could be introduced into the analysis. Obtaining such data, however, is not particularly easy. One component of Z_7, oppression, is the logarithm of the number of negative sanctions taken by the regime during the 1960 to 1961 period. Sanction counts for a number of previous years are also available, and these may be considered a crude measure of past regime oppression. Sanctions from the years immediately prior to 1960 correlate highly with the post-1960 sanctions, raising the possibility that the regression analysis would be troubled by multicollinearity. However, the number of sanctions between 1948 and 1954 is remote enough to avoid this problem. Accordingly, I defined a new variable, Z_{10};

$Z_{10} = \log_{10}$ (number of negative sanctions, 1948-54, + 1).

Z_{10} can be taken to indicate past oppressiveness of the government. The analysis shown in figure 10.4 can be redone to include Z_{10} as a sixth independent variable; the results are shown in figure 10.5. Paths with coefficients larger than .15 are shown as solid arrows; coefficients less than -.15 are indicated by dashed arrows. The actual path coefficients are presented in Appendix B.

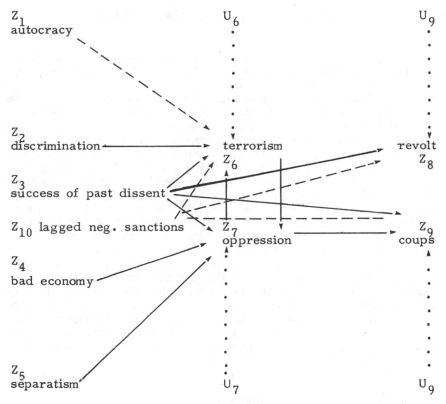

Fig. 10.5. Cross-sectional analysis with lagged
negative regime sanctions.*

*Only paths with betas ≥ .15 shown; see Appendix A for variable definitions and Appendix B for actual coefficients.

As with figure 10.4, the immediate effect of terrorism is to increase oppression, and the immediate effect of oppression is to increase terrorism. However, the long-term (i.e., lagged) effect of oppression is to decrease terrorism, decrease the occurrence of revolt or guerrilla war, and decrease the occurrences of coups d'etat. This important finding is consistent with much case historical work, and with the theory of terrorism illustrated in figure 10.3. The findings also parallel conclusions reached by Douglas Hibbs, Jr. (1973) in his own crossnational research. It appears that terrorism succeeds as short-term provocation, but succumbs to long-term oppression. In addition, long-term oppression evidently decreases the likelihood of other types of political violence as well.

CONCLUSIONS AND FURTHER RESEARCH

The data discussed thus far have been inadequate for a formal dynamic analysis. Such an analysis would, however, be preferable for investigating the questions of process raised in this chapter. Work is presently under way to pursue these questions by applying stochastic process models to time series of strife events data. Initial analysis will be focused on individual countries with high levels of strife, using a set of "contagion" models and fitting techniques developed especially for this purpose (Hamilton and Hamilton 1980). In doing time series studies of single countries, it should be feasible to keep the statistical analysis firmly grounded in historical reality. One is essentially doing a statistical case study. In the past, crossnational analyses have occasionally shown a tendency to become detached from history; this is fatal for any study intended to be taken seriously by nonstatisticians.

The indicators and the causal theory of figure 10.5 could both be improved upon. To the extent that present conclusions are supported in further research, however, it appears that a principal rationale advanced in favor of modern terrorism (fig. 10.1) is based on mistaken causal assumptions. No doubt, those committed to that rationale will find these results unpersuasive, but they are consistent with a weight of historical as well as quantitative evidence.

REFERENCES

Duncan, Otis D. Introduction to Structural Equation Models. New York: Academic Press, 1975.

Fromkin, David.   "The Strategy of Terrorism," Foreign Affairs
    53 (1975): 683–98.

Giap, Vo Nguyen. People's War, People's Army.   New York:
    Macmillan, 1962.

Guevara, Che.   On Guerrilla Warfare, edited by H. C. Peter-
    son.   New York: Frederick A. Praeger, 1961.

Hamilton, Lawrence C.   "Ecology of Terrorism," Ph.D. dis-
    sertation.   Boulder, Colorado: University of Colorado,
    1978.

Hamilton, James D. and Lawrence C. Hamilton.   "Models of
    Social Contagion," Paper presented to Pacific Sociological
    Association, San Francisco, April 11, 1980.

Heise, David R.   Causal Analysis.   New York: Wiley, 1975.

Hibbs, Douglas A., Jr.   Mass Political Violence: A Cross-
    National Causal Analysis.   New York: Wiley, 1973.

Hyams, Edward.   Terrorists and Terrorism.   London: J. M.
    Dent, 1975.

Kenny, David A.   Correlation and Causality.   New York:
    Wiley, 1979.

Laqueur, Walter.   Terrorism.   Boston: Little, Brown, 1977.

Mao   Tse-tung.   On the Protracted War.   Peking: Foreign
    Language Press, 1960.

Marighela, Carlos.   For the Liberation of Brazil.   Translated
    by John Butt and Rosemary Steed.   Hamondsworth:
    Pelican, 1971.

Richardson, Lewis F.   Arms and Insecurity.   Pittsburgh: Box-
    wood, 1960.

APPENDIX A

Summary of Variables Used

Variable	Weights[*]	Indicators (sources)
Z_1 autocracy	.50	degree of autocracy, 1960 (CSD)
	-.50	degree of democracy, 1960 (CSD)
Z_2 discrimination	.50	political discrimination, 1963 (CSD)
	.50	economic discrimination, 1963 (CSD)
Z_3 success of past dissent	.47	success in internal wars, 1850–1960 (CSD)
	.24	success in conspiracies, 1900–1960 (CSD)
	.30	success in turmoil, 1940–1960 (CSD)
Z_4 bad economy		bad economic conditions, 1960–63 (CSD)
Z_5 separatism	.11	intensity of separatism, 1960 (CSD)
	.28	proportion affected, 1960 (CSD)
	.11	size of dissident groups, 1960 (CSD)
	.23	density of dissident pop., 1960 (CSD)
	.38	extent of dissident organization, 1960 (CSD)
Z_6 terrorism	.20	log of # of political assassinations, 1961–66 (SED)
	.39	log of # of small-scale terrorist campaigns, 1961–66 (SED)
	.16	log of # of political bombings, 1961–66 (SED)
	.37	log of # of small-scale guerrilla campaigns, 1961–66 (SED)
Z_7 short-term oppression	.34	log of # of negative regime sanctions, 1960–66 (CSD)
	.41	sum of government value-depriving policies, 1960–63 (CSD)
	.31	sum of restrictions on political participation, 1960–63 (CSD)
Z_8 revolt	.50	log of # of large-scale revolts, 1961–70 (SED)
	.50	log of # of large-scale guerrilla campaigns, 1961–70 (SED)
Z_9 coups		log of # of coups and coup attempts, 1961–70 (SED)

*All weights are factor score coefficients obtained through principal-factor analysis with iterations.

Weights were applied after the indicators were standardized to zero mean and unit variance.

APPENDIX B

Path coefficients: regression of terrorism (Z_6) on its predictors.

path	beta weight
$P_{61.23\hat{7}10}$	$-.15$
$P_{62.13\hat{7}10}$	$.38$
$P_{63.12\hat{7}10}$	$.29$
$P_{67.12310}$	$.23$
$P_{610.123\hat{7}}$	$-.17$

$$R_{6.123\hat{7}10} = .63$$
$$(R_{6.123\hat{7}10})^2 = .39$$
$$P_{6U} = .78$$

Path coefficients: regression of oppression (Z_7) on its predictors.

path	beta weight
$P_{73.45\hat{6}10}$	$.26$
$P_{74.35\hat{6}10}$	$.30$
$P_{75.34\hat{6}10}$	$.23$
$P_{7\hat{6}.34510}$	$.29$
$P_{710.345\hat{6}}$	$-.01$

$$R_{7.345610} = .67$$
$$(R_{7.345610})^2 = .45$$
$$P_{7U} = .74$$

(continued)

APPENDIX B (Continued)

Path coefficients: regression of revolt (Z_8) on its predictors.

path	beta weight
$P_{81.23456710}$	.09
$P_{82.13456710}$	-.12
$P_{83.12456710}$	.19
$P_{84.12356710}$	.14
$P_{85.12346710}$	.13
$P_{86.12345710}$	.13
$P_{87.12345610}$	.08
$P_{810.1234567}$	-.32

$$R_{8.123456710} = .44$$

$$(R_{8.123456710})^2 = .20$$

$$P_{8U} = .90$$

(continued)

APPENDIX B (Continued)

Path coefficients: regression of coups d'etat (Z_9) on its predictors.

path	beta weight
$P_{91.23456710}$	-.04
$P_{92.13456710}$	.06
$P_{93.12456710}$	.52
$P_{94.12356710}$	.02
$P_{95.12346710}$	-.00
$P_{96.12345710}$	.03
$P_{97.12345610}$	.17
$P_{910.1234567}$	-.29

$$R_{9.123456710} = .58$$
$$(R_{9.123456710})^2 = .34$$
$$P_{9U} = .81$$

11 Third World Terrorism: Perspectives for Quantitative Research
John M. Gleason

INTRODUCTION

One of the top news stories in 1972 was the terrorist attack on the Israeli athletes at the Munich Olympic Games. More recently, the Bologna railroad station bombing and the seizure of the American Embassy in Iran commanded newspaper headlines. Although these were perhaps the most publicized of the recent terrorist attacks, they are indicative of the growing problem of international terrorism in the world. While Western Europe has been the focus of much terrorist activity, both terror and terrorism are growing problems in Third World countries. Alexander notes ". . . Third World countries of Asia, Africa, and the Middle East have accepted opposition violence as an expression of 'self determination.'"[1] Butler suggests ". . . inasmuch as patience is running short in Latin America and social and economc conditions do not improve substantially, we can expect that terrorists will not only continue, but will expand, their operations."[2]

The focus of this chapter is on international terrorism in Third World countries. We will examine terrorism and include a discussion of efforts to define international terrorism. Possible reasons for the growth of Third World terrorism are noted. Results are presented which suggest that the Poisson is a good model for the occurrence of events of international

---

*A version of this chapter was presented at the Joint National Meeting of the Operations Research Society of America and The Institute for Management Sciences, Los Angeles, November 13-15, 1978.

terrorism in Third World countries, based on data from 1968 to 1974. Implications of the Poisson model, the need for more quantitative research in the area of terrorism, and suggested areas for research are discussed.

TERRORISM

The increase in international terrorist activity following World War I led to several efforts to deal with the problem. One such attempt was a series of meetings held under the auspices of the International Conference for the Unification of Penal Law in the late 1920s and 1930s.(3) In years to follow, international terrorism would continue to be a concern, as evidenced by the interest of League of Nations committees and United Nations committees in the subject. Unfortunately, efforts to deal with terrorism have not always been successful; in fact, the recent United Nations ad hoc Committee on International Terrorism could not even reach a conclusion as to a definition of international terrorism.(4)

Since this definitional problem is extant, it will be useful to examine the concepts of terrorism and international terrorism. Hacker explores two kinds of fear arousal: terror and terrorism.(5) He defines terror, which is inflicted from above, as the manufacture and spread of fear by dictators, governments, and bosses. Terrorism, on the other hand, is imposed from below, and is the manufacture and spread of fear by rebels, revolutionaries, and protesters. The former is an attempt by the powerful to exert control through intimidation, and the latter is an attempt by the powerless to exert control through intimidation. Hacker also notes that terrorists can be divided into three groups according to their main motivation: the "crazies," the criminals, and the crusaders. The emotionally disturbed ("crazies") are driven by reasons of their own which do not often make sense to others. The criminal simply uses illegitimate means to obtain personal gain. The crusading terrorists are idealistic. Although there is no widely accepted definition of terrorism, several attempts at definition of the term have been made.(6)

The problem of defining international terrorism is even more difficult since it is complicated by international politics. As might be expected, definitions reflect political points of view of the different countries. Jenkins describes international terrorism as:

> a single incident or a campaign of violence waged outside the presently accepted rules and procedures of international diplomacy and war; it is often designed to attract worldwide attention to the exis-

tence and cause of the terrorists and to inspire
fear. Often the violence is carried out for effect.
The actual victim or victims of terrorist attacks and
the target audience may not be the same; the victims
may be totally unrelated to the struggle.(7)

Jenkins also indicates that the term "international terrorism"
should be applied to incidents which have clear international
repercussions; that is, incidents in which terrorists went
abroad to strike their targets, selected victims or targets that
had connections with foreign states, or created international
incidents by attacking airline passengers, personnel, and
equipment.(8)   Bassiouni's discussion of the nature of terrorism and international terrorism is consistent with those of
Hacker and Jenkins.(9)
    Possible reasons for the growth of Third World terrorism
are suggested by Bell.(10) He notes that the shift to transnational terror and away from guerrilla revolution remains a
maneuver of the truly desperate.

The turn to terror is the result of a complex con-
fluence of forces including: (1) the regular failure
of revolutionary campaigns in the third world which
have produced only escalated repression, (2) the
repeated collapse of other new strategies, (3) the
recognition of the potential for exploitation of the
mass media, and (4) political trends within the third
world.   With the end of overt colonial rule, third
world nationalists may begin to look towards the
ultimate sources of imperialism. They see the world
as controlled by an imperialist-capitalist-racist conspiracy of vast power, immune to conventional
revolutionary strategies.(11)

Having briefly reviewed the concept of terrorism, we now turn
to an analysis of incidents of international terrorism in Third
World countries which took place from 1968 to 1974.

A POISSON MODEL OF TERRORISM

There has been little quantitative effort devoted to the study
of terrorism. Any attempt to analyze terrorism in Third World
countries, to determine the effectiveness of antiterrorism
efforts in these countries, and to draw comparisons between
Third World and other countries will require an understanding
of the underlying generating processes for events of terrorism. In light of the characteristics of events of terrorism, it
appears that the Poisson model would be a good model for

occurrences of such events: (1) the probability that an event
of terrorism occurs during a time interval increases with the
length of the time interval; (2) the probability is almost negligible that two events of terrorism will occur in a very small
time interval (with the exception, of course, of coordinated
efforts); (3) generally, events of terrorism which occur during
one time interval are independent of those which occur in any
other time interval. These three factors, slightly para-
phrased, can be seen to be assumptions of the Poisson model.
It should be noted, however, that the validity of the third
factor is somewhat questionable. It is conceivable that an
event of terrorism, if given sufficient publicity, will generate
a climate which is conducive to other events of terrorism. Bell
notes that it ". . . sometimes seems as if each operation
encourages the next."(12)

This study is based upon the Jenkins and Johnson/Rand
Corporation chronology of 507 incidents of international terrorism that took place between January 9, 1968 and April 26,
1974. Tables 11.1-11.7 provide data by location and by month
for incidents of terrorism for the 76 month period under
consideration. Table 11.8 provides empirical and theoretical
data (based on the Poisson model) for the incidents of international terrorism which occurred in Third World countries
during that period. The second column of table 11.8 includes
the Poisson probabilities for the number of incidents of terrorism (indicated in the first column) in a given month.
Column four indicates the actual cumulative distribution for the
months in the sample, whereas column three indicates the
theoretical cumulative distribution based on the hypothesized
Poisson model. As may be seen in table 11.8, the Poisson
appears to be a good model for the occurrences of events of
international terrorism in Third World countries; the Komo-
gorov-Smirnov statistic is .1418 which is significant at the .10
level but not significant at the .05 level. (It should be noted
that a chi-square test based on this data does not provide
results which are supportive of a Poisson model, since the
chi-square statistic is significant at a value of .001; however,
information is lost in the chi-square test as a result of the
necessity of combining numerous classes on order to have a
valid chi-square test.)

IMPLICATIONS

The study of international terrorism has been the domain of
the psychologist, political scientist, and those in the legal
profession. Bell notes that analytical attempts to study the
problem suffer for the lack of hard data.(13) This study is a
first attempt at a quantitative analysis of terrorism. The

Table 11.1. Incidents of International Terrorism in the
Third World - 1968

Country	Jan	Feb	Mar	Apr	May	June	July	Aug	Sept	Oct	Nov	Dec	Total
Brazil										1			1
Columbia			1										1
Cuba	1												1
Guatemala	1						1						2
Mexico										1	1		2
Venezuela			1										1

Table 11.2. Incidents of International Terrorism in the
Third World - 1969

Country	Jan	Feb	Mar	Apr	May	June	July	Aug	Sept	Oct	Nov	Dec	Total
Angola						1							1
Argentina						1				6	1		8
Brazil									1	1	1		3
Columbia	1	1	1	1	1	1		1		2			9
Ecuador	1			1					1				3
Ethiopia								1	1				2
Honduras									1				1
Mexico							1						1
Pakistan						1							1
Peru	1		1										2
Syria								1					1
Turkey										1			1
Uruguay						1							1
Venezuela		1											1

Table 11.3. Incidents of International Terrorism in the
Third World - 1970

Country	Jan	Feb	Mar	Apr	May	June	July	Aug	Sept	Oct	Nov	Dec	Total
Algeria								1					1
Argentina			4						1	2			7
Bolivia						1							1
Brazil			2	2		1	1				1		7
Columbia			1		2								3
Costa Rica										1			1
Dominican Republic			1		1								2
Ethiopia	1			1									2
Guatemala	1		2										3
Iran						1				1	1		3
Jamaica					1								1
Jordan		1				4			1				6
Lebanon						1	1						2
Mexico					1		2						3
Pakistan											1		1
Paraguay					1								1
Turkey		1						1		3	2	1	8
Uganda					1								1
Uruguay	1					2	3	2	1			2	11

Table 11.4. Incidents of International Terrorism in the
Third World - 1971

Country	Jan	Feb	Mar	Apr	May	June	July	Aug	Sept	Oct	Nov	Dec	Total
Argentina				1	1								2
Bolivia					1	1							2
Brazil											1		1
Cambodia									2				2
Egypt											1		1
Ethiopia	1												1
India		1											1
Jordan				1					?		1		4
Philippines			1										1
South Korea	1												1
Turkey	2	5	3	1	2					1			14
Uruguay	1					1					1		3

Table 11.5.   Incidents of International Terrorism in the
Third World - 1972

Country	Jan	Feb	Mar	Apr	May	June	July	Aug	Sept	Oct	Nov	Dec	Total
Algeria										1			1
Argentina			1		1	2		1	1	1	2	4	13
Brazil		1											1
Cambodia									1				1
Columbia							1						1
Egypt												1	1
El Salvador											2		2
Gaza	1												1
India											1		1
Iran					1								1
Jordan											2		2
Lebanon								1				1	2
Mexico											1		1
South Vietnam							1						1
Thailand												1	1
Turkey			1		2					1		1	5
Uruguay							1						1
Venezuela												1	1

Table 11.6.   Incidents of International Terrorism in the
Third World - 1973

Country	Jan	Feb	Mar	Apr	May	June	July	Aug	Sept	Oct	Nov	Dec	Total
Afghanistan					1								1
Argentina		2	2	3	4	4	4	1	1	5	3	3	32
Brazil					1						1		2
Burma					1								1
Chile							2	2					4
Columbia					1					1			2
Cyprus	1		1	1									3
Dominican Republic									1				1
Ecuador								1					1
El Salvador				1									1
Ethiopia	1												1
Guatemala						1							1
Haiti	1												1
Honduras							1						1
Iran	1				1								2
Jordan	1	1											2
Lebanon	2		1	7	1					1	1		13
Mexico					1					1			2
Morocco			2										2
Nepal						1							1
Paraguay								1					1
Peru							2						2
Portugal									2				2
Saudi Arabia				1									1
Sudan			1										1
Venezuela					1						1		2
Zaire									1				1
Zambia									1				1

Table 11.7. Incidents of International Terrorism in the
Third World – 1974

Country	Jan	Feb	Mar	Apr	May	June	July	Aug	Sept	Oct	Nov	Dec	Total
Argentina	1	1		1									3
Columbia		1											1
Cyprus	1												1
Egypt				1									1
Ethiopia			1										1
Lebanon			1										1
Mexico		1	1										2
Pakistan		1											1
Singapore	1												1
Thailand				1									1
Venezuela			1										1

Table 11.8. Cumulative Distribution of Incidents
of International Terrorism in the Third World per Month*

Number of Incidents	Poisson Probability	Theoretical Cumulative Distribution	Actual Cumulative Distribution
0	.02613	.0261	.1579
1	.09523	.1214	.2632
2	.17354	.2949	.4211
3	.21084	.5057	.5658
4	.19212	.6979	.6974
5	.14004	.8379	.7632
6	.08507	.9230	.8026
7	.04429	.9673	.8684
8	.02018	.9874	.9079
9	.00817	.9956	.9605
10	.00298	.9986	.9737
11	.00099	.9996	.9868
12	.00030	.9999	.9868
≥ 13	.00011	1.0000	1.0000

λ = 3.64474 incidents per month

Kolmogorov-Smirnov Test: Maximum absolute deviation between
actual and theoretical cumulative distributions is .1418.

Critical value at α = .1 is .140
Critical value at α = .05 is .156

*All data have been rounded.

results suggest that the Poisson may be a good model for the
underlying generating process for incidents of international
terrorism in Third World countries.

There is an obvious need for more research of a quantitative nature in the field of terrorism. Simple hypothesis
testing of the theories of the qualitative researchers would be
of interest. For example, Hacker refers to terrorism as a
"growth industry" and notes that in the mid 1970s terrorism
increased at an alarming rate.(14)   Goldberg states that

". . . the world has been plagued during the past decade by
an alarming and unprecedented expansion of [terrorism]."(15)
The decade that Goldberg refers to is the decade from 1966 to
1976. The data which was used in the Poisson analysis in the
previous section is drawn from a 76 month period from the
middle of that ten-year period. Suppose we consider the first
38 months of our data to be a sample from the first half of the
decade, and the last 38 months of data to be a sample from the
second half of the decade. The statements of Hacker and
Goldberg relative to the alarming increase in terrorism during
this period are then subject to simple quantitative verification.
Although the details are not presented herein, it may be seen
that the Poisson model is also a good model for both 38-month
periods. (The Kolmogorov-Smirnov test statistic is not even
significant at a level of .2 for either of the 38-month periods).
The sample mean for the first 38-month period is λ = 3.105,
and the mean for the second 38-month period is λ = 4.184.
Testing the hypothesis that both samples come from the same
population results in a Kolmogorov-Smirnov statistic which is
not significant even at the .20 level (for a one-tailed test).
Thus, the "alarming" nature of the increase in terrorism is not
confirmed statistically, at least in Third World countries.

Investigation of incidents of terrorism in other countries
may be aided by the possibility of the Poisson model being
valid in those countries. For example, other research by this
author has shown the Poisson to be a good model for the
occurrence of incidents of international terrorism in the United
States.(16) The means of the samples for the two 38-month
periods based on United States terrorism data are λ = 1.0526
and λ = .6316. Testing the hypothesis that both samples come
from the same population results in a Kolmogorov-Smirnov
statistic which is not significant even at the .20 level. Thus,
it appears that there has not been an increase in international
terrorism in the United States during this period. These
findings result in several observations regarding the statements concerning the "alarming" increase in terrorism. Since
statistics in the Third World and in the United States do not
indicate an increase in terrorism, perhaps the "alarming"
increase is illusory: increased media coverage of incidents of
terrorism, or more dramatic incidents, may be causing an
incorrect perception of "alarming" increases in terrorism.

The data also indicates that, although terrorism may be a
problem in Third World countries as a group, it is less severe
in individual Third World countries than in non-Third World
countries. For example, if we consider only Third World
countries in which terrorism occurred, the mean number of
incidents per month per country is well below the mean for the
United States. A perusal of the descriptions of the incidents
certainly suggests the export of terrorism on the part of the
Third World countries.

The need for more research in the field of terrorism, of both a qualitative and quantitative nature, is evidenced by the numerous predictions of increased terrorist activity in the future. Bell notes that "There is evidence that the entire transnational system may have become a new violence zone. . . ."(17) Goldberg states that terrorism ". . . imperils both the growth and functioning of our system of international law. Indeed, modern terrorism with sophisticated technological means at its disposal and the future possibility of access to biological and nuclear weapons, presents a clear and present danger to the very existence of civilization itself."(18) Hacker suggests that the bright future of terrorism is enhanced by the present state of international disunity and the lack of imagination on the part of conventional law enforcement. He also notes that it is very likely that worldwide terrorist alliances, coalitions, and organizations will be formed and that nationalist governments will employ terrorism in a more systematic manner.(19) Hacker's observation gains increased credibility as a result of the hijacking of a Lufthansa airliner containing 86 passengers and the slaying of the pilot by a group calling itself the "Struggle Against World Imperialism." In the wake of this incident, the Washington Post notes the possibility of the ". . . existence of an international ring of terrorists that is able to coordinate acts of violence with considerable skill."(20) A London Times dispatch also indicates that it is ". . . clear that some degree of cooperation has been established between terrorist groups of various nationalities."(21)

Unfortunately, quantitative research in the area may be somewhat difficult. Bell notes that ". . . any study of terrorist activities must be largely qualitative and, since conventional academic approaches do not work in this field, dependent on less than rigorous sources."(22) He further states that terrorism theories cannot be tested through controlled laboratory experiments, that numerous variables preclude useful generalization, and that analytical attempts will suffer from a lack of hard data.(23) These statements should prove a challenge to the quantitative researcher.

Several areas of quantitative research appear to be of interest. As noted herein, the Poisson is a good model for international terrorism in both Third World countries and in the United States. However, it can be shown that the Poisson is not a good model for worldwide occurrences of international terrorism. What factors cause this incongruity? Which countries are responsible for the incongruity? What are the implications regarding the occurrence of terrorism? If one considers a block of countries in which the Poisson is a good model, and another block of countries in which the Poisson is not a good model, perhaps certain differences will be apparent among the types of countries which will suggest terrorism-inducing or terrorism-discouraging elements.

Similar questions can be raised about Third World countries. Are there obvious differences between Third World countries with a good deal of terrorist activity (such as Argentina), little terrorist activity (such as Paraguay), and no terrorist activity (such as Nicaragua)? Perhaps it can be shown that the occurrence of incidents of terrorism is dependent on only a few variables - variables which have been discussed by the qualitative researchers, but have not been analyzed by the quantitative researchers. An initial observation may be that annual per capita income may be a useful variable. However, both Argentina and Venezuela enjoy annual per capita incomes of over $1,400 and there is a noticeable difference in terrorism in those two countries.

Earlier, a question was raised about the validity of the Poisson independence assumption with respect to terrorism. That is, it is conceivable that publicity resulting from an event of terrorism triggers other such events. Nevertheless, the Poisson does appear to be a good model of international terrorism. Possibly, then, the independence assumption is not violated. An empirical investigation of the effect of publicity on terrorism would be worthwhile.

Many individuals involved in the study of international security and arms control believe that domestic considerations strongly influence decisions related to the procurement and deployment of military forces. A study of the relationship between the occurrence of terrorism and the size of the military force in various countries should prove interesting.

Studies of particular types of terrorism also should be worthwhile. For example, Senator Abraham Ribicoff recently introduced legislation which would require the suspension of United States commercial air service and munitions sales to any countries which "aid and abet" international terrorism. A study of the trade-offs between the cost of this program and the potential cost of averted hijackings should result in an interesting cost-benefit analysis of the legislation. Trade-offs also may be examined from the viewpoint of the Third World countries subject to the sanctions of the legislation. These trade-offs would occur between the consequences of the denied trade with the United States and the (partly political) costs which would be incurred in an attempt to ensure that the sanctions would not be imposed.

Two final topics should be mentioned briefly. Researchers with an interest in game theory should find the study of terrorism to be extremely challenging. Furthermore, given the terrorist activity directed at large firms, and the attendant risk faced by these firms, an effort to develop an insurance rating or a self-insurance scheme for various types of terrorism should be of interest.

NOTES

1. Y. Alexander, Ed., International Terrorism: National, Regional, and Global Perspectives (New York: Praeger, 1976), Introduction, p. xviii.

2. R. Butler, "Terrorism in Latin America," in Alexander, International Terrorism, Chap. 3, p. 60.

3. S. Finger, "International Terrorism and the United Nations," in Alexander, International Terrorism, Chap. 11.

4. United Nations, General Assembly, Report of the Ad Hoc Committee on International Terrorism, General Assembly Official Records, 28th Session, Supplement No. 28 (A/9028), 1973; see also, B. Jenkins and J. Johnson, "International Terrorism: A Chronology, 1968-1974," Rand Paper R-1597-DOS/ARFA (Rand Corporation, Santa Monica, California, 1975).

5. F. Hacker, Crusaders, Criminals, Crazies: Terror and Terrorism in Our Time (New York: W.W. Norton, 1976).

6. Inter-American Juridical Committee, "Statement of Reasons for the Draft Convention on Terrorism and Kidnapping," October 5, 1970, O.A.S. Document CP/doc. 54/70, rev. 1, of November 4, 1970; C. Leiden and K. Schmitt, The Politics of Violence: Revolution in the Modern World (Englewood Cliffs, N.J.: Prentice-Hall, 1968).

7. Jenkins and Johnson, "International Terrorism," p. 3.

8. Ibid.

9. M. Bassiouni, International Terrorism and Political Crimes (Springfield, Ill.: Charles C. Thomas, 1975).

10. J. Bell, Transnational Terror (Washington, D.C.: American Enterprise Institute, 1975), Hoover Policy Study 17.

11. Ibid., p. 76.

12. Ibid., p. 76.

13. Ibid.

14. Hacker, Crusaders, Criminals, Crazies.

15. A Goldberg, "Foreword" in Alexander, International Terrorism, p. vi.

16. J. Gleason, "A Poisson Model of Incidents of International Terrorism in the United States," Terrorism 4 (1-4) (1980), pp. 259-265.

17. Bell, Transnational Terror, p. 76.

18. Goldberg, "Foreword," p. vi.

19. Hacker, Crusaders, Criminals, Crazies.

20. M. Getler, "86 Hostages Freed in Commando Raid," The Washington Post, October 18, 1977, p. A10.

21. The Times (London), "Unity of Terrorists Believed on Rise," reprinted in Omaha World-Herald, Sunday, October 23, 1977.

22. Bell, Transnational Terror, Preface.

23. Ibid.

12 Terrorism, Alienation, and German Society
Gregory F.T. Winn

The Federal Republic of Germany (FRG) has one of the highest standards of living in the world. The West German people have more freedom than they have ever had, and the FRG's youth can look forward to participating in one of the best and least expensive educational systems in the world. As Chancellor Helmut Schmidt has stated:

> . . . never before in Germany have young people had so many rights, so much freedom, so much social security, so many opportunities in education and life in general as have opened up to them during the course of the three decades of progress in the second German democracy.(1)

Why, then, did the Federal Republic of Germany suffer so greatly from terrorism during the 1970s? And why did many German students apparently empathize or even support the terrorist atrocities of such infamous groups as the Baader-Meinhof gang and the June 2nd Movement? This study explores some of the causes of terrorism in Germany and focuses on the degree and form of alienation experienced by German university students. Potential causal (or conjunctive) factors underlying student rejection of German society are evaluated through survey research.

---

*Portions of this chapter were presented at the International Society of Political Psychology meeting, June 4-7, 1980, Boston, Massachusetts. I am most grateful to William McCown, George Witt, and Ray Russell for their invaluable research work, and to Janice Carter and Mary Sue Packer for editing and typing this essay.

Today, the Federal Republic has a total of 47 universities. In the late 1940s and in the 1950s, about 4 percent of German youth attended a university. Now, the figure is between 15 and 20 percent, and the total number of university students exceeds 900,000. These universities are state-financed (there are eleven states, or "Lander," in Germany), and are tuition free. Until the 1960s, the universities were the bastions of traditional German university principles, typified by paternalism and strict authority. In the 1960s and 1970s, students increasingly gained a stronger voice in all university affairs (Gruppenprinzip, or group principle). As students acquired greater access to administrative decision making, "left-oriented" students increasingly dominated student representative groups. According to political scientist Kurt Sontheimer of the Free University of Berlin, the increased dialogue with university students resulted in a situation where only "leftists and revolutionary students" had any say in university affairs. (2)

West German university students were not unlike their American counterparts of the late 1960s. Many were idealists who sought a better world. The students felt a form of solidarity with the American civil rights movement and also with American students opposed to the war in Vietnam. Germans who had been adults during World War II, on the other hand, did not empathize with the student Anti-War Movement in the United States. (3)   Many older Germans were obsessed by the Wirtschaftswunder (economic miracle), which they felt had to be maintained in order to avoid a demise of democracy, similar to the loss of democracy after the economic collapse of the Weimar Republic. Many younger Germans did not share their elders' perspective and were repulsed by "materialism" for its own sake. Die Leistungsgesellschaft, or "achievement society," was repugnant to many students who rebelled against the constraints of "meritocracy" and the fundamental German desire for rules, status, and order - or Grundordnung (basic order).

Those students, or former students, who subsequently expressed their frustration through terrorist actions may have been influenced by several events in the 1960s. On June 2, 1967, a student named Benno Ohnesorg was taking part in a demonstration protesting the Shah of Iran's visit to Berlin. Before the day was over, Ohnesorg was dead, shot by a policeman during the demonstration. Students in both Berlin and the Federal Republic reacted to his death with protests. A year later, on May 11, 1968, a young right-wing radical attempted to kill Rudi Dutschke. "Red" Rudi, a powerful student leader in the 1960s, was seriously injured. (He died in Denmark in 1979 from causes related to the cranial wounds he received in this attempt.) All over Germany protests took place and, in Berlin, protesters marched to the Springerhaus.

Springerhaus published a conservative newspaper that had
often sharply attacked the German student protest movement.
The protesters in Berlin blamed the newspaper for the attack
on Dutschke. They rioted at the Springerhaus and caused
heavy damage.(4)
  These events are important because of their reported
effect on German terrorist leaders. According to Die Zeit, the
shooting death of Benno Ohnesorg was one of the major factors
that brought Gudrun Ensslin down the path of terrorism.(5)
In the opinion of Jillian Becker, the attempted murder of Rudi
Dutschke was the deciding factor in favor of terrorism for
Ulrike Meinhof.(6) Similarly, Michael (Bommi) Baumann, the
founder of the June 2nd Movement, a left-wing guerilla organization, wrote that his life was irrevocably changed by the
attack on Dutschke.(7) The transformation of youthful idealists into "urban guerrillas" who advocated terrorism resulted
in a prolonged series of bombings, kidnappings, and murders.
Dozens of people were killed, as attacks evolved from indiscriminate bombings of American military installations to the
kidnapping/murders of selected German political and business
leaders. Even after the capture of the founders of the Red
Army Faction in 1972, Baader-Meinhof attacks escalated, as
evidenced in 1977 by the murder of German Attorney General
Siegfried Buback, the assassination of Jurgen Ponto (a prominent banker), and the kidnapping and eventual murder of
Hans-Martin Schleyer (a central spokesman for German industry).(8) These events culminated in the thwarted hijacking
of a German jetliner to Mogadishu, Somalia, and in the simultaneous suicides in Stuttgart's Stammheim prison of three
founders of the Red Army Faction.(9)

REASONS FOR THE TERRORIST MOVEMENT

Explanations for the existence of the terrorist movement vary
widely, but can be placed into two major categories: 1) rejection of German society, and 2) ideological/idiosyncratic pro-
clivities toward violence. There are perhaps as many theories
as there are theoreticians explaining the causes of terrorist
actions.

Societal Factors Leading to Terrorism

1. An "anti-authoritarian, extra-parliamentary opposition"
against institutions of a bourgeois German society.(10)
2. A desire to replace the "performance principle" of capitalism with a "new reality" based on human needs.(11)

3.   Contempt for Germany's "consumer society" and opposition to Germany's economic miracle.   Rejection of German society partly because of its prosperity and political success.(12)

4.   Sexual repression and frustration transformed into a public statement of "female liberation."(13)

5.   An effort to force democratic societies to crack down harshly on dissent, thereby further alienating leftist and moderate sympathizers.(14)

6.   A rather vague solidarity with the Third World combined with a rejection of the German social system.

7.   Frustration resulting from the lack of job opportunities (particularly in teaching), compounded by the fact that West Germany has the lowest birthrate of any major nation in the world.(15)

8.   Hostility to the German "loyalty check" system for civil service entrants (Berufsverbot).

9.   Frustration with a society that is overly taxed, formally rigid, and overly regulated.   Tax rates are among the highest in the world: televisions, radios, and apartments are taxed; and in some areas there is even a tax on "clean air."   Among common social restrictions are laws against mowing lawns, washing cars, and hanging out laundry on Sundays; restrictions on house designs and colors to match neighborhood "styles"; and restrictions on when one can idle a car, play music, run water, or clean carpets.(16)

10.   Disillusionment with society, due to the corruption of the political system, similitude of party policies, and the bugging/surveillance scandals.(17)

11.   Frustrations stemming from "achievement" pressures in primary and secondary schools.   In 1978, for example, 14,000 school-age youngsters attempted suicide, and one in five school-age children were under psychiatric care.(18)

12.   Alienation from an "achievement society" which has led to Germany's becoming the leading heroin country   -   in number of addicts (45,000), in 1979 deaths from over-dosage (615), and in sheer consumption.(19)

13.   Rejection of Germany's past, and association of the older generation with the atrocities of the Third Reich.

Ideological/Idiosyncratic Factors Leading to Terrorism

1.   A playing-out of nihilist/anarchist theories typified by the works of Bakunin.(20)

2.   Support for Marxist, Maoist, and Marcusian concepts justifying the liberation of "working classes" and violence "against things" (and, ultimately, "against people").(21)

3. A link between idealism, romanticism, and terror - where those inspired by "deeply romantic idealism" will stop at nothing to prove themselves. (22)

4. Terrorist violence based on purely criminal instincts without reference to any form of revolutionary theory or strategy. (23)

5. Family alienation and rejection of paternalistic authoritarianism.

6. Individual rejection of German nationalism as typified by terrorist Susanne Albrecht's statement: "I am sick and tired of all that caviar gobbling." (24)

7. Rebellion by individuals who are overly indulged in a permissive society. (25)

8. A lack of individual purpose (anomie), compounded by boredom. (26)

9. "Teutonic atavism" as evidenced by Germany's warlike traditions. (27)

10. The achievement of political consciousness through "rock music" - a causal factor defended by terrorist Bommi Baumann. (28)

11. A natural urge to "express violence as a means of ridding oneself of suppressed feelings." Acts of terrorism are seen as "appealing" to the unconscious urge for violence within all of us. (29)

12. A fear of being only "ordinary citizens" without identity in society. (30)

The wide variety of causal factors associated with German terrorism precludes any definitive conclusion concerning the motivations of individual terrorists. Specific causal factors can only be determined through direct communication with terrorists - which, for the most part, is impossible. Many terrorists have been killed or have committed suicide. In addition, the number of high-level target attacks in Germany has been greatly reduced because of: 1) more efficient computerized tracking of terrorists, 2) improved relations with other nations which previously served as terrorist sanctuaries, and 3) a series of 52 new laws since 1969 designed to tighten internal security. (31) While terrorist activities are less visible, this essay argues that the social and family conditions which led to student sympathy for terrorist motives still remain. Although the terrorists themselves are inaccessible, university students are not; and their level of alienation is the subject of the following survey research.

RESEARCH PROGRAM

The results reported here are drawn from a 1979 survey of 230 university students in central and southern Germany. Of the Federal Republic's 47 universities, six representative schools were chosen. An effort was made to select universities which were "typed" as leftist (Marburg and Heidelberg), universities considered relatively apolitical (Munich, Regensburg, and Frankfurt), and more conservative (Erlangen). The survey results did not completely confirm these typologies. At each university, students were selected at random. In part, this study complements an earlier survey by S. Robert Lichter at Tubingen and Konstanz universities. As in his works, generalizations on the patterns of behavior for all German university students are not justified.(32)

The survey questionnaire was constructed in three basic parts: 1) questions concerning personality, roles, and family conflict; 2) questions concerning both definitions of, and support for, terrorism (the dependent variable); and 3) attitudinal/informational questions on Germany's history, educational system, employment system, and materialism. Results were analyzed to determine how responses varied from university to university, and from one academic discipline to another. Differences in patterns of responses between men and women were also evaluated. Several hypotheses relating independent and dependent variables were then examined, leading to the construction of three explanatory multiple regression models.

General Survey Results

Table 12.1 lists the results of the first part of our survey research. Responses of 230 university students are summarized by university. Each of the six personality/attitude tests is described in further detail below. The assumption was made that there are several factors contributing to student alienation, and among these are: a feeling of individual lack of purpose, a conflict of personalities between generations, hostility toward an overly circumscribed society, individual rigidity against change, family alienation, and frustration resulting from sexual discrimination. Some of these assumptions were partially confirmed.

We also assumed that test scores would vary from region to region and university to university. Referring to table 12.1, "t-tests" (comparison of statistical means analyses) indicated no significant differences between regions or universities in "Normlessness," "Rigidity," and "Chauvinism" scores. In almost every case where significant differences were found, either Marburg or Erlangen universities were involved. In general, the students from Erlangen (near Nurnberg) were more authoritarian (lower average score), less alienated by their family situation, and least supportive of terrorist activities. Marburg and Regensburg students followed a reverse pattern. For example, alienation scores were lowest for Erlangen students and highest for students at Regensburg University, and the difference was significant at .01. Similarly, significant differences between Erlangen and Regensburg occurred in response to "definitional" questions on terrorism. As stated, Marburg students had the lowest scores on the authoritarian personality tests, whereas Erlangen's students had the highest. The Erlangen students were least supportive or empathetic toward terrorism, while Marburg students were most supportive (significance of .01 for question 9). On the "Powerlessness" test, the only significant difference was between Marburg and Frankfurt, and it was minimal (.05). These initial regional/university differences served as a basis for the chi-square and multiple regression analyses below. In the remainder of the study, the dependent variable is evaluated, and then general social factors contributing to terrorism are examined. The study concludes with a comparative evaluation of personality factors underlying alienation.

Alienation and Terrorist Support

Despite the nature of terrorist activities, a large segment of the German university community was willing to condone the terrorists' motives, if not their methods. Tables 12.2 and 12.3 summarize the responses to seven statements or questions concerning terrorism. The first four entries indicate the percentage of students who support (table 12.2) or at least do not refute (table 12.3) various definitions of terrorism. Similarly, entries 5, 6, and 7 represent the percentage of students who agree with (table 12.2) or at least do not disagree with (table 12.3) terrorist motives and activities. Across the board, an average of 36.5 percent of the students agreed that terrorism is directed against a political society which only allows political parties that are basically the same. When "undecided" responses are included (table 12.3), we see that 54.7 percent of the students questioned do not oppose this interpretation of terrorist motives. An almost identical number of students believe that terrorists are attempting to escape "repression within Germany's military-industrial society." Surprisingly, given the fact that many Red Army Faction terrorists trained in the Middle East, only a few students saw German terrorism as part of an international network in support of the world's working classes. In addition, a majority of the students defined "freedom" as a goal

Table 12.1. Summary Results

(■ = highest score; ■ = lowest score)

Average Scores	Erlangen	Munich	Heidelberg	Frankfurt	Regensburg
1. Authoritarian character; high score indicates less authoritarianism	X̄ 3.96 S .395 (25)	X̄ 4.21 S .657 (52)	X̄ 4.038 S .59 (58)	X̄ 4.05 S .59 (35)	X̄ 4.413 S .683 (51)
2. Normlessness (low score= acceptance of societal norms; high score=life is without purpose)	X̄ 10.48 S 4.26 (25)	X̄ 11.019 S 3.096 (52)	X̄ 11.138 S 3.337 (58)	X̄ 11.34 S 3.725 (35)	X̄ 10.588 S 3.214 (51)
3. Rigidity (higher, more exacting)	X̄ 3.016 S .794 (25)	X̄ 2.88 S .813 (57)	X̄ 3.049 S .852 (57)	X̄ 2.93 S .892 (35)	X̄ 2.918 S .805 (51)
4. Family alienation	X̄ 64.- S 12.124 (25)	X̄ 68.83 S 16.31 (52)	X̄ 67.172 S 10.301 (58)	X̄ 68.86 S 14.153 (35)	X̄ 72.51 S 13.379 (51)
5. Powerlessness (higher total=more alienation & less personal influence)	X̄ 19.56 S 4.50 (25)	X̄ 17.61 S 6.120 (52)	X̄ 18.741 S 4.564 (58)	X̄ 20.286 S 5.581 (35)	X̄ 17.33 S 4.966 (51)
6. Chauvinism (higher score= more prejudiced)	X̄ 1.58 S .694 (25)	X̄ 1.529 S .921 (52)	X̄ 1.521 S .622 (58)	X̄ 1.583 S .758 (35)	X̄ 1.398 S .660 (51)
7. Terrorism is directed against a closed political system[a]	X̄ 2.17 S 1.204 (24)	X̄ 3.0 S 1.52 (52)	X̄ 2.534 S 1.429 (58)	X̄ 2.943 S 1.513 (35)	X̄ 3.157 S 1.502 (51)
8. Terrorism is based on a desire to escape repression by the military/industrial society[b]	X̄ 2.16 S 1.18 (25)	X̄ 2.365 S 1.482 (52)	X̄ 2.534 S 1.404 (58)	X̄ 2.771 S 1.374 (35)	X̄ 2.882 S 1.595 (51)
9. Terrorists are freedom fighters[c]	X̄ 1.28 S .678 (25)	X̄ 1.66 S 1.002 (50)	X̄ 1.517 S .959 (58)	X̄ 1.86 S 1.264 (35)	X̄ 1.734 S 1.119 (51)

(continued)

Table 12.1. (Continued)

Average Scores	Marburg (N=230) Avg. X̄, S	(N=230) Avg. X̄	(N=230) Avg. S	(.05 minimum significance) t-test results	Comparison
1. Authoritarian character; high score indicates less authoritarianism	X̄ 4.52 S .34 (9)	4.11	.61	(3.66) .001 (2.35) .05 (2.24) .05	Marburg & Erlangen Marburg & Erlangen Marburg & Erlangen
2. Normlessness (low score= acceptance of societal norms; high score=life is without purpose)	X̄ 10.5 S 3.47 (9)	10.93	3.41	no significant difference	all pairs
3. Rigidity (higher, more exacting)	X̄ 2.82 S. 69 (9)	2.94 (229)	.826 (229)	no significant difference	all pairs
4. Family alienation	X̄ 66.2 S 14.52 (9)	68.6	13.56	(2.64) .01	Erlangen & Regensburg (no others)
5. Powerlessness (higher total=more alienation & less personal influence)	X̄ 15.8 S 5.43 (9)	18.38	5.30	(2.112) .05	Frankfurt & Marburg (no others)
6. Chauvinism (higher score= more prejudiced)	X̄ 1.52 S .82 (9)	1.51	.686	no significant difference	all pairs
7. Terrorism is directed against a closed political system [a]	X̄ 2.89 S 1.41 (9)	2.82 (229)	1.476 (229)	(2.78) .01 (2.054) .05	Erlangen & Regensburg Erlangen & Frankfurt (no others)
8. Terrorism is based on a desire to escape repression by the military/industrial society [b]	X̄ 3.11 S 1.45 (9)	2.70	1.45	(-1.996) .05	Erlangen & Regensburg (no others)
9. Terrorists are freedom fighters [c]	X̄ 2.33 S 1.33 (9)	1.67 (223)	1.06 (223)	(3.052) .01 (2.054) .05	Erlangen & Marburg Erlangen & Frankfurt (no others)

a. Based on the statement: "The terrorist movement in this country is directed against a political system which only allows political parties that are basically the same."
b. Based on the statement: "Terrorism in our country is based on the desire of the individual to escape from the repression within our military-industrial society."
c. Based on the statement: "The so-called terrorists in our country are really freedom fighters who deserve sanctuary in foreign countries."

12.2. Terrorism: Determination of Causes and Levels of Support
Percentage of Students Who Support Statements Indicated

	Erlangen (25)	Munich (52)	Heidelberg (58)	Frankfurt (35)	Regensburg (51)	Marburg (9)	Avg. Total
Terrorism is directed against a closed political system	16.7	44.2	27.6	40	45	44.4	36.5
Terrorism is based on desire to escape repression	24	36.5	32.8	37.1	43.1	44.4	36.1
Terrorism is part of the international workers movement	8	9.6	12.1	11.4	17.6	22.2	12.6
Freedom is obtained by struggle against government	40	55.8	50	54.5	62.7	66.7	54.4
Terrorists' rejection of society is understandable	40	59.6	60.3	47.1	66.7	77.8	58.1
Terrorists are trying to liberate our society	0	7.7	3.4	14.7	13.7	22.2	8.7
Terrorists are freedom fighters	4	6	6.9	11.4	9.8	11.1	7.9
Avg.	19	31.3	.27.6	30.9	36.9	41.3	(N=228 to 230)

12.3. Terrorism: Determination of Causes and Levels of Support
Percentage of Students Who Do Not Refute Statements Indicated

	Erlangen (25)	Munich (52)	Heidelberg (58)	Frankfurt (65)	Regensburg (51)	Marburg (9)	Avg. Total
Terrorism is directed against a closed political system	37.5	59.6	50	54.3	66.7	44.4	54.7
Terrorism is based on desire to escape repression	28	57.7	46.5	60	56.9	66.7	52.2
Terrorism is part of the international workers' movement	8	25	24.1	28.6	35.3	22.2	25.6
Freedom is obtained by struggle against the government	68	67.3	70.7	72.7	76.5	77.8	71.5
Terrorists' rejection of society is understandable	56	69.2	65.5	58.8	76.5	88.9	67.7
Terrorists are trying to liberate our society	16	30.8	20.7	32.3	29.4	33.3	26.6
Terrorists are freedom fighters	4	20	13.8	22.9	19.6	55.5	18.4
Avg.	31.1	47.1	41.6	47.1	51.6	47.0	(N=228 to 230)

attainable only through opposition to government oppression and authority. Reading across columns from left to right, it is obvious that the universities listed on the "right" (Regensburg, Marburg) were more supportive of the definitional statements concerning German terrorism.

The second part of tables 12.2 and 12.3 (entries 5, 6, and 7) indicate student support for terrorist activities. The hypothesis that German students are alienated is fully supported by the students' response to the statement: "Although I don't agree with their methods, I understand the terrorists' rejection of our society." Fifty-eight percent of the students agreed with this statement, and two-thirds of the students surveyed (table 12.3) did not refute its validity. In the specific case of Regensburg, two-thirds of the students agreed with the statement, and in a smaller Marburg sample, 78 percent were in concurrence. Responses to questions 5, 6, and 7 serve as the dependent variable for the remainder of this study.

The actual number of terrorists, active accomplices, strong supporters, and leftist sympathizers is unknown. Estimates range from 40 or 50 to 100 "hard-core terrorists" (many of whom have died or been captured), with 1,200 "highly dangerous" active accomplices, working within a wider network of 5,000 to 6,000 strong supporters.(33) As for leftist sympathizers, approximately 15 to 20 percent of Germany's university students have been characterized in the German press as "radical leftists" who believe Germany is "developing into a fascist state".(34) A German Ministry of the Interior study further concluded that 30 percent of German students belong to or have the potential to belong to leftist radical groups.(35) Our results indicate that perhaps 8 or 9 percent of the students surveyed could be considered "strong supporters" of the terrorist movement. For example, 7.9 percent agreed that terrorists are really "freedom fighters" deserving sanctuary in foreign countries. As for "left-leaning sympathizers," at least a majority of the students surveyed could belong in this category. The comparison of average totals for tables 12.2 and 12.3 clearly indicates the large numbers of students who, while not opposing terrorist activities, remain uncertain.

Although it was presumed that the students at predominantly Catholic Regensburg University would <u>not</u> be as alienated as the supposedly radicalized Heidelberg student body, the reverse was true. Test results from Frankfurt, while in the middle range on most issues, indicated a disproportionately higher number of strong supporters for terrorist activities. Column averages show that Marburg and Regensburg university students are most alienated and Erlangen students least. Since differences among university samples concerning terrorism were extensive, as were differences among several social/personality scores, the next task is to match variation in social/personality variables with the dependent variable results.

Chauvinism

In his study of German radicalism, Lichter omits women from his analysis partly because "most were ideologically moderate and very few were politically active."(36) We hypothesized that not only are women "politically active," but also that women are more likely to be supportive of terrorist activities than are men. More than half of German terrorists are women, and German cultural traditions still place women in "secondary" positions despite legal advances for equal rights.(37) Of the entire survey population, 42 percent were women. The hypothesis that women are more actively supportive of the terrorist movement was not confirmed in that approximately the same proportion of women and men gave positive replies to questions such as: 1) terrorists are trying to liberate Germany more quickly than the government will allow (40 percent); and 2) terrorists are freedom fighters (33 percent). In comparing male versus female support of terrorist alienation (statement No. 5, tables 12.2 and 12.3) there is no significant difference as can be seen in fig. 12.2.

$x^2 = .129$

		Men (58%)	Women (42%)	
Not significant at .05	yes	74	56	130
	no	41	28	69
	uncertain	13	9	22
	totals	128	93	221

Fig. 12.2. Male versus Female Support of Terrorist Alienation

While it is not possible to conclude that women are more supportive of terrorism, they appear as supportive as their male counterparts and certainly not politically inactive. Men and women supporting terrorist concepts had test score averages indicating lower authoritarianism (4.43 compared to the average 4.11); and greater family alienation (76.8 compared to the average 68.6) than other respondents. When compared to nonterrorist supporters, both these differences are significant at .001 (t = 3.64) for authoritarianism; and t = 4.51 for family alienation.(38)

An attempt was also made to determine a rough estimate of the level of sexual bias or "chauvinism" among university students. One of several "chauvinism" questions read: "Since men are naturally more intelligent than women, they should be given the jobs requiring the most responsibility." On a one to five scale (five indicating greatest prejudice), student positions were consistently antichauvinistic, regardless of the university evaluated or male versus female responses (average score 1.51). The variation in this variable was so slight, that its distribution did not lead to significant results in either contingency table (chi-square) or regression analysis.

Alienation and the Berufsverbot

Several questions in the student survey were designed simply to confirm or refute popular explanations for alienation and terrorism in Germany. One cause celebre in the early 1970s for student alienation was the German government's decision to take legal action against radicals by creating a "screening process" to prohibit their employment in public service. The 1972 "Radikalenerlass," or Radicals Decree, included these stipulations:

> the members of the public service are obligated to commit themselves positively to the free and democratic basic order in the interpretation of the fundamental law and to support stability for that order.

> The membership of public servants in parties and organizations opposing the constitutional order - as well as other support of such parties and organizations - will therefore generally result in a conflict of loyalties.(39)   (emphasis added)

The Radicals Decree also became known as the Berufsverbot, and an estimated two million investigations resulted for such "public service jobs" as apprentice gardener, mail carrier, street cleaner, as well as for professors, judges, public prosecutors, teachers, medical students, and military officers. In October 1978, the Mayor of Hamburg commented: "Twenty communists in public service are a lesser evil than 200,000 frightened young people intimidated by a state surveillance policy."(40)

While the Berufsverbot is outlawed in some German states, it continues in others. Results indicate that the German students surveyed consider the Berufsverbot an infringement upon the individual's right to work and speak out, as shown in table 12.4. Of particular interest are the final questions on "infringement on individual rights" and on allowing a teacher "with communist sympathies" to teach. A preliminary survey of people age 50 and above indicates completely reverse results, with similar majorities. One student surveyed added a note to his responses that, because of the Berufsverbot loyalty check system, some students in their bitterness have shown more sympathy for the Baader-Meinhof gang than they otherwise would have done.

Table 12.4. Student Agreement and
Disagreement with Statements on Jobs,
Alienation, and the "Civil Service" System

Do you agree with the following statements?

			% Totals
1.	Government service includes not only school teachers, but also railway workers, street cleaners, garbage collectors, and letter carriers.	yes no undecided (230)*	81.7 % 15.2 3.1
2.	The so-called "Berufsverbot" are a continuation of the tradition of German "Beamtentums" (official bureaucratic structure and orientation).	yes no undecided (230)	40.0 % 30.4 29.6
3.	The "Berufsverbot" is a legal resolution designed to protect the federal and state government against those individuals who want to "bring down" the government.	yes no undecided (230)	35.6 % 56.1 8.3
4.	The "Berufsverbot" is an infringement upon the individual's basic right to work and to speak out.	yes no undecided (230)	75.7 % 18.7 5.6
5.	A teacher who has ever joined or been associated with a communist organization cannot be trusted to teach our children fairly and without bias.	yes no undecided (229)	13.5 % 79.5 7.0

*Total number of responses for each question are indicated in parentheses.

History, Naziism, and Education

The study of modern German history among university students leads to several obvious paradoxes. The war generation accepted democratic values in the postwar era and tried to inculcate those values in the minds of their children. However, the youth were skeptical of their parents' acceptance of those values which had been fundamentally alien to Germans prior to the war.(41) The older generation did accept democratic values, but without really discussing Germany's past with its children. When asked: "What did you think about the Endlösung ('final solution')?" the typical German parent was apt to say "Es ist vorbei" ('it is over, in the past'). Students felt that parents could hardly call the younger generation moral failures when they, the older generation, were unable and perhaps unwilling to prevent the mass murder of millions of men, women, and children. A fundamental debate has evolved in recent years between those "moralists" who feel that the "Vergangenheitsbewältigung" (understanding and acknowledgement of the collective guilt for the Hitler past) is imperative to Germany's health as a nation; and those "pragmatists" who feel that, after 35 years, it is pointless to continue this self-flagellation.(42) When asked; "Do you consider Germany's past (1933-1945) as a period of disgrace or shame?" 47 percent of the students said yes, but 53 percent said no or were unsure. Desirable or not, the past is in the present; and even the proper approach for teaching German history is debated. Furthermore, memories of Naziism are revived by international concern lest it be forgotten, by ongoing war crimes trials, and by neo-Naziism.

As in the case of American history where courses tend to be divided by the Civil War and the year 1865, so modern German history is divided into pre- and post-1945 periods. Either by design or by chance, the result of this demarcation is that teachers "tend" to dwell on earlier time periods, and by the end of the first semester have reached the mid-1930s. The subsequent semester begins with 1945 and the reconstruction of Germany.(43) A clear majority of students are concerned that important topics are not openly discussed even at the university level, yet many believe the era of the Third Reich is adequately covered:

Question	%	Totals
1. Do you agree with Heinrich Böll's opinion that students and teachers are being held back from thinking and speaking freely?	yes	64.3
	no	29.6
	unsure	6.1

Question	%	Totals
2. (Do you agree) that the edu-	yes	49.6
cational system in our country	no	43.4
discourages discussion of the	unsure	7.0
period during the Third Reich?		

As indicated, almost half of the students believe that the Third Reich era is adequately presented. At the same time, fully one-third of the students surveyed agreed with a statement that Hermann Goring was German minister of propaganda. In addition, 63 percent did not know that Maidanek was one of the most notorious concentration camps and was the subject of a five-year (1975-on) war crimes trial in Düsseldorf. Despite their fear of resurgent fascism, 86 percent of the students did not know that 90 percent of "today's Generals and Admirals were former officers of the Third Reich."(44)

The issues surrounding "Nazikriegsverbrecher" (war criminals) are not particularly popular, which may partly account for student ignorance of Maidanek. When the American production "Holocaust" was first presented on German television, it was greeted by bombings at two television stations, and a former synagogue was burned. Nonetheless, the television series directly affected German attitudes. Partly in reaction to the series, the Bonn Parliament abolished all time limits on war crime cases.(45) A survey taken by West German television and the Federal Office for Political Education showed that 73 percent of a representative sample of the 14 million West Germans who watched the series found it valuable. Unfortunately, 30 percent said after seeing the series: "Nazism was a basically good idea that was only carried out badly."(46) Among university students surveyed in this study, 87 percent disagreed with a statement that the war criminals were falsely accused as a result of Allied revenge (10 percent were undecided, 3 percent agreed). Sixteen percent indicated that there should be amnesty for Nazi war criminals.

The unlimited extension on Nazi war crimes trials may have been affected by increasing concern over neo-Naziism in Germany. Although they are constrained by the German government, there are about 140 neo-Nazi groups in Germany with approximately 18,000 members.(47) Acts of anti-Semitism have increased to include the desecration of several thousand Jewish graves. The number of illegal acts (including violence) committed by the neo-Nazis rose from 319 in 1976 to 992 in 1978.(48) While ultra-right-wing actions have not matched the level of extreme violence of leftist terrorist attacks, neo-Naziism, when linked with Germany's continuing historical trauma, leads to extensive fear of a resurgent German fascist state. This sentiment is partly expressed by student response to the statement:

%	Total
47.4	yes
30.0	no
25.6	unsure

The real danger in this country is from the political "right" and not the "left."

Contingency table analysis (chi-square) suggests that there is a conjunctive if not causal link between antipathy toward Germany's past and indirect support of leftist terrorist activities. For example, in comparing a sense of historical shame/disgrace with a fear that the "real" threat is from the political right versus left, the following table results:

History - A Disgrace?

Real threat from the right?

		Yes	No/Uncertain	Total
χ^2 = 19.58	yes	66	40	106
N = 230				
P = .9999	no/uncertain	41	83	124
significant at .001				
	Totals	107	123	230

Chi Square analysis comparing both a sense of historical "shame" and perceived threat from the right with a statement concerning support for terrorist motives if not their methods yields similarly significant results. It is quite appropriate to conclude that student perception of Germany's Third Reich combined with increased concern over resurgent "rightest" movements is directly related to alienation with the German social/political system and empathy for leftist terrorist movements.

Support terrorists but not their methods	Real Threat From Right?		History - A Disgrace?	
	yes	no/unsure	yes	no/unsure
yes	83	50	74	56
no/unsure	26	71	31	64

χ^2 = 28.52 (N 23/) χ^2 = 13.01 (N = 225)
Sig at .0001   Sig. at .001

Academic Discipline and Terrorist Support

Returning to the role of the universities as "teaching" institutions, a related issue to regional university support is the
question of which disciplines, if any, within the university are
most likely to infuse students with terrorist "idealism"? While
this study does not attempt to build a "terrorist profile," we
are concerned with determining which factors contribute to
student alienation in Germany.(49)   Are terrorist supporters
more likely to be students of law, medicine, mathematics, or
sociology?   Some 70 radical lawyers, including Klaus Croissant,
Arndt Mueller, and Kurt Grunewald, have been accused of
actively supporting and even leading the terrorist movement.(50)   Schools of Psychology, Philosophy, and Social
Research at Frankfurt, Heidelberg, and Berlin Universities
have been branded as leading centers for radical indoctrination.   Nominal scale analysis of student support of terrorist
sentiments, by academic discipline, does not clearly prove that
certain disciplines are most likely to foster radical-leftist
political orientations.   Among surveyed law students, 14 were
empathetic with terrorist attitudes, 10 were not, and 3 were
undecided.   In the sciences, students of biology generally
agreed with terrorist motives; but students of chemistry,
mathematics, and physics did not.   If the subject of biology is
added to the category of "social sciences," a discernibly
significant pattern results; but one cannot necessarily conclude
that the study of some subjects will lead to greater empathy
for terrorist activities.

Academic Disciplines Contingency Table

Support terrorist philosophy but not	Liberal Arts/ Teaching	Social Sciences & Languages	Medicine/ Math Sciences	Law	Totals
action-yes	20	51	23	14	108
no	19	14	25	10	68
unsure	3	7	4	3	17
total	42	72	52	27	193

χ^2 = 14.662   d.6 = 6   (P) = .977   significant at .03

Family Alienation

Given the often hypothesized "German generation gap,"
students were asked to respond to a series of questions from
the "Minnesota Scale for the Survey of Opinions" evaluating
individual morale and adjustment to family conditions.(51)

Results support previous research on family alienation which has indicated that children resent parents, particularly fathers, who are considered punitive, lacking warmth, authoritarian, and patriarchal.(52) Comparisons with previous American test scores indicate significantly higher family alienation levels among German students.(53) Cross-analysis with statements concerning support for terrorism and freedom movements (against government repression) yield chi-square results of .05 and .001 respectively. (x^2 = 6.071. and 13.70.) That is to say, in general, the greater the student's sense of alienation from family, the more alienated the student is from the German social/political system.

Personality Factors

In addition to family attitude statements, students were given a series of standardized tests to evaluate their individual level of authoritarianism (Fromm-Adorno (F) Scale), a series of questions on personal rigidity and decision making patterns, and two tests from the Dean Scale for Measuring Alienation (Powerlessness and Normlessness Scales).(54) Neither Dean Scale Alienation test showed a wide variety in response patterns. There was no significant covariation with student support of leftist-terrorist movements. However, when compared to previous test results in the United States, German students were significantly more alienated. To a greater degree, German students felt that life was "without meaning" (Normlessness) and there was little they could do about this state of affairs [(Powerlessness) (minimum t-test differences of 6.23 or .001 significance (N), and 10.84 or .001 significance (P)].

Contingency table cross-analysis of levels of authoritarianism and personal rigidity led to predicted trends toward alienation. It was hypothesized that students with lower levels of authoritarianism (a higher score on a one to five scale; see table 12.1) and lower levels of personal rigidity would be more in favor of left-radical concepts.(55) It is perhaps plausible to argue that the terrorists themselves may be characterized by high levels of authoritarianism, i.e., simultaneously seeking increased power and service to it. However, this pattern does not apparently apply to student sympathizers with terrorism.(56) Chi-square analysis reveals a relationship between lower levels of authoritarianism and rigidity and support for terrorists (but not their methods):

	Authoritarianism (mean = 4.11)		Rigidity (mean = 2.9)	
Support for terrorists, but not their methods.	Above 4.11	Below 4.11	Below 2.9	Above 2.9
yes	92	41	72	57
no/unsure	40	57	36	61

$$x^2 = 17.901 \qquad\qquad x^2 = 7.760$$

$$N = 230 \qquad\qquad\qquad N = 226$$

$$(P) = .99997 \qquad\qquad (P) = .9846$$

$$\underline{sig} = .001 \qquad\qquad\quad \underline{sig} = .01$$

CONCLUSIONS

Multiple Regression model analyses further support contingency table comparisons of Rigidity, Authoritarianism, and Family Attitudes (table 12.5). An examination of relative degrees of explained variation indicates that Authoritarianism and Rigidity are roughly equivalent explanatory factors, followed by Family Alienation. All these factors are of some significance, with an average explained variation (Coefficient of Determination, R^2) of .82. Using the constants derived for the equation, $Z = a + a.x + a_2y$, extrapolations for changes in each (x) and (y) for each model where executed. The results indicate that the lower the level of Authoritarianism, and the lower the level of individual Rigidity, combined with greater Family Alienation, the greater the sympathy/empathy for leftist-based terrorist sentiments and/or actions. In addition, hostility toward civil service "loyalty tests" and antipathy toward Germany's past and the role played by the older generation in that past lead to increased student alienation.(57) Returning to the list of "Societal factors leading to terrorism," little evidence was derived in this study to conclude that the following factors are major sources of German student alienation: materialism and the capitalist system; sexual repression and frustration; hostility toward German societal norms; and a sense of personal futility. Before definitive conclusions can be drawn, further research on "older generation" attitudes, on nonuniversity student youthful alienation, and on the alienation of Gastarbeiter (foreign workers) is required.

As we enter the decade of the 1980s, headlines read that "terrorism is on the wane" in Germany.(58) The number of spectacular crimes has sharply dropped, but the number of

Table 12.5. Three Models Relating Society and Terrorism
(Multiple Regression, Where $Z = a_o + a_1X + a_2y$)

Model I	Model II	Model III
Authoritarianism = X ($\underline{Avg}$. 4.11)	Authoritarianism = X ($\underline{Avg}$. 4.11)	Rigidity = X ($\underline{Avg}$. 2.94)
Family Alienation = y ($\underline{Avg}$. 68.6)	Rigidity = y ($\underline{Avg}$. 2.94)	Family Alienation = y ($\underline{Avg}$. 68.6)

Test A - where = Z = % agreement

"Although I don't agree with their methods I can
understand the terrorists' rejection of our society."
(58.1% agreed, N = 230)

I	II	III
$a_o = -2.76$	$a_o = -4.892$	$a_o = 1.343$
$a_1 = .574$	$a_1 = .835$	$a_1 = -.225$
$a_2 = .014$	$a_2 = .685$	$a_2 = -.0014$
$R^2 = .885$	$R^2 = .784$	$R^2 = .796$

Test B - where Z = scale score

"The 'so-called' terrorists in our country are really
'freedom fighters' who deserve sanctuary in foreign
countries." (scale of 1-5: 1=disagree; Avg.=1.67)

I	II	III
$a_o = -6.377$	$a_o = 1.050$	$a_o = 12.086$
$a_1 = 1.560$	$a_1 = 1.092$	$a_1 = -3.528$
$a_2 = .0241$	$a_2 = -1.310$	$a_2 = .00013$
$R^2 = .82$	$R^2 = .806$	$R^2 = .71$

Test C - where Z = (opinion question = scale score)

"Terrorism in our country is based on the desire of
the individual to escape from the repression within
our military-industrial society." (scale of 1 to 5,
1=disagree; Avg.=2.70)

I	II	III
$a_o = -6.803$	$a_o = 7.552$	$a_o = 9.095$
$a_1 = 1.340$	$a_1 = .506$	$a_1 = -3.038$
$a_2 = .058$	$a_2 = -2.36$	$a_2 = .0375$
$R^2 = .942$	$R^2 = .78$	$R^2 = .85$

Test D - where Z = scale score opinion

"The terrorist movement in this country is directed
against a political system which only allows political
parties which are basically the same." (scale of
1-5; Avg. = 2.82)

I	II	III
$a_o = -2.520$	$a_o = 20.592$	$a_o = 3.139$
$a_1 = .504$	$a_1 = -.881$	$a_1 = -2.193$
$a_2 = .0148$	$a_2 = -4.280$	$a_2 = .0395$
$R^2 = .948$	$R^2 = .56$	$R^2 = .967$

terrorist incidents on both sides of the political spectrum has not; nor have the conditions disappeared which led to student alienation in the first place.

NOTES

1. Government policy statement to the Bundestag on September 15, 1979.

2. D. Sontheimer, Das Elend Unser Intellektuellen The Poverty of Our Intellectuals as quoted in Time, September 26, 1977.

3. Iring Fetscher, Terrorismus und Reaktion Europaische Verlagsanstalt (Terrorism and the Reaction of the European Publishing Community) (Cologne, Frankfurt am Main: 1977), p. 23.

4. Fetscher, Terrorismus und Reaktion, p. 104.

5. Rolf Zundel, "Die Wege zur Gewalt" ("Paths to Violence"), Die Zeit, June 9, 1978, p. 10.

6. Ibid.; Becker, the author of Hitler's Children, is quoted in the article by Zundel.

7. See Bommi Baumann, Terror or Love? trans. by Helene Ellenbogen and Wayne Parker (New York: Grove Press, 1979).

8. See Michael Getler, "The Ordeal of Terrorism Stirs Deep German Fears," International Herald Tribune (Paris), November 17, 1977; and the European Stars & Stripes, September 28 and November 14, 1977.

9. Andreas Baader, Gudrun Ensslin, and Jan-Carl Raspe died hours after a special commando unit of the West German Border Protection Force stormed a hijacked Lufthansa jet, freeing all 86 hostages aboard, and killing three of the four Arab hijackers. Baader and his colleagues may have hoped to be exchanged for the German airline hostages, as jailed terrorists had been exchanged for Peter Lorenz, a West Berlin politician, after he was kidnapped in 1975. Ulrike Meinhof, charged with murder in 1972, hanged herself before her trial ended. Two other members of the Baader-Meinhof gang also committed suicide while in prison.

10. S. Robert Lichter, "Young Rebels: A Psychopolitical Study of West German Male Radical Students," Comparative Politics 12 (1) (October 1979): 29-48.

11. Ibid., p. 28.

12. Dr. Iring Fetscher, quoted in Stern, December 1, 1977.

13. Dr. Freda Adler, quoted in European Stars and Stripes, January 28, 1978.

14. N.L. Nieburg, "The Threat of Violence and Social Change," American Political Science Review, December 1962, p. 870.

15. New York Times, April 28, 1978.

16. Time, December 26, 1977; report of John Dornberg, Munich correspondent, in International Herald Tribune, May 8, 1979.

17. International Herald Tribune, August 14, 1979; and New York Times, November 9, 1977.

18. New York Times, December 9, 1978.

19. International Herald Tribune, April 23, 1980.

20. Dr. Iring Fetscher, quoted in Time, October 31, 1977.

21. Horst Mahler, a radical lawyer, quoted in European Stars and Stripes, November 28, 1977.

22. Ibid.

23. Dr. Martin Greiffenhagen, University of Stuttgart political scientist, quoted in Time, December 19, 1977.

24. Quoted in European Stars and Stripes, September 28, 1977.

25. Dr. Iring Fetscher, quoted in Time, December 19, 1977.

26. Time, September 26, 1977.

27. Ibid., December 19, 1977.

28. New York Times Book Review, August 26, 1979.

29. Professor Karl Otto Hendrich, quoted in Die Zeit, October 7, 1977.

30. Professor Erwin Scheuch, quoted in NBC News Report, January 13, 1978.

31. Among the more controversial legal restrictions are the "Radikalenerlass" (regulations concerning radicals), the "Extremisten beschluss" (resolution concerning extremists), and the "Kontaktsperre" (regulation limiting a lawyer's access to his client if his client is a suspected terrorist). It is important to note that the thirty percent support rate for this statement, while high, is considerably less than earlier survey responses to the same question. Shifts toward a more democratic German societal structure are evident and occur generationally. See Konkret-Monatszeitschrift Fur Politik und Kulture, Herausgeber Hermann L. Gremliza 29 (2) (1976); and Der Spiegel, August 22, 1977; and Zundel, "Die Wege zur Gewalt," p. 11.

32. Lichter, "Young Rebels." This study, as was Lichter's, is phenomenological rather than causal. No offer is made to understand student "radicalism" but only to evaluate themes which may underlie moderate and left-leaning student support of terrorist actions. Generalizations for central and southern German university students may be justified. Samples at each university were randomly generated and meet fundamental parametric statistical criteria; significance is for one-tailed tests. Statistical significance is set at the conventional .05 level.

33. Interview with Bonn Ministerial Counsellor Ernst Gunter Patzold, January 13, 1976 (Bonn); and statistics derived from the Bundeskriminalamt (parallel to the American FBI), published in Lichter, "Young Rebels," p. 27.

34. Stanley Rothman, Smith College political scientist, quoted in Time, December 19, 1977; and West German legislator, Peter Glotz, quoted in International Herald Tribune, November 14, 1977.

35. The Ministry of the Interior study was completed by the West German Infra-Test Institute; and the findings were published in Bild am Sonntag, January 21, 1979, and Die Welt, January 22, 1979.

36. Lichter, "Young Rebels," p. 31.

37. See "A Criminologist's View of Women Terrorists," an interview with Dr. Freda Adler, New York Times, January 9, 1978.

38. In comparing Authoritarian and Family Alienation scores of terrorist sympathizers with the average score, obviously these scores should not be double counted. Subtracting "terrorist" supporter scores from the total results in an average score of 4.04, with s.d. of .606; and the family alienation score average becomes 66.77 with s.d. of 13.10.

39. Willibald Fink, Angriff auf unsere Demokratie, Hanns-Seidel-Stiftung e.v. Munchen 1974, p. 10.

40. Quoted by John Durnberg, in an analysis of the radicals decree, International Herald Tribune (Paris), October 24, 1978.

41. Rolf Zundel presents this argument in "Die Wege zur Gewalt," p. 12.

42. Gitta Sereny, "Germany: The 'Rediscovery' of Hitler," The Atlantic 242 (2) (August 1978): 8.

43. Frederick Weibgen, "Compensating for a Childhood in Germany," New York Times, January 17, 1978. As Weibgen describes his education, "Two hours were spent on some of the more questionable aspects of the Nazis' reign (including camps), some days on the German Army's heroic exploits, and some weeks on more lasting aspects of the Third Reich like the Fuhrer's doing away with unemployment, building highways, and curbing inflation."

44. See Michael Getler, "Dusseldorf's Lengthy War - Crimes That May be the Last Big One," International Herald Tribune, January 31, 1978; and "Maidenak," December 9, 1977, and "Bundeswehr," European Stars and Stripes, June 1978.

45. Among various reports, see The New York Times, February 7, May 9, and July 4, 1979; The International Herald Tribune, January 23, March 15, April 24, May 10, and July 24, 1979, and February 13, 1980; and European Stars and Stripes, January 20 and February 8, 1979.

46. "Germans Surveyed on TV 'Holocaust'," New York Times, May 9, 1979.

47. International Herald Tribune, November 29, 1977; and the European Stars and Stripes, October 14, 1978. It is important to note that the thirty percent support rate for this statement, while high, is considerably less than earlier survey responses to the same question. Shifts toward a more democratic German societal structure are evident and occur generationally.

48. For specific reference to neo-Nazi statistics, see European Stars and Stripes, October 14, 1978 and July 11, 1979. Among other English language news references on this subject are: New York Times, March 30 and May 22, 1979; European Stars and Stripes, December 1, 1977, February 22 and October 14, 1978, and February 5 and June 28, 1979; and the International Herald Tribune, November 29, 1977, February 6 and September 18, 1978, July 6 and November 13, 1979, and January 21, 1980. One neo-Nazi group of particular concern is led by Karl-Heinz Hoffmann, has about 400 members, and is heavily armed.

49. See Gregory F.T. Winn and George W. Witt, "German Terrorists: A Profile," (Unpublished paper, University of Southern California, 1980).

50. Time, October 31, 1977; European Stars and Stripes, January 19, 1978; and International Herald Tribune, November 15 and 16, 1977, and January 12, 1978.

51. See Delbert C. Miller, Handbook of Research Design and Social Measurement (New York: David McKay, 1970), pp. 230-52; and Jack M. Wright, Scales for the Measurement of Attitudes (New York: McGraw Hill, 1967).

52. Lichter, "Young Rebels," pp. 30-42. Lichter uses the "Parent-Child Questionnaire" (PCQ), a test which not only evaluates family alienation, but also attempts to discern the causes of that alienation. His test groups are divided by level of "radicalism," and the more radical the student, the more critically he or she evaluates the parents. Mothers were considered punitive, harsh, and not particularly caring.

53. The German student test results were 1.2 standard deviations higher than the mean scale level of alienation, $t=10.38$, or significant at .001.

54. Miller, Handbook of Research Design and Social Measurement, pp. 366-76 and 323-26; William Erbe, "Social Involvement and Political Activity: A Replication and Elaboration," American Sociological Review 29 (April 1964): 198-215; and Dwight G. Dean, "Alienation and Political Apathy," Social Forces 38 (March 1960): 185-89. Two previous test results of American universities gave the following results: Normlessness, $X=7.62$, $N=384$, $s.d.=4.7$; and Powerlessness, $X=13.65$, $N=1000$, $s.d.=6.1$.

55.   The F Scale Test first developed by Teodor Adorno, in Authoritarian Personality (New York: Harper, 1950), has been the subject of much criticism and lengthy analysis. See, for example, John Kirscht and Ronald Dillehay, Dimensions of Authoritarianism (Lexington, Ky.: Univ. of Kentucky Press, 1967), pp. 29-34; and Bernard M. Bass, "Authoritarianism or Acquiescence?" Journal of Abnormal and Social Psychology 51 (November 1955): 616-23.

56.   Lichter, in "Young Rebels," pp. 27-48, argues that the authoritarian personality has strong power needs. He evaluates authoritarian ambivalence using a Thematic Apperception Test (TAT). His test results indicate that the most radical students had scores indicating a high degree of authoritarianism. His result is the reverse of this study's, unless the authoritarian pattern tends to follow a J curve. In that case, sympathizers are less authoritarian depending on their increasing support of terrorist's motives, but the terrorists themselves are authoritarian, thus reversing the trend. Previous test results of American and Korean foreign policy elites by the author using the same scale indicate that the overall level of German student authoritarianism is very low. See "Conflict and Korea: A Comparison of Korean Foreign Policy Beliefs, Perceptions, and Orientation Toward Conflict," Korea and World Affairs 4 (2) (Summer 1980).

57.   Because of the nature of these variables (minimum variation), it was not appropriate to include them in the construction of the multiple regression models.

58.   New York Times, May 19, 1979; and Los Angeles Times, December 6, 1979.

13 A Multivariate Time Series Analysis of the Northern Irish Conflict 1969-76

Steve Wright

INTRODUCTION

The difficulties encountered when attempting to produce an accurate, objective, and comprehensive analysis of an episode of substate violence usually prove to be fundamental as well as formidable. Each approach brings with it a range of inherent assumptions that exclude from consideration certain forms of information produced by the conflict. Each person has a different perspective, a different training, and a different set of prejudices. How is it possible for any conflict researcher to avoid the accusation of bias when simple and objective criteria for making an interpretation rarely exist? It is, therefore, necessary for us to assume that the mode of analysis chosen to clarify the dynamics of a conflict will limit in many ways the forms of explanation and understanding that emerge from it. We can expect that these limitations will shape, in turn, the various means proposed to effect conflict resolution. They are also likely to determine the outcome of any attempt to apply them.

So few people are currently working in peace and conflict research that it is not surprising that our understanding of human conflict processes remains at a relatively primitive level. Even just specifying the boundary conditions required to trace the roots and the geographical extent of any particular conflict's impact can prove to be problematic. Open questions persist in their challenge to the often heavily qualified or oversimplified models of reality that have been developed by the conflict research done so far. How could it be otherwise when most conflicts are complex, involve multiple issues and perspectives, and a different form of conflict resolution is required by the various groups participating? Many people have adopted the sensible strategy of making a critical assessment and synthesis of a range of different perspectives and analytical frameworks when attempting to enhance their understanding of a particular conflict.

An eclectic attitude is certainly useful to anyone who wishes to assimilate the already substantial literature on the Northern Irish "troubles." The task of explaining the causes which are responsible for generating and sustaining this conflict has for example produced analyses based upon social,(1) political,(2) sectarian,(3) historical,(4) game simulation,(5) technological,(6) psychological,(7) Marxist,(8) metagame,(9) survey,(10) and peace(11) perspectives to name but a few.

The literature offers many valuable insights into why this conflict has become so intractable, and it will no doubt continue to expand as a rich resource to contribute to our understanding. However, like many other studies of internal wars, the existing accounts of the "troubles" have tended to focus on conflict points rather than conflict processes. This is unfortunate since, if only certain events and periods are viewed as critical, it becomes necessary to establish and explain the relationships between them by reference to selected facts and arguments. Naturally, what emerges from any particular time point analysis is likely to prove contentious to those who don't happen to share the same view.

If all the conflict processes in a conflict system could be described, it would be possible to make an holistic description of its dynamics that would enable the contribution of all the participants' conflict transactions to be clarified and assessed. Such an holistic perspective involves the consideration of a conflict as a living organism, consisting of many complex, interconnected, systemic relationships. Of course, the ideal is unreachable since, no matter how good our models are, it is impossible for them to incorporate as much variety as the reality to which they are supposed to correspond. Nonetheless, the ideal may provide us with an invaluable focus for our work, if we can begin by foregoing the luxury of assuming simple, static, linear cause and effect relationships when performing conflict analysis. A long-term aim could be the provision of a new multimethod, multitrait set of research tools. These could be derived from a wide range of disciplines and designed to help us integrate the various forms of information produced into a coherent framework that could create a truly ecological description of conflict.

The creation of such a multidimensional gestalt form of approach to conflict description will pose many difficulties. The attempt would involve producing an understanding of every act of conflict considered, whether from a nongovernmental or governmental participant, and its relationships and effects on all the other conflict acts considered. A set of cybernetic descriptions could then be produced to enable the researcher to explore the configuration of different processes responsible for structuring and sustaining the conflict system.

Unfortunately, the production of any holistic form of research tool appears to still be a long way off. However, what follows in the discussion below is an account of a tentative attempt in that direction. It is based on an application of a set of statistical social science techniques to empirical data covering a range of conflict indicators in Northern Ireland during the period 1969-76. The methodological tools used in the empirical analysis presented below were developed as part of this explorative study. Therefore, it must be emphasized that the approach remains in an embryonic form and the provisional findings described here must be treated with some caution. A statistical study of this type inherently suffers from many of the limitations referred to above. It isn't meant to replace but, rather, to augment existing studies. Following a suitable period of development, it is hoped that this form of approach may reveal unsuspected dynamics in the conflict and possibly lead to the development of new theory.

THE BACKROUND TO THIS STUDY

This study first took form as an undergraduate thesis on New Police Weapons, which had as one its themes the unforeseen impacts associated with the use of violent means of coercion by the state during times of sociocultural crisis.(12) It was argued that violence is a form of process and, like pollution, it doesn't just disappear from the environment when it is spilled. In the case of new forms of crowd control, similarities emerged between the use of pesticides and the evolution of resistance in insects, and the responses of people when faced with less lethal weapon deployment.(13) In both instances the, deployment of the control technology became ineffective and required more intense levels of use to retain the same efficacy as the target population adapted to its effects. Similarly, new, more severe forms of control technology were used to replace the ineffective forms and, not surprisingly, the cycle repeated itself. The mechanism by which resistance was evolved and transmitted is, of course, vastly different; in insects it is biological whereas in humans it is psychological in origin.(14)

Given that crowd versus police/military confrontations often initiate a trigger effect during episodes of substate violence, it is vitally important that changes in crowd psychology and behavior when faced with violently coercive policing tactics are fully understood. Conversely, it is just as important to understand the changes in police psychology and behavior when they are called on to handle violent sociopolitical actions.   Hopefully, this work will be undertaken fairly soon.

In the case of pesticide use, the unforeseen developments of resistance and the concentration of chlorinated hydrocarbon residues in food chains led to numerous, localized, ecological crises. Fortunately, the dynamics of the problem were recognized(15) soon enough for corrective measures to begin. However, the development and deployment of safer forms of pest control is a process that is still far from being successfully completed. If the use of coercive technologies and tactics during civil disturbances can produce an analogous destabilization in the political ecology of a nation, the implications could prove to be far more frightening. The parallels were, to say the least, sufficiently interesting to warrant further study.

THE NORTHERN IRISH CONFLICT

The historical backround to the Northern Irish conflict is long, involved, and complex. A thorough overview is beyond the scope of this chapter, but there are numerous good sources available to place the current conflict into historical perspective. Of more relevance to this study are the applications of certain conflict management strategies during the course of its more recent past. The British media usually portray Northern Ireland as a purely sectarian conflict and the British Army as a neutral actor undertaking a peacekeeping role.(16)   This portrayal is open to question.

The traditional method of conflict resolution used by most states undergoing an escalating internal disturbance is very often some form of military or paramilitary "peacekeeping force." It is, therefore, vital that the peace research community should analyze the short, medium, and long-term effects of new developments in crisis policing.

Northern Ireland is an appropriate place to begin such an appraisal. Not only do the "troubles" form the longest episode of substate violence in the Western world during recent times, the strategies and technologies of both nonstate and state participants are also being adapted and transferred to other groups engaged in similar struggles elsewhere. Another important consideration is the fact that the Northern Irish conflict has become one of the most accurately and comprehensively documented of all episodes of substate violence.

When the British Army was sent in to give assistance to the Royal Ulster Constabulary ten years ago, they arrived with a set of "peacekeeping" strategies that they had heuristically evolved as a result of their participation in over 30 colonial wars following World War II.(17)   Almost the entire gamut of these phased strategies has subsequently been deployed in the Province.

It has been suggested that the use of less lethal weaponry in conjunction with what the army terms "counterrevolutionary operations," may lead to a conflict sustaining rather than a peacekeeping process.(18) Briefly stated, the theory goes roughly something like this. If, in response to the deployment of less lethal weapons, a community becomes more hostile, this will be met with intensified military activity. If more military activity breeds a further increase in acts of overt hostility by the community, the military response may require the deployment of the next (more severe) phase of their operations. If such aggressive feedback circuits are allowed to develop unchecked, then the counterinsurgency phase system may become successively deployed in a self-fulfilling fashion. Thus, military activities gradually take on more severe manifestations in a mutually reinforcing set of responses to nongovernmental terrorists who are persuaded to pump even more aggression into the conflict processes by reploying in kind. At some stage in the evolution of the conflict network, the acts of all the participants can be considered to be self-legitimating.

When changes in the deployment of military counter insurgency phases and technologies used by the British Army in Northern Ireland were compared with the monthly total number of political killings, a pattern emerged which was consistent with this theory. (See Fig. 13.1.) It was obvious, however, that since this description was based on the changes in only one empirical conflict indicator, it could only be a crude simplification of a vastly more complex set of conflict dynamics. The result was still fruitful in that it suggested that significant relationships existed between state and non-state conflict activities which might somehow be measured. It also provided a rudimentary framework to consider these linkages, and implied that the influence of particular conflict actions may persist within a system long after the event.

As it stood, the description was limited by a two-dimensional quality which gave a false impression of the formation of static phases in the conflicts progression. What was required was a means of describing the relationships between many different forms of conflicting behavior, covering as many of the conflicts contributors as possible.

In attempting to develop even a very basic holistic approach, the same fundamental problems emerge. What criteria should be used to select representative conflict indicators? Where can such information be located? How can extensive amounts of information on a conflict be presented in a meaningful way? How can the process of interpretation be separated from the actual description so that subjective bias is eliminated as far as it is possible? The attempt to solve these problems -

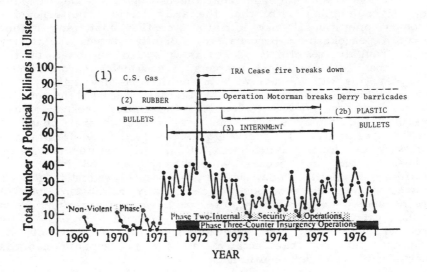

Fig. 13.1.   Military Deployment vs. Political Killings

or at least understand the existing limitations, has become the
theme of the author's current research and, of course, the
rest of this chapter.

RELIABILITY AND VALIDITY OF DATA

Representative conflict indicators were chosen by referring to
the kind of incident which are typically regarded as being
symtomatic of internal war.   These include such activities as
shooting incidents and bomb attacks as well as house searches
and imprisonment without trial.   They fell roughly into three
categories, a full breakdown of which is listed below.   Some of
these variables are composite.   A fuller breakdown is included
in Appendix A.

Statistics:

Category A. Activities of Nongovernmental Terrorists

The Total Number of Shooting Attacks
The Total Number of Bomb Attacks
The Number of Catholics Assassinated
The Number of Protestants Assassinated
The Number of Military Personnel Killed (Army & UDR)
The Number of Military Personnel Injured/Wounded (Army & UDR)
The Number of RUC Injured/Wounded
The Number of Catholics Kneecapped
The Number of Protestants Kneecapped

Category B. Activities of State Enforcement Personnel

The Number of Terrorists Killed
The Number of Catholic Terrorists Out of Action
The Number of Protestant Terrorists Out of Action
The Number of Catholics Interned
The Number of Protestants Interned
The Number of Weapons Recovered From Catholics
The Number of Weapons Recovered From Protestants
The Amount of Ammunition Recovered From Catholics
The Amount of Ammunition Recovered From Protestants
The Number of Vehicles Searched
The Number of Occupied Houses Searched
The Total Number of CS Gas Projectiles Fired
The Total Number of Baton Rounds Fired

Category C. Victims of the Conflict Process

The Number of Civilians Injured/Wounded
The Number of Civilians Killed

Taken together, these variables provide a significant measure of the conflict's level and intensity, revealed through the behavior of a variety of identifiably participating groups. Future studies may consider extending the number of different groups examined by increasing the number of representative indicators taken into account.

A number of variables included in this current study have omissions where information is either unavailable or cannot be considered to be reliable. Every attempt has been made to cross-check the information which has been given but there are, of course, the obvious difficulties in ascertaining the reliability of data which relate to an ongoing violent conflict. The figures for wounded and injured should, for example, be treated as minimal numbers in the case of civilians, since some people will not have sought hospital treatment. On the whole, however, the authorities who provided the information can be regarded as having done a fairly competent job of data collection. Of course, this does not mean that their neutrality in the interpretation of the statistics can be unquestionably relied upon. The labels "Protestant and Catholic Terrorists Out of Action" incorporate a range of implied assumptions which the author does not share. Nonetheless, it is reasonable to suggest that the statistical information included in this range of variables comprises the most accurate and comprehensive data currently available on this conflict. The full data file is included with this chapter as Appendix A, along with a list of sources from whom the information was obtained. This should enable anyone who is particularly interested in utilizing these statistics to verify their accuracy.

It should be noted that the figures for each variable are given in the form of a monthly breakdown, and each incident of a particular type is regarded as being the same. A finer breakdown of the data would obviously be preferable but, until it becomes accessible, it is necessary to utilize the information at hand. The homogeneous nature of incidents forms an unintended implication of statistical analysis which can prove to be problematic. However, if any particular incident is suspected of being critical, means exist to assess its impact on the conflict dynamics, and these are further discussed below.

SOME METHODOLOGICAL CONSIDERATIONS

A time series approach was chosen as the most appropriate analytic framework for making an attempt to achieve the explorative aims of this study. Among the reasons considered in coming to this conclusion were the following.

The examination of time serial relationships over the entire span of the conflict obviates the criticism of bias that can be justifiably made when only selected time points are described. The investigation of sequential serial relationships may also reveal conflict processes which are operating over longer periods of time than those normally considered. This possibility is sometimes referred to as the time level problem of analysis. The concept is a difficult one to grasp but, essentially, it calls for a more precise definition of what we mean by an event. The term event is commonly used for the sake of convenience but, in reality, its span may be of vital importance. In subatomic phenomena an event may last only millionths of a second, whereas some astronomical events take place over millenia. Most so called events can be thought of as processes reaching different thresholds. If the phenomenon under investigation is to be adequately conceptualized, it is necessary to choose a means of description which is sensitive to the appropriate time level. A comparison can be made with movie photography which is, in fact, a form of interrupted time series observations.

Slow moving changes such as a flower opening or closing can be observed with elapsed-time photography, using only relatively few frames per minute. Conversely, fast moving changes such as the beat of a humming bird's wings, for example, can only be recorded using a relatively enormous number of frames per minute. Ordinary film speeds would simply be too insensitive to record the changing processes manifested by either of these phenomena. Yet, a film passing through the camera lens at an appropriate time level can reveal and clarify what would have otherwise been invisible processes. In time series analysis, the frame interval is analogous to the number of data points sequentially considered as a time series and termed the series length. The series length used in a particular scan can be varied and, hence, facilitate research for evidence of any conflict processes operating beyond the time levels which are normally considered.

Another important reason for using time series techniques of serial and autocorrelation was the descriptive form of their output. Because the results of the analysis are relatively near to the raw data, they are also free of the kind of statistical artifacts used by techniques such as factor analysis.

There also exists a fair amount of time series expertise in the Richardson Institute, and this proved to be an important and indeed invaluable factor in the development of this particular approach. Of the three related time series techniques used in this study, two of them (the univariate and bivariate time series analyses), were adopted and adapted from Paul Smoker's Time Series Analysis of Sino-Indian Relations.(19) The third, more complex, multivariate cluster time series analysis was developed by Paul Smoker for the purposes of this study. The utility of each of these techniques in attempting to develop a more holistic approach to conflict analysis is further elaborated on in the discussion below.

The Univariate Time Series Analysis

Univariate time series analysis (t.s.a.) enables a description to be made of the level of influence which any variable's past behavior exerts on that variable's subsequent activity. The autocorrelation level (as it is termed) provides a measure of the extent to which any variable's behavior over a particular time series (comprised of time points t_1, t_2, t_3 . . . t_n) is implicated in that variable's future behavior over the subsequent series (t_2, t_3, t_4 . . . t_{n+1}) and so on, where n equals the selected series length.

The autocorrelation measure is an important indicator of emergent processes. In conflict analysis, we are concerned with discovering the factors which determine the formation of the processes which are associated with the development of the conflict. The measure of autocorrelation helps in this regard by providing us with a sensitive means of discovering whether a particular variable's behavior has structured sufficiently to be considered as self-legitimating or self-sustaining. The behavior of any such self-generating variable is highly dependent upon the pattern of its earlier behavior and reveals a significant level of autocorrelation. The higher the autocorrelation, the more predictable or systemically deterministic the behavior of the variable has become.

A familiar example of a phenomenon which would reveal a highly structured process if described using this technique is the pattern of buses of any selected service passing by any particular stop. Over a time period of seven days (i.e., the scope of changes covered by most timetables), the behavior of buses along the chosen route would be more or less predictable. In fact, any form of behavior governed primarily by routine or habit will reveal a high level of autocorrelation when described in the terms of a univariate time series analysis. Other examples include behavior based on drug dependence, the number of people dying from lung cancer, television licenses bought, car accidents per annum, and so on. Conversely, there are many other phenomena which are stochastic and, because they are far less structured, remain much less predictable. Examples include the amount of rain falling today or the number of goals scored in football matches next Saturday.

Obviously, the discovery of highly autocorrelated behavior in any of the activities of a conflict's participants should be regarded as of particular significance. It indicates a loss of behavioral freedom in the activities represented by any variable where it is found. Such variables should be thoroughly investigated since high autocorrelation in this context is a powerful indicator of processes tending to "lock" participants into conflict-sustaining traps. If any form of self-legitimating behavior is revealed by this analysis, it is important to establish whether it occurs more frequently in one group of participants than in others and why.

The Bivariate Time Series Analysis

Bivariate t.s.a. enables a description to be made of the influence one variable's behavior has on another or, more precisely, it provides measure of the extent to which processes associated with the formation of variable A are implicated in the processes associated with the formation of variable B. The method works on the basis of a correlation analysis of the leads and lags in the behavioral changes of the respective time series of the chosen variable pair. In use, the technique actually maps out the relative strength and direction of any flow of implicated influences, as a set of graph traces. Since each type of influence is indicated by a different colored trace, it is a simple matter in practice to establish whether a flow of influence travels from A to B; and/or from B to A; and/or if both variables interact by rising and falling in strength together. Any feedback that exists between a particular variable pair is revealed as a contoured set of correlation traces which represent each type of associated influence. As was the case in the univariate t.s.a., the correlation strength between any pair of variables can be assumed to be a measure of the significance of any implicated influences which are discovered.

The Multivariate Cluster Time Series Analysis

Multivariate cluster t.s.a. is a more complex technique which enables a description to be made of the extent to which one variable's behavior is implicated in the influences responsible for generating all the others. In more precise terms, it provides a measure of the overall connectivity of the infuences implicated in the generation of all the variables; a measure of the strength of particular linkages together with an indication of the direction of any flows of influence which are revealed.

As the label "multivariate cluster time series analysis" suggests, the technique really consists of an amalgam of two different techniques, i.e., a clustering procedure and a time series analysis. The clustering procedure is essentially a form of typal analysis that has been derived from the work of McQuitty.(20) As a component of this methodology, it defines each variable's time series as a member of a type, if its behavior is more like the behavior of some other member of that type than it is like anything else. The time series component is derived from the work of Smoker,(21) Quenouille,(22) and Wold.(23) It serves to define the direction and strength of any influences discovered to be flowing within and between the clusters of variables described.

The technical details of the construction and operation of this methodology deserve a more comprehensive dissertation. Athough such an account is outside the scope of this chapter, it is formally presented as the subject matter of another work.(24) The body of the discussion which follows is mainly devoted to clarifying and interpreting the form of results which emerge from the multivariate cluster t.s.a. However, if anyone is interested in learning more about the technical details, the various computer programs used in this study will be made available by the author on request.

Conventions, Concepts, and Measures

The actual computer printout obtained from running the
multivariate t.s.a. consists of a series of large correlation
matrices. Each matrix covers a certain <u>time period</u> containing
a preselected number of time points, i.e., <u>the series length</u>.
Since the data is in the form of a monthly breakdown, the real
interval between time points is one month and the period of
the conflict studied (Jan. 1969 to Dec. 1976) covers 96 time
points. The point at which a particular matrix begins, as well
as the series length selected, can be altered for purposes of
investigation. Each correlation matrix is, therefore, labeled
with a time period reference together with the number of time
points covered by the scan of the analysis. For example,
<u>Time Period 16, Series Length 24</u>, identifies an analysis which
began at time point 16, ended at time point 40, and described
the extent to which all the variables were implicated in one
another's formation during the intervening 24 time points.
Each correlation matrix yields a numerical representation of the
most dominant links discovered by the multivariat t.s.a. It
should be emphasized, however, that, although strongly
correlated linkages between variables implies an associated
influence in the factors responsible for their generation, a
causal connection cannot be directly inferred. Causal connection is only one form of a possible range of explanations.
This rather cautious inference is a more precise description of
the implication represented by each link. Given the complexity
of the context, such a reservation must be made when interpreting the results of the analyses since intermediate variables
may exist which have not been considered.
    The numerical information contained in each correlation
matrix needs to be visually accessible if a more holistic
perspective is to be developed. To this end, the flows
measuring the extent to which particular variables are implicated in each other's formation have been presented as
conflict systems diagrams, or systemograms.
    Each systemogram is constructed from its correlation
matrix by drawing out the connections between variables
according to the following conventions:

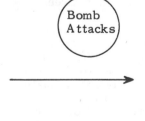

1. A short legend is used to identify each
    variable.
2. A single arrowheaded line is used to
    indicate the direction of a flow of
    influence discovered between pairs of
    variables with a lag of <u>one</u> time point.
3. Similarly, a double arrowheaded line is
    used to indicate the direction of a flow
    of influence discovered to be asso-

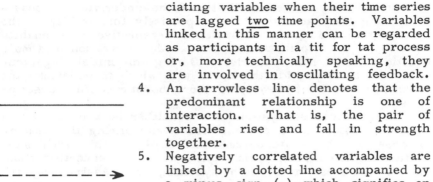

ciating variables when their time series are lagged <u>two</u> time points. Variables linked in this manner can be regarded as participants in a tit for tat process or, more technically speaking, they are involved in oscillating feedback.

4. An arrowless line denotes that the predominant relationship is one of interaction. That is, the pair of variables rise and fall in strength together.

5. Negatively correlated variables are linked by a dotted line accompanied by a minus sign (-) which signifies an inverse relationship. That is, the process generating one variable waxes in strength while that associated with the other variable wanes, and vice versa.

6. The number which appears boxed inside the connecting links represents the measure of correlation between that variable pair. It should be noted that the conventional Pearson Product Moment Correlation Coefficient is the one used throughout this study and is expressed as a percentage.

Since our main concern is the investigation of the strongest linkages between variables, a filter has been incorporated into each form of time series analysis discussed above to exclude any correlations which are less than 50. This enables the output of the empirical analysis to be kept within limits which can be realistically appraised. Of course, if more automatic drawing out techniques can be successfully created, these weaker influences can be brought into context. Even with this limit, the systemograms presented below remain information rich to say the least. In the discussion which follows, an attempt is made to define some concepts and measures which can be used to clarify their contents.

The first thing to note when examining the systemograms is their overall form, the number of variables and links, and any nodes which appear to be connected to a large number of other variables.

Within each systemogram, the flow of arrows shows the direction and extent of influences implicating variables in each other's formation. If these arrows are followed through from variable to variable, the path of a particular circuit of aggression can be traced. This is an important exercise if the violent transactions between participants are to be understood in terms of the interconnectivity of the underlying processes associating their activities. It is precisely this facility of the systemograms to create a systemic perspective that enables them to be used to further work toward the creation of a more holistic set of conflict theories. During this initial stage, our main task is to provide the means with which to undertake the preliminary work of developing more holistic conflict descriptions.

In practice, subsystems emerge either between or within variable clusters as a consequence of performing this tracing exercise on the systemograms. Variables within each subsystem develop certain typical patterns of influence that stand out as features within each systemogram. Assimilating the meaning of these features is a key purpose of this analysis since it enables five main types of variables to be distinguished:

Active variables have only strands of influence emanating out from them and do not receive influence from any other variable (see fig. 13.2). They therefore act on other variables rather than being significantly acted on themselves.

Reactive variables have only strands of influence feeding into them and do not significantly push influence into other variables (see fig. 13.3). They are therefore acted on by other variables whose influence they receive.

Mixed variables both give and receive influence to and from other variables (see fig. 13.4). They not only act on other variables but are themselves acted upon.

Interactive variables neither receive nor give influence but correspond their influence with the other variables to which they are linked (see fig. 13.5).

Highly autocorrelated variables feed a large part of their influence back into themselves indicating a pattern of self-generation. Such variables are quite easy to spot in the systemograms since they are represented by conspicuous concentric circles or semi-circles (see fig. 13.6). In their most developed form, highly autocorrelated variables can be considered to be autistic, neither giving nor receiving influence to or from any other variable but themselves. In the systemograms, autistic variables can be recognized by the fact of being completely decoupled from the rest of the influence system. Interpreting such curious behavior is obviously important since the factors responsible for generating such phenomena have structured into a pattern akin to the bus timetable, which results in the same number of buses traveling, regardless of the number of passengers getting on or off.

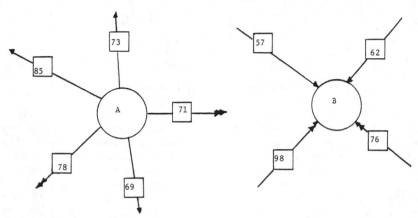

Fig. 13.2.   Active Variable   Fig. 13.3.   Reactive Variable

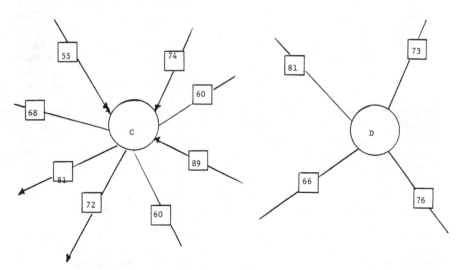

Fig. 13.4.   Mixed Variable   Fig. 13.5.   Interactive Variable

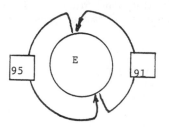

Fig. 13.6.   Autocorrelated Variable

If the conflict time sequence is examined systemogram by systemogram, it is possible to discover whether the changing influence processes between different variables or within subsystem variable clusters are growing stronger or weaker. The change in the strength of a systemic process is revealed by the change in the level of correlation over the selected time sequence.   Strengthening processes are associated with an increase in the level of correlation, while processes which are weakening exhibit a decline in the level of correlation as time goes on.

It is important to emphasize that the systemograms describe the processes influencing the dynamics of the conflict over the whole province.   They do not relate to regional manifestations of these processes except insofar as they relate to the conflict system as a whole.   Of course, the time series methodologies could be used for a regional subsystem conflict analysis providing that the necessary data could be located. Individual incidents are also placed in the context of their significance as a manifestation of the overall conflict process. However, the relative impact of any individual incident; political, military, or nongovernmental decision, policy, or tactic, can be empirically measured if it is possible to determine exactly when it first enters a chronological sequence considered by the systemograms.

If it is possible to establish the chronological period during which a particular "event" occurred, it becomes a straightforward matter to locate the systemogram in which it may have produced a measurable effect.   If we define the influence horizon of an event as being the time period limit of the systemogram where its influence is first felt, then:

The relevant systemogram TP = t - n+L

        Where t = The   chronological   number   of   the
               appropriate month
          n = The Series Length
          L = The maximum time lag used.

For example, if we are interested in discovering whether or not the decision to introduce internment produced a measurable influence on the dynamics of the conflict, then we can find the first relevant systemogram if we know the following:

t = August 1971 (= 12 + 12 + 8) = 32
n = 24 (In the sequence described below)
L = 2 (In this particular study)
TP = 32 - 24 + 2
TP = 10

Therefore, the required <u>systemogram</u> is TP 10.

In practice, the period of transition involving the systemograms for the time periods 9, 10, and 11 would be examined. The sequence is, in effect, a conflict profile which allows us to assess any changes in the pattern of conflict relationships before, during, and after the implementation of this decision.

In a similar fashion, it is possible to discover whether or not the presence of any particular variable or variable cluster is associated with a higher or lower level of conflict intensity. It may also be possible to determine if the presence of certain variables is sustaining or constraining the behavior of the remaining variables. Any structuring of particular conflict configurations into phases would be noticeable as relatively stable patterns of variable correlations through a sequence of systemograms.

In concluding this methodological section, it can be said that the most significant feature of the presentation of the results of the empirical analysis as systemograms is that it creates a clear set of cybernetic conflict descriptions. The format allows the pathways and flow circuits associating the various acting and reacting conflict indicators to be traced with relative ease. In spite of the underlying complexity of the techniques, even someone without any formal training in applied social science can quickly learn to interpret the systemograms. Once the path of influence concept is grasped, it is possible to distinguish activities which actively influence the conflict process from those which are reacting to it. Merely by looking at the distribution of the arrows, it is possible to discover which factors play the most important role in structuring the conflict.

What follows is a sequential set of selected systemograms produced by performing a multivariate cluster time series analysis on the 24 variables listed in Appendix A. The next section deals with some of the problems encountered in attempting to interpret these results and includes a brief discussion of their implications in the specific case of Northern Ireland.

Time Period: 1
Series Length 24

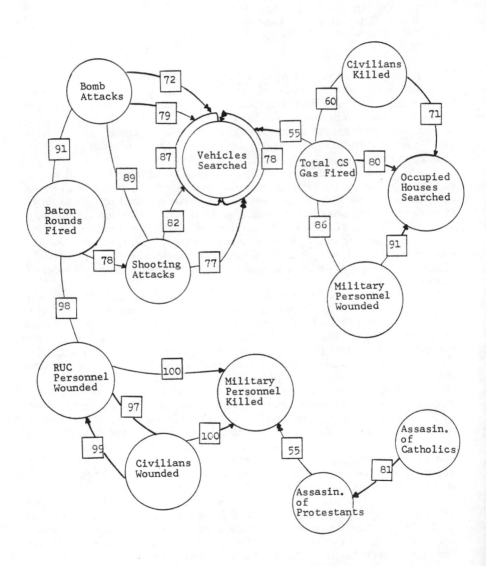

Systemogram 1.

Time Period: 6
Series Length 24

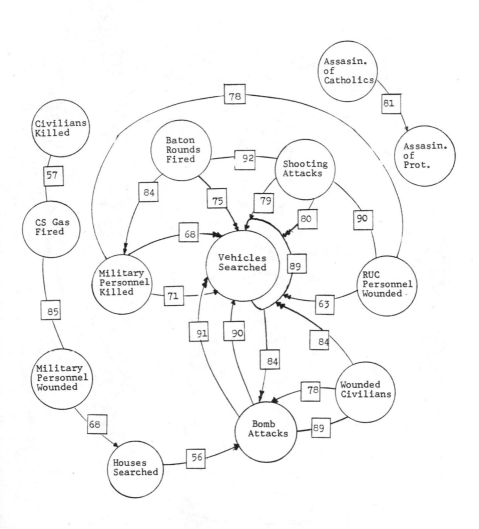

Systemogram 2.

Time Period: 16
Series Length 24

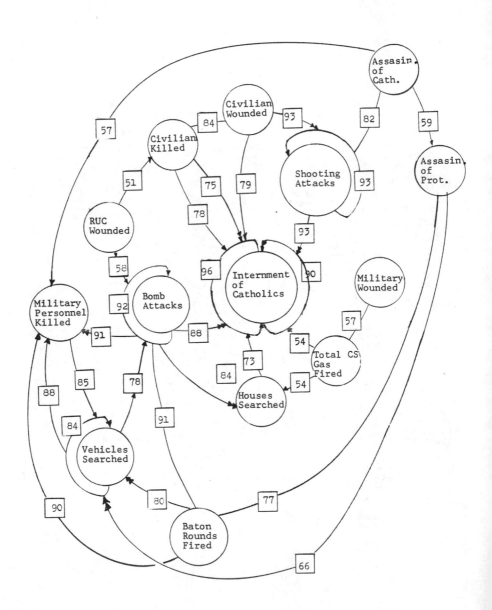

Systemogram 3.

Time Period: 21
Series Length 24

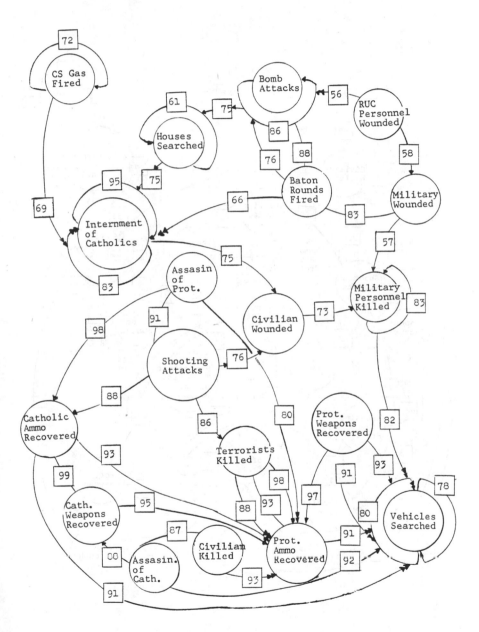

Systemogram 4.

Time Period: 36
Series Length 24

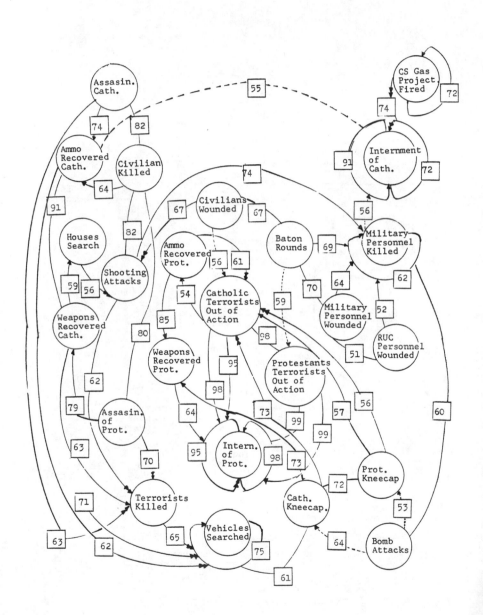

Systemogram 5.

Time Period: 41
Series Length 24

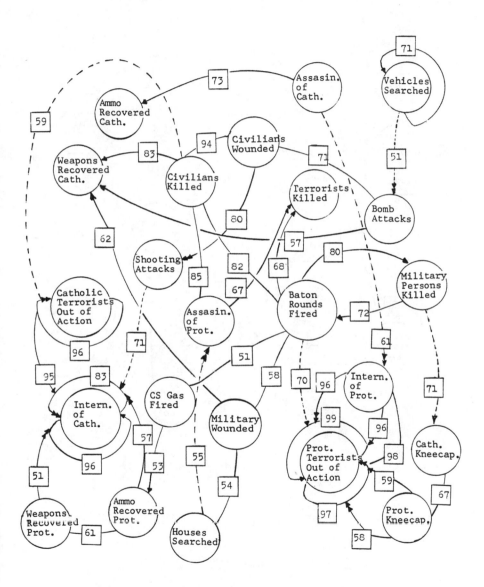

Systemogram 6.

Time Period: 56
Series Length 24

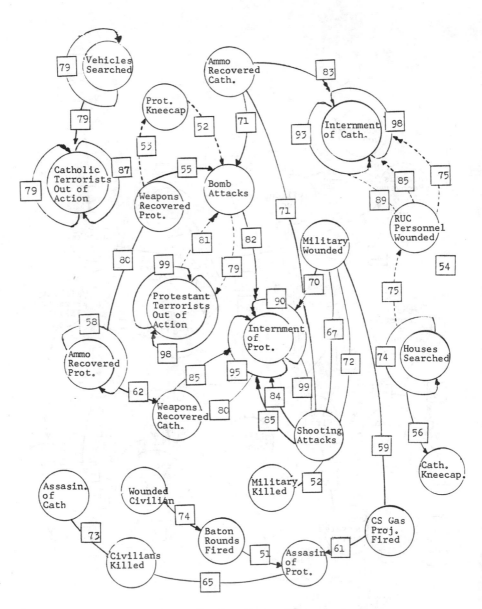

Systemogram 7.

Time Period: 71
Series Length 24

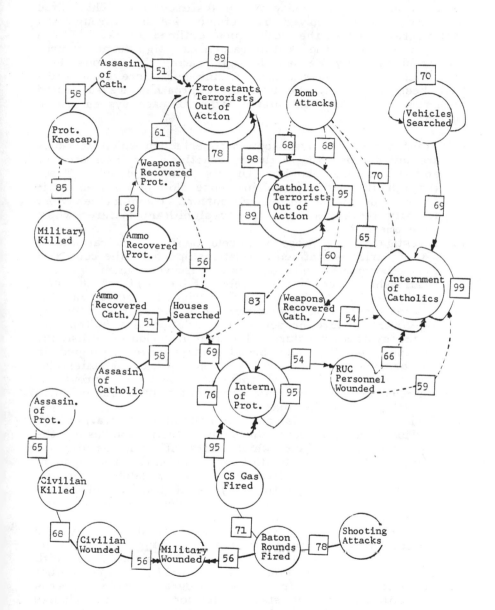

Systemogram 8.

Interpreting the Results of the Multivariate T.S.A.

The first difficulty usually encountered when attempting to interpret the results of the multivariate t.s.a. is one of coming to terms with the complexity of the systemograms. This initial difficulty is best resolved by actually working through the systemograms using the techniques outlined below. With a little perseverance, the skill of recognizing significant features can be heuristically learned through tracing the various flows of influence along their chains of linkage. Once these skills have been developed, the following approaches are suggested as a means of making an interpretation of each systemograms' contents:

1. Examine the first systemogram to establish which variables are initially behaving actively, reactively, or interactively, and which are mixed or highly autocorrelated. Trace through the pathways of influence flowing between variables to determine the overall pattern of conflict behavior. Identify the components of any significant features which have emerged.

2. Investigate the process of development in each variable or set of variables' influence relationships over the course of the subsequent systemograms. Discover which variable relationships remain relatively stable and which ones change. If destabilization in any particular set of variable relationships is found to occur, note the emergence of any significant feature or set of new relationships in the rest of the systemogram during the overall period of transition.

3. Determine whether any broad phases have developed in the behavior of any variable or set of variable interrelationships. Discover whether any particular group of participants becomes more frequently involved in such stereotyped behavior than others.

4. Decide, on the basis of the multivariate t.s.a., which variables merit a more thorough investigation using the univariate t.s.a., and which pairs of variables likewise warrant further investigation over the entire time span of the conflict using a bivariate t.s.a. Establish, through the combination of all three types of t.s.a., which participants became "locked into" conflict relationships and during which time periods.

5. Compare the chronology of any political, military, or nongovernmental policy change, operation, tactics, or incident suspected of having particular significance, with the empirical description of the dynamics of the conflict processes contained in the systemogram profile. Assess the difference in the stated intention behind the change and the measurable results of any implementation. Use the results of this exercise to create new theory, and to

suggest which other variables ought to be considered including, perhaps, more positive strategies for social change.

The full, formal presentation of the results of the time series analysis of the Northern Irish conflict using these approaches is beyond the scope of this chapter. However, the actual implementation of these interpretive approaches can be illustrated here by referring to the selected sequence of systemograms presented above. Throughout the discussion which follows, the correlation strength of any links that are referred to is given in brackets.

INTERPRETING THE SYSTEMOGRAMS

The most significant patterns of influence which emerge from the first systemogram are associated with the reactive variables. These include the process of house searches which are influenced by processess related to the wounding of military personnel (91), the firing of CS gas projectiles (80), and the number of civilians killed (71); the number of military personnel killed, a process which is almost deterministically influenced by the processes leading to the wounding of civilians and RUC personnel received (100), in addition to a weaker process of influence received from that associated with the assassination of protestants; and the process of vehicle searches which is a reaction to processes implicated in shooting attacks (82 & 77), bomb attacks (72 & 79) and CS gas projectiles fired (55). The process of vehicles searched also revealed significant levels of autocorrelation (87 & 78).

In systemogram 2 the searching of vehicles has developed into the most likely response to other conflict processes. Thus, the military deployment of vehicle searches becomes the standard reaction to processes associated with shooting attacks (79 & 80), RUC personnel wounded (63), baton rounds fired (75), military personnel killed (71 & 68), civilians wounded (84), and bomb attacks (90 & 91). Vehicle searching remains a highly autocorrelated process (89) but, at this sixth time period, has become actively implicated in the process of bomb attacks (84), and feedback between these two variables is apparent. Other active variables include baton rounds fired which is implicated in the process of military personnel killed (84) and vehicles searched (75), as well as interactively with shooting attacks and the assassinations of catholics which is the only process link into the assassination of protestants (81). The overall sectarian assassination process at this time period is completely separate from the other conflict processes. In the main cluster, chains of implicated influence have begun to emerge. The process associated with the killing of civilians is interacting with CS gas firings (57), and is associated interactively with the process of military woundings (85) which are actively influencing the number of houses searched (68), a process which has become implicated in the number of bomb attacks (56) which are interactively involved in the number of civilians wounded (89) as well as being part of a reactive process to them (78), which ultimately actively (91 & 90) and reactively (84) feed the process leading to vehicles searched. Even at this stage of the conflict's development, it would appear that the dominant mode of behavior associated with all the participants' conflict transactions involves a mutually adaptive struggle to overcome the influence of each other's activities.

Moving along the conflict profile to time period 16 (which is described in systemogram 3) we find that a new pattern has emerged. The process of catholic internment has replaced vehicle searches as most probable military response to all the other conflict processes. The process of catholic internment is highly autocorrelated to an almost mechanistically deterministic extent (96 & 90). It is behaving reactively to processes implicated in the number of civilians wounded (79), the number of civilians killed (75 & 78), bomb attacks (88), houses searched (73 & 84), CS gas projectiles fired (54), and the number of shooting attacks (93). Numerous pathways can be traced between the various conflict indicators which have as their ultimate destination the internment of catholics sink. For example, the process of catholic assassinations is actively implicated in the process of protestant assassinations (59) which is, in turn, interactively implicated in the process of baton rounds fired (77), which is actively implicated in the formation of the military personnel killed variable (90) that has a feedback relationship with vehicles searched (85 & 88). This is actively influencing the number of bomb attacks (78) that actively influence, in turn, the formation of the process of catholic internment (88).

Vehicles searched remains as the only other highly autocorrelated indicator of state enforcement behavior (84). A quick check across the subsequent systemograms indicates that this variable remains highly autocorrelated during the remaining sequence.

Nongovernmental terrorist behavior has become highly autocorrelated for the first time in this systemogram. The processes of bomb (92) and shooting attacks (93) show extremely high levels of autocorrelation. This is an important development since, when both governmental and nongovernmental participants' behavior exhibits high levels of autocorrelation and hence predictability, we have the circumstances which are classically associated with a conflict "lock in." During such an episode of "lock in" we can, expect the con-

flict to rapidly escalate since many of the conflict's participants
have lost their freedom of decision.

Over the time period covered by the fourth systemogram,
the new variables of protestant and catholic weapons and
ammunition recovered, along with terrorists killed are considered by the analysis for the first time. All of these
variables are linked into a conflict subsystem which is associated with sectarian assassination, and shooting incidents,
and actively involved in influencing the process of vehicle
searching. The other subcluster involves the autocorrelated
CS projectiles fired variable actively influencing catholic
internment (69). RUC wounded actively influences the process
of military wounded (58), which interactively influences baton
rounds fired (83), which form an active component in the
processes leading to bomb attacks (76) which, in turn, actively influence the number of houses searched (77). That is
also actively implicated in the Catholic Internment process,
which remains in effect as a highly autocorrelated variable (95
& 83). A check over the subsequent systemograms reveals
that the internment of catholic variable continues to exhibit
high levels of autocorrelation for the rest of the sequence (see
fig. 7). The univariate t.s.a. succinctly indicates the nature
of the process. The only variable actively influenced by
internment of catholics is the process associated with civilian
woundings (75) which actively influences the number of military personnel killed (73) which is actively associated with the
process of vehicle searching (82) that forms the node of the
subclusters. Other variables which have become autocorrelated during time period 21 include the governmental houses
searched (61) and the nongovernmental process associated with
military personnel being killed.(83)

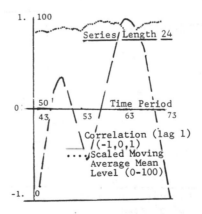

Fig. 13.7.   Internment of Catholics

Moving much further along the conflict profile to time period 36 described in systemogram 5, we find a much more complicated set of conflict dynamics. Five new variables have entered the conflict system, namely, catholic kneecappings, protestant kneecappings, internment of protestants, and catholic and protestant terrorists out of action. The protestant internment process, like its catholic counterpart, enters the conflict system with an extremely high level of autocorrelation (98 & 95). Checking through the subsequent systemograms we find that the process of protestant internment continues to be a highly predictable indicator for the remainder of the period covered by the analysis.

During time period 41 (systemogram 6), a transition occurs. While there are no longer any highly autocorrelated variables associated with nongovernmental terrorist behavior, the governmental activities responsible for taking catholic and protestant terrorists out of action have become very highly autocorrelated. The protestant terrorist out of action variable (99 & 97) is highly reactive to the process of protestant internment (96). The catholic terrorist out of action variable is also highly autocorrelated (96) and is an active process associated with catholic internment (95). A check through the subsequent systemograms reveals that the protestant and catholic terrorists out of action variables retain their high levels of autocorrelation.

In the last time period considered by this analysis (TP 71) and described here as systemogram 8, we find that the processes of catholic and protestant terrorists out of action have become highly interactive (98) and to all intents and purposes can be regarded as one unified process. The overall cohesiveness of other processes (except for this removal effect) are much weaker among the remaining indicators, revealed by the comparatively lower levels of correlation. The

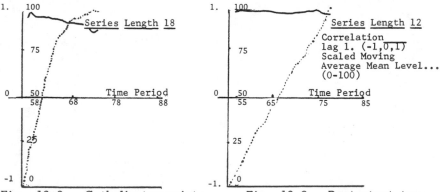

Fig. 13.8.   Catholic terrorists out of action

Fig. 13.9.   Protestant terrorists out of action

univariate t.s.a. of the terrorist removal processes have been included to show how structured this process of activist removal became (See figures 13.8 and 13.9). Note that the mean level scaled moving average which appears on the univariate t.s.a. traces is a direct measure of the actual figures involved.

Most of what has been said above can be regarded as an illustrative set of remarks on how to follow the first four of the five approaches suggested above. They can only be a sketch of the many interlocking processes described by the systemograms. The fifth approach entails a full and formal conflict assessment which will require a far more detailed analysis of the various changes, and paying particular regard to the possibility of spurious correlations emerging when new variables enter the frame of analysis. Such a problem is anticipated and can be accommodated by the use of a time window criterion which excludes relationships which cannot be viewed as having strict statistical validity. The specific relationships of other variables during such periods of transition can also be cross-checked using the univariate and bivariate t.s.a.

Although it is too early to make any policy recommendations on the basis of such a preliminary analysis, the conflict processes which have been described have some serious policy implications if the are corroborated by further research.

Over the time levels used in this study, the Northern Irish conflict can be regarded as a set of remarkably structured processes. Reactive rather than active processes have played the most important role in sustaining the high level of structured behavior which has been revealed. Reactions rather than actions are more frequently associated with a loss of freedom of decision. The nonrandom processes of response in particular have played an important role in sustaining the structure of the Northern Irish conflict. This is most apparent from the way that military behavior, once it becomes a predictable standard operating procedure, tends to persist in that mode. For example, vehicles searched initially becomes the standard military response to the various conflict processes, and it is a phenomenon which then continues to persist as a feature of the conflict. Likewise, catholic internment after introduction also persists as a predictable process - the new standard operating procedure. A lock-in phase developed when nongovernmental terrorists' bombing processes became their highly structured response. This lock-in phase was followed by protestant internment as the new, highly-structured governmental response. As internment was phased out, two more severe forms of standard operating procedure were developed as the dominant form of military reaction to the overall processes of conflict - namely, keeping protestant and catholic terrorists out of action.

The final systemogram indicates that, for all intents and purposes, the reactive military response to terrorist activities is a unified, highly-structured program which has become deterministic. Exactly why so many of the military reactions have developed such highly deterministic traits is a question which must be answered by future studies. Obviously, military behavior, by definition, is variety-reducing while guerilla activists depend on the unpredictability and variety-increasing aspects of their behavior to remain active, alive, and at large. The possibility which must be faced is that of governmental behavior having become dysfunctional. Adversaries need each other to maintain their respective roles. The presence of so much evidence of self-legitimating behavior in the conflict activities of military personnel should be of concern. Traditional counterterrorist theory suggests that such wars must be fought by directing activities toward getting the hard men. When freedom of decision is lost in the military group of participants on the level described above, the efficacy of such an approach to conflict resolution must be deeply questioned. The range of associated activities in this process appear to have just as much efficacy in evolving more hard men to get.

Given that, since World War II, internal wars are far more the norm than the external variety,(25) it is vital that we begin a critical appraisal of the more hidden dynamics of counterterrorist versus terrorist activities. The time series approaches outlined above may be of assistance in this endeavor by seperating the descriptive conflict analysis from the process of interpretation.

CONCLUSIONS

Although the results of any time series conflict analysis cannot be regarded as a substitute for a working knowledge of its social, political, and historical bases; they may augment existing knowledge by directing the descriptions which are produced into explanations and theory which can find application.

Conflicts which often appear to be interminable, such as the one in Northern Ireland, seem to produce different effects on different people. Activists are conflict thrivers and become naturally stronger in the war environment. Other, often unwilling, participants are severely debilitated by the conflict processes. Tracing the effects of conflict on this second group might involve the analysis of a range of psychosocial indicators such as drug use, mental hospital admissions, heart attacks, and so forth. If we assume a holistic analysis, it is necessary to put structural factors such as unemployment into perspective. The data for these variables has been collected and will be analyzed in due course. The attempt will continue to follow through the aim of examining as many related factors as possible. The theory being developed by this study suggests that conflict processes during an internal war permeate almost every sphere of social existence. It may be that the tensions produced by the conflict emerge in many more dimensions than currently considered. For example, more people in Northern Ireland have been damaged and killed by car accidents than by political violence. A possible relationship is a worthy focus for future analysis.

Of course, as emphasized previously, the techniques themselves are still in their formative stages and a period of further development will follow. Part of this work involves the task of computerizing the drawing out procedure used to create the systemograms. If this rather laborious work could be automated, it could speed up the process of research enormously. Work is also continuing to make the contents of the systemograms clearer by displaying them as three-dimensional models.

The techniques are not just parochially applicable, and it is hoped that a series of comparative studies can be initiated to discover whether similar processes to those found in the Northern Ireland province are a common currency of the internal war process. If the appropriate data can be obtained, the Palestinian, Cypriot, Aden, and Italian conflicts might be suitable for such a comparative approach, or even the Irish troubles of an earlier time.

In the meantime, an exposition covering the chronological sequence of developments in the Northern Irish conflict in relation to the changes in a systemogram conflict profile will be prepared and made available in due course.

NOTES

1. D.P. Barritt and C.F. Carter, The Northern Ireland Problem: A Study of Group Relations (London: Oxford University Press, 1962).

2. M. Farrel, The Orange State (London: Pluto Press, 1977). Also R.N. Hill, The Irish Triangle: Conflict in Northern Ireland (Princeton, N.J.: Princeton University Press, 1976).

3. M. Dillon and D. Lehane, Political Murder in Northern Ireland (Hammondsworth: Penguin, 1973). Also R.N. Lebow, "The Origins of Sectarian Assassination: The Case of Belfast," Journal of International Affairs 32 (1) (1978).

4. K. Deutsch and V. Magowan, Northern Ireland - A Chronology of Events (Belfast, Northern Ireland: Blackstaff Press, 1973) Volumes 1& 2.

5. J. McCormick, Ulster in Your Hands. A Simulation in Politics (New University of Ulster, Coleraine N.I. (UK): The Education Centre).

6. Ackroyd et al., The Technology of Political Control. (London: Pelican, 1977). Also S. Wright, "An Assessment of the New Technology of Repression," in Repression & Repressive Violence, ed. M. Hoefnagels (Amsterdam: Swets & Zeitlinger, 1977).

7. R.M. Fields, Society Under Siege - A Psychology of Northern Ireland (Philadelphia: Temple University Press, 1977); H.A. Lyons, "Psychiatric Sequelae to the Belfast Riots," The British Journal of Psychiatry, March 1971.

8. M.B. Probert, Orange & Green (London: Zed Press, 1978).

9. J.R. Faulkner, "An Operational Researcher Looks at the Situation in Ulster" (M.Sc. thesis, University of Sussex, UK, 1976).

10. A truly prophetic example can be found in J.C. Macrae, Polarization in Northern Ireland (Peace Research Centre, Lancaster, UK. 1966).

11. M. Lumsden, "Peace by Peace? - Socio-Economic Structures and the Role of the Peace People in Northern Ireland" Current Research on Peace & Violence 1 (1978): 96-107.

12. S. Wright, "New Police Weapons" (thesis, University of Manchester, U.K. 1975).

13. Hoefnagels, Repression and Repressive Violence.

14. S. Wright, "New Police Technologies," Journal of Peace Research 15 (4) (1978).

15. Initially by biologists such as Rachel Carson whose book, Silent Spring (New York: Houghton Mifflin, 1962), provided a powerful contribution to our awareness of the insidious dangers presented by indiscriminate pesticide use.

16. Campaign for Free Speech in Northern Ireland, The British Media and Ireland (London: The Russell Press, 1979).

17. Formally set out in the British Army's Land Operations Manual Vol. III, ("Counter Revolutionary Operations") 1969. See the London magazine Time Out, January 10, 1975 for a succinct description.

18. Wright, "New Police Technologies."

19. P. Smoker, "A Time Series Analysis of Sino-Indian Relations," The Journal of Conflict Resolution 2 (June 1969): 172-91.

20. L. McQuitty, "Elementary Linkage Analysis for Isolating both Othogonal Types and Typal Relevancies," Educational & Psychological Measurements 17 (1957): 207-29.

21. Smoker, "A Time Series Analysis."

22. M.H. Quenouille, Associated Measurements (New York: Academic Press, 1952).

23.   H. Wold, "On Least Squares Regression with Auto-correlated Variables & Residuals" (A paper presented to a meeting of the International Statistics Institute, Berne, 1949).

24.   Wright S., "A Time Series Analysis of the Northern Irish Conflict 1969-78" (Ph.D. dissertation, The University of Lancaster, United Kingdom, 1980).

25.   H. Eckstein, Internal War (New York: Free Press of Glencoe, 1964).

APPENDIX A: STATISTICS RELATING TO OVERT VIOLENCE

Assassinations of Protestants

	Jan	Feb	Mar	Apr	May	Jun	Jul	Aug	Sep	Oct	Nov	Dec
1969	0	0	0	0	0	0	0	1	1	0	0	0
1970	0	0	0	0	0	0	0	0	0	0	0	0
1971	0	1	0	0	0	0	0	1	1	2	0	1
1972	1	1	1	1	1	5	16	5	4	2	0	6
1973	2	5	2	3	1	8	2	4	2	1	0	2
1974	4	0	3	3	1	2	3	1	3	3	13	1
1975	0	3	5	6	2	9	3	6	8	3	2	2
1976	12	2	3	1	4	5	0	1	0	1	2	0

Assassinations of Catholics

	Jan	Feb	Mar	Apr	May	Jun	Jul	Aug	Sep	Oct	Nov	Dec
1969	0	0	0	0	0	0	0	2	0	0	0	0
1970	0	0	0	0	0	0	0	0	0	0	2	0
1971	1	0	0	0	0	0	0	4	1	0	0	1
1972	1	1	1	3	10	5	21	9	6	10	8	12
1973	6	7	7	0	7	6	3	9	3	1	3	1
1974	5	7	4	2	9	2	2	1	4	7	13	2
1975	1	12	3	12	4	7	3	3	3	10	6	0
1976	10	4	2	0	0	0	2	0	0	5	5	0

Number of Terrorists Killed

	Jan	Feb	Mar	Apr	May	Jun	Jul	Aug	Sep	Oct	Nov	Dec
1969	-	-	-	-	-	-	-	-	-	-	-	-
1970	-	-	-	-	-	-	-	-	-	-	-	-
1971	-	-	-	-	-	-	-	-	-	-	-	-
1972	-	-	-	-	-	-	6	9	10	7	3	3
1973	1	11	3	4	5	4	2	6	2	0	4	4
1974	0	2	2	2	4	2	0	3	1	3	2	2
1975	3	0	1	2	0	3	3	0	1	4	0	4
1976	2	5	0	2	0	1	2	1	0	3	0	0

Total Number of Civilians Killed

	Jan	Feb	Mar	Apr	May	Jun	Jul	Aug	Sep	Oct	Nov	Dec
1969	0	0	0	0	0	0	0	8	2	2	0	0
1970	0	0	0	0	0	11	6	0	2	0	3	1
1971	1	8	2	0	2	0	2	28	11	17	10	33
1972	18	15	27	14	31	16	75	35	27	30	11	25
1973	12	27	14	9	17	26	11	18	8	4	16	9
1974	13	14	17	10	22	10	8	10	11	15	28	8
1975	6	18	12	36	9	20	9	27	23	27	14	15
1976	42	23	13	14	20	34	24	17	11	24	15	7

(continued)

APPENDIX A (Continued)

Weapons Recovered From Protestants

	Jan	Feb	Mar	Apr	May	Jun	Jul	Aug	Sep	Oct	Nov	Dec
1969	-	-	-	-	-	-	-	-	-	-	-	-
1970	-	-	-	-	-	-	-	-	-	-	-	-
1971	-	-	-	-	-	-	-	-	-	-	-	-
1972	-	-	-	-	-	-	12	32	18	63	20	50
1973	26	53	87	75	32	44	40	50	265	67	65	34
1974	41	93	52	90	27	97	48	37	29	33	23	21
1975	5	36	46	49	35	53	20	30	35	41	41	21
1976	18	16	23	26	28	25	11	11	26	15	17	16

Weapons Recovered From Catholics

	Jan	Feb	Mar	Apr	May	Jun	Jul	Aug	Sep	Oct	Nov	Dec
1969	-	-	-	-	-	-	-	-	-	-	-	-
1970	-	-	-	-	-	-	-	-	-	-	-	-
1971	-	-	-	-	-	-	-	-	-	-	-	-
1972	-	-	-	-	-	-	89	221	98	82	73	45
1973	51	66	97	84	67	56	57	73	49	55	60	42
1974	75	42	62	84	79	63	47	45	43	50	38	41
1975	18	24	34	42	36	31	22	25	31	45	72	33
1976	27	45	58	80	60	36	36	43	62	58	39	55

Ammunition Recovered From Protestants

	Jan	Feb	Mar	Apr	May	Jun	Jul	Aug	Sep	Oct	Nov	Dec
1969	-	-	-	-	-	-	-	-	-	-	-	-
1970	-	-	-	-	-	-	-	-	-	-	-	-
1971	-	-	-	-	-	-	-	-	-	-	-	-
1972	-	-	-	-	-	1101	3298	5984	5984	5256	899	7805
1973	3231	4237	9362	7803	16910	5936	4330	34286	2903	11139	8205	10990
1974	2950	18987	6444	18036	3826	11444	8314	8595	1708	2065	1160	1404
1975	98	3181	5472	3068	9758	1496	2228	2350	6271	4121	2526	2167
1976	1260	1632	3074	2236	2943	1186	450	6300	2905	652	714	3892

Ammunition Recovered From Catholics

	Jan	Feb	Mar	Apr	May	Jun	Jul	Aug	Sep	Oct	Nov	Dec
1969	-	-	-	-	-	-	-	-	-	-	-	-
1970	-	-	-	-	-	-	-	-	-	-	-	-
1971	-	-	-	-	-	-	-	-	-	-	-	-
1972	-	-	-	-	-	-	12811	30966	11317	7786	11270	12016
1973	3236	3661	9904	7209	3930	6448	3147	7361	9015	6831	3508	3817
1974	5686	6961	3625	5511	7540	6936	4707	3491	2463	5874	6350	3118
1975	1178	1546	1487	1795	1522	1082	524	7565	4189	2387	4427	3166
1976	2442	4624	5830	4792	6305	3419	2742	1254	3096	5436	1942	1180

(continued)

APPENDIX A (Continued)

Protestant Terrorists Out of Action

	Jan	Feb	Mar	Apr	May	Jun	Jul	Aug	Sep	Oct	Nov	Dec
1969	-	-	-	-	-	-	-	-	-	-	-	-
1970	-	-	-	-	-	-	-	-	-	-	-	-
1971	-	-	-	-	-	-	-	-	-	-	-	-
1972	-	-	-	-	-	-	-	-	-	-	-	-
1973	-	97	116	116	151	174	185	195	195	215	238	249
1974	257	277	308	334	370	354	346	342	352	388	393	420
1975	447	461	479	481	491	530	512	517	527	583	586	593
1976												

Catholic Terrorists Out of Action

	Jan	Feb	Mar	Apr	May	Jun	Jul	Aug	Sep	Oct	Nov	Dec
1969	-	-	-	-	-	-	-	-	-	-	-	-
1970	-	-	-	-	-	-	-	-	-	-	-	-
1971	-	-	-	-	-	-	-	-	-	-	-	-
1972	-	-	-	-	-	-	-	-	-	-	-	-
1973	-	687	752	818	884	981	1035	1070	1095	1123	1148	1094
1974	1082	1112	1079	1111	1131	1120	1279	1255	1273	1278	1343	1347
1975	1315	1349	1286	1233	1225	1212	1184	1173	1197	1189	1097	1016
1976												

Internment Figures For Republicans

	Jan	Feb	Mar	Apr	May	Jun	Jul	Aug	Sep	Oct	Nov	Dec
1969	0	0	0	0	0	0	0	0	0	0	0	0
1970	0	0	0	0	0	0	0	0	0	0	0	0
1971	0	0	0	0	0	0	0	240	290	372	503	651
1972	758	609	913	760	553	372	346	239	248	273	293	294
1973	303	358	372	408	459	508	557	576	600	619	620	547
1974	538	534	531	581	577	573	540	529	502	504	516	517
1975	488	472	371	319	304	270	241	213	191	172	93	0
1976	0	0	0	0	0	0	0	0	0	0	0	0

Internment Figures For Loyalists

	Jan	Feb	Mar	Apr	May	Jun	Jul	Aug	Sep	Oct	Nov	Dec
1969	0	0	0	0	0	0	0	0	0	0	0	0
1970	0	0	0	0	0	0	0	0	0	0	0	0
1971	0	0	0	0	0	0	0	0	0	0	0	0
1972	0	0	0	0	0	0	0	0	0	0	0	0
1973	0	9	22	23	21	27	33	33	38	39	49	47
1974	47	49	51	48	70	59	49	44	37	31	24	25
1975	15	4	0	0	0	0	0	0	0	0	0	0
1976	0	0	0	0	0	0	0	0	0	0	0	0

(continued)

APPENDIX A (Continued)

Vehicles Searched (in hundreds)

	Jan	Feb	Mar	Apr	May	Jun	Jul	Aug	Sep	Oct	Nov	Dec
1969	-	-	-	-	-	-	-	-	-	-	-	-
1970	-	-	-	-	10	63	299	194	192	209	266	234
1971	225	219	640	898	698	596	655	883	752	1489	1055	1082
1972	734	889	1014	1321	1507	1340	1085	2430	2410	6088	5691	6022
1973	4590	1704	1975	2024	2223	2769	4594	4356	4559	4712	3761	2250
1974	2409	2743	4504	6040	6072	7129	7441	7340	7024	7410	5994	5376
1975	5307	4479	5391	6667	3031	2816	2745	3171	3821	4310	3568	3732
1976	3617	3267	3393	3662	3422	3618	3098	2491	2500	2038	1672	1634

Total Number of Military Deaths

	Jan	Feb	Mar	Apr	May	Jun	Jul	Aug	Sep	Oct	Nov	Dec
1969	0	0	0	0	0	0	0	0	0	0	0	0
1970	0	0	0	0	0	0	0	0	0	0	0	0
1971	0	2	4	0	2	0	2	7	7	11	7	6
1972	4	7	8	8	9	18	18	20	13	7	7	7
1973	2	8	15	7	13	3	6	2	2	2	4	2
1974	4	1	6	3	1	2	4	3	0	3	6	2
1975	0	1	0	0	0	1	4	2	0	2	8	2
1976	2	1	5	4	0	1	3	2	0	3	7	1

Number of CS Gas Cartridges Fired

	Jan	Feb	Mar	Apr	May	Jun	Jul	Aug	Sep	Oct	Nov	Dec
1969	-	-	-	-	-	-	-	-	-	-	-	-
1970	0	0	0	127	195	3090	1433	853	1519	453	1	0
1971	0	0	0	0	0	7	189	2165	2391	1700	791	1481
1972	1692	2364	527	77	9	0	141	10	15	23	27	28
1973	51	3	19	325	49	136	272	30	24	39	25	0
1974	13	19	5	11	42	31	3	0	0	359	31	0
1975	0	0	0	0	0	0	0	7	0	0	0	0
1976	0	0	0	0	0	0	0	0	0	0	0	0

Total CS Gas Projectiles Fired

	Jan	Feb	Mar	Apr	May	Jun	Jul	Aug	Sep	Oct	Nov	Dec
1969	-	-	-	-	-	-	-	-	-	-	-	-
1970	-	-	-	140	354	3496	1700	928	1705	497	1	0
1971	0	1	0	0	0	15	258	2404	2779	2169	962	2245
1972	2112	2771	694	95	19	0	235	16	30	30	37	76
1973	73	5	29	366	58	166	357	43	55	63	28	0
1974	18	21	6	13	68	32	6	1	1	937	41	0
1975	0	0	0	0	0	0	0	7	0	0	0	0
1976	0	0	0	0	0	0	0	0	0	0	0	0

(continued)

APPENDIX A (Continued)

Total Death Count

	Jan	Feb	Mar	Apr	May	Jun	Jul	Aug	Sep	Oct	Nov	Dec
1969	0	0	0	0	0	0	0	8	2	3	0	0
1970	0	0	0	0	0	11	6	2	2	0	3	1
1971	1	12	6	0	4	0	4	35	19	32	21	39
1972	26	22	39	22	40	35	95	55	40	39	20	34
1973	17	37	30	16	30	30	17	21	10	8	20	14
1974	19	15	26	14	25	14	12	14	12	19	35	11
1975	8	19	13	36	11	21	15	29	23	31	24	17
1976	47	27	17	20	26	37	28	20	12	28	23	11

Security Force Personnel Killed

	Jan	Feb	Mar	Apr	May	Jun	Jul	Aug	Sep	Oct	Nov	Dec
1969	0	0	0	0	0	0	0	0	0	1	0	0
1970	0	0	0	0	0	0	0	2	0	0	0	0
1971	0	4	4	0	2	0	2	7	8	15	11	6
1972	8	7	12	8	9	19	20	21	13	9	9	9
1973	5	10	16	7	13	4	6	3	2	4	4	5
1974	6	1	9	4	3	4	4	4	1	4	7	3
1975	1	1	1	0	2	1	6	2	0	4	11	2
1976	5	4	5	5	6	3	4	3	1	4	8	4

Number of Baton Rounds Fired

	Jan	Feb	Mar	Apr	May	Jun	Jul	Aug	Sep	Oct	Nov	Dec
1969	0	0	0	0	0	0	0	0	0	0	0	0
1970	0	0	0	0	0	0	0	12	27	199	0	0
1971	259	1033	255	243	50	27	1718	2975	3292	3419	1554	1927
1972	1563	3813	1588	2170	2588	1560	3480	2545	1429	1649	573	405
1973	1416	2289	1032	2013	1152	1507	1843	847	314	219	75	58
1974	92	210	170	437	265	105	32	152	20	1209	134	2
1975	0	17	4	303	97	145	50	2383	573	26	41	39
1976	7	541	49	108	66	192	171	2137	63	71	22	37

Kneecappings of Catholics

	Jan	Feb	Mar	Apr	May	Jun	Jul	Aug	Sep	Oct	Nov	Dec
1969	-	-	-	-	-	-	-	-	-	-	-	-
1970	-	-	-	-	-	-	-	-	-	-	-	-
1971	-	-	-	-	-	-	-	-	-	-	-	-
1972	-	-	-	-	-	-	-	-	-	-	-	-
1973	7	6	7	4	1	0	3	9	5	5	4	2
1974	7	11	5	11	5	7	13	11	8	2	2	2
1975	7	11	9	16	7	8	8	19	7	35	10	1
1976	10	2	1	3	3	4	9	12	5	2	6	5

(continued)

APPENDIX A (Continued)

Kneecappings of Protestants

	Jan	Feb	Mar	Apr	May	Jun	Jul	Aug	Sep	Oct	Nov	Dec
1969	-	-	-	-	-	-	-	-	-	-	-	-
1970	-	-	-	-	-	-	-	-	-	-	-	-
1971	-	-	-	-	-	-	-	-	-	-	-	-
1972	-	-	-	-	-	-	-	-	-	-	-	-
1973	1	4	3	2	4	0	0	1	1	0	3	2
1974	1	8	2	5	3	3	3	2	3	4	6	4
1975	4	7	3	3	6	2	2	6	5	8	2	2
1976	0	1	1	3	3	3	6	7	3	4	1	4

Total Number of Kneecappings

	Jan	Feb	Mar	Apr	May	Jun	Jul	Aug	Sep	Oct	Nov	Dec
1969	-	-	-	-	-	-	-	-	-	-	-	-
1970	-	-	-	-	-	-	-	-	-	-	-	-
1971	-	-	-	-	-	-	-	-	-	-	-	-
1972	-	-	-	-	-	-	-	-	-	-	-	-
1973	8	10	10	6	5	0	3	10	6	5	7	4
1974	8	19	7	16	8	10	16	13	11	6	8	6
1975	11	18	12	19	13	10	10	25	12	43	12	3
1976	10	3	2	6	6	7	15	19	8	6	7	9

Security Force Personnel Injured and Wounded

	Jan	Feb	Mar	Apr	May	Jun	Jul	Aug	Sep	Oct	Nov	Dec
1969	-	-	-	-	-	-	-	-	-	-	-	-
1970	-	-	-	-	-	-	-	-	-	-	-	-
1971	20	36	7	27	23	9	82	91	70	58	33	39
1972	36	55	53	60	79	43	89	77	58	42	39	41
1973	59	70	74	95	55	42	43	54	36	39	30	45
1974	46	67	72	78	48	19	36	36	18	92	25	4
1975	13	15	23	29	46	26	29	57	47	46	43	56
1976	33	47	50	40	35	58	48	62	34	74	31	47

Total Number of People Injured and Wounded

	Jan	Feb	Mar	Apr	May	Jun	Jul	Aug	Sep	Oct	Nov	Dec
1969	-	-	-	-	-	-	-	-	-	-	-	-
1970	-	-	-	-	-	-	-	-	-	-	-	-
1971	64	141	30	68	119	57	179	399	345	286	300	345
1972	269	297	784	258	655	361	554	319	327	293	161	207
1974	134	211	269	201	277	122	247	116	91	310	200	43
1973	186	283	279	228	223	223	181	234	111	156	192	156
1975	71	150	192	283	181	218	118	447	222	267	128	197
1976	279	221	162	286	238	338	198	282	159	210	175	181

(continued)

APPENDIX A (Continued)

Military Personnel Injured and Wounded

	Jan	Feb	Mar	Apr	May	Jun	Jul	Aug	Sep	Oct	Nov	Dec
1969	0	0	0	0	0	0	0	0	0	0	0	0
1970	0	6	41	17	8	331	15	54	57	86	3	2
1971	19	30	7	27	22	9	20	86	64	42	28	36
1972	26	49	47	52	65	35	78	73	47	38	33	35
1973	51	57	65	70	54	37	41	43	33	38	25	36
1974	39	59	63	70	45	16	30	32	17	89	19	4
1975	3	5	10	5	21	4	15	30	12	32	11	19
1976	8	25	23	13	9	21	17	53	13	57	12	13

Total RUC Personnel Injured and Wounded

	Jan	Feb	Mar	Apr	May	Jun	Jul	Aug	Sep	Oct	Nov	Dec
1969	-	-	-	-	-	-	-	-	-	-	-	-
1970	-	-	-	-	-	-	-	-	-	-	-	-
1971	1	6	0	0	1	0	62	5	6	16	5	3
1972	10	6	6	8	14	8	11	4	11	4	6	6
1973	8	13	9	25	1	5	2	11	3	3	5	9
1974	7	8	9	8	3	3	6	4	1	3	6	0
1975	10	10	13	24	25	22	14	27	35	14	32	37
1976	25	22	35	27	26	37	31	9	21	17	19	34

Army Personnel Injured and Wounded

	Jan	Feb	Mar	Apr	May	Jun	Jul	Aug	Sep	Oct	Nov	Dec
1969	0	0	0	0	0	0	0	0	0	0	0	0
1970	0	6	41	17	8	331	15	54	57	86	3	2
1971	19	28	7	27	19	9	20	86	64	42	28	33
1972	25	45	43	47	63	31	77	66	45	35	31	34
1973	47	56	63	70	51	34	39	41	33	35	24	32
1974	37	51	56	67	44	15	27	32	16	89	15	4
1975	2	5	5	4	21	4	15	29	11	29	11	15
1976	6	22	23	10	7	19	15	53	11	56	9	12

Total Number of Civilians Injured and Wounded

	Jan	Feb	Mar	Apr	May	Jun	Jul	Aug	Sep	Oct	Nov	Dec
1969	-	-	-	-	-	-	-	-	-	-	-	-
1970	-	-	-	-	-	-	-	-	-	-	-	-
1971	44	105	23	41	96	48	97	308	275	228	267	306
1972	233	242	731	198	576	318	465	242	269	251	122	166
1973	129	213	205	133	168	181	138	180	75	117	162	111
1974	88	144	197	123	229	103	211	80	73	218	175	39
1975	58	135	169	254	135	192	89	390	175	221	85	141
1976	246	174	104	246	203	280	150	220	125	136	144	134

(continued)

APPENDIX A (Continued)

Rubber Bullets Fired

	Jan	Feb	Mar	Apr	May	Jun	Jul	Aug	Sep	Oct	Nov	Dec
1969	0	0	0	0	0	0	0	0	0	0	0	0
1970	0	0	0	0	0	0	0	12	27	199	0	0
1971	259	1053	255	243	50	27	1718	2975	3292	3419	1554	1927
1972	1563	3813	1588	2170	2588	1560	3480	2545	1429	1649	573	405
1973	1416	2248	1032	2013	1151	1507	1843	847	314	219	75	58
1974	92	210	170	437	265	105	32	152	20	1034	95	0
1975	0	17	0	0	0	1	9	70	12	10	3	0
1976	0	0	0	0	0	0	0	0	0	0	00	0

Plastic Bullets Fired

	Jan	Feb	Mar	Apr	May	Jun	Jul	Aug	Sep	Oct	Nov	Dec
1969	0	0	0	0	0	0	0	0	0	0	0	0
1970	0	0	0	0	0	0	0	0	0	0	0	0
1971	0	0	0	0	0	0	0	0	0	0	0	0
1972	0	0	0	0	0	0	0	0	0	0	0	0
1973	0	41	0	0	1	0	0	0	0	0	0	0
1974	0	0	0	0	0	0	0	0	0	175	39	2
1975	0	0	4	303	97	144	41	2313	561	16	38	39
1976	7	541	49	108	66	192	171	2137	63	71	22	37

Number of CS Gas Grenades Fired

	Jan	Feb	Mar	Apr	May	Jun	Jul	Aug	Sep	Oct	Nov	Dec
1969	-	-	-	-	-	-	-	-	-	-	-	-
1970	0	0	0	13	159	406	267	75	186	44	0	0
1971	0	1	0	0	0	8	69	239	388	469	171	762
1972	420	407	167	18	10	0	94	6	15	7	10	48
1973	22	2	10	41	9	30	85	13	31	24	3	0
1974	5	2	1	2	26	1	3	1	1	578	10	0
1975	0	0	0	0	0	0	0	0	0	0	0	0
1976	0	0	0	0	0	0	0	0	0	0	0	0

Occupied Houses Searched (In hundreds)

	Jan	Feb	Mar	Apr	May	Jun	Jul	Aug	Sep	Oct	Nov	Dec
1969	-	-	-	-	-	-	-	-	-	-	-	-
1970	0	0	4	2	6	21	599	71	20	11	9	6
1971	21	179	173	150	252	333	335	145	349	1353	2579	1385
1972	1514	916	627	117	196	857	764	1572	1933	218	1829	822
1973	801	1570	1910	1539	1280	856	1215	1003	1504	1075	988	598
1974	1159	888	1890	1776	993	1032	1431	1573	2738	2237	2110	1749
1975	175	198	72	138	605	138	199	124	417	972	581	290
1976	431	568	694	915	1038	976	1314	1317	843	964	922	767

(continued)

APPENDIX A (Continued)

Total Number of Shooting Attacks

	Jan	Feb	Mar	Apr	May	Jun	Jul	Aug	Sep	Oct	Nov	Dec
1969	-	-	-	-	-	-	-	-	-	-	-	-
1970	1	4	11	18	8	18	37	17	12	24	35	28
1971	17	75	53	17	33	39	185	182	278	420	243	314
1972	336	391	399	724	1223	1215	2778	640	747	812	634	729
1973	678	695	799	477	369	303	283	237	266	298	312	299
1974	297	229	292	329	353	227	240	317	222	266	280	154
1975	110	112	141	199	121	139	128	244	175	185	180	73
1976	124	208	110	154	157	137	171	266	138	167	149	127

Shooting Incidents Which Involved the Security Forces

	Jan	Feb	Mar	Apr	May	Jun	Jul	Aug	Sep	Oct	Nov	Dec
1969	-	-	-	-	-	-	-	-	-	-	-	-
1970	0	1	2	2	2	4	24	12	1	12	1	6
1971	6	49	18	3	16	17	62	148	256	378	234	298
1972	336	391	399	563	828	730	1900	457	578	611	486	390
1973	421	465	516	361	281	230	231	163	156	195	165	181
1974	177	131	184	213	215	153	125	202	101	164	151	88
1975	37	36	21	48	27	26	40	98	72	58	56	34
1976	52	124	56	83	78	57	92	174	69	73	73	82

Shooting Incidents Which Did Not Involve Security Forces

	Jan	Feb	Mar	Apr	May	Jun	Jul	Aug	Sep	Oct	Nov	Dec
1969	-	-	-	-	-	-	-	-	-	-	-	-
1970	1	3	9	16	6	14	13	5	11	12	34	22
1971	11	26	35	14	17	22	23	34	22	42	9	16
1972	0	0	0	161	395	485	878	183	169	201	148	339
1973	257	230	283	116	82	73	52	74	110	103	149	118
1974	120	98	108	116	138	74	115	115	121	102	129	66
1975	73	76	120	151	94	113	86	148	103	125	124	39
1976	72	84	54	71	79	80	79	92	69	94	76	45

Number of Bomb Explosions

	Jan	Feb	Mar	Apr	May	Jun	Jul	Aug	Sep	Oct	Nov	Dec
1969	0	0	2	3	0	0	0	0	0	1	0	1
1970	3	10	8	12	4	10	16	26	17	23	18	6
1971	11	36	30	39	51	53	79	142	186	155	117	123
1972	156	140	136	105	94	117	184	126	87	96	82	57
1973	57	73	104	65	104	110	67	79	64	79	118	58
1974	63	90	111	44	64	69	55	42	28	32	49	38
1975	24	46	19	26	17	25	26	25	47	72	37	35
1976	47	82	78	83	50	48	83	79	56	82	33	45

(continued)

APPENDIX A (Continued)

Number of Bombs Neutralized

	Jan	Feb	Mar	Apr	May	Jun	Jul	Aug	Sep	Oct	Nov	Dec
1969	0	0	0	1	0	0	0	1	0	0	0	0
1970	1	1	3	0	0	3	1	3	3	4	0	1
1971	13	51	28	15	21	32	34	53	69	75	45	57
1972	31	39	29	37	34	62	48	53	43	23	37	35
1973	25	36	47	53	48	61	47	42	37	57	54	30
1974	39	45	46	39	62	28	31	25	26	32	22	33
1975	21	31	10	8	14	8	7	29	20	27	21	40
1976	28	70	31	61	28	28	25	45	36	26	18	28

Total Number of Bomb Attacks

	Jan	Feb	Mar	Apr	May	Jun	Jul	Aug	Sep	Oct	Nov	Dec
1969	0	0	2	4	0	0	0	1	0	1	0	1
1970	4	11	11	12	4	13	17	29	20	27	18	7
1971	24	87	58	54	72	85	113	195	255	230	162	180
1972	187	179	165	142	128	179	232	179	130	119	119	92
1973	82	109	146	118	152	171	114	121	101	136	182	88
1974	102	135	157	83	126	97	86	67	54	64	71	71
1975	45	77	29	34	31	33	33	54	67	99	58	75
1976	75	152	109	144	78	76	108	124	94	108	51	73

Note: A dash (-) indicates that data is unavailable on that conflict indicator during this period.

The figures used to compile Appendix A were obtained from the following sources:

The Army Information Services, H.Q. Lisburn, BFPO 825, Northern Ireland.

Protestant & Catholic Assassinations; Terrorists Killed; Weapons recovered from Protestants & Catholics; Ammunition recovered from Protestants & Catholics; Protestant & Catholic Terrorists Out of Action. (Supplied in a letter to the author dated January 20, 1977.)

CS Grenades Fired; Rubber Bullets Fired; Plastic Bullets Fired; Occupied Houses Searched & Vehicles Searched. (Supplied in a letter to the author dated February 10, 1977.)

CS Cartridges Fired. (Supplied in a letter to the author dated March 5, 1977.)

Kneecappings of Protestants & Catholics. (Supplied in a letter to the author dated March 29, 1977.)

Royal Ulster Constabulary Press Office, Knock Road, Brooklyn, Belfast, Northern Ireland BT5 6LF.

Civilians Killed; Army Killed; UDR Killed; RUC & RUC 'R' Killed. (Supplied in a letter to the author dated February 10, 1977.)

The Northern Ireland Office, Government Offices, Great George Street, London SW1.

Republicans and Loyalists Interned. (Supplied in a letter to the author dated January 7, 1977.)

Bombs exploded; Bombs neutralised; Total number of Bomb Attacks; Shooting Incidents Involving the Security Forces; Shooting Incidents not Involving the Security Forces; Total Number of Shooting Attacks; Number of Army Personnel Injured & Wounded; Number of RUC Personnel Injured & Wounded; Number of Civilians Injured & Wounded. (Supplied in a letter to the author dated February 22, 1978.)

Dillon M., & Lehane D., 'Political Murder in Northern Ireland', Penguin Books 1973.

Protestant & Catholic Assassinations during the period January 1969 to June 1972.

Deutch K., & Magowan V., 'Northern Ireland. - A Chronology of Events Volume I. Blackstaff Press, Belfast, Northern Ireland 1973.

The Number of Bombs exploded and neutralized during the period January to December 1969.

14 Terrorism, Violence, and the International Transfer of Conventional Armaments
William P. Avery

Acts of terrorist violence are more visibly prominent today than ever before. Terrorism has been a part of the global scene at least since World War II, and scarcely any modern nation can claim to have escaped its effects.(1) Terrorist acts normally have sought to bring about radical changes in societies, forced capitulation by governmental authorities to specific demands, and often simply the undermining or weakening of the current political authority. The thrust of scholarly research on political violence has tended to focus on "causes" or conditions influencing levels of violence.(2) Research dealing with objectives and consequences of terrorism generally have concluded that acts of terrorism seldom succeed. Cooper observes that "perhaps the most signal lesson from an international perspective is the invariable failure of terrorism to attain its objectives."(3) Terrorist violence seems particularly ineffective in bringing about long-term social and political change.

But whether they are Montoneros of Argentina, the Red Brigades of Italy, or Weathermen of the United States, terrorists generate perhaps far more attention than their success rate or the consequences of their behavior in harm to life and property might merit.(4) During the Mau Mau terrorism in Kenya, for instance, more Europeans died in Nairobi traffic accidents than were killed by terrorists in the whole nation.(5)

*An earlier version of this chapter was presented at the annual meeting of the Midwest Political Science Association, Chicago, Illinois, April 20-22, 1978. The author gratefully acknowledges support for this project by the Research Council of the University of Nebraska.

Of the effects of terrorism, it has been said that "never have so few succeeded in causing so much concern to so many."(6) The consequences of terrorist violence cannot, however, be meaningfully measured only in terms of harm to life and property. The responses of governments must also be taken into account, in particular their coercive actions and capabilities.

Governments, of course, respond to political violence in a variety of ways. Coercive actions are taken to neutralize, suppress, or eliminate the threat through censorship, restrictions on political activities, espionage, and military force.(7) The present study is concerned with governmental responses of the latter sort. Serious terrorist campaigns and protracted political violence almost universally lead to some form of military response. In some countries, particularly in Latin America, military involvement to thwart terrorist violence has resulted in direct assumption of political power by the military. During the Mau Mau insurgency, the Kenyan and British governments were estimated to have expended nearly $165 million in counter insurgency actions. Search and destroy missions are regular features of Israeli responses to Palestinian terrorism. The objective of this inquiry is an exploratory examination of the effects of political violence on the international transfer of conventional armaments. The central question to be examined is: To what extent do levels of terrorist political violence influence countries to increase their coercive capacity through greater acquisitions of conventional weaponry?

DATA, MEASUREMENT, AND METHODS

Broadly speaking, terrorism is violence with a politically-based motive. But is is also political violence with special characteristics. Terrorist violence is characterized by randomness, a high degree of cruelty and indifference toward victims, and an overriding sense that even the most bizarre and barbaric means are always justified by the ends. As Cooper has observed there is a "subtle difference between the deliberate elimination of a hated police chief and a systematic campaign to terrorize, that is to coerce through fear, through the killing of individual police officers against whom no particular animosity might be felt."(8) Perhaps the most distinguishing feature of terrorism is, thus, the attempt to coerce through fear. It is violence designed to produce a "psychological state of anguish, fright, uncertainty, desperation, or despair - or some combination of these."(9) Further, the violence is usually action carried out by organized and ideologically oriented groups.

As an analytic concept, terrorism presents a number of problems in definition and measurement.(10) Terrorist violence may only comprise a small part of global political violence. In order to determine accurately how much is terroristic, however, requires determinations as to motives and intentions that are not always possible. How, for example, does one determine when acts of sabotage are terroristic? They may be nothing more than covert acts of warfare designed to destroy something of value to the enemy, and may have no terroristic objectives. Assassinations are similarly sometimes difficult to classify unambiguously as terroristic. The murder of President Kennedy apparently was not an act of terrorism. But the assassination of Rafael Trujillo in the Dominican Republic is much more difficult to classify.

These are but some of the problems one confronts when attempting to operationalize terrorism. Equally important is that available data on political violence do not specifically distinguish terrorist events from other acts of political violence. Thus, for purposes of the present analysis, and with full recognition of the limitations, the political violence variables thought most likely to include acts of terrorism have been drawn from the well-known data collections of Taylor and Hudson(11) and Banks.(12) Those variables are as follows:

> Armed Attacks - acts of violent political conflict carried out by (or on behalf of) an organized group. They are characterized by bloodshed, physical struggle, or the destruction of property.
> Deaths from Political Violence - the number of persons reported killed in events of domestic political conflict. These data refer to numbers of bodies and not the events in which political deaths occurred. Assassinations are not included.
> Assassinations - any politically motivated murder or attempted murder of a high government official or politician.
> Guerrilla Warfare - armed activity, sabotage, or bombings carried on by independent bands of citizens or irregular forces and aimed at the overthrow of the present regime.
> Riots - a violent demonstration or disturbance involving a large number of people and characterized by material damage or bloodshed.

Among these variables, armed attacks would appear to approximate acts of terrorism most closely. Deaths resulting from terrorism would be included in the body counts of all deaths from various forms of political violence. Assassinations, while not always clearly terroristic, may be presumed to be frequently terroristic in character. The remaining variables may not reflect terrorism as closely as the others, although acts of terrorism are regular features of guerrilla warfare. Riots are included because, at times, they have their origin in terrorist-led or terrorist-inspired agitation and organization. Data on these variables (cumulative totals) were collected for the most recent year for which they were reported on all the variables (1966).

Data on arms transfers are taken from estimates of the U.S. Arms Control and Disarmament Agency (ACDA).(13) As defined by ACDA, "arms transfers represent the international transfer under grant, credit or cash sales terms of military equipment usually referred to as 'conventional,' including weapons of war, parts thereof, ammunition, support equipment, and other commodities considered primarily military in nature."(14) Thus, by definition, arms transfers include such items as aircraft, naval vessels, nonstrategic missiles and rockets, communications and electronic equipment, ordnance materials, parachutes, uniforms, vehicles, artillery, and the like. Nuclear, chemical, and biological weapons are not included, nor are mechanical equipment, foodstuffs, and other items with civilian uses which may also be useful to the military. Also excluded are transactions involving technical services and training. Arms data were collected for each year during the period 1966-1970.

The reliability of the arms data may be open to dispute, or at least require some qualification. In the first place, arms transfers are presented as the dollar value (in constant dollars) of transactions. Dollar value data are a poor indication of the numbers of weapons transferred. Increases in dollar value of imports may result from the purchase of more sophisticated and thus more expensive weaponry, without necessarily meaning that an increase has occurred in the rate or volume of acquisitions. Also, the term "dollar value" may be, at times, misleading when applied to arms transactions. There is some indication of the presence of "package deals" in arms trading, "whereby arms are given or sold on official credit at very low prices in exchange for commercial (often nonmilitary) sales at going rates."(15) Such package dealing results in highly variable pricing policies from one transaction to another. Data problems of this sort are not uncommon in crossnational analyses, especially studies involving public expenditure data, providing some basis for thinking of these data as approximations.

Countries included in the investigation are all the arms importing nations except those designated by ACDA as "major" suppliers.(16) It was felt that a better test of the relationship between terrorist violence and arms acquisitions could be achieved by examining those countries which, in order to meet their arms needs, must go outside their domestic arms production capacity to international suppliers. Countries thus excluded are the United States, the USSR, Great Britain, France, Poland, Czechoslovakia, the Peoples' Republic of China, West Germany, and Canada.

Statistical testing procedures in the study are product moment correlation and multiple regression. Correlation coefficients (Pearson r) are employed to test the degree of bivariate association, by regions, between each of the violence variables in the year 1966 and arms imports for each of the five years during the period 1966-1970. In this manner, a "time lag" procedure is introduced into the analysis. There is a solid theoretical basis for lagging the violence variables against the arms import data. Countries which experience acts of terrorist violence may require a certain amount of response time to calculate arms needs, to arrange procurements, and then to secure deliveries. Thus, the effects of violence on decisions to import armaments are most likely to appear sometime after the violence has occurred. It should be made clear, however, that this research design allows but a pre-liminary venture into the question of the temporal process associated with terrorism and arms. A more complete testing of the temporal relationships must await later analysis of time series data of the sort not readily available.

The regression analysis is employed only for the ag-gregate of the countries due to problems of multicollinearity that appear when grouping the countries by regions. Multi-collinearity, or high interdependence among the independent variables, can be a serious problem in regression analysis. When interdependence is present, the regression estimates are misleading and often lead to inaccurate interpretations.(17) Assessing the severity of interdependence, however, is often difficult; many analysts merely state that it must not be "too large."(18) Klein has suggested that interdependence may be harmful if any simple correlation (among the independent variables) is equal to or greater than the multiple correlation (R).(19) Applying this check on the regression equations for the aggregate of countries in this study indicates that multi-collinearity is not a problem; but severe interdependence exists when the countries are grouped by regions, rendering regression estimates unreliable. We can, thus, only interpret the simple correlations when controlling for regions, thereby sacrificing some important information concerning the multiple effects of types of violence on arms imports in the various regions.

FINDINGS

Bivariate Analysis

The bivariate correlations between each violence variable and arms transfers by regions are summarized in table 14.1. The coefficients represent the strongest statistically significant relationships, after taking into account whatever lag effects may be present. Arms transfers to African states, after "incubation" periods of one to three years, are strongly influenced by all of the violence variables. In Asia, all but riots are significantly related to arms; and, in each case, the strongest relationships appear after a four-year lag. Three of the variables have some effect on Europe's arms purchases, with deaths by political violence apparently being most strongly related to arms. Deaths by political violence, with a two-year lag effect, is the only variable affecting Mideast arms imports. Latin American arms seem to be related only to riots and, then, only moderately after a three-year lag.

Table 14.1. Bivariate Correlations Between Terrorist Violence and Arms Transfers, by Region and Type of Violence (lagged correlations)

Region	Armed Attacks	Deaths by Political Violence	Assassinations	Guerrilla Warfare	Riots
Africa	.79 (t-2)	.70 (t-2)	.98 (t-3)	.86 (t-1)	.86 (t-1)
Asia	.97 (t-4)	.96 (t-4)	.63 (t-4)	.55 (t-4)	n.s.
Europe	n.s.	.57 (t)	.38 (t-1)	n.s.	.36 (t-4)
Middle East	n.s.	.50 (t-2)	--	--	n.s.
Latin America	n.s.	n.s.	--	n.s.	.48 (t-3)

All coefficients are significant at $p < .05$ unless otherwise indicated.

n.s. = no significant relationship identified.

It is not readily apparent why acts of political violence seem relatively unimportant in Latin America and the Mideast. The rather low correlations for the European data are more understandable. Acts of terrorism have become prominent in Europe only during the past five years or so. If more recent violence data were available, terrorist violence possibly would be more strongly related to European arms imports. The high level of Latin American armed violence is historically rooted and well documented, as are the almost routine military responses to violence by the incumbent elites. However, political violence in many Latin American countries has become so endemic that it frequently goes unreported in daily newspapers which are the basis for the data collections employed here.(20) It should be noted further that such findings for Latin America are not completely unexpected since they are roughly consistent with the broad thrust of much of the existing literature on the impact of Latin American violence.(21) The near absence of any significant influence of violence variables on arms to the Mideast is especially puzzling, since that area is one of the world's most conflictive. Most of the Mideast conflict, however, takes the form of interstate violence rather than internal conflict. Further, arms supplies to the Mideast are partly responding to arms race dynamics largely unaffected by internal political strife.(22)

In Africa and Asia, political violence variables are almost uniformly significant; and the strength of the relationships across all variables suggests that they share some common variance. Indeed, attempts to employ regression analysis were unsuccessful because of high interdependence among the violence variables, indicating that they measure a common underlying dimension. Such methodological problems unfortunately prevent a more detailed analysis in which multiple regression techniques are employed for each region. However, the general finding that acts of political violence significantly affect levels of arms imports, and usually after some time lags, is an important one. Previously, such relationships have been assumed to exist, but without empirical testing and verification.

Regression Analysis

The problems encountered when attempting to employ multiple regression in the analysis of the regional samples of nations are not present when all the countries are aggregated. Those results are in table 14.2. Clearly, for all the countries taken together, armed attacks have by far the greatest impact on arms imports. In three of the time points, armed attacks account for fully half or more of the weapons transferred. However, the strongest effect of armed attacks, after con-

trolling for the effects of the other acts of violence, appears
at t-3 and accounts for virtually all of the explained variance.
Inference suggests that acts of armed attacks occurring in
1966 account for 65 percent of weapons deliveries in 1969. A
similar relationship obtains at t-4. As suggested earlier,
countries experiencing acts of terrorist violence apparently
require some "lag" time between the violence and arms deliveries.

Table 14.2.   Variance Explained in Arms Transfers
for All Recipients
(Increments to R^2)

VARIABLE	t	t-1	t-2	t-3	t-4
Armed Attacks	.485*	.003	.500	.646*	.548*
Assassinations	.002	.000	.001	.000	.000
Deaths by Political Violence	.008	.206	.000	.000	.000
Guerrilla Warfare	.005	.004	.005	.009	.013*
Riots	.014*	.000	.001	.000	.000
R	.717*	.461	.712	.809*	.749*
R^2	.514*	.213	.507	.655*	.561*

* = Significant at p = $\leq$ .05

Only two other variables - riots and guerrilla warfare -
make significant contributions to explaining arms in the
multiple regression. And with each variable, after the effects
of armed attacks are accounted for, very little additional
variance is explained. Without time (t), riots explain just
over 1 percent of the variance in armaments. Guerrilla
warfare does no better, contributing roughly an equal amount
at t-4. Deaths by political violence and assassinations have no
significant effects on arms shipments even after lagging. In
the aggregate, these two types of violence are not significant
considerations in decisions concerning levels of conventional
armaments. Riots and guerrilla warfare are only marginally
important in decisions on armaments, leaving armed attacks as
practically the sole type of political violence exerting important
influence on arms procurements. It is interesting to note also

that no significant coefficients appear at t-1 and t-2. It would seem that responses to acts of terrorist violence in the form of arms purchases are either immediate or lag behind the violence by three to four years.

CONCLUSIONS

This has been an exploratory examination of the relationship between terrorist political violence and the international transfer of conventional armaments. No attempt has been made to explain all the variance in arms imports. The focus has been explicitly on a subset of variables in the total array of possible influences on arms acquisitions.(23) Clearly, the findings are more suggestive than conclusive. Although armed attacks seem to approximate our conceptualization of terrorism more closely than any other violence measures (and, interestingly, was the variable most consistently correlated with arms imports), it falls short of the measurement precision necessary to achieve more complete tests of the relationships posited in this analysis. For example, data and measurement criteria are needed on political kidnappings, skyjackings, bombings, and many other acts of violence that are more directly terroristic in nature. Variables employed in the present study are largely "proxy" variables, which cannot provide the direct test one would hope eventually to achieve. Their analysis is important, however, because it is suggestive of trends and patterns of relationships that require further study. Future research might well be directed toward these ends.

NOTES

1. Yonah Alexander, ed., International Terrorism: National, Regional and Global Perspectives (New York: Praeger, 1976); and Marcia McK. Trick, "Chronology of Incidents of Terroristic, Quasi-Terroristic, and Political Violence in the United States: January 1965 to March 1976," in Disorders and Terrorism (Washington: National Advisory Committee on Criminal Justice Standards and Goals, Law Enforcement Assistance Administration, 1976), pp. 507-595.
2. I.K. Feierabend and R.L. Feierabend, "Aggressive Behaviors Within Polities, 1948-1962: A Cross-National Study," Journal of Conflict Resolution 10 (September 1966): 249-71; Ted Gurr, "A Causal Model of Civil Strife," American Political Science Review 62 (December 1968): 1104-24; D.A. Hibbs, Jr., Mass Political Violence: A Cross-National Causal Analysis (New

York: Wiley, 1973); Michael C. Hudson, "Conditions of Political Violence and Instability," Sage Professional Papers, Comparative Politics Series, 1 (1970); R.J. Rummel, "Dimensions of Conflict Behavior Within and Between Nations," General Systems Yearbook 8 (1963): 1-50; and Raymond Tanter, "Dimensions of Conflict Behavior Within and Between Nations, 1958-1960," Journal of Conflict Resolution 10 (March 1966): 41-64.

3. H.H.A. Cooper, "The International Experience with Terrorism: An Overview," in Disorders and Terrorism, p.420.

4. Brian M. Jenkins, International Terrorism: A New Mode of Conflict (Los Angeles: Crescent Publications, 1975).

5. I. Henderson and P. Good, Man Hunt in Kenya (New York: Doubleday, 1958), p. 13.

6. Cooper, "The International Experience with Terrorism," p. 419.

7. Brian M. Jenkins, Soldiers Versus Gunmen: The Challenge of Urban Guerrilla Warfare (Santa Monica, CA: Rand, 1974).

8. Cooper, "The International Experience with Terrorism," p. 421.

9. Murray C. Havens, Carl Leiden, and Karl M. Schmitt, Assassination and Terrorism: Their Modern Dimensions (Manchaca, Texas: Sterling Swift Publishing, 1975), p. 148.

10. On this topic, see: J. Dugard, "International Terrorism: Problems of Definition," International Affairs 50 (January 1974): 75ff.

11. Charles L. Taylor and Michael C. Hudson, World Handbook of Political and Social Indicators, II (New Haven, Conn.: Yale University Press, 1972).

12. Arthur S. Banks, Cross-Polity Time-Series Data (Cambridge, Mass: MIT Press, 1971).

13. U.S. Arms Control and Disarmament Agency, World Military Expenditures and Arms Transfers, 1966-1975 (Washington: Government Printing Office, 1976).

14. Ibid., p. 8.

15. Philippe C. Schmitter, "Foreign Military Assistance, National Military Spending and Military Role in Latin America," in Military Role in Latin America, ed. P.C. Schmitter (Beverly Hills, CA: Sage Publications, 1973), p. 128.

16. Some countries were omitted from the analysis due to missing data on key variables or to negligible levels of arms imports. The 95 countries included in the analysis are the following: 1) Africa - Cameroon, Central African Republic, Chad, Congo, Dahomey, Ghana, Guinea, Ivory Coast, Kenya, Liberia, Malagasy Republic, Mauritania, Nigeria, Senegal, South Africa, Tanzania, Togo, Uganda, Upper Volta, Zaire, and Zambia; 2) Asia - Afghanistan, Burma, Cambodia, India, Indonesia, Japan, Nepal, North Korea, South Korea, Laos, Malaysia, Pakistan, Philippines, Sri Lanka (Ceylon), Thailand,

North Vietnam, and South Vietnam; 3) <u>Europe</u> - Albania, Austria, Belgium, Bulgaria, Denmark, East Germany, Finland, Greece, Hungary, Iceland, Ireland, Italy, Luxembourg, Netherlands, Norway, Portugal, Rumania, Spain, Sweden, Switzerland, Turkey, Yugoslavia, plus Australia and New Zealand; 4) <u>Mideast</u> - Algeria, Cyprus, Egypt, Ethiopia, Iran, Iraq, Israel, Jordan, Lebanon, Libya, Morocco, Saudi Arabia, Somalia, Sudan, Syria, and Tunisia; 5) <u>Latin America</u> - Argentina, Bolivia, Brazil, Chile, Colombia, Cuba, Dominican Republic, Ecuador, El Salvador, Guatemala, Honduras, Mexico, Nicaragua, Paraguay, Peru, Uruguay, and Venezuela.

17. H.M. Blalock, Jr., "Correlated Independent Variables: The Problem of Multicollinearity," <u>Social Forces</u> 43 (December 1963): 233-37.

18. D.R. Heise, "Problems in Path Analysis and Causal Inferences," in <u>Sociological Methodology</u>, edited by E.F. Borgata (San Francisco: Jossey-Bass, 1969), p. 57.

19. L.R. Klein, <u>An Introduction to Econometrics</u> (Englewood Cliffs, NJ: Prentice-Hall, 1962), p. 101.

20. On this problem, see: Edward Azar, Stanley Cohen, Thomas Juckham, and James McCormick, "The Problem of Source Coverage in the Use of International Events Data," <u>International Studies Quarterly</u> 16 (September 1972): 373-88.

21. Schmitter, "Foreign Military Assistance," pp. 117-87; and William P. Avery, "Domestic Influences on Latin American Importation of U.S. Armaments," International <u>Studies Quarterly</u> 22 (March 1978): 121-42.

22. See, for example: H. Rattinger, "From War to War: Arms Races in the Middle East," <u>International Studies Quarterly</u> 20 (December 1976): 501-31; Rattinger, "Econometrics and Arms Races," <u>European Journal of Political Research</u> 4 (1976); and J.C. Lambelet, "A Dynamic Model of the Arms Race in the Middle East: 1953-1965," <u>General Systems Yearbook</u> 14 (1971): 145-67.

23. Elsewhere this author has dealt with a larger set of explanatory variables in U.S. arms transfers to the Third World and to Latin America (Avery, "Domestic Influences on Latin American Importation of U.S. Armaments"; and, William P. Avery, "Recipient Influences on U.S. Arms Trade with the Third World," <u>Mondes en Developpement</u> 18 [1977]: 342-59).

IV

**Terrorism:
Future Prospects**

15 Super-Terrorism
Yonah Alexander

It is a generally accepted notion that terrorism - ideological and political violence utilized by subnational groups seeking to achieve imaginary or realistic tactical and strategic objectives(1) - is relevant to the concept of high-technology weapons.(2) The seriousness of this relationship was succinctly observed by Justice Arthur J. Goldberg:

> Modern terrorism, with sophisticated technological means at its disposal and the future possibility of access to biological, chemical, and nuclear weapons, presents a clear and present danger to the very existence of civilization itself.(3)

Such an awesome eventuality forces us to think about the "unthinkable"(4) with grave concern. The purpose of this brief report is to examine these novel aspects of contemporary ideological and political violence and particularly to focus on the potential threat of nuclear terrorism.

DANGERS OF UNCONVENTIONAL TERRORISM

Pragmatic and symbolic terrorist acts - including arson, bombing, hostage-taking, kidnapping, and murder - undertaken by extremist groups for the purpose of producing pressures on governments and peoples to concede to the demands of the perpetrators have already victimized, killed, and maimed thousands of innocent civilians. These casualties include government officials, politicians, judges, diplomats, military personnel, police officers, business executives, labor leaders, university professors, college students, school children, travelers, pilgrims, and Olympic athletes.(5) Also, considerable damage has been inflicted on nonhuman targets.(6) Terrorists have already attacked government offices and police stations; pubs, restaurants, and hotels; banks, supermarkets, and department stores; oil pipelines, storage tanks, and refineries; railroad stations, air terminals, and jetliners; broadcast stations, computer and data centers, and electric power facilities.

This record provides evidence that no mass casualties and widespread disruptions to vital systems of industrialized nations have resulted from a single terrorist attack. Terrorist groups have usually used guns and bombs, and only rarely more sophisticated weapons such as man-portable antitank rockets and ground-to-air missiles when they became available.(7) Having achieved considerable tactical success, terrorists found it politically and morally expedient to restrain the level of violence. Had it been otherwise, they could have used conventional weapons to cause major disasters in our extremely vulnerable society by attacking, for example, hazardous chemical plants.(8)

There are, however, no guarantees that the self-imposed constraints of terrorist groups will persist indefinitely and that future incidents will not be much more costly in terms of human lives and property. Three considerations suggest such a probable draconic development. First, assuming that conventional terrorism would be brought under substantial control in the foreseeable future through national and international legislation as well as through increased security and enforcement measures, this may in fact have the effect of hastening the advent of mass destruction terrorism. After all, terrorist groups tend, whenever possible, to attack "soft targets," those without security or the appearance thereof. This worldwide trend has been noted clearly over the 1970-78 time span, and accounts for an evolution in terrorist targeting from the primacy accorded attacks on police/military facilities (1970-72), to a shift toward assaulting diplomatic and related activities (1973-75), to an emphasis on business targets (1976-78). In each stage, the primary target group selected for assault was less secure, and thus easier to attack, than the previous one. Today, however, many business firms are following the lead of police and diplomatic establishments by upgrading their security.(9) As a result of this trend, other vulnerable targets created by technological advances of contemporary society are likely to become more attractive to terrorists.

A second consideration for the probable shifting from conventional to mass destruction violence is the propaganda and psychological warfare value of such operations to terrorist groups. Since the strategy of terrorism does not prescribe instant victories over adversaries, an extension of the duration and impact of violence is indispensable.(10) As a keen observer stated, "The media are the terrorist's best friend. The terrorist's act by itself is nothing; publicity is all."(11) Should effective governmental and intergovernmental responses deny terrorists their sought-after publicity, they are likely to change tactics, increase their audacity, and escalate their symbolic-oriented acts through high-technology weapons, if available.

A third consideration which might encourage nonconventional terrorism is the fact that, since ideological and political violence is usually a means to an end, it progresses in proportion to the aims envisioned. If the goals are higher, then the level of terrorism must necessarily be higher. The only constraints to such violence are the limits of available weaponry. Thus, it is conceivable that a highly motivated and desperate terrorist group with technological and financial assets will attempt to improve its bargaining leverage by resorting to mass destruction violence. Such a determined group would be willing to take numerous risks in acquiring and using such weapons. Because the confrontation is seen by many groups as an "all-or-nothing" struggle, in case of failure the terrorists are prepared to bring the government to submission, to actually use these weapons and, in the process, to bring devastation and destruction to many lives including their own. Surely, for these terrorists, the fear of deterrence or retaliation does not exist as it does in the case of states.

It is obvious that the prospects of success for such a group would be enhanced if it had previously demonstrated high technological capabilities and a strong willingness to incur high risks involved in similar ventures. Even if there were some skepticism about the credibility of the threat, no rational government would lightly risk a nonconventional incident. The danger here is that if one subnational body succeeds in achieving its goals, then the temptation for other terrorist groups to use, or threaten to use, similar weapons may become irresistible.

CHEMICAL AND BIOLOGICAL TERRORISM

In view of these considerations, experts do not exclude the possibility that the arsenal of tomorrow's terrorist might include chemical, biological, and nuclear instruments of massive death and destruction potential.(12) These weapons are capable of producing from several thousand to several million casualties in a single incident, and cause governmental disruption of major proportions and widespread public panic.

To be sure, there are inherent differences among weapons of high technology in terms of their characteristics and modes

of action.(13)   The resort to chemical and biological weapons is
regarded more achievable than the use of nuclear explosives.
More specifically, there are no insurmountable technological
impediments in the utilization of chemical agents (e.g.,
fluoroacetates, organophosphorous compounds, and botulinum
toxin).(14)   They are relatively easily obtainable, their
delivery systems are manageable, and their dispersal techniques are efficient.(15)   For example, it has recently been
reported that "terrorists wanting to make deadly nerve gases
can still find the formulas at the British Library despite
attempts by the Government to remove them from public access."(16)
     Once in possession of such information, a terrorist with
some technical "know-how" could synthesize toxic chemical
agents from raw materials or intermediates.   In fact, many
chemical toxins (e.g., Cobalt-60 and TEPP insecticides) are
commercially available.   They could either be bought or stolen.
     Also, covert and overt options for dispersing chemical
agents are virtually limitless, including poisoning of water
systems, contamination of food supplies, generation of gases in
enclosed spaces with volatile agents, generation of aerosols in
enclosed spaces with nonvolatile agents, and dispersal with
explosives.
     There have already been a number of chemical-related
terrorism incidents.   In 1975, German authorities were threatened that mustard gas, stolen from an ammunition bunker in
the country, would be used against the population of Stuttgart
unless all political prisoners were granted immunity.   Only
some of the stolen canisters were later found.(17)   The
following year, U.S. postal authorities intercepted a package,
presumably mailed by an Arab terrorist group, containing a
small charge designed to explode a vial of nerve gas when the
package was opened.(18)   More recently, Israeli citrus fruit
was contaminated with liquid mercury.   This particular event
proved to be more of an economic hazard than a human one
because Israel had to cut back its export of oranges by 40
percent.(19)
     As in the case of chemical violence, biological terrorism -
the use of living organisms to cause disease or death in man,
animals, or plants - is technologically possible.   Warfare
agents such as brucellosis (undulant fever), coccidioidomycosis
(San Joaquin Valley or desert fever), and psittacosis (parrot
fever) are easy to acquire, cultivate, and disseminate.   The
poison Ricin, for example, is developed from castor beans;
about half a milligram is fatal.
     Evidence indicates that terrorists have seriously con-
sidered resorting to biological terrorism.   In 1970, members of
the Weather Underground were planning to steal germs from
the bacteriological warfare center at Fort Detrick, Maryland,
for the purpose of contaminating a city water supply;(20)

organizers of Rise - a group of young people dedicated to creating a new master race - were arrested in 1972 in an abortive plot to poison Chicago's water system with typhoid bacteria;(21) and, in 1975, technical military manuals on germ warfare were found in a San Francisco hideout of the Symbionese Liberation Army.(22)

NUCLEAR TERRORISM

Notwithstanding the assumption that, in the short-term future, chemical and biological terrorism is more feasible technologically, nuclear terrorism - the explosion of a nuclear bomb, the use of fissionable material as a radioactive poison, and the seizure and sabotage of nuclear facilities - has received far greater public attention. As one observer remarked, "It cannot be assumed that these possibilities have been ignored by existing or potential terrorists or that they will not be considered in the future."(23)

Awareness of this danger is, indeed, growing. Warnings that thefts from nuclear plants might provide terrorists with material to make a crude bomb have been issued in the United States(24) and abroad.(25) Concern has also been expressed that attacks on nuclear power plants discussed in the European "underground" publications may encourage domestic groups to escalate their violence.(26) And, more recently, Joseph Hendrie, Chairman of the Nuclear Regulatory Commission, reported that his "agency has concluded the possibility of terrorist interest in nuclear capability cannot be discounted."(27)

Also, scholars have provided numerous scenarios of nuclear terrorism over the years.(28) Examples of some of the more obvious possibilities that are technically feasible and politically plausible could include the threat or use of a nuclear option by: a group of psychopaths and sociopaths, with suicidal tendencies, whose incentive is to use nihilistic violence for its own sake; political or environmental extremists seeking to carry out acts of symbolic violence against nuclear facilities; a revolutionary group against its own government or against a foreign country in order to increase the pressure on the home government to meet the revolutionaries' demands; a national liberation movement against the imperialist government in the mother country; or a terrorist group engaged in a "proxy-war" initiated by an "outside state" or even nuclear power.

Such developments are indeed serious because they could result in a broad-scale nuclear war or increase the risk of such a war. This likelihood increases in situations where nuclear terrorism would be used as form of war by "proxy" or as a tactical weapon by desperate terrorist groups. It is conceivable, for example, that if Israel were a target of a "surrogate" nuclear attack by the PLO, the United States and the Soviet Union could reach a point of confrontation that greatly increases the dangers of a nuclear war between them.

It is clear that a major factor encouraging this frightening reality is the profound negative effects of nuclear proliferation, both vertically and horizontally. At present, there are tens of thousands of nuclear weapons, including tactical ones, in military stockpiles. Although the current "Nuclear Club" is limited in membership, it is expected that some 40-50 states will have access to peaceful nuclear material and technology by the end of the century. Therefore, it will not be difficult for states desiring to manufacture their own nuclear weapons to do so. They could build a small processing plant at the cost of several million dollars, sufficient to produce enough fissionable weapons-grade plutonium 239 for three or four bombs a year.(29) India's manufacture of a nuclear device with technology supplied by Canada, and the recent deals between West Germany and Brazil, and France and Pakistan, Libya and the Soviet Union involving pilot reprocessing plants certainly charts a new trend.

Other "threshold" nuclear nations are Argentina, Egypt, Israel, Iran, South Korea, Taiwan, and South Africa. Some nations, such as Indonesia and Turkey, have the motivation to go nuclear but not the capability to join the club yet. There are over a dozen states, including Austria and Japan, that have the capability but no incentive at the present.(30) Future projections are that, by 1990, developing countries alone would be capable of making 3,000 nuclear bombs a year;(31) and, at the beginning of the twenty-first century, the world could make more than 100,000 nuclear explosives each year.(32)

This enormous expansion in the nuclear arsenal is indeed alarming, not only in terms of the total number of weapons stockpiled but also because most of them will be without the electronic safety locks and coded permissive action links (known as PAL's) protecting weapons of the more advanced nuclear powers.(33)

While stealing or seizing a tactical nuclear weapon from a less sophisticated nuclear nation might be more tempting to a terrorist group, an attempt to acquire weapons from the superpowers should not be ruled out. For instance, weaknesses and shortcomings in the security system of some United States Armed Forces' storage depots highlight questions of command, inventory control, and communications. Furthermore, the transit of nuclear warheads between missile sites (identifiable storage sites, unsafe transport, etc.) improve the chances of a terrorist group to succeed.(34) Even if difficulties of detonation of a stolen bomb prove impossible to overcome, the terrorist group will be able to use the weapon as a credible threat.

To be sure, concern over the risk of theft or seizure of tactical and strategic weapons at home and abroad has been expressed by many observers. One test scenario describes the seizure of a Launch Control Center at a Minuteman site by terrorists, thereby providing them with the capability of launching a nuclear attack. In this particular case, it was concluded that "there is little reason to have confidence that Minuteman safeguards are inviolable."(35)

Even if the shortcomings in safeguards and physical security measures of the United States and other advanced nuclear countries were corrected, the fact remains that lesser technological states will not always introduce similar improvements and, therefore, will still be vulnerable to seizure or theft of nuclear weapons. In such circumstances, the security of the more sophisticated nuclear states could well be in jeopardy. Clearly, protection and safety can be improved on all levels, but the risks can only be reduced and not completely eliminated.

Moreover, as a consequence of the use of the oil embargo and the political unreliability of some oil producing countries, industrial nations have been motivated to develop alternative sources of energy. Nuclear power has figured largely in these efforts. Currently, more than 300 nuclear power plants are either operating, under construction, or planned in 26 countries, the vast majority in the United States. Thus, as the world moves deeper into the plutonium economy, the potential dangers of diversion, theft, or seizure of fissionable nuclear material produced by private industry will become greater.(36)

This vulnerability in the United States and elsewhere has already generated various recommendations on the international and national levels to improve the physical protection of nuclear material in civilian hands. Cases in point are the reports, suggestions, guidelines, and regulations provided by the International Atomic Energy Agency (IAEA), the Non-Proliferation Treaty Review Conference, and the U.S. Atomic Energy Commission. Despite these and other efforts, current international safeguards are totally inadequate.(37) The conclusion of some analysts is that there "is no systematic exchange among states of technical, administrative, or intelligence information regarding physical protection of nuclear facilities and materials or of information concerning terrorist threat potentials. Similarly, there appears to be no contingency plan for, nor international coordinative mechanism to deal with, a theft of nuclear materials from one state to another."(38)

This vulnerability is expected to result in the opening up of opportunities for a black market of plutonium, and thereby increasing the chances of success in obtaining the needed fissionable material. Only some 11 to 20 pounds of such material is necessary to construct a crude explosive device which would probably have a yield in the range between several hundreds and several thousands of high explosives. If this device were detonated in a crowded metropolitan area, as many as 10,000 people might be killed directly, while tens of thousands of others might suffer from severe fallout exposure.

To be sure, with fissionable material available, a determined terrorist group wishing to manufacture its own "home-made" weapon can do so without insurmountable difficulty. As early as the 1960s, various reports have indicated that persons using only unclassified information as well as publicly available literature could design a crude device that may function in the nuclear mode. For example, in 1975 an M.I.T. undergraduate designed a workable bomb of low yield.(39) Similarly, in 1976, a Princeton student put together a design for an explosive with half the power of the Hiroshima yield; the bomb could be built for $2,000.(40) And, more recently, an economics major at Harvard with only one year of physics designed a series of nuclear bombs in five months.(41)

If bright undergraduates have the technological know-how to design nuclear bombs, it is obvious that any proficient terrorist group that could obtain the fissionable material and do what these students have done will have a reasonable chance of building, quite skillfully and safely, a home-made bomb at an expense of $10,000-$30,000.(42) It is even more conceivable, because possibly some of the tens of thousands of scientists, engineers, and other trained personnel in the nuclear field might be motivated by political convictions or economic and personal considerations, and, therefore, would be willing to participate in a nuclear operation. Additionally, experts might be kidnapped and forced to contribute their expertise in exchange for their lives and/or the lives of their families.(43)

Another aspect of nuclear terrorism is the problem of radiological weapons dispersal.(44) A plausible alternative to the explosion or threat of explosion of a nuclear device is the utilization of plutonium or any other radioactive nuclides for the dispersal of radioactivity in any given area, or the contamination of natural resources. A dispersal threat would be more credible if only because it requires less material and a lower level of technological expertise. Thus, a determined terrorist group could place only 3 1/2 ounces of plutonium (its toxicity is at least 20,000 times that of cobra venom or potassium cyanide) in a dispersal device such as an aerosol canister. This could be used as an effective radiological weapon if introduced into the air conditioning system of a large government office building. The effect would be devastating. Several thousand people would die over a period of time depending on the level of dosage absorbed. Additionaly, there are likely to be significant psychological effects which could create immediate panic and spontaneous mass exodus, and result in intolerable political, economic, and social implications. (45)

Another threat of radioactivity release could occur as a consequence of the sabotage of nuclear power stations. Since an expansion in the number of these stations is expected, the likelihood of such incidents increases. To succeed in such operations, the terrorists must disable the cooling system to the reactor core of the power station, where radioactive material is contained, causing it to melt and resulting in the release of the poisonous substance. Although such a task is most difficult, experts agree that it is not impossible. Once the reactor core melts down, the released material would cause thousands of casualties and serious environmental contamination with short and long-term effects. As a keen observer of nuclear developments has predicted: "Because of its toxic and fissile properties, plutonium offers a unique and powerful weapon to those who are sufficiently determined to impose their will. In these circumstances I do not believe it is a question whether someone will deliberately acquire it for purposes of terrorism and blackmail, but only of when and how often."(46)

This prediction is not baseless if one examines the historical record. There have already been several hundreds of nuclear-related incidents which have serious implications for future trends. Some unclassified examples in the United States, selected at random, include the theft in 1973 of "extremely harmful" capsules of Iodine 131 from a hospital in Arcadia, California;(47) the loss in 1969 of a container of highly enriched Uranium Hexafluoride (UF-6) which was shipped from Ohio to Missouri;(48) the 1972 threatened crash of a hijacked airliner into the Oak Ridge National Laboratory in Tennessee;(49) the arson at the Indian Point No. 2 plant near Buchanan, New York in 1974;(50) the intrusion attempt in 1977 of the Vermont Yankee Nuclear Power Corporation;(51) the 1976 bomb threat at the B&W Naval Nuclear Fuel facility at Lynchburg, Virginia;(52) and the bomb detonation next to the visitors' center at Trojan Nuclear Power Plant in Oregon in 1977.(53) Thus far, thousands of pounds of low-enriched uranium and plutonium have already disappeared during the past several years. According to a recent report, more than 50 tons of fissionable material was unaccounted for in some 34 facilities operated by the Energy Research and Development Administration. (54)

Similar incidents took place overseas, including the theft of fuel rods from atomic power stations in England in 1966;(55) the apparent uranium smuggling operation uncovered in India in 1974;(56) and the apparent intrusion attempts, surveillance operations, and disturbances at perimeter fences and areas outside nuclear weapons storage sites in Europe.(57) It is worth mentioning two specific cases. A lone terrorist, calling himself a "justice guerrilla" protesting against prison conditions in Austria, dispersed radioactive material in two trains in 1974. Several people became ill in these incidents and the perpetrator escaped.(58)   Also during the same year, right-wing Italian terrorists planned to poison the country's water supply with radioactive uranium stolen from a nuclear center. The scheme also involved a plan to assassinate top government officials and the communist party leader. The alleged purpose of the plot was to create public panic and compel the army to intervene and open the way for a rightist government take-over.   The plot was uncovered with the arrest of several members of the group.(59)

Finally, since 1970, there have been over a dozen ter-rorist attacks against nuclear facilities. According to available data, these incidents represent 6.8 percent of the total of 192 terrorist attacks against utilities around the world.(60)   For instance, in 1973, members of the People's Revolutionary Army (Ejercito Revolucionario del Pueblo - ERP)(61) seized the nearly completed Atucha nuclear station in Argentina. The attackers escaped after painting a political slogan on the building, stealing weapons, and wounding several guards.(62)

In 1975, several bombs exploded at the site of a French nuclear power station under construction in Fessenheim, south of Strasbourg. There was some damage, but no significant delay in the completion of the reactor.(63)   The "Meinhof-Puig Antioch" group claimed credit for this incident.(64)   During the same year, two explosions caused minor damage to a nuclear power plant in Brittany. A local separatist group has been suspected of this act of sabotage.(65)   Other attacks occurred in 1976 when a group known as Commando d'Oppo-sition par Explosifs l'autodestruction de l'univers (COPEAU) - "Commando of Opposition by Explosives to the Self-Destruction of the Universe" - bombed the Paris offices of a manufacturer of nuclear fuel elements and a uranium mine in southwestern France, causing extensive damage at both locations.(66)

And, more recently, two incidents are noteworthy. In March 1978, the Basque Separatist terrorist organization (E.T.A.)(67) bombed the partially built nuclear plant at Lemoniz, Spain, the second largest in Western Europe. The bombing caused $8.1 million in material damage to the plant, killing two workers and injuring fourteen. Several months earlier, members of the same group opened fire at the site but were beaten back by police.(68)   And in a related nuclear facility issue, the German Revolutionary Cells(69) have claimed responsibility for a May 1978 explosives attack on a private security firm contracting at a nuclear works site at Kalkar, West Germany, and for an incendiary attack on a vehicle belonging to the police chief who handled violent demonstra-tions at that location.(70)

Limited as these incidents are, they should not be construed to mean that the world in the years ahead will face only isolated cases of nuclear terrorism. It is likely that changing political, economic, and social patterns in the domestic and international situations which will occur over the next two decades might give rise to pressures and tensions that could motivate terrorists to engage in nuclear terrorism.

CONCLUSIONS

The intrinsically complicated threats arising from any sort of chemical, biological, and nuclear terrorism may become an ominous future reality. If modern society is to provide a reasonable degree of protection against superterrorism, developments in this area of public concern must continuously and patiently be monitored by all involved. Also, emergency preparedness countermeasures must necessarily include contingency planning and sound crisis management policies at various governmental, intergovernmental, and nongovernmental levels.

Faced with potential dangers of unconventional terrorism, democratic states would have to ask themselves what price they ought to be prepared to pay, in terms of expenditure and in terms of diminution of their citizens' convenience and civil liberties. Although precise answers are virtually impossible, one should take into account the following fundamental guidelines recommended at the 1978 Ditchley Conference on Terrorism:(71)

1. Exceptional measures of law enforcement should be kept to the lowest necessary level.
2. All such measures should be specifically expressed as temporary deviations from the norm. They should be subject to review, renewal, and revision.
3. They should be tightly framed so as to ensure that the civil liberties of the people as a whole are affected as little as possible. The use of any special powers should be linked to a discernible and defined threat: such powers should not be available for the suppression of dissident opinion at large.

Notwithstanding these considerations, one can concur with Walter Laqueur that, if an actual emergency arose, and if a choice had to be made between state survival and foregoing citizens' civil liberties and fundamental freedoms, there is no doubt what a responsible government would do.(72)

NOTES

1. For recent studies on terrorism, see, for example, Yonah Alexander, Ed., International Terrorism (New York: Praeger, 1976); Yonah Alexander and Seymour M. Finger, Eds., Terrorism: Interdisciplinary Perspectives (New York and London: John Jay Press and McGraw-Hill, 1977); Yonah Alexander, David Carlton, and Paul Wilkinson, Eds., Terrorism: Theory and Practice (Boulder, Colorado: Westview Press, 1979); Yonah Alexander and Robert A. Kilmarx, Eds., Political Terrorism and Business (New York: Praeger, 1979); J. Bowyer Bell, Terror Out of Zion (New York: St. Martin's Press, 1976), and On Revolt (Cambridge, Mass.: Harvard University Press, 1976); David Carlton and Carlo Schaerf, Eds., International Terrorism and World Security (London: Croom Helm, 1975); Richard Clutterbuck, Kidnap and Ransom: The Response (London and Boston: Faber and Faber, 1978); Ronald D. Crelinsten, Danielle Laberge-Altmejd, and Denis Szabo, Eds., Terrorism and Criminal Justice (Lexington, Mass., and Toronto: Lexington Books, 1978); John D. Elliot and Leslie K. Gibson, Contemporary Terrorism: Selected Readings (Gaithersburg, Md.: International Association of Chiefs of Police, 1978); Alona E. Evans and John F. Murphy, Eds., Legal Aspects of International Terrorism (Lexington, Mass. and Toronto: Lexington Books, 1978); Richard W. Kobetz and H. H. Cooper, Target Terrorism (Gaithersburg, Md.: International Association of Chiefs of Police, 1978); Walter Laqueur, Terrorism (Boston and Toronto: Little, Brown 1977); Maurius H. Livingston, Lee Bruce Kress, and Marie G. Wanek, Eds., International Terrorism in the Contemporary World (Westport, Conn.: Greenwood Press, 1978); Terrorism: An International Journal 1 (1977-78); and Paul Wilkinson, Political Terrorism (London: The Macmillan Press, 1974) and Terrorism and the Liberal State (New York: John Wiley and Sons, 1977).

2. See, for example, B.J. Berkowitz et al., Superviolence: The Civil Threat of Mass Destruction Weapons, Adcon Corp. report A72-034-10, Sept. 29, 1972 (Santa Barbara, CA.: The Adcon Corp, 1972); Bernard L. Cohen, "The Potentialities of Terrorism," The Bulletin of the Atomic Scientists 32 (6) (June 1976): 34-35; Brian Jenkins, "International Terrorism: A New Kind of Warfare" (Santa Monica, CA.: The Rand Corp., June 1974); Robert H. Kupperman, "Crisis Management: Some Opportunities," Science 187 (1975), and "Treating the Symptoms of Terrorism: Some Principles of Good Hygiene," Terrorism: An International Journal (1) (1977); R. W. Mengel, "Terrorism and New Technologies of Destruction: An Overview of the Potential Risk" in Disorders and Terrorism: A Report of the Task Force on Disorders and Terrorism (Washington, D.C.: National Advisory Committee on Criminal Justice Stan-

dards and Goals, 1976), pp. 443-73; Miliaglo Mesarovic and Eduard Pestal, Mankind at the Turning Point (New York: E. P. Dutton, 1974); Robert K. Mullen, "Mass Destruction and Terrorism," Journal of International Affairs 32 (1) (Spring/ Summer 1978): 63-91; Eric D. Shaw et al. "Analyzing Threats from Terrorism," CACI-Inc., April 1976 (mimeographed); Roberta Wohlstetter, "Terror on a Grand Scale," Survival 18 (May-June 1976): 98-104; and "Latest Worry: Terrorists Using High Technology," U.S. News and World Report, March 14, 1977.

3. Alexander, International Terrorism.

4. Herman Kahn, Thinking About the Unthinkable (New York: Avon, 1971).

5. According to available data from 1970 to September 10, 1978, 2,118 persons were killed, 3,472 wounded, and 3,286 held hostage. There was a total of 4,899 terrorist incidents. These statistics were presented by Charles Russell at a Corporate Policy Conference, Washington, D.C., September 25, 1978. For other data see "International Terrorism In 1977," (CIA: National Foreign Assessment Center, August 1978); and Edward J. Mickolus, "Statistical Approaches to the Study of Terrorism" in Alexander and Finger, Terrorism: Interdisciplinary Perspectives, pp. 209-69.

6. According to Russell's statistics, material damage (including thefts) totals $381,835,000 for the 4,899 incidents.

7. Examples of utilization of advanced weapons are the Palestinian January 1975 attack on an El-Al airline at Orly Airport with a RPG-7 rocket; the employment of the Strela SA-7 missile by Palestinian groups in abortive plots in Rome (1973) and Kenya (1975); and the destruction of a civilian Rhodesian airliner with an SA-7, apparently used by guerrillas.

8. See Kenneth A. Solomon, "Meteorological Aspects of Chemical Spill Study," Hazard Prevention, May-June 1975, pp. 6-11; and K. A. Solomon, M. Rubin, and D. Okrent, On Risks from the Storage of Hazardous Chemicals, University of California, Los Angeles, School of Engineering and Applied Science, December 1976.

9. See "Terrorism and U.S. Business: Conference Report," CSIS Notes, July 1978.

10. For detailed discussions on this subject see Yonah Alexander, "Terrorism, the Media and the Police," Police Studies 1 (2) (June 1978): 45-62; and "Communication Aspects of International Terrorism," International Problems 16 (1-2) (Spring 1977): 55-60; and Alexander and Finger, Terrorism: Interdisciplinary Perspectives, pp. 141-208; and "Terrorism and the Media," Terrorism: An International Journal 2 (1) (1979).

11. Walter Laqueur, "The Futility of Terrorism," Harper's 252 (1510) (March 1976): 104.

    12. See, for instance, Brian M. Jenkins and Alfred P. Rubin, "New Vulnerabilities and the Acquisition of New Weapons by Nongovernment Groups," in Evans and Murphy, Legal Aspects of International Terrorism, 221-76; and David Carlton and Carlo Schaerf, The Dynamics of the Arms Race (London: Croom Helm, 1975), pp. 170-93.
    13. See, for example, Richard Dean McCarthy, The Ultimate Folly: War by Pestilence, Asphyxiation and Defoliation (New York: Random House, 1969); and Stockholm International Peace Research Institute, The Rise of CB Weapons: The Problem of Chemical and Biological Warfare, Vol. 1. (New York: Humanities Press, 1971).
    14. Frederick Lewis Maitland Pattison, Toxic Aliphatic Fluorine Compounds (New York: Elsevier, 1959).
    15. Mullen, "Mass Destruction and Terrorism."
    16. The Observer (London), November 19, 1978.
    17. "Terrorist Use of Gas Feared," Washington Post, May 13, 1975.
    18. "Terrorist Gangs Reaching for Nerve Gas, Gruesome New Weapons," Boston Globe, November 7, 1976. See also "Australian Police Nab Poison-Gas Producers," Ottawa Citizen, March 2, 1976; and "Terrorist Use of Gas Feared," Washington Post, April 13, 1975.
    19. The New York Times, February 10, 1978; and The Guardian (Manchester, Eng.), February 7, 1978.
    20. George W. Griffith, "Biological Warfare and the Urban Battleground," Enforcement Journal 14 (1) (1975): 4, citing a Jack Anderson column for November 20, 1970.
    21. "Chicago Pair with Plot to Poison Midwest Water Supply," Los Angeles Times, January 19, 1972; and Chicago Tribune, January 19, 1972.
    22. Reported by Lowell Ponte, KABC Radio Broadcast, Los Angeles, October 23, 1975, 9:00-10:00 p.m.
    23. Brian Jenkins, "The Potential for Nuclear Terrorism" (Santa Monica, CA.: The Rand Corporation, May 1977), and "Will Terrorists Go Nuclear?" (Santa Monica, CA.: The Rand Corporation, 1975), p. 5541. See also A. and M. Adelson, "Please Don't Steal the Atomic Bomb," Esquire, May 1969; Louis Rene Beres, "Terrorism and the Nuclear Threat in the Middle East," Current History (January 1976), pp. 27-29; Thomas M. Conrad, "Do-it-Yourself A-bombs," Commonweal (July 1969); Forrest R. Frank, "Nuclear Terrorism and the Escalation of International Conflict," Naval War College Review 29 (Fall 1976); The International Clandestine Nuclear Threat (Gaithersburg, MD.: International Association of Chiefs of Police, 1975); "International Terrorism and World Order: The Nuclear Threat," Stanford Journal of International Studies 12 (Spring 1977); David Krieger, "Terrorists and Nuclear Technology," The Bulletin of the Atomic Scientists 31 (6) (June 1975): 28-34; "The Nuclear Threat of Terrorism," International

Journal of Group Tensions 6 (1-2) (1976); Lowell Ponte, "Better Do As We Say: This is an Atom Bomb and We're not Fooling," Penthouse, February 1972; "Will Terrorists go Nuclear?" (paper presented at California Seminar on Atomic Control and Foreign Policy, November 1975); and Mason Willrich, "Terrorists Keep Out!" The Bulletin of the Atomic Scientists 31 (5) (May 1975): 12-16. For press reports see Jack Anderson, "Will Nuclear Weapons Fall into the Hands of Terrorists?" Parade (September 20, 1974); "California Thinks Unthinkable: A-Blackmail," International Herald Tribune, February 24, 1977; "The Danger of Terrorists Getting Illicit A-Bombs," Los Angeles Times, April 25, 1976; Robert A. Jones, "Nuclear Terror Peril Likely to Increase," Los Angeles Times, April 25, 1976; "Keeping Nuclear Bombs out of the Wrong Hands," The Times (London), February 5, 1977; and "Nuclear Terrorism Fear," The Times, (London), January 4, 1977.

    24. For an FBI warning see The Washington Post, January 4, 1975.

    25. See, for example, statement made by the Salzburg Conference on Non-Nuclear Future cited in The Times (London), May 2, 1977; and The New York Times, May 2, 1977.

    26. See U.S. Senate, Subcommittee on Internal Security of the Senate of the Senate Judiciary Committee, "Terrorist Activity: International Terrorism," May 14, 1975, p. 197. The New York Times of March 12, 1978, reported that danger from "urban terrorists" and "sabotage" was cited by New York City in a legal argument when it sought to establish a local right to block the use of a 250-kilowatt research reactor by Columbia University on its Morningside Heights campus.

    27. U.S. Senate, Hearings before the Committee on Governmental Affairs, An Act to Combat International Terrorism, January, February, and March, 1978, pp. 67-81; and U.S. Senate, Report of the Committee on Governmental Affairs, An Act to Combat International Terrorism, May 23, 1978.

    28. See, for instance, William Epstein, The Last Chance: Nuclear Proliferation and Arms Control (New York: The Free Press, 1976), pp. 19-22, and "Nuclear Terrorism and Nuclear War" an unpublished paper for the Pugwash International Symposium on Nuclear War by the Year 2000, at Toronto, May 4-7, 1978; Mason Willrich and Theodore B. Taylor, Nuclear Theft: Risks and Safeguards (Cambridge, Mass.: Ballinger, London: Croom Helm, 1975); Ted Greenwood, Harold A. Feireson, and Theodore B. Taylor, Nuclear Proliferation: Motivations, Capabilities and Strategies for Control 1980s Project (Council on Foreign Relations, New York: McGraw-Hill, 1977), pp. 99-107; Albert Wohlstetter et al. Moving Toward Life in a Nuclear Armed Crowd? (Los Angeles: Pan Heuristics, 1976); David M. Rosenbaum, "Nuclear Terror," International Security (Winter 1977), pp. 140-61; and A. Dunn, "Nuclear

Proliferation and World Politics," Annals of the American Academy of Political and Social Science (March 1977), pp. 96-109.

29. Epstein, The Last Chance, p. 231.

30. For details, see Andrew J. Pierre, Nuclear Proliferation: A Strategy for Control (New York: Foreign Policy Association, Headline Series, October 1976).

31. U.S. Atomic Energy Commission, Energy Research and Development (ERDA) Report (1976). See also Robert Henderson, "Making Nuclear Weapons - Easily," The Washington Post, December 14, 1978 ("Letter to the Editor").

32. International Atomic Energy Agency (IAEA) Report, 1976.

33. John Larus, Nuclear Weapons: Safety and the Common Defense (Columbus: Ohio State University Press, 1967).

34. See, for example, Lloyd Dumas, "National Insecurity in the Nuclear Age," The Bulletin of the Atomic Scientists (May 1976); The New York Times, November 15, 1977; and Lloyd Norman, "Our Nuclear Weapons Site: Next Target of Terrorists?" Army 27 (June 1977): 28-31.

35. Bruce G. Blair and Garry D. Brewer, "The Terrorist Threat to World Nuclear Programs," Journal of Conflict Resolution 21 (3) (September 1977): 389. See also Blair and Brewer, "The Terrorist Threat to U.S. Nuclear Programs" (Unpublished paper, October 1976), and Lawrence L. Whetten, "Legal Implications of the Theft of U.S. Nuclear Weapons on German Soil" (unpublished paper, March 1978).

36. GIST, October 1976; S. Burnham, Ed., The Threat to Licensed Nuclear Facilities (Washington, D.C.: The Mitre Corporation, September 1975), pp. 72, 95-96; and P.A. Karber et al. "Analysis of the Terrorist Threat to the Commercial Nuclear Industry," Draft Working Paper B, Summary of Findings, Report to the U.S. Nuclear Regulatory Commission, The BDM Corp. Report BDM/w-75-176-TR (Vienna, VA: The BDM Corp., September 1975).

37. Brian Jenkins, "Rand's Research on Terrorism," Terrorism: An International Journal 1 (1) (November 1977): 90; and Jerry Peter Coleman, "International Safeguards against Nongovernment Nuclear Theft: A Study of Legal Inadequacies," International Lawyer 10 (Summer 1976).

38. Evans and Murphy, Legal Aspects of International Terrorism, pp. 179-180.

39. The New York Times, February 27, 1975.

40. The Princeton Alumni Weekly, October 25, 1976, p. 6; and The New York Times Magazine, July 18, 1977, p. 66.

41. The New York Times, March 26, 1978, and June 10, 1978; and John Aristotle Phillips and David Michaelis, "If a Guy Like Me Designed an A-Bomb, Don't You Think Terrorists Could?" Washington Star (Comment), September 24, 1978.

42. Martha Crinshaw Hutchinson, "Defining Future
Threat: Terrorism and Nuclear Proliferation," in Alexander and
Finger, Terrorism, p. 302. See also "Threat of Home-made
A-bomb," Guardian, June 13, 1977.
43. In March 1977, it was feared that the German terrorist Hans-Joachim Klein had contact with and was even a
house guest of one of the three managing directors of a
Cologne nuclear research firm, Interatom G.m.b.H.   The
nuclear scientist, Dr. Klaus Traube, was eventually cleared of
any suspected wrongdoing. See "Protection for Atom Scientists," Guardian, May 2, 1977.
44. The New York Times, April 15, 1978; Robert R.
Jones, "Nuclear Reactor Risks - Some Frightening Scenarios,"
Chicago Sun-Times, April 30, 1976; and The Wall Street
Journal, December 12, 1975.
45. Thomas C. Schelling, "Who Will Have the Bomb?"
International Security 1 (1) (1976): 77-91; David Krieger,
"What Happens If . . . ? Terrorists, Revolutionaries and
Nuclear Weapons," Annals of the American Academy of Political
and Social Science (March 1977), pp. 44-57; John W. Simpson,
"Managing and Safeguarding Wastes and Fissionable Material,"
Fortune (May 1975).
46. Sir Brian Flowers, "Nuclear Power and the Public
Interest: A Watchdog's View," The Bulletin of the Atomic
Scientists (December 1976), p. 27.
47. L. Douglas DeNike, "Radioactive Malevolence,"
Bulletin of the Atomic Scientists 30 (2) (1974): 16-20. For
details on other theft incidents see "Radioactive Plates Stolen
from the Lab," Los Angeles Times, October 3, 1974; "Radioactive Needle Sought After Theft Suspect is Arrested," Los
Angeles Times, November 28, 1974; "Cesium Sources Stolen,
Found; Damage Reported," Nuclear News, February 1975, p.
59; United States Atomic Energy Commission, News Release,
October 29, 1974, and November 13, 1974.
48. DeNike, "Radioactive Malevolence." For other examples of missing or lost material see Homer Bigart, "Engineers
Pursue Lost Radium Hunt," The New York Times, August 19,
1966, and "Second Shipment of Radium is Lost," The New York
Times, September 6, 1966; and Donald P. Gessaman, "Plutonium and the Energy Decision," Bulletin of the Atomic Scientists 37 (2) (1971): 33-35.
49. Los Angeles Times, November 12, 1972, and The New
York Times, November 12, and 13, 1972. For another plot see
Ralph E. Lapp, "The Ultimate Blackmail," The New York Times
Magazine, February 4, 1973, p. 13.
50. See The New York Times, December 12, 1971;
January 30, 1972; September 13, 1973; and November 14, 1974.
51. U.S. Senate, Hearings, p. 649.
52. Ibid., p. 643.
53. Ibid., p. 958. See also The Washington Post,
December 8, 1971.

54. The New York Times, August 6, 1976. See also "FBI, CIA Block GAO Study on Missing Uranium," Washington Star, December 28, 1978.

55. Tom Margarison, "Buying Doom in Sealed Packages?" Daily Telegraph (London), February 14, 1975, pp. 12-13.

56. The Times of India, April 30, and May 1, 2, 7, 15, 1974; The Times (London), May 2 and October 8, 1974; Los Angeles Times, December 30, 1974; and Environment, December 1974.

57. The Congressional Record, April 30, 1975, pp. S7184-90; and The Washington Post, May 1, 1975.

58. The Washington Post, April 18 and 20, 1974; and Los Angeles Times, April 20, 1974.

59. The Washington Post, October 24, 1974.

60. Utilities covered in this data base include electrical, telephone, petroleum, nuclear, and waterworks facilities. Statistics were provided by Charles Russell, supra.

61. The ERP was the military arm of the Trotskyite Revolutionary Workers' Party (Paritido Revolucionario de los Trabajadores - PAT). It was established in August 1970, when the Party adopted a policy of "armed struggle." See Ernst, Terrorism in Latin America (CSIS, The Washington Papers, 1976); and James Petras, "Building a Popular Army in Argentina," New Left Review (January-February 1971), p. 54.

62. La Razón, March 26, 1973, p. 4; La Nación, March 26, 1973, p. 3; and Applied Atomics, March 28, 1973, p. 4.

63. The New York Times, May 4, 1975; The Washington Post, May 4, 1975; and The Times (London), May 5, 1975.

64. This group was apparently named for Ulrike Meinhof, leader of the West German terrorist Red Army Faction, and Salvador Puig Antioch, an anarchist executed by the Spanish government in 1974. Since no information is available on this group it has been suggested that antinuclear extremists in France may have used the cover of a terrorist "group" to publicize their cause.

65. Lester A. Sobel, Ed., Political Terrorism, Vol. 2, 1974-78 (New York: Facts on File, 1978), p. 204.

66. Cited in Peter deLeon, Brian Jenkins, Konrad Kellen, and Joseph Kronfcheck, "Attributes of Potential Criminal Adversaries to U.S. Nuclear Programs," Santa Monica, CA: Rand Corp., February 1978, p. 29.

67. The E.T.A. ("Freedom for the Basque Homeland") was founded in 1959 by a militant splinter group of the Basque Nationalist Party (PNV). This separatist organization is influenced by Marxist-Leninist ideologies. For details see Brian Crozier, Ed., Annual of Power and Conflict 1976-77 (London: Institute for the Study of Conflict, 1978), pp. 50-57; and Sobel, Political Terrorism, pp. 240-47.

68. The New York Times, March 18 and 22, 1978; and The Guardian, March 18, 1978.

69. For a recent survey on German Revolutionary Cells see Jillian Becker, Hitler's Children: The Story of the Baader-Meinhof Gang (London: Granada Publishing, 1977).

70. Frankfurter Allgemeine Zeitung, May 9, 1978.

71. The Ditchley Conference on Terrorism was held November 24-26, 1978. A published summary of the deliberations is forthcoming.

72. Laqueur, Terrorism, p. 221.

Selected Bibliography

Adelson, Alan. SDS: Profile. New York: Charles Scribner's Sons, 1972.

Aizcorbe, Roberto. Argentina, The Peronist Myth. Hicksville, New York: Exposition Press, 1975.

Alexander, Robert J. The Bolivian National Revolution. New Brunswick, New Jersey: Rutgers University Press, 1958.

Alexander, Yonah. The Role of Communications in the Middle East Conflict: Ideological and Religious Aspects. New York: Praeger Publishers, 1973.

_____. ed. International Terrorism: National, Regional and Global Perspectives. New York: Praeger Publishers, 1976.

_____. Browne, Nargorie Ann and Names, Allan S., eds. Control of Terrorism. New York: Crane, Russak & Company, 1979.

_____. Carlton, David and Wilkinson, Paul, eds. Terrorism: Theory and Practice. Boulder: Westview Press, 1979.

_____. and Friedlander, Robert A., eds., Self-Determination: National Regional and Global Perspectives. Boulder: Westview Press, 1979.

_____. and Kilmarx, Robert A., eds. Political Terroriom and Business: The Threat and Response. New York: Praeger Publishers, 1979.

_____. and Kittrie, Nicholas, eds. Crescent and Star: Arab-Israeli Perspectives on the Middle East Conflict. New York: AMS Press, 1972.

_____. and Nannes, Allan, eds., The United States and Iran: A Documentary History. Frederick, Maryland: University Publications of America, 1980.

_____. and Seymour, M. Finger, eds. Terrorism: Interdisciplinary Perspectives. New York: John Jay Press, 1977 and Maidenhead: McGraw Hill Book Co., 1978.

Ali, Tariq, ed. The New Revolutionaries: A Handbook of the International Radical Left. New York: William Morrow and Co., 1969.

Alves, Marcio Moreira. A Grain of Mustard Seed. Garden City, New York: Doubleday Anchor Press, 1973.

American University, Washington, D.C. Special Operations Research Office. Human Factors Considerations of Undergrounds in Insurgencies. Washington, 1966.

Andreski, Stanislav. Parasitism and Subversion: The Case of Latin America. New York: Pantheon, 1967.

Annual of Power and Conflict 1979 - 80. London: Institute for the Study of Conflict, 1980.

Arey, James A. The Sky Pirates. New York: Charles Scribner's Sons, 1972.

Ariel, Dan. Explosion! Tel Aviv: Olive Books, 1972.

Avineri, Shlomo, ed. Israel and the Palestinians: Reflections on the Clash of the Two National Movements. New York: St. Martin's Press, 1971.

Avner (Pseudo.) Memoirs of an Assassin. New York: Yoseloff, 1959.

Avrich, Paul. The Russian Anarchists. Princeton: University Press, 1967.

Bassiouni, M. Cherif, ed. International Terrorism and Political Crimes. Springfield, Illinois: Thomas, 1975.

Baudovin, Jean. Terrorisme et Justice. Montreal: Editions du Jour, 1970.

Baumann, Bommi. Terror or Love? Bommi Baumann's Own Story of His Life as a West German Urban Guerrilla. New York: Grove Press, 1979.

Baumann, Carol Edler. The Diplomatic Kidnappings: A Revolutionary Tactic of Urban Terrorism. The Hague: Marinus Nifhoff, 1973.

Bayo, Alberto. 150 Questions to a Guerrilla. Translated by R.I. Madigan and Angel de Lumus Medina. Montgomery: Air University, n.d.

Becker, Jillian. Hitler's Children: The Story of the Baader-Meinhof Terrorist Gang. Philadelphia: Lippincott, 1977.

Bell, J. Bowyer. A Time of Terror: How Democratic Societies Respond to Revolutionary Violence. New York: Basic Books, 1978.

_____. The Myth of the Guerrilla: Revolutionary Theory and Malpractice. New York: Knopf, 1971.

_____. On Revolt. Cambridge: Harvard University Press, 1976.

_____. The Secret Army: The IRA 1916-1974. Cambridge: MIT Press, 1974.

_____. Terror out of Zion: The Irgun, Lehi, Stern & the Palestine Underground, 1929-1949. New York: St. Martin's Press, 1977.

_____. Transnational Terror. Washington, D.C.: American Enterprise Omstotire. 1975.

Beres, Louis Rene. Terrorism and Global Security: The Nuclear Threat. Boulder, Colo.: Westview Press, 1979.

Berkman, Alexander. Now and After: The ABC of Communist Anarchism. New York: Vanguard Press, 1929.

_____. Prison Memoirs of an Anarchist. New York: Schocken Books, 1970.

Berry, Steve. The Prevention of Terrorism Act: Legalized Terror. London: Socialist Work Printers and Publishers, 1977.

Bewaffneter Kampf in Iran Isari Komitte, 1975.

Black, Cyril E. and Thornton, Thomas P. Communism and Revolution. Princeton: University Press, 1964.

Blackstone Associates. Risk Assessment for Italy. Washington: Blackstone Associates, 1978.

Bloomfield, Louis M. and Fitzgerald, Gerald F. Crimes Against Internationally Protected Persons: Prevention and Punishment: An Analysis of the U.N. Convention. New York: Praeger Publishers, 1975.

Bocca, Geoffrey. The Secret Army. Englewood Cliffs: Prentice-Hall, 1968.

Bodelsen, Anders. Operation Cobra. Translated by Joan Tate. New York: Elsevier Nelson Books, 1979.

Borisov, J. Palestine Underground: The Story of Jewish Resistance. New York: Judea Publishing Co., 1947.

Boston, Guy D.; Marcus, Marvin; and Wheaton, Robert J. Terrorism: A Selected Bibliography. Washington, D.C.: National Criminal Justice Reference Service, March, 1976.

Botha, Andries Jakob. SWAPO. Sandton, South Africa: Southern Africa Freedom Foundation, 1977.

Bowden, Tom. The Breadkdown of Public Security. London and Beverly Hills: Sage, c1977.

Brigham, Daniel T. Blueprint for Conflict. New York: American-African Affairs Association, 1969.

Brinton, Crane. The Anatomy of a Revolution. Englewood Cliffs: Prentice-Hall, 1965.

Broehl, Wayne G. The Molly Maguires. Cambridge: Harvard University Press, 1964.

Brown, Richard M. Strain of Violence: Historical Studies of American Violence and Vigilantism. London: Oxford University Press, 1975.

Burton, Anthony M. Revolutionary Violence: The Theories. New York: Crane, Russack & Co., 1978.

_____. Urban Terrorism: Theory, Practice and Response. New York: Free Press, 1975.

Button, James W. Black Violence: Political Impact of the 1960's Riots. Princeton, New Jersey: Princeton University Press, 1978.

Canadian Council on International Law. International Terrorism: Proceedings of the Third Annual Conference held at the University of Ottawa, Ottawa, Canada, October 18-19, 1974. Ottawa: Faculte de droit de L'Universite d'Ottawa, 1974.

Carlton, David and Schaerf, Carlo, eds. International Terrorism and World Security. London: Croom Helm, 1975.

Carmichael, Joel. Stalin's Masterpiece. New York: St. Martin's Press, 1976.

Carr, E. H. Studies in Revolution. New York: Grosset and Dunlap, 1964.

Catholic Commission for Justice and Peace in Rhodesia. Civil War in Rhodesia: Abduction, Torture, and Death in the Counter-insurgency Campaign. Salisbury: The Commission, 1976.

Chailand, Gerald. The Palestinian Resistance. Baltimore: Penguin, 1972.

Chase, L.J., ed. Bomb Threats, Bombings and Civil Disturbances: A Guide for Facility Protection. Corvallis, ORE: Continuing Education Publications, 1971.

Clark, Michael K. Algeria in Turmoil. New York: Praeger Publishers, 1959.

Clark, Richard C. Technological Terrorism. New York: Devin-Adair Co., 1978.

Clark, Robert P. The Basques: The Franco Years. Reno, Nevada: University of Nevada Press, 1980.

Clutterbuck, Richard L. Guerrillas and Terrorists. London: Faber and Faber, 1978.

_____. Kidnap and Ransom: The Response. London and Boston: Faber and Faber, 1978.

_____. Living with Terrorism. London: Faber and Faber, 1975.

Clyne, P. Anatomy of Skyjacking. London: Abelard-Shumann, 1973.

Cole, Richard B. Executive Security. New York: John Wiley & Sons, Inc., 1980.

Conquest, Robert. The Great Terror. New York: MacMillan, 1968.

_____. The Human Cost of Soviet Communism. Washington: U.S. Government Printing Office, 1970.

Contemporary Terrorism. Gaithersburg, Maryland: Bureau of Operations and Research. International Association of Chiefs of Police, 1978.

"Convention to Prevent and Punish the Acts of Terrorism taking the Form of Crimes Against Persons and Related Extortion that are of International Significance." U.S. Government Printing Office, 1971.

Coogan, Tim Patrick. The IRA. New York: Praeger Publishers, 1970.

Cormier, Robert. After the First Death. New York: Pantheon Books, 1979.

Council of Europe. Explanatory Report on the European Convention on the Suppression of Terrorism. Strasbourg: Council of Europe, 1977.

Crelinsten, Ronald S.; Laberge-Altmeja, Danielle; and Szabo, Denis, eds. Terrorism and Criminal Justice. Lexington: Lexington Books, 1978.

Crooty, William J. Assassination and the Political Order. New York: Harper and Row, 1971.

Crozier, Brian, ed. Annual of Power and Conflict, 1973-1974: A Survey of Political Violence and International Influence. London: Institute for the Study of Conflict, 1975.

_____. Annual of Power and Conflict, 1974-1975: A Survey of Political Violence and International Influence. London: Institute for the Study of Conflict, 1975.

_____. Annual of Power and Conflict, 1975-1976: A Survey of Political Violence and International Influence. London: Institute for the Study of Conflict, 1976.

_____. Annual of Power and Conflict, 1976-1977: A Survey of Political Violence and International Influence. London: Institute for the Study of Conflict, 1977.

_____. South-East Asia in Turmoil. Baltimore, Penguin Books, 1965.

_____. The Study of Conflict. London: Institute for the Study of Conflict, 1976.

_____. Ulster: Politics and Terrorism. London: Institute for the Study of Conflict, 1973.

Cunningham, William C. Prevention of Terrorism. McLean, Virginia: Hallcrest Press, 1978.

Curtis, Michael. et al., eds. The Palestinians: People, History, Politics. Edison, New Jersey: Transaction Books, 1975.

Dallin, Alexander and Breslauer, George W. Political Terror in Communist Systems. Stanford: University Press, 1970.

Davies, Dave. The Ustahsa in Australia. Sydney: Communist Party of Australia, 1972.

Davies, Jack. Political Violence in Latin America. London: International Institute for Strategic Studies, 1972.

Davies, James C., ed. When Men Revolt and Why. New York: Free Press, 1971.

Davis, James R. The Terrorists. San Diego, California: Grossmont Press, 1978.

Debray, R. Revolution on the Revolution. New York: Monthly Review Press, 1967.

DeGrazia, Sebastian and Stecchini, Livio C. The Coup d'Etat: Past Significance and Modern Technique. China Lake: U.S. Ordinance Test Station, 1965.

Demaris, Ovid. Brothers in Blood: The International Network. New York: Scribner, 1977.

Dillon, Martin and LeHane, Denis. Political Murder in Northern Ireland. Baltimore: Penguin Books, 1974.

Dobson, Christopher. Black September: Its Short, Violent History. New York: MacMillan, 1974.

_____. The Terrorists. New York: Facts on File Publications, 1979.

_____. and Payne, Ronald. The Carlos Complex: A Study in Terror. New York: Putnam, 1977.

Dortzbach, Karl and Debbie. Kidnapped. New York: Harper and Row, 1975.

Draper, Theodore. Castro's Revolution: Myths and Realities. New York: Praeger, 1962.

Duncan, Patrick. South Africa's Rule of Violence. London: Methuen, 1964.

DuPlessis, Jan A. South Africa. Pretoria: Foreign Affairs Association, 1977.

Eckstein, Harry, ed. Internal War. New York: Free Press, 1964.

Elliot, John D. and Gibson, Leslie K., eds. Contemporary Terrorism: Selected Readings. Gaithersburg: International Association of Chiefs of Police, 1978.

Ellis, Albert and Gullo, John. Murder and Assassination. New York: Stuart Lyle, 1971.

European Convention on the Suppression of Terrorism. Strassbourg: Council of Europe, 1977.

Evans, Alona E. and Murphy, John F., eds. Legal Aspects of International Terrorism. Lexington: Lexington Books, 1978.

Evans, Ernst. Calling a Truce to Terror: The American Response to International Terrorism. Westport, Conn.: Greenwood Press, 1979.

Evans, Robert D. Brazil, The Road Back from Terrorism. London: Institute for the Study of Conflict, 1974.

Fairbairn, G. Revolutionary Guerrilla Warfare: The Countryside Version. Middlesex, England: Penguin Books, 1974.

Fanon, Franz Toward the African Revolution: Political Essays. Translated by Haadon Chevalier. New York: Grove Press, 1967.

_____. The Wretched of the Earth. New York: Grove Press, 1968.

Farhi, David. The Limits to Dissent. Palo Alto, California: Aspen Institute for Humanistic Studies, 1978.

Faul, Denis. SAS Terrorism. Dungannon, The Authors, 1976.

Ferguson, J. Halcro. The Revolution of Latin America. London: Thames and Hydson, 1963.

Fitzgerald, Charles P. Revolution in China. New York: Praeger, 1952.

Fleming, Marie. The Anarchist Way to Socialism. Totowa, New Jersey: Rowman and Littlefield, 1979.

Footman, David. Red Prelude. Westport, Conn.: Hyperion Press, 1979.

Frank, Gerold. The Deed. New York: Simon and Schuster, 1963.

Freed, Donald and Landis, Fred. Death in Washington: The Murder of Orlando Letelier. London: U.S. Distributors for Zed Press, 1980.

Friedlander, Robert A. Terrorism: Documents of International and Local Control. Dobbs Ferry, New York: Oceana Publications, 1979, 2 vols.

Fromm, Erich. The Anatomy of Human Destructiveness. New York: Rinehart and Winston, 1973.

Fuqua, Paul Q. and Wilson, Jerry. Terrorism - The Executives Guide to Survival. Houston: Gulf Publishing Company Book Division, 1978.

Gablonski, Edward. Terror from the Sky: Airwar. Garden City, New York: Doubleday, 1971.

Gale, William. The Compound. New York: Rawson Associates Publishers, 1977.

Galula, Davis. Counterinsurgency Warfare: Theory and Practice. New York: Praeger, 1964.

Gaucher, Roland. The Terrorists: From Tzarist Russia to the O.A.S. Translated by P. Spurlin. London: Secker and Warburg, 1968.

Gellner, J. Bayonets in the Streets: Urban Guerrilla at Home and Abroad. Ontario: Collier-MacMillan Canada, Ltd., 1974.

Giap, Vo-nguyen. People's War, People's Army: The Viet Cong Insurrection Manual for Underdeveloped Countries. New York: Praeger, 1962.

Gibson, Brian. The Birmingham Bombs. Chichester: Rose, 1976.

Gillo, M. E. The Tupamaro Guerrillas. New York: Ballantine, 1970.

_____. The Tupamaro Guerrillas. Translated by Anna Edmonston. Introduction by Robert Alexander. New York: Saturday Review Press, 1972.

Goode, Stephen. Guerrilla Warfare and Terrorism. New York: F. Watts, 1977.

Goodhart, Philip. The Climate of Collapse. Richmond: Foreign Affairs Publishing Co., 1975.

Gott, Richard. Guerrilla Movements in Latin America. London: Thomas Nelson and Sons, 1970.

Graham, Hugh D. and Gurr, Ted R., eds. Violence in America: Historical and Comparative Perspectives. Washington, D.C.: National Commission of the Causes and Prevention of Violence, 1969.

Great Britain. Committee of Privy. Counsellors Appointed to Consider Authorized Procedures for the Interrogation of Persons Suspected of Terrorism. Report. London: H.M. Stationary Off., 1972.

Great Britain. Foreign Office. Report by Mr. Roderic Bowen, Q. C., on Procedures for the Arrest, Interrogation and Detention of Suspected Terrorists in Aden. London: H.M.S.O., 1966.

Greene, T. N., ed. The Guerrilla: And How to Fight Him. New York: Praeger Publishers, 1962.

Grimshaw, Allen. Racial Violence in the United States. Chicago: Aldine, 1970.

Gross, Feliks. Violence in Politics: Terror and Political Assassination in Eastern Europe and Russia. The Hague: Mouton, 1972.

Grundy, Kenneth W. Guerrilla Struggle in Africa: An Analysis and Preview. New York: Grossman, 1971.

Guevara, Che. Reminiscences of the Cuban Revolutionary War. Translated by V. Ortiz. New York: Monthly Review Press, 1968.

Guevara, Ernesto. Che Guevara on Guerrilla Warfare. Translated by Harries-Clichy Peterson. New York: Praeger, 1961.

_____. Obra Revolucionaria. 4th ed. Mexico: Ediciones Era, 1971.

Guillaume, Gilbert and Lerasseur, Georges. Terrorisme International. Paris: A Pedone, 1977.

Guillen, Abraham. Philosophy of the Urban Guerrilla. Translated by D. C. Hodge. New York: Morrow, 1973.

Gurr, Ted Robert. Why Men Rebel. Princeton: University Press, 1970.

Gusman, Campos, et al. La Violencia en Columbia. Bogota: Ediciones Tercer Mundo, 1963.

Gwyn, David. Idi Amin: Death-Light of Africa. Boston: Little, Brown, 1977.

Hacker, Frederick F. Crusaders, Criminals, Crazies: Terror and Terrorism in Our Time. New York: Norton, 1976.

Hackey, Thomas, ed. The Problem of Partition: Peril to World Peace. New York: Rand McNally, 1972.

_____. Voices of Revolution: Rebels and Rhetoric. Dryden Press, 1973.

Hale, H. W. Political Trouble in India, 1917-1937. Allahabad: Chush Publications, 1974.

Halperin, Ernst. Terrorism in Latin America. Beverly Hills: Sage Publications, 1975

Harkabi, Y. The Arab's Position in Their Conflict with Israel. Jerusalem: Israeli Universities Press.

Havens, Murray Clark. Assassination and Terrorism. Manchaca, Texas: S. Swift Publishing Col, 1975.

Heilbrunn, Otto. Partisan Warfare. New York: Praeger Publishers, 1962.

Hills, Denis Cecil. Rebel People. New York: Africana Publishing Co., 1978.

Hodges, Donald Clark. National Liberation Fronts: 1960-1970. New York: Morrow, 1972.

_____. Philosophy of the Urban Guerrilla. New York: Morrow, 1973.

Hofstadter, Richard, and Wallace, Michael, eds. American Violence: A Documentary History. New York: Knopf, 1970.

Horn, Stanley. Invisible Empire: The Story of the Ku Klux Klan, 1866-1871. Boston: Houghton Mifflin Co., 1939.

Horowitz, Irving Louis, ed. The Anarchists. New York: Dell Publishers, 1964.

_____. The Struggle is the Message: The Organization and Ideology of the Anti-War Movement. Berkeley: Glendessary Press, 1970.

Horrell, Muriel, Terrorism in South Africa. Johannesburg: South African Institute of Race Relations, 1968.

Hosmer, Stephen T. Viet Cong Repression and Its Implications for the Future. Lexington: Heath Lexington Books, 1970.

The Human Cost of Communism in Vietnam. Washington: U.S. Government Printing Office, 1970.

The Human Cost of Communism in Vietnam: A Compendium. Washington: U. S. Government Printing Office, 1972.

Humberman, Leo, and Sweezy, Paul M. Cuba: Anatomy of a Revolution. 2nd ed. New York: Monthly Review Press, 1960.

Hutchinson, Martha Crenshaw. Revolutionary Terrorism: the FLN in Algeria, 1954–1962. Stanford, California: Hoover Institution Press, Stanford University, 1978.

Hyams, Edward. Terrorist and Terrorism. New York: St. Martin's Press, 1974.

Hyde, Douglas Arnold. The Roots of Guerrilla Warfare. Chester Springs, PA: Dufour Editions, 1968.

The Impact of Terrorism and Skyjacking on the Operations of the Criminal Justice System. Montreal: International Centre for Comparative Criminology. Universite de Montreal, 1976.

Indira Devi, M. G. Terrorist Movement in South India. Trivandrum: Kercila Historical Society, 1977.

Institute for the Study of Conflict. Ulster, Politics and Terrorism. London: Institute for the Study of Conflict, 1974.

International Defence Aid Fund. Terror in Tete. London: International Defence Aid Fund, 1973.

International Terrorism. Milwaukee: Institute of World Affairs, University of Wisconsin-Milwaukee, 1974.

Israel. Misrael ha-huts. ha-Lish kah le-hasbarah Jerusalem: Israel Ministry for Foreign Affairs, Information Division, 1972.

Irish Republican Army. Provisional IRA. Freedom Struggle. London: Red Books, 1973.

Jackson, Sir Geoffrey. Surviving the Long Nights: An Auto- biographical Account of a Political Kidnapping. New York: Vanguard, 1974.

Jacobs, Walter Darnell. Terrorism in Southern Africa: Por- tents and Prospects. New York: American African Affairs Association, 1973.

Jenkins, Brian M. The Five Stages of Urban Guerrilla War- fare. Santa Monica: Rand, 1974.

_____. International Terrorism: A New Kind of Warfare. Santa Monica: Rand Corp., 1974.

_____. International Terrorism. Los Angeles, California: Crescent Publications, 1975.

_____. Numbered Lives. Santa Monica: Rand Corp., 1977.

_____. Soldiers versus Gunmen; The Challenge of Urban Guerrilla Warfare. Santa Monica: Rand Corp., 1974.

_____. Terrorism and Kidnapping. Santa Monica: Rand Corp., 1974.

_____. Terrorism Works - Sometimes. Santa Monica: Rand Corp., 1974.

_____, and Johnson, Janera. International Terrorism: A Chronology, 1968-1974. A Report prepared for the Department of State and Defense Advanced Research Projects Agency. Santa Monica, Cal.: Rand Corp., 1975.

Johnson, Chalmers A. Revolutionary Change. Boston: Little, Brown, and Co., 1966.

Johnson, John H. The Military and Society in Latin America. Stanford: University Press, 1964.

Joll, James. The Anarchists. New York: Grosset and Dunlop, 1964.

Joyner, Nancy D. Aerial Hijacking as an International Crime. Dobbs Ferry, N.Y.: Oceana, 1974.

Jurjevie, Marjan. Ustasha Under the Southern Cross. Melbourne: M. Jurjevie, 1973.

Kaplan, Morton, A., ed. The Revolution in World Politics. New York: Wiley, 1962.

Karagueuzian, Dikran. Blow It Up! Gambit: Boston Press, 1971.

Katz, Robert. Days of Wrath: The Ordeal of Aldo Moro, the Kidnapping, the Execution, the Aftermath. Garden City, New York: Doubleday, 1980.

Kautsky, Karl. Terrorism and Communism: A Contribution to the Natural History of Revolution. Translated by W. H. Kerridge. London: George Allen and Unsin, 1920.

Kirkham, J. F. and Levy, S. Assassination and Political Violence. National Commission on the Causes and Prevention of Violence. Washington, D. C.: GPO, 1969.

Kitson, Frank. Low Intensity Operations: Subversion, Insurgency, Peace-Keeping. London: Faber Publishers, 1972.

Kobeertz, Richard W. Target Terrorism. Gaithersburg, Maryland: Bureau of Operations and Research: International Association of Chiefs of Police, 1978.

Kohl, J. and Litt, J. Urban Guerrilla Warfare in Latin America. Cambridge: MIT Press, 1974.

Kuper, Leo. The Pity of It All: Polarisation of Racial and Ethnic Relations. Minneapolis: University of Minnesota Press, 1977.

Kupperman, Robert H. Facing Tomorrow's Terrorist Incident Today. Washington, D.C.: Law Enforcement Assistance Administration, Office of Operations Support, 1977.

_____, and Trent, D. Terrorism: Threat, Reality, Response. Stanford, Cal.: Hoover Institution Press, 1979.

Laffin, John. Fedayeen. New York: MacMillan, 1973.

Lambrick, H. T. The Terrorist. London: Rowman, 1972.

Laqueur, Walter. Guerrilla: A Historical and Critical Study. Boston: Little, Brown and Co., 1976.

_____. Terrorism. Boston: Little, Brown and Co., 1977.

_____. The Terrorism Reader: A Historical Anthology. Philadelphia: Temple University, 1978.

Lasswell, Harold, and Lerner, Daniel, eds. World Revolutionary Elites: Studies in Coercive Ideological Movements. Cambridge: MIT Press, 1965.

Laushey, David M. Bengal Terrorism & the Marxist Left. Calcutta: Firma K. L. Mukhopadkyay, 1975.

Leach, Edmund Ronald. Custom, Law and Terrorist Violence. Edinburgh, University Press, 1977.

Legal and Other Aspects of Terrorism. New York: Practicing Law Institute, 1979.

Leiden, Carl and Schmitt, Karl M. eds. The Politics of Violence. Englewood Cliffs: Prentice Hall, 1968.

Leites, Nathan and Wolf, Charles, Fr. Rebellion and Authority: An Analytical Essay on Insurgent Conflicts. Chicago: Markham, Lieuwen, Edwin Publishing Co., 1970.

Lens, Sidney. Radicalism in America. New York: Thomas Y. Cromwell Co., 1966.

Lesch, Moseley. The Politics of Palestinian Nationalism. Los Angeles: University of California Press, 1973.

Lewytzkyj, Borys, comp. The Stalinist Terror in the Thirties: Documentation from the Soviet Press. Stanford, Cal.: Hoover Institution Press, 1974.

LiBonachea, Ramon. The Cuban Insurrection. Brunswick, New Jersey: Marta San Martin, 1964.

Lineberry, William P., ed. The Struggle Against Terrorism. New York: H. W. Wilson, 1977.

Liston, Robert A. Terrorism. Nashville: Nelson, 1977.

Livingston, Maurius, ed. International Terrorism in the Contemporary World. Westport, Conn.: Greenwood Press, 1978.

Lorch, Netanel. The Edge of the Sword: Israel's War of Independence, 1947-1949. New York: Putnam, 1961.

Lun, Dyer. A Concise History of the Great Trial of the Chicago Anarchists. Chicago: Socialistic Publishing Co., 1887.

MacDonald, Peter G. Stopping the Clock. London: Hale, 1977.

MacStiofan, Seam. Revolutionary in Ireland. London: G. Cremonesi, 1975.

Maksimov, Grigorii Petrovich. The Guillotine at Work. Brooklyn, New York: Revisionist Press, 1975.

Mallin, Jay, ed. Terror and Urban Guerrillas: A Study of the Tactics and Documents. Coral Gables, Florida: University of Miami Press, 1971.

_____. Terror in Vietnam. Princeton, New Jersey: D. Van Nostrand Co., 1966.

Malloy, James M. Bolivia: The Uncompleted Revolution. Pittsburg: University Press, 1970.

Mao Tse-tung. Basic Tactics. New York: Praeger Publishers, 1966.

_____. On Guerrilla Warfare. New York: Praeger Publishers, 1961.

Mardor, Munya. Haganah. New York: New American Library, 1966.

_____. Strictly Illegal. London: Robert Hale, 1964.

Marighella, Carlos. For the Liberation of Brazil. Harmondsworth: Penguin, 1972.

_____. Minimanual of the Urban Guerrilla. Havana: Tricontinental, n.d.

Masotti, Louis H. and Bowen, Don R., eds. Riots and Rebellion: Civil Violence in the Urban Community. Beverly Hills: Sage Publications, 1968.

Matekalo, Ivan. Les Dessous du Terrorisme International. Paris: Jilliard, 1973.

Mathur, L. P. Indian Revolutionary Movement in the United States of America. Delhi: S. Chand, 1970.

Max, Alphonse. Guerrillas in Latin America. The Hague: International Documents and Information Center, 1971.

_____. Tupamaros - A Pattern for Urban Guerrilla Warfare in Latin America. The Hague: International Documentation and Information Center, 1970.

McDonald, Lawrence Patton. Trotskyism and Terror: The Strategy of Revolution. Washington, D.C.: ACU Education and Research Institute, 1977.

McKnight, B. Mind of the Terrorist. London: Michael Joseph, Ltd., 1974.

McWhinney, E. W., ed. Aerial Piracy and International Law. Eiden: A. W. Sijthoff, 1971.

The Media and Terrorism. Chicago: Field Enterprises, 1977.

Mercader, A. and de Vera, J. Tupamaros: Estratagia y Accion. Montevideo: Editorial Alfa, 1969.

Merleau-Ponty, Maurice. Humanism and Terror: An Essay on the Communist Problem. Boston: Beacon Press, 1969.

Metrowich, F R. Terrorism in Southern Africa. Pretoria: Africa Institute of South Africa, 1973.

Mickolus, Edward F. The Literature of Terrorism: A Selectively Annotated Bibliography. Westport, Conn.: Greenwood Press, 1980.

_____. Transnational Terrorist: A Chronology of Events, 1968-1979. Westport, Conn.: Greenwood Press, 1980.

Milbank, David L. International and Transnational Terrorism. Washington, D.C.: Central Intelligence Agency, 1976.

Miller, Abraham H. Terrorism and Hostage Negotiations. Boulder, Colo.: Westview Press, 1980.

Miller, Michael J. and Gilmore, Susan. Revolution at Berkley. New York: The Dial Press, 1965.

Momboisse, R. M. Blueprint of Evolution: The Rebel, The Party, The Techniques of Revolt. Springfield, Ill.: Charles C. Thomas, 1970.

Morf, Gustave. Terror in Quebec. Toronto: Clarke, Irwin, 1970.

Morris, Michael. Armed Conflict in Southern Africa. Cape Town: Jeremy Spence, 1974.

_____. Terrorism. Cape Town: Howard Timmins, 1971.

Morton, Marian J. Terrors of Ideological Politics. Cleveland: Case Western Researve, 1972.

Mosbey, John C. The Prison-Terrorist Link. Bessemer, Ala.: Cerberus, 1977.

Moss, Robert. Urban Guerrillas. London: Temple Smith, 1972.

_____. The War for the Cities. New York: Coward, 1972.

Naipaul, V. S. Guerrillas. New York: Alfred A. Knopf, 1975.

Nasution, Abdul Haris. Fundamentals of Guerrilla Warfare. New York: Praeger Publishers, 1965.

National Advisory Committee on Criminal Justice Standards and Goals. Task Force on Disorders and Terrorism. Disorders and Terrorism. Washington, D.C.: National Advisory Committee on Criminal Justice Stnadards & Goals, 1976.

National Council for Civil Liberties. Prevention of Terrorism (Temporary Provisions) Act, 1974. London: National Council for Civil Liberties, 1976.

Nieburg, H. L. Political Violence: The Behavorial Process. New York: St. Martin's Press, 1969.

Nkrumah, Kwame. Handbook of Revolutionary Warfare. New York: International Publishers, 1972.

Nolin, Thierry. La Haganah: L'Armee Secrete d'Israel. Paris: Ballard, 1971.

Nomad, Max. Aspects of Revolt: A Study in Revolutionary Theories and Techniques. New York: Noonday Press, 1959.

Norton, Augustus R. and Greenberg, Martin H. International Terrorism: An Annotated Bibliography and Research Guide. Boulder, Colo.: Westview Press, 1980.

O'Ballance, Edgar. Language of Violence: The Blood Politics of Terrorism. San Rafael, Dal.: Presidio Press, 1979.

O'Farrell, Patrick. Ireland's English Question. London: Batsford, 1971.

O'Flaherty, Liam. The Terrorist. London: E. Archer, 1926.

O'Neill, Bard E., Heaton, William R., and Alberts, Donald J., eds. Insurgency in the Modern World. Boulder, Colo.: Westview Press, 1980.

Oppenheimer, Martin. The Urban Guerrilla. Chicago: Quadrangle Books, 1969.

Oruka,   H.   Odera.   Punishment and Terrorism in Africa.
Kampala: East African Literature Bureau, 1976.

Osanka,   Franklin   Mark.   Modern Guerrilla Warfare: Fighting
Communist Guerrilla Movements 1941-1961.   New   York:
Free Press, 1962.

Paine, Lauran.   The Terrorists.   London: Hale, 1975.

Paret, Peter and Shy, John W.   Guerrillas in the 1960's.   rev.
ed. New York: Praeger Publishers, 1962.

Parry,   Albert.   Terrorism: From Robespierre to Arafat.   New
York: Vanguard Press, 1976.

Pasadas, J.   Terrorism and the Struggle for Democratic Rights
and Socialism in Germany.   London: Fourth   International
Publications, 1978.

Payne, Pierre Stephen Robert.   The Terrorists: The Story of
the Forerunners of Stalin.   New York: Funk and Wagnals,
1967.

_____.   Zero, The Story of Terrorism.   New   York: Day,
1950.

Peres,   Shimon.   David's Sling.   New   York: Random   House,
1970.

Piasetzki, J. Peter.   Urban Guerrilla Warfare and Terrorism.
Monticello,   Ill.:   Council   of   Planning   Librarians, 1976.

Pike, Douglas Eugene.   Hanoi's Strategy of Terror.   Bangkok,
Thailand: South-East   Asia   Treaty   Organization,   1970.

Pisano,   Vittorfranco   S.   Contemporary Italian Terrorism.
Washington,   D.C.:   Library   of   Congress,   Law   Library,
1979.

The Politics of Terrorism.   New   York: M.   Dekker,   1979.

Pomeroy,   William   J.   Guerrilla Warfare and Marxism.   New
York: International Publishers, 1968.

Porzicanski,   A.   C.   Uraguay's Tupamaros: The Urban Guerrilla.   New York: Praeger, 1973.

Possony,   Stefan   T. and Bouchey, L. Francis.   International
Terrorism   -   The   Communist   Connection.   Washington,
D.C.: American Council for Freedom, 1978.

Pryce-Jones, David.   The Face of Defeat: Palestinian Refugees
and Guerrillas.   London: Weiderfeld and Nicholson, 1972.

Pustay,   John S.   Counterinsurgency Warfare.   New York: The
Free Press, n.d.

Pye,   Lucian.   Guerrilla Communism in Malaya: Its Social and
Political Meaning.   Princeton: University   Press,   1956.

Radvanyi, Miklos K. Anti-Terrorist Legislation in the Federal
    Republic of Germany. Washington, D.C.: Library of
    Congress, Law Library, 1979.

Radwanski, George. No Mandate But Terror. Richmond,
    Ont.: Simon and Schuster of Canada, 1971.

Rapoport, David C. Assassination and Terrorism. Toronto:
    Canadian Broadcasting System, 1971.

The Red Brigades. New York: Manor Books Inc., 1978.

Reed, David. 111 Days in Stanleyville. New York: Harper
    and Row, 1965.

Regush, Nicholas, M. Pierre Vallieres: The Revolutionary Pro-
    cess in Quebec. New York: Dial, 1973.

Rotberg, R. J. and Mazrui, Ali, eds. Protest and Power in
    Black Africa. New York: Oxford University Press, 1970.

Russell, D. E. H. Rebellion, Revolution and Armed Force.
    New York: Harcourt, Brace, Jovanovich Publishers, 1974.

Sale, Kirkpatrick. SDS. New York: Random House, 1973.

Schiff, Zeev and Rothstein, Raphael. Feyadeen: Guerrillas
    Against Israel. New York: David McKay, 1972.

Schreiber, Jan Edward. The Ultimate Weapon: Terrorists and
    World Order. New York: Morrow, 1978.

Scorer, Catherine. The Prevention of Terrorism Acts, 1974
    and 1976. London: The Council, 1976.

Selzer, Michael. Terrorist Chic. New York: Hawthorn Books,
    Inc., 1979.

Shay, Res. The Silent War. Salisbury, Rhodesia: Galaxie
    Press, 1971.

Shultz and Sloan, eds. Responding to the Terrorist Threat.
    Elmsford, New York: Pergamon Press, Inc., 1981.

Silvert, Kalman H. Reaction and Revolution in Latin America.
    New Orleans: Hauser Press, 1961.

Sinclair, Andrew. Guevara. London: William Collins and
    Sons, 1970.

Skobnick, Jerome, ed. The Politics of Protest. New York:
    Ballantine Books, 1969.

Sobel, Lester A., ed. Palestinian Impasse: Arab Guerrillas
    and International Terror. New York: Facts on File, 1977.

_____. Political Terrorism. New York: Facts on File,
    1975.

_____. Political Terrorism, 1974-1978 vol. 2. New York:
    Facts on File, 1975.

Sorel, George. Reflections on Violence. New York: Collier Books, 1961.

South Africa Department of Foreign Affairs. South West Africa: Measures Taken to Combat Terrorism. Cape Town, 1968.

Stewart, Anthony Terence Quincey. The Ulster Crisis. London: Faber and Faber, 1967.

Studies in Nuclear Terrorism. Norton and Greenberg, eds. Boston: G. K. Hall, 1979.

Styles, George. Bombs Have No Pity. London: Luscombe, 1975.

Suchlicki, Jaime. University Students and Revolution in Cuba, 1920-1968. Coral Gables: University of Miami Press, 1969.

Taber, Robert. The War of the Flea. New York: Lyle Stuart, 1965.

Tanham, George Kilpatrick. Communist Revolutionary Warfare. New York: Praeger Publishers, 1961.

Teixeira, Bernardo. The Fabric of Terror: Three Days in Angola. New York: Devin-Adair, 1965.

Ten Years of Terrorism: Collected Views. Jennifer Shaw, ed. London: Royal United Services Institute for Defense Studies, New York: Crane, Russak, 1979.

Terror in East Pakistan. Karachi: Pakistan Publications, 1971.

The Terrorism Reader. New York: New American Library, 1978.

Trautman, Frederic. The Voice of Terrorism: A Biography of Johann Most. Westport, Conn.: Greenwood Press, 1980.

Trelease, Allen W. White Terror: The Ku Klux Klan Conspiracy and Southern Reconstruction. New York: Harper and Row, 1971.

Trotsky, Leon. Against Individual Terrorism. New York: Pathfinder Press of New York, 1974.

Truby, J. David. How Terrorists Kill: The Complete Terrorist Arsenal. New York: Paladin Press, 1978.

Turi, Robert T. et al. Descriptive Study of Aircraft Hijacking. Huntsville, Texas: Institute of Contemporary Corrections and the Behavioral Sciences, 1972.

United Nations. General Assembly. Ad Hoc Committee on International Terrorism. Report. New York: United Nations, 1973.

United States Central Intelligence Agency. Annotated Bibliography on Transnational and International Terrorism. (Prepared by Edward F. Mickolus) Washington, D.C.: CIA, 1976.

United States Central Intelligence Agency. Directorate of Intelligence. International Terrorism in 1976. Washington, D.C.: CIA, 1977, 1978.

United States Congress. House. Committee on Foreign Affairs, Subcommittee on the Near East and South East Asia. International Terrorism. Ninety-third Congress, second session. Washington, D.C.: U. S. Government Printing Office.

United States Congress. House. Committee on International Security. The Symbionese Liberation Army: A Study. Ninety-third Congress, second session. Washington, D.C.: U. S. Government Printing Office, 1974.

United States Congress. House. Committee on Public Works and Transportation, Subcommittee on Aviation. International Terrorism. Ninety-fifth Congress, second session on H. R. 13261. Washington, D.C.: U. S. Government Printing Office, 1978.

United States Congress. Senate. Committee on Foreign Relations. Combating International and Domestic Terrorism. Ninety-fifth Congress, second session on S. 2236, June 8, 1978. Washington, D.C.: U. S. Government Printing Office, 1978.

United States Congress. House. Committee on Internal Security. Terrorism: Hearings before the Committee on Internal Security, House of Representatives. Ninety-third Congress, second session. Washington, D.C.: U. S. Government Printing Office, 1974.

United States Congress. Senate. Committee on Foreign Relations, Subcommittee on Foreign Assistance. International Terrorism. Ninety-fifth Congress, first session. Sept. 14, 1977. Washington, D.C.: U. S. Government Printing Office, 1977.

United States Congress. House. Committee on Internal Security. Terrorism: A Staff Study. Ninety-third Congress, second session. Washington, D.C.: U. S. Government Printing Office, 1974.

United States Congress. Senate. Committee on Governmental Affairs. An Act to Combat International Terrorism. Ninety-fifth Congress, second session, on S. 2236. Washington, D.C.: U. S. Government Printing Office, 1978.

United States Congress. Senate. Committee on the Judiciary, Subcommittee to Investigate the Administration of the Internal Security Act and other Internal Security Laws. Ninety-third (Ninety-fourth, second session) Congress. Washington, D.C.: U. S. Government Printing Office, 1974.

United States Congress. Senate. Committee on the Judiciary, Subcommittee on Criminal Laws and Procedures. The Terrorist and his Victim. Ninety-fifth Congress, first session. July 21, 1977. Washington, D.C.: U. S. Government Printing Office, 1977.

United States Congress. Senate. Committee on the Judiciary, Subcommittee on Criminal Laws and Procedures. West Germany's Political Response to Terrorism. Ninety-fifth Congress, second session. April 26, 1978. Washington, D.C.: U. S. Government Printing Office, 1978.

United States Congress. Senate. Committee on the Judiciary, Subcommittee to Investigate the Administration of the Internal Security Act and Other Internal Security Laws. Trotskyite Terrorist International. Ninety-fourth Congress, first session. July 24, 1975. Washington, D.C.: U. S. Government Printing Office, 1975.

United States Congress. Senate. Committee on the Judiciary. Washington, D.C.: U. S. Government Printing Office, 1973.

United States Embassy (Vietnam) Viet Cong Use of Terror. Saigon, 1967.

United States. Private Security Advisory Council. Prevention of Terroristic Crimes. Washington, D.C.: The Administration, 1976.

Vajpeyi, J. N. The Extremist Movement in India. Allahabad: Chush Publications, 1974.

Values in Conflict: Blacks and the American Ambivilance Towards Violence. ed., Frye, Charles A. Washington, D.C.: University Press of America, 1980.

Van den Haag, Ernest. Political Violence and Civil Disobediance. New York: Harper and Row, 1972.

Waddis, Jack. New Theories of Revolution. New York: International Publishers, 1972.

Walker, Walter. The Bear at the Back Door. Richmond, Surrey: Foreign Affairs Publishing Co., 1978.

Wallace, Michael, ed. Terrorism. New York: Arno Press, 1979.

Index

About the Contributors

YONAH ALEXANDER is professor of International Studies and Director of the Institute for Studies in International Terrorism at the State University of New York. He is also a staff associate of the Center for Strategic and International Studies, Georgetown University, and fellow, Institute of Social and Behavioral Pathology (Chicago). An author, editor, and co-editor of fifteen books, Dr. Alexander is editor-in-chief of Terrorism and Political Communication and Persuasion, both international journals. His graduate degrees are from Columbia University and the University of Chicago.

JOHN M. GLEASON is College of Business Administration Research Professor, Decision Sciences Program, University of Nebraska at Omaha. His D.B.A. degree, with majors in quantitative business analysis and logistics, was granted by the Indiana University Graduate School of Business. His research interests include the quantitative analysis of urban and public sector issues. He has served as a visiting professor with the Boston University Overseas Graduate Program in West Germany and England, and is a member of the Board of Editors of Terrorism: An International Journal.

WILLIAM P. AVERY is Associate Professor of Political Science at the University of Nebraska-Lincoln. Among his published works, are recent articles on global arms transfers appearing in International Studies Quarterly, Journal of Political and Military Sociology, and Mondes en Developpement. He is co-editor of two books on the politics of rural transformation and is currently engaged in research on the effects of international economic instability on domestic political strife. During 1980-81, he was Visiting Associate Professor in the Institute of Foreign Relations, Warsaw University, Poland.

EZZAT A. FATTAH is Professor and former Chairman, of the Department of Criminology, Simon Fraser University (Vancouver, British Columbia). Educated at the University of Cairo (law degree), the University of Montreal (Master's and Doctoral degrees), and the University of Vienna (Criminology studies), he has authored or co-authored six books and over sixty articles. In 1975 he received a presidential citation from the American Society of Criminology for outstanding contributions to the quality of criminal justice in Canada.

RONA M. FIELDS is a Psychologist and Sociologist who does private practice and consulting. She is on the Board of Directors of SIFKU in Kiel, FRG; a Research Associate for Transnational Family Research Institute of Bethesda, Md. and the Institute for Behavioral Research in Silver Spring, Md. She has served as a consultant on terrorism and victims in the United States and several European countries. Among her books are Society Under Siege; A Psychology of Northern Ireland, Temple University Press 1976 and The Portuguese Revolution and the Armed Forces Movement, Praeger, 1976.

FREDERICK J. HACKER is Professor of Psychiatry (Clinical) at the University of Southern California (USC); Professor of Psychiatry at Law, USC Law Center; Chief of Staff of the Hacker Clinic; Diplomate, American Board of Neurology and Psychiatry in Psychiatry; Founder and former President of the Sigmund Freud Society in Vienna; Director of the Institute for Conflict Research in Vienna and Certificate Program in Psychopolitics and Conflict Research at USC.

LAWRENCE C. HAMILTON received his Ph.D. in Sociology from the University of Colorado in 1978, and is presently an Assistant Professor in the Department of Sociology and Anthropology at the University of New Hampshire. He is currently working on the application of new stochastic contagion models to data on international terrorism 1968-1978.

EDWARD HEYMAN studied terrorism and guerrilla warfare at Wesleyan University, Middletown, Connecticut, and at the University of North Carolina at Chapel Hill. He is presently an associate at CACI. His previous research includes studies on political violence in Argentina and human rights violations in Latin America.

BRIAN M. JENKINS, Director of the Security and Subnational Conflict Research Program at The Rand Corporation, is a recognized authority on terrorism and low-level conflict. He is the author of International Terrorism: A New Mode of Conflict (1975) by Crescent Publications and co-author of The Fall of South Vietnam (1980), published by Crane, Russak & Co., New York.

ABRAHAM KAPLAN is the Chairman of the Philosophy Department at Haifa University, and serves as President of the Israel Philosophical Association. He has lived in Israel since 1972. He is the author of Power and Society (with H.D. Lasswell), American Ethics and Public Policy, The Conduct of Inquiry, In Pursuit of Wisdom and other works.

JEANNE N. KNUTSON holds earned doctorate degrees in both Political Science and in Psychology. She is a practicing clinical psychologist and is expert in psychodiagnostic evaluation. She is Associate Research Professor, Department of Psychiatry and Biobehavioral Sciences, University of California, Los Angeles, and President, Psychological Diagnostic Services, Inc., in Los Angeles. She has written widely on aspects of political behavior. For the past three years, she has been engaged in a research project evaluating persons in prison convicted of crimes for a political purpose. Her contribution to this volume is an outgrowth of this on-going study, as were "The Dynamics of the Hostage Taker," in Forensic Psychology and Psychiatry, The New York Academy of Sciences (1980) and "The Terrorists' Dilemmas: Some Implicit Rules of the Game," Terrorism, IV, 1-4 (1980).

EDWARD F. MICKOLUS is an Intelligence Analyst in the Office of Policy Analysis, U.S. Central Intelligence Agency. His articles have appeared in International Studies Quarterly, Journal of Irreproducible Results, Orbis, and many other journals and books. He is the author of Transnational Terrorism: A Chronology of Events, 1948-79.

THOMAS STRENTZ is a Special Agent Supervisor, F.B.I. academy of Quantico, Virginia. A graduate of California State University at Fresno (A.B. in Social Science and M.A. in Social Work), he is currently completing his Ph.D. in Social Work-Sociology from Virginia Commonwealth University. His research focuses on human behavior patterns as they relate to terrorist activity.

GREGORY F.T. WINN is the former Director of the University of Southern California's Graduate School of International Relations in West Germany. He is an area specialist on East Asian and German international relations, and was a Fulbright scholar in Japan and Korea. In addition to analyses of German and Northern European security issues, Dr. Winn has written extensively on East Asian national security and decision making problems, and has also published articles on "New Perspectives on Soviet Foreign and Defense Policy" and a "Comparison of Western and Soviet Systems/Social Science Theories." Dr. Winn now works as a research analyst on Western European affairs in the Office of Research of the United States International Communications Agency.

STEVE WRIGHT received his B.Sc. in Liberal Studies in Science from the University of Manchester (1975). He has conducted post-graduate research in the Programme of Peace and Conflict Research (1976-1978), and the Richardson Institute (1978-1980), at the University of Lancaster.